FRIENDS AND ENEMIES

Essays in Canada's Foreign Relations

FRIENDS AND ENEMIES

Essays in Canada's Foreign Relations

J.L. GRANATSTEIN

UNIVERSITY OF TORONTO PRESS
Toronto Buffalo London

© University of Toronto Press 2024
Toronto Buffalo London
utorontopress.com

ISBN 978-1-4875-4983-1 (cloth)   ISBN 978-1-4875-4985-5 (EPUB)
ISBN 978-1-4875-4984-8 (paper)   ISBN 978-1-4875-4986-2 (PDF)

Library and Archives Canada Cataloguing in Publication

Title: Friends and enemies : essays in Canada's foreign relations / J.L. Granatstein.
Names: Granatstein, J.L., author.
Description: Includes bibliographical references.
Identifiers: Canadiana (print) 20230591140 | Canadiana (ebook) 20230591175 | ISBN 9781487549831 (cloth) | ISBN 9781487549848 (paper) | ISBN 9781487549862 (PDF) | ISBN 9781487549855 (EPUB)
Subjects: LCSH: Canada – Foreign relations – 1945–
Classification: LCC FC242 .G685 2024 | DDC 327.71 – dc23

Cover design: EmDash Design
Cover image: President Franklin D. Roosevelt, Rt. Hon. W.L. Mackenzie King, and Rt. Hon. Winston Churchill at the Citadel during the Quadrant Conference, Library and Archives Canada, RG53, WR-4966

We wish to acknowledge the land on which the University of Toronto Press operates. This land is the traditional territory of the Wendat, the Anishnaabeg, the Haudenosaunee, the Métis, and the Mississaugas of the Credit First Nation.

University of Toronto Press acknowledges the financial support of the Government of Canada, the Canada Council for the Arts, and the Ontario Arts Council, an agency of the Government of Ontario, for its publishing activities.

Canada Council for the Arts   Conseil des Arts du Canada

ONTARIO ARTS COUNCIL
CONSEIL DES ARTS DE L'ONTARIO
an Ontario government agency
un organisme du gouvernement de l'Ontario

Funded by the Government of Canada   Financé par le gouvernement du Canada

Canada

Contents

Preface vii

Permissions ix

Introduction 3

Section One: Canada and the United States

1 Getting on with the Americans: Changing Canadian
  Perceptions of the United States, 1939–1945   13

2 Canada and the Marshall Plan, June–December 1947   30
  WITH R.D. CUFF

3 The Rise and Fall of Canadian-American Free Trade,
  1947–1948   51
  WITH R.D. CUFF

4 Too Close for Comfort: John Diefenbaker and the
  Political Uses of Anti-Americanism   79

5 When Push Came to Shove: Canada and the
  United States   102

6 The Importance of Being Less Earnest: Promoting
  Canada's National Interests through Tighter
  Ties with the US   123

Section Two: Canada and Britain

7 The Anglocentrism of Canadian Diplomacy — 155

8 Dealing with London — 171

9 How Britain's Weakness Forced Canada into the Arms of the United States — 199

10 From Mother Country to Far Away Relative: The Canadian-British Military Relationship from 1945 — 218

Section Three: Canada in the World

11 Canada as an Ally: Always Difficult, Always Divided — 227

12 When the Department of External Affairs Mattered – and When It Shouldn't Have — 253

13 Peacekeeping Is Our Profession? — 263

14 Peacekeeping: Did Canada Make a Difference? And What Difference Did Peacekeeping Make to Canada? — 270

15 What's Wrong with Peacekeeping? — 284

16 War and Peacekeeping in the Canadian Psyche — 296

17 Changing Alliances: Canada and the Soviet Union, 1939–1945 — 302

18 From Gouzenko to Gorbachev: Canada's Cold War — 318

19 Multiculturalism and Canadian Foreign Policy — 338

20 Can Canada Have a Grand Strategy? — 351

Preface

This book contains twenty essays on Canadian foreign policy. It primarily covers the period from the Second World War through to the early 2000s and treats policy under Prime Ministers Mackenzie King, Louis St. Laurent, John Diefenbaker, Lester Pearson, and Pierre Trudeau.

These essays are not theoretical; instead, they are narrative accounts based on extensive research into archives and interviews conducted in Canada, the United States, and Britain. I was very fortunate in acquiring early access to many hitherto closed collections of government and private papers, and the references, I believe, still remain a useful guide to the sources. An earlier collection of my essays, *Canada at War: Conscription, Diplomacy, and Politics* (2020), covered the period from the Great War through the Second World War and its aftermath. The two volumes together cover much of my writing on Canadian foreign policy, Canada-US and Canada-UK relations, and the Canadian military.

I have chosen to group the essays thematically in three sections focusing on Canada's relationship with the United States, with the United Kingdom, and with the world. Some might have preferred a chronological organization, but it should be easy enough for anyone who so wishes to read the articles in the order they originally appeared by simply checking the publication dates on the permissions pages.

Because the chapters were written some years ago, they will not seem current. I talk in chapter 6 of NATO winning the Cold War, for example, and keeping the peace since the 1990s. Clearly that does not take into account President Putin's Russia and its aggression against Ukraine since 2012. How could it? These are historical essays written by a historian. I have views on present events, and I have sometimes expressed them in the media. I have, however, not felt obliged to bring the chapters up to date. Indeed, that would destroy their value as historical artefacts. If I wrote of NATO's success in the 1990s, that was true at the time the essay first appeared. Are the chapters thus irrelevant today? I do not think so – only by understanding the past can we make sense of the present. That is the spirit in which this collection has been published.

I must note as well that the chapters in this volume were written over many years and first published in sometimes obscure places. The styles employed in documenting sources necessarily varied, and I have not tried to standardize them here. In every case, I trust that enough information is provided to help other researchers find the material without difficulty.

I have also been fortunate in having generous friends, colleagues, and students who assisted me in my work with advice, criticism, and helpful leads to papers and people. I must thank John Saywell, David Bercuson, Norman Hillmer, Roger Sarty, Desmond Morton, Robert Bothwell, and many others. I am greatly indebted to them all.

JLG

Permissions

"Getting on with the Americans: Changing Canadian Perceptions of the United States, 1939–45," *Canadian Review of American Studies* 5, no. 1 (1974): 3–17. Reprinted with permission.

"Canada and the Marshall Plan, June–December 1947," *Historical Papers* 12, no. 1 (1977): 196–213. Reprinted with permission.

"The Rise and Fall of Canadian-American Free Trade, 1947–48," *Canadian Historical Review* 58, no. 4 (1977): 459–82. Reprinted with permission.

"Too Close for Comfort: John Diefenbaker and the Political Uses of Anti-Americanism," in *Yankee Go Home? Canadians and Anti-Americanism* (Toronto: Harper Collins, 1996), 121–45. Reprinted with permission.

"When Push Came to Shove: Canada and the United States," in *Kennedy's Quest for Victory, 1961–1963*, ed. Thomas G. Paterson (New York: Oxford University Press, 1989), 86–104. Reprinted with permission.

The Importance of Being Less Earnest: Promoting Canada's National Interests through Tighter Ties with the US (Toronto: C.D. Howe Institute, Benefactors Lecture 2003), 1–32. Reprinted with permission.

"The Anglocentrism of Canadian Diplomacy," in *Canadian Culture: International Dimensions*, ed. Andrew Cooper (Waterloo, ON: Centre on Foreign Policy and Federalism/Canadian Institute of International Affairs, 1985), 27–44. Reprinted with permission.

"Dealing with London," in *Canada's War: The Politics of the Mackenzie King Government, 1939–1945* (Toronto: Oxford University Press, 1975; Oakville, ON: Rock's Mills Press, 2016), 42–71. Reprinted with permission.

How Britain's Weakness Forced Canada into the Arms of the United States (Toronto: University of Toronto Press, 1989), 43–62, 72–7. Reprinted with permission.

"From Mother Country to Far-Away Relative: The Canadian-British Military Relationship from 1945," *Canadian Military History* 18, no. 1 (2009): 55–60. Reprinted with permission.

"Canada as an Ally: Always Difficult, Always Divided," in *Entangling Alliances: Coalition Warfare in the Twentieth Century*, ed. Peter Dennis and Jeffrey Gray (Canberra: Army Historical Unit, 2005), 254–76. Reprinted with permission.

"When the Department of External Affairs Mattered – and When It Shouldn't Have," in *In the National Interest: Canadian Foreign Policy and the Department of Foreign Affairs and International Trade, 1909–2009*, ed. Greg Donaghy and Michael K. Carroll (Calgary: University of Calgary Press, 2011), 69–79. Reprinted with permission.

"Peacekeeping Is Our Profession?," *International Journal* 25, no. 2 (1970): 414–19. Reprinted with permission.

"Peacekeeping: Did Canada Make a Difference? And What Difference did Peacekeeping Make to Canada?," in *Making a Difference? Canada's Foreign Policy in a Changing World Order*, ed. John English and Norman Hillmer (Toronto: Lester Publishing, 1992), 222–36. Reprinted with permission of the author.

"What's Wrong with Peacekeeping?," in *Canada and the New World Order: Facing the New Millenium*, ed. Michael J. Tucker, Raymond B. Baker, and P.E. Bryden (Toronto: Irwin, 2000), 45–54. Reprinted with permission of the author.

"War and Peacekeeping in the Canadian Psyche," *Descant*, no. 108 (2000): 97–103. Reprinted with permission.

"Changing Alliances: Canada and the Soviet Union, 1939–1945," in *Canada and the Soviet Experiment: Essays on Canadian Encounters with Russia*, ed. David Davies (Toronto: Canadian Scholars' Press, 1994), 75–87. Reprinted with permission of the author.

"From Gouzenko to Gorbachev: Canada's Cold War," in *Canadian Military Journal* 12, no. 1 (2012): 41–53. Reprinted with permission.

"Multiculturalism and Canadian Foreign Policy," in *The World in Canada: Diaspora, Demography, and Domestic Politics*, ed. David Carment and David Bercuson (Montreal: McGill-Queen's University Press, 2008), 78–91. Reprinted with permission.

Can Canada Have a Grand Strategy? (Calgary: Canadian Defence and Foreign Affairs Institute, 2011), 1–3. Reprinted with permission.

FRIENDS AND ENEMIES

Essays in Canada's Foreign Relations

Introduction

As I look at what I have written over the years, the consistent thread is a realistic assessment of Canada's national interests. What was truly crucial for us?

Our interests are very easy to state, and I doubt many would quarrel with this list:

- we must protect our territory, the security of our people, and our unity;
- we must enhance our independence and sovereignty;
- we must promote economic growth to support the prosperity and welfare of our population; and
- we must work with our friends and allies to protect, promote, and enhance freedom around the world.

There can be subheadings, qualifiers, additions, and changes in wording, but any such list, I suggest, would include these national interests. These are the basics, the key factors that determine Canadian security and success. These are the interests that, above all others, should concern our governments.

We also have core values that matter greatly in shaping our lives and the way Canadians have viewed and continue to see the world. These include a belief in democracy, the rule of law, and human rights. These are important and, much as our national interests, worth fighting for. Today, some expand Canadian values to include such things as multiculturalism, diversity, gender equality, LGBTQ rights, medicare, civility, good governance, and even flexible federalism. But these are relatively new concerns, hardly in place long enough to be pronounced immutably Canadian. The yet-to-be-achieved goal of full rights and acceptance for homosexuals, for example, is very recent, flexible federalism is a swear word to some Canadians, and Canada's good governance these days is not quite the model for the world we might wish it to be. Values that are not long-lived and widely cherished by the Canadian people may be seen more as government propaganda than as expressions of the popular will.[1]

Some Canadians wish us to be a moral superpower, setting out to make the world more like us every day. They forget that we are a relatively small nation in terms of population with a very limited ability to affect superpowers like the United States and China and those nations like Russia, Iran, and Saudi Arabia that have different belief systems. Our values matter, of course, but primarily to us, not so much for the rest of the world. Canadians are unlikely to go into battle for multiculturalism or federalism. We have, however, been willing on critical occasions to go to war for our national interests. Interests and core values both matter, but interests will always trump values.

But I suggest that national interests have not always determined our course in the past. Did it necessarily serve Canadian national interests to go to war in 1899 in South Africa? In Europe in August 1914? Or in Europe again in September 1939? Participation in each of those great events – from a Canadian perspective – is arguable, at least at the date we chose to begin hostilities. I would suggest, however, that going to war against Japan in December 1941 was without question an absolute necessity in the Canadian interest. North America, or its outlying islands, was under attack, and we had to respond. Similarly, the threat from the Soviet Union to North America after 1945 was real, and Canada's national interests demanded that we rearm, cooperate with the United States in defence of the continent, and join the North Atlantic alliance in the defence of Western Europe.

A more recent example of Canada's failure to recognize its national interests might be the decision made in the early 2000s by the Paul Martin Liberal government not to sign on to the Ballistic Missile Defence program with Washington. Canada was asked for nothing – neither money, nor people, nor territory – and the US offer was made simply on the assumption that as a neighbour under threat from a potential missile attack, Ottawa might wish to have a seat at the table. Despite the fact that some of his key ministers apparently favoured accession to the plan, Prime Minister Martin astonishingly said no – to the puzzlement of the US administration but to the cheers of much of the Canadian population (who, for other reasons, promptly rejected the Liberals in the 2005–6 election). Why? Because anti-Americanism, our secular religion, always seems more important to present-day Canadians than the national interest. Indeed, the very idea of national interests seems almost unknown to most Canadians. No government since Martin's has moved towards acquiring anti-missile defences despite increasing threats from Russia, China, North Korea, and soon Iran.

What is striking to me is that the debate in the United States, hyperpartisan as it is, very often seems to be based around great issues, around national interests. Americans know their nation has interests, and they can and do discuss them. That does not seem to be the case here. None of our political parties talks of national interests, not even the Bloc Québécois, which purports to advance the interests of an eventual separate, independent Quebec. Programs take priority; special interests prevail; and ten-dollar-a-day childcare remains more important to Canadians than national security. This is not sensible, and Canadians, and especially our leaders, need to face up to the reality that Canada's most important long-term national interests are not being considered seriously. Defence of our security and our people matter.

Consider peacekeeping, the subject of several of the chapters in section 3 of this volume, the foreign policy and defence subject that first interested me when I was an officer cadet at the Royal Military College at the end of the 1950s. Lester Pearson had won the Nobel Peace Prize for his role in creating the United Nations Emergency Force in the autumn of 1956, and I, like virtually every Canadian, was thrilled, so thrilled that I wrote a very long undergraduate thesis on peacekeeping in my final year at RMC.[2] At the time I thought peacekeeping was a natural role for our military. I knew we had 10,000 men on the ground and in the air in Western Europe in NATO and most of our navy patrolling the North Atlantic for Soviet submarines. But with a military numbering some 120,000 soldiers, sailors, and airmen, we had enough personnel in uniform to do peacekeeping at the same time. I hadn't anticipated the defence cutbacks that began under Diefenbaker and continued to the present, the wars in Afghanistan and Ukraine notwithstanding.

Canadian enthusiasm for peace operations remained strong, and successive governments liked this because peacekeeping was both popular and cheap. The Canadian Armed Forces began to fall in strength and its equipment grew obsolete as budgets declined in real terms from the 1960s onward. By the 1990s, as cutbacks intensified and personnel numbers were cut further after the end of the Cold War, peace operations increased; inevitably problems arose as soldiers spent more time overseas. The situation erupted in Somalia with killings of Somalis by Canadian troops – while no officer or sergeant did anything to intervene. Almost as bad, peacekeeping was never very successful on the ground, some operations (as in Cyprus and the Middle East) seemed never to end, and there were casualties, all of which Canadians failed to notice in their continuing and never-ending support for the concept. My opinions on the worth of peace operations began to change, and the shift can be traced in section 3.

My RMC thesis was important in another key way. It was the first time I did sustained research. I had briefly met the army's adjutant general, General Robert Moncel, at a Camp Borden mess dinner in the summer of 1960, and I wrote to him when I returned to RMC in September. To my surprise, he gave me access to the files of the Historical Section at National Defence Headquarters in Ottawa, where I saw – for the first time – confidential documents, most notably on the Suez crisis. I was hooked, and my BA thesis formed the basis for one of my first publications after I left the military, *Peacekeeper: International Challenge and Canadian Response*, published by the Canadian Institute of International Affairs in 1968.[3]

The army in 1961 allowed me to accept a scholarship to do a master's degree at the University of Toronto. Then, two years later, it again permitted me to go on leave without pay to take up a fellowship at Duke University in North Carolina and do a PhD in history. There, a seminar in British history in 1963–4 was taught by William Hamilton. He assigned each student another's draft paper; we would then dissect it, mark it up stylistic infelicity, and note every factual or interpretative error. This meant that the critic had to research the topic quickly, probe for strengths and weaknesses, and criticize the paper constructively in class. This was a terrific learning experience, and after I left the army and began to teach at York University in 1966, I used this technique in my fourth-year and graduate seminars. It was wondrously effective.

My PhD dissertation was on the Conservative Party during the Second World War,[4] and again this involved sustained research. New archival collections were beginning to be available, Xeroxes were beginning to be offered by archives, and while notes written by pen were still the product of most of my digging into the files, piles of copies and five-by-eight notecards began to be amassed. I developed simple organizational systems and carried them through to the 1990s.

The first book that brought me into research on foreign policy in a major way was *Canada's War: The Politics of the Mackenzie King Government, 1939–1945*, published in 1975.[5] This involved Canadian-American relations and our dealings with Britain during the war. A chapter on relations with Britain can be found in section 1. Canada was starting to become a player, and the Departments of External Affairs and Finance had impressive public servants who led the way and shaped Canadian policy. This soon led directly to a biography of Norman Robertson, O.D. Skelton's successor as undersecretary of state for external affairs,[6] and to a collective biography of the key officials in the years 1935–57, men (they were all male) that I dubbed "the Ottawa men."[7]

All three of these books were heavily tilted towards foreign policy with substantial space devoted to economic foreign policy. I began to realize that Britain, acting in its own national interests during the Second World War and after, had been forced by its economic and military weakness to push Canada to deepen its economic links to the United States. Only by doing that could Ottawa acquire the American dollars it needed to pay for the components from the United States it required for munitions manufacturing; only in that way could the British get the economic assistance they needed from Canada. The result was the Ogdensburg and Hyde Park Agreements tying Canada much more closely than ever before to its neighbour. This process continued after the war when the British, still short of dollars and still rationing key commodities, again needed financial assistance. Ottawa had to provide aid in order to get Canadian exports into the UK market. Two chapters in section 1, both co-authored with Robert Cuff, my colleague at York University, detail Ottawa's efforts to find a way to get the American dollars it needed to pay for critical imports from the south, and that almost led to a free trade agreement in 1947–8, a move ultimately vetoed by Mackenzie King in his last months as prime minister.

Motivated by a searing anti-Americanism (and without any research into the primary sources!), two of Canada's great historians, Donald Creighton and W.L. Morton, painted these increasing links with the Americans as a shameful Liberal sellout to the United States and a betrayal of Canada's ties to the mother country. My research, however, had convinced me that this was not Ottawa's deliberate choice, but rather actions forced upon us by British weakness. In a series of three sardonic Joanne Goodman Lectures at the University of Western Ontario in 1988, I argued this case. The lectures turned into a small book that I had hoped to have the title "How Britain's Economic, Military and Political Weakness Forced Canada into the Arms of the United States: A Melodrama in Three Acts." Gerry Hallowell, my able editor at University of Toronto Press, balked at this, and the book, appearing in 1989, had an abbreviated title.[8] In sum, Britain receded in importance to Canada, and the United States replaced it as our lodestar. The post-war chapter from *Britain's Weakness* in this present book, along with one on the surprising persistence of Anglocentrism in Canadian foreign policy and another on the gradual collapse of military links to Britain, can be found in section 2.

Those Goodman Lectures made me interested in the history of Canadian anti-Americanism. I was and remain a strong Canadian nationalist, and I had been quite anti-American especially during the Vietnam War. But I gradually came to realize that anti-American feeling was frequently used in a shameless fashion by politicians to win votes and by Canadian industries to press Ottawa to keep protective tariffs high and subsidies flowing. The result was *Yankee Go Home? Canadians and Anti-Americanism*, published in 1996.[9] The publisher told me American tourists were upset by the title when they saw it in bookstores, and officials at the US Consulate General in Toronto criticized me to my face. I pointed out to no avail that there was a question mark in the title and that the book was an argument *against* anti-Americanism. The critics at the consulate and the tourists, of course, did not read (or buy!) the book. A chapter from *Yankee Go Home?* focused on the anti-Americanism of the Diefenbaker government in 1962–3 is here in section 2. The Conservatives, of course, were not the only political party to use anti-Americanism. Both the Liberals and the New Democratic Party had no qualms about railing against Washington whenever it suited their purposes.

There was more to Canadian foreign policy than Britain and the United States. I have already mentioned peacekeeping, but Canada was heavily involved in the Cold War with the Soviet Union, the major post-war threat to North America and Western Europe. First, Canada was never very united in responding to threats from overseas; the conscription crises in the two world wars, opposition in Quebec to participation in the Korean War, the wars against Saddam Hussein's Iraq, and to missile defence are proof of this. Canada had been an ally of the USSR during the Second World War, lasting until the defection of Igor Gouzenko in September 1945 and revelations about Moscow's spying began to make Soviet intentions clear. Two chapters in section 3 discuss these and the subsequent events of the Cold War.

Multiculturalism became Canadian policy under Pierre Trudeau, and immigration from Latin America, Asia, and Africa began to change the face of the nation. This soon came to have substantial influence on the nation's foreign policy, a subject I tackled in another of the essays in section 3. To me, the desires of diaspora groups that Canada should take strong positions on their former nations' travails did not sit well. I argued once again that Canada's national interests must determine our policies abroad, not the wishes of diaspora communities. We are not a superpower with great resources that can resolve all the world's problems, and we can have no grand global strategy. The Americans have these resources and strategies for this, as do the Chinese, but a middle power cannot. The only way for Canada to exercise real influence is to work within alliances and with our friends abroad. That will always be

Introduction 9

in our national interest – but we must pull our weight. Unfortunately, we did and still do not always do that.

I ended the introduction to *Canada at War*[10] with the following observation (slightly revised here for present purposes): Canada's national history still matters. It seems very odd to me that Canadian historians now pay so little attention to such subjects as those covered in this volume. Could it be that some believe that the political events of the First and Second World Wars in Canada and the battles overseas are of no consequence? That Canada's shift from the British to the American sphere of influence is unimportant? That Canada's role in dealing with the Soviet Union during the Cold War should not be studied and taught? To me and to the literate Canadian public, such issues matter. The past is a foreign country, to be sure, but if we do not examine the issues that once tormented Canadians we will never understand how we reached our present condition and status.

In other words, the past has genuine relevance for the present and the future. As George Orwell put it in *1984*, "Who controls the past controls the future: who controls the present controls the past." Canada has had its history wars in the past, and they continue to the present. We can learn from the past, and what we learn will shape the nation in the future.

NOTES

1 This subject is discussed in chapter 6.
2 "Canada and United Nations Forces" (honours thesis, Royal Military College, 1961).
3 Alastair Taylor, David Cox, and J.L. Granatstein, *Peacekeeping: International Challenge and Canadian Response* (Toronto: CIIA, 1968).
4 "The Conservative Party of Canada, 1939–1945" (PhD diss., Duke University, 1966). Published as *The Politics of Survival: The Conservative Party of Canada, 1939–45* (Toronto: University of Toronto Press, 1967).
5 (Toronto: University of Toronto Press, 1985).
6 *A Man of Influence: Norman A. Robertson and Canadian Statecraft, 1929–1968* (Ottawa: Deneau Publishers, 1981).
7 *The Ottawa Men: The Civil Service Mandarins, 1935–1957* (Toronto: Oxford University Press, 1982).
8 *How Britain's Weakness Forced Canada into the Arms of the United States* (Toronto: University of Toronto Press, 1989).
9 (Toronto: Harper Collins, 1996).
10 *Canada at War, 1914–45: Conscription, Diplomacy, and Politics* (Toronto: University of Toronto Press, 2020), 11.

SECTION ONE

Canada and the United States

Chapter One

Getting on with the Americans: Changing Canadian Perceptions of the United States, 1939–1945

The Second World War is regularly trumpeted as the period in which Canada came of age. The nation contributed very substantially to the Allied victory in men, materiel, and foodstuffs, and as a result of this effort Canada emerged from the war as perhaps the leader of a group of middle powers. There was a very great distance between a middle and a great power, to be sure, but there can be no doubt that fortunate geographical circumstance and economic power had combined to give Canada a status far beyond anything she had enjoyed before.

But in a sense this was artificial. During the war, as Professor C.P. Stacey has effectively demonstrated in his magisterial study of Canadian war policies, Canada was essentially unsuccessful in getting much of a share in Allied decision-making.[1] Power was concentrated in the hands of the "Big Three" and there was no disposition to share it, no matter how valuable the contribution of Canada and other lesser states might be.

This was no less true of the United States than of the Soviet Union or Great Britain, and this came as something of a shock to Canadian statesmen. Relations with the Americans had become increasingly warm after 1935, and Prime Minister Mackenzie King for a time was fully convinced that his destiny was to serve as the linch-pin that would link Great Britain and her erstwhile colonies. With their heavy capital investment in Canada and a growing trade surplus to protect, American leaders reciprocated Mackenzie King's friendship, and a special relationship seemed firmly established. The outbreak of war made this a valuable asset to Canada and to Britain, and King was exceedingly successful in the way he exploited his position in the period before Pearl Harbor.

Perhaps he was too successful, for the war linked the two North American states into economic lockstep, while the military exigencies led to a large American presence in Canada. This state of affairs might have been marginally acceptable to Canada if there had been an accretion of influence in Washington to offset it, but if such an intangible as influence can be measured, after mid-1941 there was probably an absolute decline. The effects were serious to Canada, and they preoccupied planners more and more as the war progressed and planning for the peace began. For the ordinary-sized, relations with giants must always be careful, and it is this delicate condition that forms the subject of this essay.

The requirements of defence began to force closer cooperation on Canada and the United States even before war began in 1939. A first meeting between military staff officers of both countries, arranged in secret and with the direct authorization of President Franklin Roosevelt and Prime Minister King, took place in January 1938, and a second meeting followed eleven months later.[2] More important, since offered in a public statement, was Roosevelt's pledge in a speech at Queen's University in Kingston, Ontario in August 1938: "The Dominion of Canada is part of the sisterhood of the British Empire. I give to you assurance that the people of the United States will not stand idly by if domination of Canadian soil is threatened by any other Empire."[3] "What I said at Queen's University," Roosevelt wrote in a private letter to Lord Tweedsmuir, the Governor-General of Canada, "was so obvious that I cannot quite understand why some American President did not say it half a century ago."[4]

The importance of the American pledge became evident after September 1939. The war was supposed to be one of "limited liability" for Canada, one that could be won without huge expenditures of men or money. The British and French shared similar views, too, and the Allied leaders and press talked optimistically of the blockade that would force Germany to its knees. The dreams of easy victory, however, dissolved into the reality of May and June 1940. Suddenly Britain found herself in danger of invasion and bereft of her French ally. For Canada, the character of the war altered overnight, and the Dominion all at once became England's ranking ally. The prospect of a British defeat was real, and in the circumstances Canadians cautiously began to look to their own safety.

The United States was Canada's only salvation. This was clear. Fortunately, there had been no major gaffes to alienate the Roosevelt administration or the American public. War measures that would affect the United States, its citizens or its corporations had been canvassed fully in Washington before implementation.[5] And with a few exceptions Canadians managed to restrain themselves while the isolationists and interventionists hammered away at one another in the United States.[6]

The deliberate and cautious low profile maintained by Canada in the first months of the war was probably appreciated in Washington. As a result Canada was in a good position to deal with the United States in this time of troubles. The first task was to play the role of middleman between London and Washington. King had hoped for this earlier, but now in the very different circumstances of the spring of 1940 he found this chore very difficult and taxing indeed.

The future of the Royal Navy in the event of a British defeat was obviously of great importance to Roosevelt. With the fleet in its hands, Germany could be a direct threat to America; without it or with the fleet in the American service, there would be no practical risks at all. The problem was that some Empire statesmen, most notably Menzies of Australia, saw the fleet as a bargaining counter that could induce the United States to give aid to the foundering Allies. An appeal cast in those terms clearly offended Roosevelt, who told a Canadian emissary that the message seemed to say, "If you don't help us at once we will let the Germans have the Fleet and you can go to Hell."[7] But what would happen to the Royal Navy "in the event of certain possible eventualities which could not possibly be mentioned aloud"?[8]

Roosevelt wanted Mackenzie King to convey to Winston Churchill the American hope that the Royal Navy would be preserved if the worst came to pass. In the event of a surrender, the President told H.L. Keenleyside, the External Affairs officer who served as King's emissary, the fleet should be dispersed to the Empire and King George VI despatched to Ottawa, perhaps, or to some other safe location. By that time, American opinion would be ready to help the Allies. But if Hitler took the Royal Navy, the result would be disaster. Japan would gain a virtually free hand in the Pacific and the Empire would be divided between Germany and Italy. Then came the difficult part for Mackenzie King. Keenleyside told the Prime Minister that the President wanted him to persuade the other Dominions to make a joint appeal to Churchill not to surrender the fleet.

King was appalled since such a request could only imply a lack of faith in Churchill's determination. As he recorded in his diary, "for a moment it seemed to me that the United States was seeking to save itself at the expense of Britain. That it was an appeal to the selfishness of the Dominions at the expense of the British Isles ... I instinctively revolted against such a thought. My reaction was that I would rather die than do aught to save ourselves or any part of this continent at the expense of Britain." The worst was yet to come. After he sent Keenleyside back to see Roosevelt to clarify the point, King learned that he was expected to present the President's view as if it were his own. The result was that King spent a very difficult May 30 trying to draft a message so as to "meet the President's wishes ... of having the message appear to be from myself rather than from him, while at the same time taking care to see that it was wholly his point of view that I was putting over and not my own."[9] The middleman's role was not an easy one, and Churchill's understandable irritation showed through his answering despatches. "Although the President is our best friend," he telegraphed to King, "no practical help has yet been forthcoming from the United States,"[10] a hard but true statement.

For Mackenzie King this period was an agonizing one. His world was crumbling, and he was near despair. Grant Dexter, a reporter for the *Winnipeg Free Press* with the best contacts in Ottawa, saw J.L. Ralston, King's Minister of Finance, on June 7 and was told of the Prime Minister's condition:

> Ralston had found King in his office at 2 a.m. working on this proposition [one of the liaison roles he was filling between Churchill and Roosevelt]. King had said that he was played out, finished and couldn't carry the load, or words to this effect. Ralston told me he said: "Chief you've got to go through. The despatch you are working on may mean victory, the saving of civilization." King agreed.[11]

Of equal importance, particularly from the Canadian point of view, was the formal defence tie that was made with the United States in the summer of 1940. The idea was not a new one,[12] but before the fall of France few would have believed it either necessary or expedient. Justice Felix Frankfurter, a close confidant of the President, told the Canadian Minister in Washington in early July that a common defence scheme was necessary.[13] Similarly a group of influential Canadians, mainly academics, younger politicians, and lawyers associated through the Canadian Institute of International Affairs, had drawn up a "Program of Immediate Canadian Action" at a meeting in July. Their concerns were fixed on the potential economic difficulties Canada faced with much of Europe closed to her trade now, but even more they argued the need for "conversations with the United States aiming at a continental defence scheme ... Public opinion in Canada," they claimed, "is ready for a frank recognition by the government of the need for action." Time was of the essence and Canada had to take the initiative: "If Canada allows this opportunity to go by default and the United States is consequently [later] obliged to require us to cooperate, we might as a result be unable to maintain our independent identity."[14]

Economic issues also concerned official Ottawa. The Bank of Canada had set up a committee in June to explore what steps would be necessary if, as it was euphemistically stated, communications with the United Kingdom were cut. The results, the subsequent study argued, would be catastrophic, and there would be heavy unemployment as industries lost their overseas markets. Canada would have to appeal to the United States for assistance, Graham Towers of the Bank wrote to King, and almost the only card that Canada held was that "The United States will have to plan its defence on continental terms at least, and Canada will be an integral and necessary part of their plan."[15]

Certainly the Americans knew this, for their exports to Europe and Britain were in much the same position as Canada's. The result was a sharp turn toward hemispheric thinking in Washington. Bruce Hutchison, the reporter for the Sifton newspapers, visited Washington early in June and had an astonishing conversation with A.A. Berle, the theorist of the large-scale corporation who had served in Roosevelt's brains trust. By 1940, Berle was an Assistant Secretary of State and, as Hutchison put it a bit too fulsomely, "the President's very closest adviser and brain man." Berle's studies, the reporter noted in a memorandum that found its way to Mackenzie King, "now relate to the new American Empire. I can describe it as nothing else. He has been working, he said, on the reorganization of the economy of all North and South America, the new hemispheric concept." Where, Hutchison asked, did Canada fit in all this?

> Well [Berle said], it's a problem, but not as great as you might think. Don't forget that we are going in for huge armaments. This will provide a large employment for Canadians. Then, there are such factors as the end of Scandinavian paper exports. You will get this business in the US. Wheat is the headache. But there, too, we will have to make concessions. You people still talk Manchester Liberalism. All right, we'll apply it to wheat. We'll say to the wheat producers, we can take so much wheat at a fixed price guaranteed by the government. You can produce more than that if you please, but you'll take whatever price the market will pay. In the end, your wheat men will get less and many of them will move into other industries. That has to come with us and with you, too. It was coming anyway. My feeling, in fact, is that the war has made it possible to settle many such problems, including the future of trade between the US and Canada, which we could not settle in peace times. In these times Congress will be willing to do many things it would never do before.

"His whole assumption," Hutchison concluded, "was that Canada's economy would be merged with that of the US, but he did not foresee political union."[16] Berle's scheme seemed predicated on a British defeat, of course.

Canadians could not publicly concede a British defeat as a possibility, although the Bank of Canada study indicated that planning for such an eventuality was in hand. H.L. Keenleyside wanted something more. "It is no longer any secret," Keenleyside wrote, "that the Government of the United States has been giving detailed and serious consideration to the possibility of re-organizing the whole economic life of the Western Hemisphere." Canadians had not studied this question at all, he argued, nor had they given much thought to the "military necessity for a revision of our external policies":

> It would seem to be improbable that the United States, in the chaotic and dynamic world that is likely to emerge from the present war, will be prepared to continue indefinitely to protect Canada without demanding a measure of active co-operation in return. It is a reasonable assumption that the United States will expect, and if necessary demand, Canadian assistance in the defence of this continent and this Hemisphere. Concrete steps such as the construction of the Alaska Highway, the defensive development of the Pacific coast and the Maritime Provinces, the coordination of Canadian and United States war materiel ... – these are lines along which Washington is likely to require Canadian co-operation. If the United States is forced to defend the Americas against encroachments from across either Ocean, Canada will be expected to participate; thus the negotiation of a specific offensive-defensive alliance is likely to become inevitable.[17]

Indeed it would, and when Roosevelt telephoned Mackenzie King and invited him to Ogdensburg, New York in mid-August, King was only too pleased to go. The result of this meeting was the Ogdensburg Agreement, a simple statement that announced the creation of a Permanent Joint Board of Defence charged with beginning "immediate studies relating to sea, land and air problems ... It will consider in the broad sense the defence of the north half of the Western Hemisphere."[18]

The Agreement was a logical extension of Roosevelt's pledge of 1938. What was striking about it, however, was that the PJBD was declared to be permanent. Seen in retrospect, the Agreement marked the shift from Canada as a British dominion to Canada as an American protectorate. Some people realized this at the time,[19] but in the general relief that Canada's safety was assured in the face of Axis power only the very foolish felt obliged to say so in public.[20] There was one very important, very cool response from abroad, however. Churchill wired King that

> I am deeply interested in the arrangements you are making for Canada and America's mutual defence. Here again there may be two opinions on some of the points mentioned. Supposing Mr. Hitler cannot invade us and his Air Force begins to blench under the strain, all these transactions will be judged in a mood different to that prevailing while the issue still hangs in the balance.[21]

Churchill's pique at Canada's scurrying to protect itself was understandable. But the British Prime Minister was wrong to assume that Canadian public opinion would permit the defences of Canada to be stripped so that aid could be sent to England without some guarantee of Canada's security. No Canadian government, charged above all with the defence of Canada, could have acted otherwise. The Ogdensburg Agreement, in addition, tied the United States closer to the belligerents, a positive gain for the Allied cause. In the long run, however, Churchill was prophetic.

The post-Ogdensburg linkages between the two North American states developed apace. The PJBD began its meetings almost immediately and soon the Board was drafting plans and making recommendations to the two governments.[22] One of its suggestions, apparently advanced by the Canadian secretary to the PJBD, was that a Joint Committee should be appointed to report on the possibilities of increased economic coordination between Canada and the United States. This idea was extensively discussed within the Canadian government and with some Washington officials, including Berle, and it formed the subject of a formal Canadian note to the United States, delivered on March 17, 1941. "It is the belief of the Canadian Government," the *aide-mémoire* stated, "that the promotion of economy and efficiency during the present period of crisis, the solution of the problems which will be posed during the period of transition from war to peace, and adequate and effective provision for the continuing requirements of hemisphere defence, all demand that early and detailed study be given to this question." The upshot was the establishment of the Joint Economic Committee in June 1941. Its task was to study and report on the "possibilities of 1) effecting a more economic, more efficient and more coordinated utilization of the combined resources of the two countries in the production of defence requirements ... and 2) reducing the probable post-war economic dislocations consequent upon the changes which the economy in each country is presently undergoing."[23] The Committee was a Canadian initiative toward closer integration of the North American economy.

There was another major initiative in this direction, too. On April 20, 1941, King and Roosevelt agreed to the Hyde Park Declaration. This agreement declared the President's intention to ease Canada's shortage of United States dollars by buying more in Canada. In addition, the President agreed that components the United States was lend-leasing to Britain could be shipped to Canada for incorporation in Canadian goods destined for England. These were measures of crucial concern to the Canadians, and Roosevelt's willingness to assist was vital.[24]

The Canadian aim in these critical months of 1940 and 1941 had been to bind the Dominion to the United States. In part this was a plain and simple desire for the protection that could be afforded by the American government. Also important was a clear desire to involve the United States more closely with a belligerent, to tie America and the Commonwealth closer together. To help Canada was to help Britain, and this was certainly the case with the Hyde Park Declaration, which ensured that Canada would not fall victim to an exchange shortage that could interrupt the flow of supplies to England.

In strictly Canadian terms, however, there were both assets and liabilities on the new balance sheet. The gains were in terms of security, the jobs, economic stability, and access to vital components that the new relationship with the United States brought. There was also a new influence in Washington. But Canada was also being linked inextricably into an American-dominated nexus, and its production and resources were increasingly coining to be thought of as joint assets. The *Canadian Forum* noted in June 1941 that the Americans "are more and more tending to look upon the military and economic integration which is taking place between Canada and the United States as the starting-point ... They are hinting more and more openly that Canadian-American plans, military and economic, are not merely for the duration of the war."[25]

Even as the *Forum* wrote, however, the shift in American planning was in process. Talks with the British military had begun early in 1941, and joint planning was already far advanced. From the point of view of the War and Navy Departments in Washington it was much easier to negotiate with Britain alone rather than individually with Britain and her passel of Dominions. As a result when the Canadians tried in mid-1941 to secure US permission to establish a military mission in

Washington they were rebuffed. Repeated efforts were dealt with in a similar way, and it was not until July 1942 that a full-fledged Canadian Joint Staff was created in Washington.[26] The hemispheric vision was gone after a year's existence. In its place was a global dream. Pearl Harbor forcibly fixed the new vision firmly in place.

For Canada the results would be pronounced. From being a vital link in the defence of the hemisphere in 1940–41, Canada had become a mere appendage of limited importance. The Canadian government had made agreements of far-reaching importance based on the continuance of an American hemispheric scheme, and now that scheme was dead. Roosevelt and King would still meet and talk in a friendly way, but no longer would the President feel obliged to deliver messages through the medium of Mackenzie King. He and Churchill met for the first time in August 1941 off Newfoundland, a meeting at which the Canadian Prime Minister was prominent only by his absence. The realities had intervened.

The new Canadian position vis-à-vis the United States greatly concerned the Department of External Affairs, and Norman Robertson, the Undersecretary, prepared a long memorandum on the subject for the Prime Minister a few weeks after Pearl Harbor. Canadians, Robertson wrote, "have tended to take it for granted" that the United States would "always regard Canadian interests as a close second to their own and appreciably ahead of those of any third country." Now this was no longer so:

> It is probably an inevitable consequence of the increasing involvement of the United States in the war and of its acceptance of leadership of the democratic cause that the President should tend more and more to deal directly with the Great Powers and find less time to spend on the specifically Canadian aspects of American international relations. Canada naturally loomed much larger in the American scheme of things when the President and both political parties in the United States were thinking primarily in terms of continental and hemispheric defence. Now that the world war is joined on both oceans, the United States is, not unnaturally, inclined to take Canadian concurrence and support entirely for granted.

The result was a shift in the tenor of Canadian-American relations, a shift that Robertson believed to be "rather abrupt and not too tactfully handled." Part of the problem was caused by the scattering of responsibility for foreign affairs among a plethora of new agencies and offices in Washington and partly by the growing pressure there for a unification of Allied representation in the United States. Canadian matters were no longer always checked with the Department of State, as they had been before the war; and indeed the Department was rapidly declining in influence with the President at this time. Of course, contact between opposite numbers in the various agencies in Ottawa and Washington was close and a useful aid to a speedy resolution of technical problems. But, Robertson argued, this gain was "offset by the loss ... of the preferred position Canada had gradually consolidated through long years of close and friendly collaboration with the President and the Department of State."

Equally important was the shift in the American perception of power. Before the war, Robertson claimed, the US believed it could save the world by "its example, by minding its own business, pursuing a fair and friendly policy toward its neighbours." This era was over now and "we can see the United States turning everywhere to more direct and forceful methods of exerting its influence." This had been shown, for example, in the way the Americans had taken over the negotiations with Vichy France and in the way they had monopolized dealings with Japan before Pearl Harbor. The effect of this "new appreciation of the enormous strategic importance and strength of the United States" was a "new sense of ... 'manifest destiny' and a corresponding disposition to take decisions and accept responsibilities. This change of attitude is very encouraging from the standpoint of the world in general but," Robertson warned, "it does imply quite an important modification of the special relationship in which Canada has hitherto stood with regard to the United States."

There were a host of examples that showed that the special relationship was gone. Robertson cited the "gradual assumption by the United States of hegemony in Newfoundland" as one and the negotiation of the Atlantic Charter by Roosevelt and Churchill alone as another. Equally important in his view was Canada's omission from the Anglo-American discussions of post-war commercial relationships then in progress although "the field of these negotiations is one in which, up until this year, Canada has taken a much greater initiative than any other part of the British Commonwealth."

Robertson was probably painting an idealized picture of the pre-1941 period, but that there was a shift in Canadian-American relations was clear. What was to be done? Probably the most able civil servant of his generation, Robertson could only suggest that Canada upgrade its Legation in Washington to Embassy status and appoint as Ambassador an individual who would also sit in the Cabinet War Committee in Ottawa.[27] The first part of this recommendation was to be carried out in 1943 without noticeable effect. Quite likely, nothing that Canada could have done would have achieved much. The United States was now well and truly launched on a search for world power as pronounced as the reluctance to accept binding commitments had been during the interwar years.

Curiously, just at the time that some Canadians were beginning to worry about their declining relationship with Washington, the British were beginning to think that Canada's links with the United States were too close, that Ogdensburg and Hyde Park marked the seduction of Canada out of the Empire and into the arms of America. Malcolm MacDonald, the British High Commissioner in Ottawa, who was very close to Mackenzie King, noted that "There may be some danger that Mr. Mackenzie King will be inclined to associate Canada too closely as a North American country with the United States as distinct from the United Kingdom." King's friendship with the President worried MacDonald, but the High Commissioner concluded that King's loyalty to the Commonwealth was "paramount in his mind as it is in the minds of his fellow countrymen."[28] Other British ministers were by no means as certain. "Bobbetty" Cranborne, the Secretary of State for Dominion Affairs, worried often about Canada's too-close relationship with the United States, and in a 1942 minute to a file he observed that "I do not like feeling that [Canada's] closest contacts are with Washington in matters of national defence."[29]

What of Mackenzie King? His career had been based in part on his desire to create closer ties with the United States and to cut away the bonds that entangled Canada in the affairs of Empire.[30] But, as MacDonald properly assessed him, he was a sentimental imperialist, a devotee of the British connection, and an almost fawning courtier before British royalty. To King, however, Roosevelt was almost a monarch, and the correspondence from Prime Minister to President was sometimes almost embarrassing in its devotion. After a visit to Washington in May 1942, for example, King wrote that "I could not, if I would, begin to tell you how much I enjoyed its every hour and, particularly, the intimate personal talks with yourself."[31]

This kind of hyperbole aside, King was very capable of assessing Canada's American problem realistically. He liked Roosevelt and admired him deeply – "Give him my love," he told one visiting American in 1941[32] – and he knew that he could win important concessions for his country simply because his access to the President allowed Canada often to bypass the bureaucracy. In 1940, for example, he noted that "there is real purpose behind my seeing the President … I can do more in one week spent to that end than might be accomplished in months by remaining at Ottawa."[33]

Still, Roosevelt was not the United States. The Alaska Highway, begun in 1942, was one issue that impressed upon King the need to protect Canada's sovereignty against the Americans. The road, he told Malcolm MacDonald in March 1942, "was less intended for protection against the Japanese than as one of the fingers of the hand which America is placing more or less over the whole of the Western hemisphere."[34] He told the same thing to another visitor: "it was not without some concern that ... I viewed the Alaska Highway and some other things growing out of the war, ... [and it] was clear to my mind that America has had as her policy, a western hemisphere control which would mean hemispheric immunity ... from future wars but increasing political control by US."[35] In Cabinet, King "held strongly to the view with one or two others that we ought to get the Americans out of the further development there [Norman Wells, NWT], and keep complete control in our hands."[36] Again and again, King told his callers the same thing. With some it was what they wanted to hear, to be sure. He told the anglophilic Vincent Massey that "Canadians were looked upon by Americans as a lot of Eskimos,"[37] for example, but the refrain is so consistent that King certainly believed what he said.[38] Whether he did enough to counter American penetration is another question entirely.

King was not alone in feeling uneasy about American policy as a whole series of assessments penned in the Department of External Affairs in 1943 and 1944 make clear. H.L. Keenleyside, for example, had detected a coordinated American effort to obtain post-war advantages in Canada as a result of United States wartime expenditures in the Northwest. The American people, he argued, "have begun to think in terms of postwar advantage ... a popular feeling in the United States that the Administration will be failing in its duty if it does not provide now for the acquisition of post-war profit from wartime expenditure in foreign countries."[39] Lester Pearson, the second-ranking officer in Washington, was similarly worried, and he regretted "that we should be so often forced into a position where we have to complain to the State Department about slights or injuries or omissions." There was another danger, Pearson added, "On instructions from Ottawa, we take a firm stand in Washington in opposition to certain United States demands. But as soon as pressure is exerted by the US Government either here or in Ottawa, we give in ... This kind of diplomacy, the strong glove over the velvet hand, has nothing to commend it."[40] The same kind of feeling was expressed by Escott Reid, a young and able nationalist who before the war had been one of the leading neutralists in Canada. Reid had served in Washington early in the war and now was back in Ottawa. Some Canadians, he observed in a memo sent to Norman Robertson, were expressing the fear that Canada was becoming an adjunct of the United States "without the formalities of annexation" simply because the Americans were becoming more insistent about demanding and getting their own way. To many Americans, their participation in the war "is a favour which the United States is conferring on humanity and which carries with it the right to run things their own way." This was particularly true of recent dealings with Canada, Reid said. Before the war, a patronizing "Good Neighbour" attitude had not been shown to Canada but now it was, and one reason for this change was just plain aggressiveness. One example Reid cited dealt with an argument over wheat sales. The American Embassy in Ottawa had told the Deputy Minister of Trade and Commerce "that if we did not sell the wheat at the low price demanded by the United States they would be forced to announce publicly that because of Canada's decision the United States would have to cut down on wheat shipments to the United Kingdom and the USSR." The message was clear: Canada would have to be prepared for "energetic, aggressive and at times inconsiderate policies on the part of the Administration in Washington and as close neighbours we may see more of this than most other people."[41]

All these fears nothwithstanding, the realities of geographical propinquity, of economic dependence, and of the potential problems of continental defence gave Canada little room for manoeuvre. The Cabinet War Committee finally decided in July 1945 to maintain defence ties with the United States into the post-war world. The ministers' deliberations for more than a year had centred around successive drafts of a paper on "Post War Defence Arrangements with the United States," the major thrust of which was that the United States "may be expected to take an active interest in Canadian defence preparations in the future." The reason was clear: "Canada lies astride the overland route between the United States and the USSR." Any deterioration in Soviet-American relations would be embarrassing to Canada, the paper said, but in the event of any such embarrassment it was clear that Canada stood with the United States. As the paper also noted, "This closer tie-up with the United States need not conflict with the Canadian tradition of basing military policy and training upon British practice. However," the drafters of the report said, surely realizing the import of their words, "if Canada and the United States are to be efficient in the defence of North America, common experience between the national forces will be desirable."[42]

The government's decision was made, and so evidently was that of the informed public. This became very clear in 1945 when the Canadian Institute of International Affairs, its membership comprising virtually the entire Canadian foreign policy community, met at Kingston on May 26–27, 1945. The Canadian desk officer at the State Department in Washington, J. Graham Parsons, attended and addressed the meeting. His remarks and the reaction they received were reported to London by a British observer:

> There was a high degree of acceptance of the proposition that Canada's future political alignment would be with the United States, and only secondarily with the British Commonwealth ... The view ... was tactfully encouraged by Mr. Parsons ... He said that Canada's views and wishes exerted an influence on the United States administration out of all proportion to Canadian power, and added that on commercial policy Canada already enjoyed a consideration accorded to Great Powers alone. The enormous gratification of the company at this remark could not be concealed, and it apparently occurred to no one that it might be a bit exaggerated and of questionable validity in relation to the future.
>
> Mr. Parsons went on to describe as a source of some embarrassment to the United States the elasticity of the present system under which Canada's interests are presented sometimes through Canadian diplomatic channels and sometimes through London ... He said that the effect was that the State Department did not always know where Canada stood on particular issues.[43]

The shift was almost complete. Most Canadians now recognized that they lived in a North American nation and, although it would take a decade to become completely apparent, the Commonwealth tie was now in decay.

Two Canadian officials who spent much of the war in Washington summed it all up in an academic article written in 1945 that described the kind of cooperation that had existed in Washington:

> There has been the open exchange of confidence between the Americans and Canadians, the warm welcome, the freedom from formality, the plain speaking, and the all-pervading friendship. Neither is it easy to enumerate the conditions which made the high degree of co-operation possible. Co-operation was, of course, a sensible course to follow. It stood on its own merits. However, commonsense is not always able to prevail over sovereignty, and self-interest, and special national interests. That the course was followed, or at least adopted so readily and successfully, is due in part to the friendly disposition that existed, attributable no doubt to our common background of language and culture, and to the close trade and industrial relationship: in part it is due to the fact that our approach to problems is similar.[44]

Canadians and Americans were almost the same.

Over the course of the next few years, the pressing demands of international politics would force Canadians and Americans still closer together. Canadian policy-makers generally wanted this and pressed for it, seeing certain advantages for Canada in it. Their caution remained, however, and eventually they would begin to seek with increasing desperation for new makeweights to the United States. The United Nations, the North Atlantic Treaty Organization, even finally the Commonwealth – all would be tried and found wanting. The links that had been forged during the war were too strong. Those were "the ties that bind."

NOTES

1 C.P. Stacey, *Arms, Men and Governments* (Ottawa, 1970), esp. chapter 4.
2 Public Archives of Canada, W.L.M. King Papers, "Memorandum to the Minister on Conversations held in Washington ... 26 Jan 38," ff. C112708ff.; F.D. Roosevelt Library, Hyde Park, Roosevelt Papers, PSF State Dept., S. Welles to FDR, 20 Dec 37; ibid., PSF Welles, Welles to FDR, 10 Jan 38 and 14 Jan 38; Directorate of History, Canadian Forces Headquarters, 000.4 (D14), Memo, Gen. Anderson to Minister of National Defence, 23 Nov 38.
3 [United States Information Service], *Canadian-American Relations 1867–1967* (Ottawa, 1967), III, 34.
4 Roosevelt Papers, PPF 3396, FDR to Tweedsmuir, 31 Aug 38.
5 *E.g.*, King Papers, Loring Christie to King, 23 Feb 40, ff. 241080ff.
6 See Stephen Leacock, *All Right Mr. Roosevelt* (Toronto, 1939). Even more foolish was a speech by Gordon Conant, Ontario Attorney-General. See *Toronto Star*, 4 Apr 40; King Papers, Christie to Secretary of State for External Affairs, 4, 11 Apr 40, ff. 241188, 241233–4. For a British response to Conant, see Public Record Office, London, Foreign Office Records, FO 800/398, Campbell to Lothian, 8 Apr 40, and FO 371/25224, Cavendish-Bentinck to Garner, 11 Apr 40.
7 King Papers, Black Binders, vol. 19, I, Memo by Keenleyside, 29 May 40.
8 Ibid., III, Memo by Keenleyside, 23 May 40.
9 J.W. Pickersgill, *The Mackenzie King Record*, Vol. I: *1939–1944* (Toronto, 1960), 117ff. The message is on pp. 120–1.
10 King Papers, Black Binders, vol. 19, III, Secretary of State for Dominion Affairs to Secretary of State for External Affairs, 5 Jun 40.
11 Queen's University, Grant Dexter Papers, Memorandum, 7 Jun 40. The memo goes on: "Which indicates Ralston's position fairly well. Willie may be doing all he says but, in any event, he sure has J.L. buffaloed."

12 Library of Congress, Washington, Cordell Hull Papers, folder 194, Memo of Conversation with Canadian Chargé, 17 Jun 40; US National Archives, Washington, State Department Records, 740.0011 Eur War 1939/4700, Memo by A.A. Berle, 12 Jul 40.
13 King Papers, Black Binders, vol. 20, file 77, Typed Diary Note, 13 Jul 40.
14 Copy in University of British Columbia, Alan Plaunt Papers, Box 9, file 1. Among the group were Brooke Claxton, MP, John Baldwin of the CIIA, Frank Scott of the McGill law faculty, Sen. Norman Lambert, and others. See ibid., Box 8, file 20, Plaunt to Baldwin, 13 Aug 40. I am indebted to William R. Young for allowing me to use his notes from this collection.
15 King Papers, Towers to King, 15 Aug 40, ff. 25269ff.
16 Ibid., Black Binders, vol, 19, Memorandum, 12 Jun 40.
17 PAC, Department of External Affairs Records, vol. 781, file 394, "An Outline Synopsis for a Reconsideration of Canadian External Policy with particular reference to the United States," 17 Jun 1940.
18 *Canadian-American Relations 1867–1967*, II, 3.
19 See J.L. Granatstein, "The Conservative Party and the Ogdensburg Agreement," *International Journal*, XXII (Winter, 1966–7), and James Eayrs, "The Road from Ogdensburg," *Canadian Forum*, L (February, 1971), 364ff.
20 For press response, see King Papers, Notes and Memoranda, vol. 139, and ibid., Christie to Secretary of State for External Affairs, 10 Sep 40, ff. 241378ff.
21 Ibid., Black Binders, vol. 20, file 77, Message of 22 Aug 40.
22 On the PJBD, see C.P. Stacey, "The Canadian-American Permanent Joint Board of Defence," *International Journal*, IX (Spring, 1954).
23 See documents on file 1497-40, part I, at the Department of External Affairs, Ottawa. See also, External Affairs Records, vol. 780, file 383, and vol. 826, file 725; State Department Records, 842.20 Defense/71, Memo by A.A. Berle, 17 Mar 41.
24 On Hyde Park, see J.L. Granatstein and R.D. Cuff, "The Hyde Park Declaration of April 1941: Origins and Significance," *Canadian Historical Review*, LV (March 1974).
25 "Pax Americana," *Canadian Forum*, XXI (June, 1941), 69ff, See also the notes on an interview with Berle in External Affairs Records, file 1497-40, 4 Feb 41.
26 The negotiations for the military mission are well handled in Stacey, pp. 354–7. Cf. S.W. Dziuban, *Military Relations Between the United States and Canada 1939–1945* (Washington, 1959), pp. 71ff. See also British documents on this question. Documents on PRO, Dominions Office Records, DO 35/1010 pt. III/WG 476/4/6 and on DO 114/114, pp. 127ff.
27 External Affairs Records, vol. 810, file 614, Memo for the Prime Minister, 22 Dec 41. Cf. memos by Keenleyside in ibid., 27 Dec 41 and 14 Apr 42. For a US appraisal of the new sensitivity in Ottawa, see State Department Records, 711.42/237, "Memo of Conversation with Norman

Robertson ... 19 Feb 42." Prof. F.R. Scott characterized the new relationship with Washington as imposing a "dual colonialism" on Canada, adding the US brand to the existing UK one. F.R. Scott, "Canadian Nationalism and the War," *Canadian Forum*, XXI (March, 1942), 361.
28 PRO, Prime Minister's Office Records, Premier 4/44/10, extract from letter Aug 1941.
29 Dominions Office Records, DO 35/1010 A III/WG 476/141, minute, n.d. /early, 1942/.
30 See, e.g., King's remarks to the Liberal caucus on 5 Jun 40 in Pickersgill, I, 87.
31 Roosevelt Papers, PSF Canada 1–42, King to FDR, 4 May 42.
32 Ibid., PSF–1, Diplomatic correspondence – Canada, Archibald MacLeish to FDR, 15 Feb 41.
33 King Papers, Diary, 20 Apr 40, f. 392.
34 Ibid., 21 Mar 42, f. 251.
35 Ibid., 18 Mar 42, f. 243.
36 Pickersgill, I, 644–5.
37 Vincent Massey, *What's Past Is Prologue* (Toronto, 1963), p. 397.
38 But see State Department Records, 711.42/255, Memo, Hickerson to Hull, 20 May 43, which indicates real complacency about Canada-US relations.
39 King Papers, "Evidence Relating to United States Efforts ...," 11 Dec 43, ff. C241909ff.
40 Ibid., "Certain Developments in Canada-United States Relations," 18 Mar 43, ff. C241878ff.
41 External Affairs Records, vol. 110, file 702, Memo for Undersecretary, 29 Feb 44.
42 External Affairs Records, file 7-AD(s), part II, and James Eayrs, *In Defence of Canada*, Vol. III: *Peacemaking and Deterrence* (Toronto, 1972), 320–31, 375–80.
43 Foreign Office Records, FO 371/50365, "Notes on Annual Conference ..." att. to Holmes to Stephenson, 15 Jun 45. For a US view of the same meeting, see State Department Records, 842.00/6–145, Atherton to Secretary of State, 1 Jun 45 and atts.
44 S.D. Pierce and F.W. Plumptre, "Canada's Relations with War-Time Agencies in Washington," *Canadian Journal of Economics and Political Science*, XI (1945), 410–11.

Chapter Two

Canada and the Marshall Plan, June–December 1947

J.L. GRANATSTEIN AND R.D. CUFF

Pragmatic self-interest in tension with idealistic internationalism is one characteristic theme of Canadian foreign policy in the postwar era and no more so than in those revolutionary years immediately after 1945 when Canada, too, was "present at the creation." From the vantage point of a rich and powerful North American continent untouched by war, Canada contemplated the devastation of Europe. At the same time, however, like the European nations, Canada nervously eyed its fundamental dollar dependency on the United States. The world had changed, but what R.S. Sayers has called Canada's "bilateral unbalance within a balanced 'North Atlantic Triangle'" remained.[1]

It was Lester Pearson's central historic task to resolve for Canadians in ideology this tension between political hope and economic necessity, and there can be no question of his great success. But the tensions remained in practice: between moralism and military security; between United Nations universalism and NATO regionalism; between peacekeeping idealism and material contributions to the American stockpile; between the quest for national autonomy and the bilateral basis of Canadian prosperity. Leading a nation not at all different than the others, Canadian officials had to negotiate their way between the superpowers in a new, nuclear world. And it was both their burden and their opportunity in the late 1940s to be near the geographic centre of the most powerful imperial superpower of all.

How did Canadian officials perceive and respond to America's postwar "creation"? Close study of a variety of relationships is, of course, required for a comprehensive overview. Nevertheless, a case study of Canada's relationship and reactions to the early stages of the Marshall Plan initiative is a microcosm of what we believe to be characteristic patterns of Canadian-American economic relations in the postwar years.

I

"I need not tell you, gentleman, that the world situation is very serious." With those words, Secretary of State George C. Marshall began the core of his address to the graduating class at Harvard University on June 5, 1947. The world situation did seem to be deteriorating rapidly. The British and European economies were in ruins, shattered by the impact of the war, and their rehabilitation seemed threatened by a growing and general shortage of American dollars.[2] "The truth of the matter," Marshall said flatly, "is that Europe's requirements for the next three or four years of foreign food and other essential products – principally from America – are so much greater than her present ability to pay that she must have substantial additional help or face economic, social and political deterioration of a very grave character." Such a collapse would hurt the American economy. And although this was only implicit in what the Secretary of State said, it could also lead to the loss of Western Europe to the Communists, possibly through military action from the Soviet Union but more likely through the election of Communist governments in the disheartened democracies.

The solution to this problem, Marshall said in a carefully worded statement that had been the product of substantial discussion within the Department of State, was for the United States to assist in alleviating the crisis. Before this could occur, however, "there must be some agreement among the countries of Europe as to requirements of the situation and the part those countries themselves will take in order to give proper effect to whatever action might be undertaken by this Government ... The role of this country," General Marshall said, "should consist of friendly aid in the drafting of a European program and of later support of such a program ..."[3]

Although lacking in specifics, the American proposal was a generous one and the Europeans were not slow to take advantage of it. Through the summer of 1947, the meetings and suggestions came with great speed, and by the fall the ground was cleared for action. The Soviet Union and the East European nations in its sphere of influence chose not to participate in the Marshall Plan, a decision that one may confidently assume did not trouble the United States or most of the Western European states very much.[4] The "shopping lists" had been prepared by the Europeans with some American help and direction;[5] now all that remained was to pass the Plan and its huge appropriations through the United States Congress and to work out the details. That would be difficult enough.

For Canada, the Marshall Plan proposals were welcome ones, promising stability in a reconstructed Europe that could only be in Canada's long-term economic and security interests. Lester Pearson, the Undersecretary of State for External Affairs, told Prime Minister Mackenzie King on June 28 that the Marshall suggestion would be "not only of fundamental international value, but would, incidentally, help very greatly to solve our dollar problem as it would put European countries in possession of American dollars, some of which could be used for purchases in Canada."[6] There was an opportunity there, a way of possibly resolving the growing shortage of American dollars that was troubling the Ottawa bureaucracy through mid-1947.[7] In 1946 and 1947 Canada had loaned some $2 billion to Western Europe in an effort to re-build Canadian markets there as well as to contribute to European recovery. Those loans, when linked to a great domestic post-war spending spree on imported American consumer goods, were primarily responsible for the catastrophic drop in Canada's US dollar reserves from $1,667 million in May 1946 to $480 million in November 1947.[8] Now the Marshall Plan, in its great generosity to Europe, could provide a way out of the morass. To secure as much of the benefits as possible for Canada would become the first task of the Departments of External Affairs and Finance.[9]

The real Canadian difficulty was with Congress, for under the American system of government there were few certitudes. The Secretary of State might propose but Congress would dispose. And in 1947, Congress was dominated by fractious, often isolationist Republicans who were convinced that after the 1948 elections they would be in power and Harry Truman's Democrats would be out. In its present mood, Congress seemed dubious about giving much aid to Europe; if any was given, the benefits that could be secured by purchasing needed supplies would have to stay in the United States.

For example, when the Senate Foreign Relations Committee was considering a bill providing $350 million for "Relief to the People of Countries Devastated by War" in April 1947, Senator Wallace White, Republican of Maine, was blunt on this point in a closed Committee session: "I think one of the objections that will be raised, and raised with some loud voice, is the possibility that substantial amounts of these relief goods ... can be purchased abroad with the American market in a position to furnish them. There are going to be a lot of fellows, in my opinion," the Senator orated, "who would much prefer to vote all of this should be of American origin rather than any of it should be of foreign origin, and I would go the very limit in giving assurance by the letter of this legislation that American goods are to be purchased just to the limit of possibilities." Only with some difficulty was the Committee persuaded to accept the State Department's importunings that as much as 6 per cent of the money appropriated could be spent outside the United States.[10]

Hume Wrong, the Canadian Ambassador in Washington, was well aware of the potential difficulties that the Marshall Plan itself might face and equally concerned with the difficult task of getting Canada some of its benefits. On June 20 he reported to Ottawa on a conversation with Dean Acheson, the Undersecretary of State and a close personal friend. Wrong had told Acheson, then in the last few days of his tenure of office, that Canada's deteriorating dollar holdings would probably necessitate import restrictions unless the Marshall Plan came into effect within a few months. Acheson's reply was bleak: "He said that he did not see how the Marshall Plan could be developed so as to operate before the beginning of next year."[11] Charles Bohlen, one of the State Department's Soviet experts, was somewhat more optimistic when he told Wrong that the Marshall Plan proposal marked the first time the West had seized the initiative since 1945. "General Marshall as a soldier, knew the importance of gaining the initiative ... He was determined to do his best to keep [it] ..., and would do his utmost to carry the majority of Congress with him."[12] George Kennan, another Soviet expert now heading the State Department's planning staff, could only suggest to Wrong that "He was fairly sure ... that the public had much greater trust in the Administration than Congress had and that in time Congressional opinion would be modified as a result."[13]

Bleakest of all was the advice Wrong received from Robert Lovett, Acheson's successor as Undersecretary of State, at the end of July. He said, Wrong wrote to Pearson in Ottawa, "that the advice which they had received from political leaders at the Capitol was that if Congress were convened in the autumn to consider further US aid to Europe, not a dollar would be appropriated." The best that Lovett could suggest was that this might alter "because of a growing sense of crisis," presumably with the Soviet Union, but he was not at all confident. Wrong tried to raise the Canadian dollar shortage with Lovett, pointing out that the Dominion's crisis would affect the American position:

> with our US dollar deficit, we could not continue to finance from loans Canadian exports to Europe on the present scale and that, if these exports were reduced, it would increase the pressure on the US to provide goods of the same type and thus have the effect of adding to inflationary tendencies in the United States. He was not, however, impressed by these arguments.[14]

Worse still, Lovett, thinking no doubt about the State Department's difficulties with Congress' attitude to "off-shore purchases" in April 1947, "appeared to think that any funds [appropriated by Congress for European aid] would be tied to purchases in the United States ..."[15]

The *Financial Post*, looking at the situation from Bay Street, had "grave fears ... that some American leaders do not yet realize the urgency of prompt and generous backing of the Marshall Plan ... After the first Great War, the United States made the tragic mistake of turning her back on Europe. In the economic chaos which followed all hopes of democracy were extinguished in the greater part of that continent. A similar mistake by Washington this time," the *Financial Post* said, "might well eliminate the last foothold."[16]

That was one lesson that could be drawn by comparing past and present. Another was possible. To a quite extraordinary degree, the situation in that summer of 1947 was remarkably analogous to that in the spring of 1941. Then Canada had been facing a major drain of her holdings of American dollars caused by the large purchases her munitions industries had to make in the still-neutral United States. Those munitions were being manufactured for Britain, and the irony was that the more Canada helped arm the United Kingdom, the further into difficulty she was plunged with the United States. The whole problem was complicated by the building Congressional and public debate over the Lend-Lease Bill, for Canada faced the prospect of seeing "free" American goods drive her munitions out of the British market, an argument that tough-minded British negotiators did not hesitate to make. That crisis had been resolved by the Hyde Park Declaration, that product of "a grand Sunday" in April, negotiated by Mackenzie King and Franklin Roosevelt. Hyde Park had provided the relief Canada needed, charging the British lend-lease account for the materials and components Canada required to produce munitions for overseas. In addition the Americans agreed to buy more from Canada and both measures at a stroke relieved the dollar crisis of 1941.[17]

Now six years later, Canada faced a similar crisis caused largely by her too generous aid to Britain and Europe since the end of the war. Again as in 1941 Canada was caught in the middle, pondering the consequences and watching the Americans and Europeans manoeuver and search for solutions. About all Canadians could do was to observe closely from their vantage points in Washington, London, and Paris, looking for openings, seeking to make the special Canadian case...[18] And again the attitude of Congress would be critical.

Ambassador Wrong returned to this theme of Congressional reluctance in an important despatch on September 26. "It is difficult to realize from a distance the uncertainty that prevails here over the attitude of Congress toward further large-scale assistance to Europe," he said. "... Congress either may refuse to vote any new funds or may whittle down whatever is recommended by the Administration so that the program would be wholly inadequate in both size and duration. Another possibility is that the President, fearful of the reactions of Congress, may not ask enough of Congress." Wrong added that he, himself, was not pessimistic "because of the high stakes at issue, especially in the 'cold war,' as [Walter] Lippman calls it, with the Soviet Union." Then in a particularly provocative passage, Wrong argued that

> the behaviour of the Soviet Government provides the strongest popular reason for supporting the Marshall Plan. There is truth in the paradox that, to secure the adoption of a plan for world economic recovery, it is necessary to emphasize the division of the world between the Soviet bloc and the rest. This indicates one ground on which the position of Canada (as a beneficiary from the expenditure of Marshall Plan funds in Canada) might receive special consideration – long-term defence policy. There is both substance and popular appeal in the argument that the defence of the United States requires a strong and productive Canadian economy.[19]

In other words, Wrong seemed to be suggesting that the threat to the free world posed by the Soviet Union might have to be accentuated, if not exaggerated, in order to see the Marshall Plan gain passage through Congress.[20] The Ambassador seemed to see nothing improper in this; indeed he pointed out that Canada might be in a good position to make a case for special treatment as a result of it, particularly if the strategic importance of the Dominion to the United States could be emphasized. What Canada must do, Wrong's message was saying, was stress anew the pervasive theme of common cooperation between the United States and Canada. But even if this was done, there still might be difficulties in convincing the American public and Congress that Marshall funds should be spent in Canada. Senator Taft, the powerful Ohio Republican, had said on September 25 that there should be no off-shore purchasing. "Even if the Administration is satisfied on this point," Wrong's telegram noted, its "views might well be overridden in Congress."[21]

Other officials of External Affairs were also grappling with the problem of the Congress and they too were beginning to focus on the ways Canada could secure special treatment. British and French planning for the Marshall Plan referred to "the needs (in quantities and values) to be covered by aid from outside Europe" and that phrase – "outside Europe" rather than "from the United States" – frightened Ottawa as did the estimate of aid from "other American countries" at $6.6 billion.²² Could Canada itself make a contribution to the Plan when it sought US dollars too? But to D.V. LePan at the Canadian High Commission in London, there were opportunities here. In a memorandum on September 25, LePan first noted that a "clear distinction must be drawn between the possibility that Canada might contribute financially to the plan and the possibility that the United States might buy commodities in Canada in implementation of the plan." No one in London or Paris had suggested that Canada should bear any of the financial burden, but if "the United States were prepared to make large purchases for European reconstruction in Canada, I feel that we would probably be able to make some contribution of our own on top of that."²³ Indeed, LePan suggested, the Americans would probably buy more in Canada if "we were to join them in this enterprise and were to make some financial contribution." Secondly, it was in Canada's long-term interest to assist in the reconstruction of Europe. Most important, LePan argued that any Canadian contribution, however small,

> would also be of political advantage, I think, to the United States Administration. In selling the Marshall programme to public opinion in the United States, the State Department would find it useful to be able to point to at least one other country which was bearing a share of the burden. More generally, a Canadian contribution would also help to introduce some of the shading which the existing world political picture more and more requires. As the gulf deepens between the United States and the Soviet Union and as the general dollar famine spreads, the United States occupies an increasingly solitary position which invites attack ... Canadian cooperation in the Marshall Plan would tend to show that the western world is not to be pictured as a single giant towering above a cluster of mendicant clients ... but rather as a group of freely associated states ... held together by ... ligaments both of interest and of sentiment.²⁴

LePan's argument was clever indeed. As did Wrong he was stressing the importance of cooperating with the United States so that Canada could achieve its economic ends. He also sounded much like Louis St. Laurent, the Secretary of State for External Affairs, who a few months before had remarked that "we know that peoples who live side by side on the same continent cannot disregard each others interests, and we have always been willing to consider the possibility of common action for constructive ends."²⁵ The new wrinkle in LePan's despatch, much as in Wrong's, was the use of fear of the Soviet Union as a weapon to secure Canadian ends.

Nonetheless, LePan's ideas met little positive response in an Ottawa that was reluctantly moving to the certainty of imposing import restrictions on United States' goods as part of an effort to stem the outflow of American dollars. Compounding the cool reception was the widespread belief that Canada's dollar difficulties stemmed in large part from the already vast sums loaned to Europe since the war. No more money could be given, certainly not until Canada could learn how the United States intended to proceed with the Marshall Plan. Indeed, the entire shape of Canada's restrictions would depend on the Marshall Plan. As Wrong put it on September 26:

> On the assumption that action must be taken by Canada before the end of the year to conserve United States dollars, the extent and character of that action depend in part on whether Canada may expect to benefit directly from "Marshall Plan" dollars by the purchase of some Canadian products either from those now going to Europe mainly on credit or as the result of expanded production, or whether Canada may benefit only indirectly through the easing of the United States dollar shortage in Europe.

In the first case, Wrong added, the benefits would be substantial; in the second they would be both indirect and delayed. What concerned the Ambassador was his growing realization that only the Marshall Plan could rescue the Canadian position. His Embassy had worked hard to stimulate American defence-related purchases in Canada, but for three or four months of effort all that could be shown was $72,000 in sales.[26]

The difficulties for the hard-pressed Ambassador were compounded by the caution and coolness of the State Department officials with whom he had to deal. A meeting with Andrew Foster of the British Commonwealth division on September 25 produced little, beyond a comment that it would be unrealistic to expect any American initiatives to help Canada out of its difficulties. In particular, Foster said, it was unrealistic for Canada to expect anything from the Marshall Plan.[27] Foster had also been present a week earlier at a meeting with Clifford Clark, the Deputy Minister of Finance, who similarly had asked if Canada was being included in the planning for the Marshall Plan.

> If Canada was included in our thinking, [Foster wrote] and he appreciated that we couldn't say what Congress may do, his Government would apply the least drastic remedies to the present emergency and would declare them to be temporary. But if Canada was not included ... Canada would be obliged to apply very drastic and long-term remedies.[28]

Clark, in other words, was holding out a *quid pro quo*: help Canada by giving some indication of access to Marshall Plan procurement or else Canada would be forced to take drastic action against American imports on a long-term basis.[29] That was about as tough as any Canadian could talk in Washington, but as two American political scientists observed of the Canadian capacity to take economic retaliation against the United States in the 1970s and 1980s, "The deterrence value of Canada's ability to inflict pain upon the United States would depend on Canada's will to suffer great pain itself."[30] That was obviously true in 1947 as well. To restrict imports from the United States would hurt American exporters,[31] but it would hurt Canadians, eager to buy refrigerators and expensive automobiles, even more and that was a political factor that no government could ignore.

If the Americans grasped the nature of the suggestion made by Clark – they could scarcely have missed it – they did not seem overly impressed. At a State Department meeting on September 30, a meeting that brought together almost all the American officials concerned with Canada, including Ray Atherton, the Ambassador in Ottawa, the general response was one of friendly incapacity to act. "The group devoted most of its discussions to the prospects for the Marshall Plan," Foster's memorandum on the discussions noted.

> It was agreed that the Plan is in too early a stage for any prudent man to be able to give any sort of assurance as to its prospects. It was further felt that although the executive branch of the Government may decide to ask Congress for considerable flexibility [which would permit procurement under the Plan to be placed in Canada or would make American dollars available to Western Europe for purchases in Canada] no one could say whether Congress would grant such flexibility. It was noted that there are straws in the wind which indicate that Congress might conceivably allow no flexibility at all and might adopt a relief program under which commodities are purchased in the United States with US dollars and shipped to Europe as straight relief or possibly on a barter basis ...
>
> It was noteworthy that every officer present feels deeply concerned about the Canadian problem and is convinced that we should do everything possible to assist the Canadians. At the same time it was clear that at the moment there is practically nothing of major substance that lies within our power to do.[32]

There seemed no reason to doubt both the good will of the State Department officers or their inability to do anything in the face of Congressional uncertainties. In fact, it seemed obvious that the American foreign policy elite was in favour of cooperating to the fullest with the Canadians.³³ Foster's memorandum of the meeting, for example, held out the first hints that the Truman administration might go to bat for off-shore purchases, for the greatest degree of flexibility possible in the implementation of the Plan. There had not been any indication of that before.

At their next meeting with the Canadians on October 1, State Department officials gave the first suggestions of this: "we hoped for such flexibility under the Plan as would permit us to assist Canada by placing procurement but ... no assurance could be given at present in this regard."³⁴ Wrong's account of the same meeting stressed one official's comment that "No prudent man could base his decision on the action which ought to be taken on the assumption of Congress voting unrestricted funds for the execution of a generous Marshall Plan." Wrong added this assessment for the Department of External Affairs: if approaches to Senate leaders showed that the whole Plan could be jeopardized by pressing for off-shore purchases, the Americans "might quite probably not even ask for such funds. It is clear, however," Wrong said, demonstrating that he had not missed the tinge of optimism in the American officials' remarks, "that the officials concerned will urge on the Administration the great advantage of 'a considerable measure of flexibility' ..."³⁵

All this was heartening to the Canadians. The task now was to keep the pressure on so that the State Department and the Administration would make the strongest possible pitch to Congress. Douglas Abbott, the Minister of Finance, had been assured by the Secretary of the Treasury and by the American Ambassador to Britain that this would be done,³⁶ and Wrong continued his efforts with key officials in the State Department. In a conversation on October 14 with Jack Hickerson, the head of the European division under which all Commonwealth matters fell, he returned to the idea of Canada's making a contribution to the Marshall Plan. "With regard to the political importance here of some offer from us to do what we could" toward a contribution to European recovery,

> Hickerson said that he believed that this would be of substantial help. He urged, however, that such an offer, if we were prepared to make it, should be made at a time and in a manner previously agreed with them, so that they could use it to extract the maximum domestic political benefit from it.³⁷

Simultaneously, however, the inexorable trend in Ottawa toward the imposition of import controls continued. The choice now was not between controls and no controls; matters had gone too far for that. The options now – and Clifford Clark was bringing them to Washington on October 28 – were between two plans, one "very drastic and discriminatory and the other not."[38]

Discussions on the Canadian dollar-saving plans took place between October 28 and 31, the Canadians being represented by Clark, John Deutsch of the Department of Finance, and Hector McKinnon, the chairman of the Tariff Board. The major American participants were from the Departments of State, Treasury, Commerce and Agriculture, and from the Export-Import Bank. The tough Canadian plan, Plan A, hinged around brutal import restrictions. "Every identifiable consumer item from the United States would be completely banned," Foster's memorandum of the talks observed, "except that citrus fruits, prunes, cabbages, carrots, and textiles would be put under quotas and reduced by one-third to one-half. Capital goods would also be stringently reduced. The second plan, Plan B, would be much less discriminatory against American products but it too would involve quotas." Another feature of Plan B, the carrot along with the stick of Plan A, was described by Foster: "Long-term measures ... would include diversion of Canadian exports perhaps under a trade treaty whereby the US tariff was reduced and participation of Canada in the Marshall Plan. In the latter connection, Canada hopes that the US may be able to place some of the procurement for the Plan in Canada or make US dollars available in the UK or Western Europe for the purchase of commodities in Canada."

The Americans' response was firm but tactful, particularly so in the light of the stark choices put before them by the Canadians, choices that would certainly cause difficulties with American business interests, farmers, and others exporting to Canada. Foster noted:

> We endeavoured to persuade the Canadians of our deep concern over their problem and of our anxiety of assist. At the same time, we took considerable pains to place before them the difficulties at our end. As to the Marshall Plan, we indicated that it was still impossible to give any sort of assurance that we would get flexibility from Congress. However, we said that by November 15 it should be possible to tell the Canadians what the Administration's intentions were ...
>
> We expressed the strong hope that it might be possible for them to adopt Plan B and we emphasized the unfortunate consequences that would follow from Plan A. Plan A would be far more difficult to get out from under and far more difficult for us to defend in the US.

The Canadian summary was fuller on the Marshall Plan aspects. On October 30, one senior American official said "that in the two days since the start of the talks the Administration's Marshall Plan policy had firmed up sufficiently to allow him to report that the Executive branch of the Government would make a strong stand to obtain the flexibility which they wish in order to make 'off-shore procurement' possible, although he specifically said he would not wish to have this statement quoted back against him in the event they did not obtain the desired flexibility."

Clearly, both sides were now close to making their trade-offs. "The Canadians had said that they would be compelled to put Plan A or Plan B into effect about the middle of November," Foster wrote, "and it was noted that this would coincide with the summoning of Congress to consider the Marshall Plan ..." The Americans also pointed out that it would facilitate matters if they could tell Congress that certain items needed for the Marshall Plan and not available in the United States could be provided by Canada. Both sides agreed to work on this, the Americans insisting that the list could not include items Canada was already contracted to supply to Britain and Europe, such as wheat. The list was to be focussed on products which could not be expected to move from Canada unless American dollars were made available for them.[39]

II

The opening battles for Canada's access to Marshall Plan dollars were now virtually over. A meeting on November 6 between Canadian and American officials went over the lists of supplies that Canada could provide.[40] The next day in Washington, the President's Committee on Foreign Aid, chaired by Averell Harriman, the Secretary of Commerce, reported that

> European recovery can be prevented or halted just as effectively by the inability to obtain wheat from Argentina or Canada for example, as it could by a lack of dollars to buy foods from the United States. Many of the materials and products which Europe needs most urgently are in short supply here. For these items it is clearly in the interests of the people of the United States that European countries buy a maximum of their imports elsewhere. A number of these countries which supply Europe with food and raw materials have been generous in extending aid in the last two years ... However, a number of countries are beginning to experience serious difficulties ... [such as] Canada ...[41]

The Harriman Committee, a blue ribbon group carefully structured to command wide support, suggested further that the United States would have to provide almost $2 billion to cover Western Europe's trade deficit with the Western Hemisphere exclusive of the United States.

The next week, Secretary Marshall told a joint meeting of the House and Senate Foreign Relations Committees that Marshall Plan dollars should be made available for purchases in Canada and other countries.[42] The proposal to be submitted, Marshall said,

> contemplates the use of funds provided under the program for purchases outside the United States of commodities not readily available in sufficient quantities in this country. This policy will tend to protect our home economy against inflationary price movements which might result from concentrated buying in our markets.
>
> It seems clearly in our interest that the greatest possible amount of these supplies be obtained for Europe from other countries. Such countries should be encouraged to contribute directly as much as they can to the recovery programs through grants-in-aid or by extending credits for export to Europe.
>
> The European Recovery Program will be quickly reflected on other countries if the important element of flexibility in purchasing is provided. To the extent that supplies for Europe are procured from nonparticipating countries for dollars, the trade position of these countries with the United States will be improved. In this way we feel that the problems of other Western Hemisphere countries can be met through a combination of the European Recovery Program purchases and normal Export-Import Bank transactions.[43]

Marshall's statement and Harriman's report obviously held much for the Canadian interest.

And in return, as promised, the Canadian government opted for the milder, temporary approach in imposing its restrictions against American imports, a policy announced a few days after Marshall's statement to the Congressional committees.[44] As Kenneth Wilson of the *Financial Post*, a reporter with excellent sources of information in the Cabinet and among the mandarins of the civil service, pointed out two days before the restrictions were put into place, had there been no suggestion of Marshall Plan help, "it is more than likely that the measures which Canada would have had to take to curb US imports would have been far more drastic and more lasting in their import than those which are shortly to be announced."[45]

For the Canadian negotiators the capstone to their efforts came on December 19 when President Truman delivered his message to Congress on the Marshall Plan proposals. Truman slated the obvious fact that the United States would have to put up most of the aid to Europe. "We expect," he added, "that other countries which have it within their power will also give what assistance they can to Europe. Canada, for example, has been lending assistance to Europe fully as great in proportion to its capacity as that which we have given." A few moments later Truman reaffirmed the Harriman and Marshall proposals for off-shore purchasing: "The funds we make available to aid European recovery ... should not be restricted to purchases within the United States."[46]

The statements in Washington marked the successful completion of Canada's campaign to get access to Marshall Plan dollars. A variety of details would require attention in subsequent months, including just what financial contribution, if any, Canada might be expected to make. But the general principle of Canadian access to ECA funds for off-shore purchases had been established. The campaign had been arduous and much credit was owed to Wrong and Clark and the others who had argued with such skill. Nonetheless it seems clear that a major reason for the American decision to support off-shore purchasing was domestic. In a confidential interview he gave historians working on the Marshall Plan in 1952, General Marshall said that "The selling of the European Recovery Program to the American people was an exacting task ... I had good success in enlisting the cooperation of special interest groups although it was particularly tough to get the cooperation of those groups representing items in short supply (wheat ...) ..."[47] Clearly, to get the required support for the Plan, Marshall had to indicate that no further strain would be placed on domestic supplies of scarce commodities. Off-shore purchases were the way out for everyone, not least Canada.

There is further confirmation of this in the records of the Senate Foreign Relations Committee in November 1947 when it considered an interim emergency foreign aid bill. The Committee staff in a memorandum to the Majority and Minority leaders of the Committee recommended that 20 to 25 per cent of the appropriation should be available for purchases "from any source," that is off-shore. "This would seem desirable in view of the petroleum, coal and fertilizer which must be furnished for the program and some of which must be procured from abroad. The State Department agrees that it would not be objectionable ..." And when the Committee reported to the Senate on November 21, its attitude was markedly different than it had been in the spring of 1947. It noted:

> At the present time the situation with regard to commodities in short supply has changed considerably. Given a shortage of grain, petroleum and

fertilizer in the United States, it would seem desirable to encourage the purchase of more commodities in other countries. To this end, the committee amended section 6 of the bill to provide that not more than 25 percent of the total amount authorized should be used to procure supplies outside the United States ... [48]

There would be difficulties of similar and different sorts when the Marshall Plan itself came before Congress in the winter of 1948, but so long as domestic shortage existed in the United States it seemed that Canadian interests would be safe.

III

As John Holmes has noted, "... the extent to which the [Canadian] national interest was in fact subordinated to do-goodism by previous governments has been considerably exaggerated."[49] The story of the Canadian search for access to the largesse of the Marshall Plan certainly bears out this observation. Pragmatic considerations of national self-interest were uppermost in the minds of Canadian officials in the early stages, and they would remain there as Canadian negotiators fought to maintain their place in the face of subsequent attacks by a variety of American interest groups and their spokesmen both in Congress and the Administration. It was a cast of mind that would lead Ambassador Wrong to observe to his friend and superior, Lester Pearson, in April 1948, the month that Congress finally approved the appropriation of funds for the Marshall Plan, that "We now seem to be moving rapidly into a new period of close economic and political cooperation which, it seems to us, calls for the United States government to take a broad, statesmanlike view of its economic relations with Canada, and to do so in a concrete way in the common interest of the two countries (chiefly the political interests of the United States and the economic interests of Canada)."[50]

The common task of historical scholarship in Canada and the United States is to explore the balance between "do-goodism" and national interest in the postwar policies of the two nations, to move beyond official rationalizations to understand the self-interested trade-offs on which postwar arrangements rested. It is probably true that Canadians, less idealistic than their North American compatriots, are not likely to be so surprised at the importance of economic concerns in national decision-making or at the eagerness with which Canadian officials sought to aid the Truman Administration in its end-runs around Congress, even if this required some exaggeration and manipulation of the

Soviet threat. But the findings should be instructive nonetheless. For it is now almost a truism to point out that the relationships begun in the First and Second Worlds Wars and renewed and reinforced in the late 1940s established the basic framework for the Canadian-American relationship with which we live today.

NOTES

1. R.S. Sayers, *Financial Policy, 1939–1945* (London, 1956), pp. 322–3.
2. For a good account of Norwegian problems and attitudes to the Marshall Plan (many of which are not dissimilar to Canada's), see Helge Pharo, "Bridge-Building and Reconstruction, Norway Faces the Marshall Plan," *Scandinavian Journal of History*, 1 (1976), pp. 125ff.
3. Margaret Carlyle, ed., *Documents on International Affairs 1947–8* (London, 1952), pp. 23ff. Recent accounts of the Plan's origins are D.S. McLellan, *Dean Acheson: The State Department Years* (New York, 1976), pp. 123ff; John Gimbel, *The Origins of the Marshall Plan* (Stanford, 1976), passim; Dean Acheson, *Present at the Creation* (New York, 1969), pp. 226ff; and Joyce and Gabriel Kolko, *The Limits of Power* (New York, 1972), pp. 359ff. Earlier accounts include Howard Ellis, *The Economics of Freedom* (New York, 1950); and Harry B. Price, *The Marshall Plan and Its Meaning* (Ithaca, 1955). None of these accounts pay serious attention to off-shore purchasing, or to Canada.
4. See Blair Bolles, "American Policy Abroad," *Behind the Headlines*, IX (February, 1949), p. 13; Gimbel, p. 267; Kolko, pp. 362–3; Francis Williams, *A Prime Minister Remembers* (London, 1961), pp. 172–3. For contradictory views, see Pharo; Department of External Affairs, External Affairs Records, file 264(s), LePan to Pearson, June 11, 1947. Hume Wrong's view of the Soviet refusal to go along with the Marshall Plan is in Department of External Affairs Records, file 264(s), Wrong to Pearson, July 3, 1947: "My impression is that the break-up of the Conference should assist in stimulating support for further aid to the countries that are willing to cooperate with the United Kingdom and France ... It is, of course, tragic that the 'one-world' conception has been blatantly discarded two years after the signature of the [UN] Charter ... It has, however, been dead for some time ... Fortunately," the Canadian Ambassador in Washington said, "there is no doubt about who killed it ..."
5. Descriptions of the process can be found in External Affairs Records, file 264(s). One example is a memo, "The Marshall Plan," July 17, 1947.
6. Ibid., Memo, Pearson to King, June 28, 1947; External Affairs Records, file 265(s), T. Stone to Pearson, June 12, 1947; *Financial Post*, June 14. 1947, p. 1.

7 Britain and Western Europe took virtually all of Canada's wheat exports, nearly two-thirds of her flour, one-third her nickel, half her lead and zinc, and two-thirds her aluminum. "The continued prosperity of virtually every region of Canada, from east to west, was thus bound up with this trade and so dependent on the future of Europe." R.A. Spencer, *Canada and World Affairs 1946–1949* (Toronto, 1959), p. 230.

8 A good analysis is in Public Archives of Canada [PAC], C.D. Howe Papers, vol. 87, file S48-10, "The Canadian Exchange Problem," August 18, 1947, by Alex Skelton. See also R.C. McIvor and J.H. Panabaker, "Canadian Post-War Monetary Policy, 1946–52," *Canadian Journal of Economics and Political Science*, XX (May, 1954), p. 215; J.D. Gibson, "Post-War Economic Developments and Policy in Canada," *CJEPS*, XX (November, 1954), pp. 446–7; and J.D. Gibson, "General Review," in J.D. Gibson, ed., *Canada's Economy in a Changing World* (Toronto, 1948) pp. 285ff.

9 PAC, External Affairs Records, Washington Embassy files, vol. 2158, "Economic Cooperation, Canada-US," Memo re Discussions at State Department, June 11, 1947. See also the good account by W.A. Mackintosh, "Dependence on Export Markets Overseas," in Gibson, ed., pp. 130ff.

10 *Hearings Held in Executive Session Before the Committee on Foreign Relations, United States Senate, 80th Congress ... on H.J. Res. 152 ... and S. 1774 ...* (Washington, 1973), pp. 55–6. On the general theme of Congressional-Executive relations in the period see Susan M. Hartmann, *Truman and the 80th Congress* (Columbia, Mo., 1971). Cf. External Affairs Records, file TS 264(s), Memo for the Prime Minister, 2 June 1947.

11 Ibid., file 265(s), Tel. Wrong to Pearson, June 20, 1947.

12 Ibid., file 2AE(s), Wrong to Pearson, July 14, 1947 and encl.

13 Ibid., file 264(s), Wrong to Pearson, July 17, 1947.

14 But one officer at the Canadian desk in the State Department was concerned. He had talked with Dick Murray, second secretary at the Canadian embassy, he reported, and Murray was concerned at the disillusionment in Ottawa on the prospects of any help from the United States. "From the political point of view, this shortage of US dollars is bad for the Liberals who believe in free trade and free enterprise and close friendship with the US. The Conservatives believe in free enterprise but not free trade, the CCF believes in neither. If the Liberals are desperately embarrassed by the dollar shortage, and Canada's economy falters, it would obviously strengthen one or both wings of the opposition." US National Archives, State Department Records, 842.5151/8-1447, Memo, M.J. Tibbetts to Andrew Foster, August 14, 1947, Cf. Foster to Atherton, September 8, 1947, ibid., 842.5151 /9-847.

15 Ibid., file 265(s), Wrong to Pearson, July 30, 1947.

16 *Financial Post*, July 26, 1947. For the different views of a counterpart American periodical, see *Wall Street Journal*, September 11, 16, 1947.

17 See on Hyde Park, R.D. Cuff and J.L. Granatstein, *Canadian-American Relations in Wartime* (Toronto, 1975), chap. IV.
18 E.g., External Affairs Records, file 264(s), Bryce to Clark, August 30, 1947; ibid., Wrong to Secretary of State for External Affairs, September 4, 6, 1947; *Canadian Mining Journal*, October, 1974, editorial.
19 External Affairs Records, file 264(s), Wrong to SSEA, September 26, 1947. Cf. ibid., Moran to Pearson, September 27, 1947. A good source for Congressional attitudes in A.H. Vandenberg, Jr., *The Private Papers of Senator Vandenberg* (Boston, 1952), pp. 373ff.
20 There were others than Wrong thinking in this way. Gimbel, p. 267, cites a State Department planning report of May 23, 1947 that did not see "communist activities as the root of the difficulties of western Europe." Maurice Pope, *Soldiers and Politicians* (Toronto, 1962), p. 332, noted J.D. Hickerson's comment that "Molotov's tactics" had "been damn fool enough to hook the US into the European jackpot – something the State Department could not possibly have done for themselves." Cf. Kolko, p. 376; David Horowitz, *From Yalta to Vietnam* (London, 1971), p. 78.
21 External Affairs Records, file 264(s), Wrong to SSEA, September 26, 1947.
22 Ibid., Memo, "Canadian interest in the Marshall Plan for the Reconstruction of Europe," n.d.; PAC, Department of Finance Records, vol. 843, file 800-4-4, R.M. Keith to R.B. Bryce, September 27, 1947; *Financial Post*, October 4, 1947; External Affairs Records, file 264(s), Memo for Mr. Wheelock, September 22, 1947. Earlier, Mackenzie King had written in his diary that Canada "would find it increasingly difficult to loan abroad or make further advances for relief, etc. This may not be a misfortune. The sooner the country or more the Gov't, realizes that we can't go on spending at will the better." J.W. Pickersgill and D.F. Forster, *The Mackenzie King Record*, Vol. IV: *1947–48* (Toronto, 1970), p. 84.
23 LePan's point was made by Wrong, too, in External Affairs Records, file TS 265(s). Wrong to Clark, October 2, 1947. John Deutsch confirmed the existence of this idea in an interview. August 22, 1975. See also the *King Record*, IV, pp. 126–7.
24 External Affairs Records, file 264(s), Memo, "Canada and the Marshall Plan," September 25, 1947; ibid., Robertson to Pearson, September 24, 1947; ibid., Memo, Escott Reid to Pearson, October 8, 1947. Cf. *Financial Post*, October 18, 1947, which closely parallels Reid's memo.
25 L.S. St. Laurent, *The Foundations of Canadian Policy in World Affairs* (Toronto, 1947), pp. 31–33.
26 External Affairs Records, file 264(s), Wrong to SSEA, September 26, 1947; ibid., file 265(s), Wrong to Clark, September 26, 1947; ibid., file 264(s), Beaudry to Robertson, September 26, 1947. Earlier US estimates of defence purchases in Canada had put the best figures at $25–50 million, admittedly

insufficient to affect the dollar shortage. United States National Archives and Records Service, State Department Records, 842.5151/6-2347, Secretary of State to US Embassy, London, June 23, 1947, and 842.5151/6-2547, Memo, Hickerson to Acheson, June 25, 1947. Two comments by J. Douglas Gibson are germane. "A certain lack of realism is suggested by the spectacle of Canada postponing action in the face of a rapidly deteriorating exchange position in the hope that the European Recovery Program would be promptly implemented ..." (*CJEPS*, XX, p. 447). Later he would write ("The Changing Influence of the United States on the Canadian Economy," *CJEPS*, XXII [November, 1956], p. 423) that "we have had no practicable alternative to increasing our exports to the United States ... No remotely comparable opportunity ... has been available in the sterling area or elsewhere, particularly in the early post-war period ..."

27 External Affairs Records, Washington Embassy files, vol. 2158, Economic Co-operation, Canada-US, "Memo of Conversation ...," September 25, 1947. Cf. ibid., file 264(s). Wrong to SSEA, September 30 and October 2. 1947.

28 State Department Records, 842.5151/9-2747, Memo, Foster to Hickerson, September 27, 1947. This memo is printed in *Foreign Relations of the United States 1947* (Washington, 1970), III, pp. 124–6.

29 Clark may have been simply carrying out the policies of his minister, Douglas Abbott. In a confidential interview with Max Freedman of the *Winnipeg Free Press*, Abbott said "that we are extremely conscious of the United States but they don't know we are here at all. Therefore, if we punched them in the nose they would become aware of us and would realize that we are trying to solve our dollar problem." Abbott also pointed out the extent to which luxury items were responsible for the dollar shortage – "we spent $45,000 a month on juke boxes" (Queen's University, Grant Dexter Papers, "Telephone Call from Maxie," October 15, 1947).

30 Robert Keohane and Joseph Nye, Jr., "Introduction: The Complex Politics of Canadian-American Interdependence," in Annette Baker Fox, et al., *Canada and the United States: Transnational and Transgovernmental Relations* (New York, 1976), p. 9.

31 "Canada is the United States' best customer. During 1947, the United States sold to Canada over $2,000 millions worth of goods – more than the combined sales to her second and third largest customers, Britain and France." Bank of Nova Scotia, *Monthly Review*, July, 1948. See D.C. MacGregor, "Dependence on Imports from the United States," in Gibson, ed., pp. 180ff.

32 State Department Records, 842.5151/9-3047, Memo, "The Canadian Dollar Problem," September 30, 1947.

33 Some in the State Department treated the Canadian problem in a hard-boiled fashion, however. Paul Nitze, Deputy Director of the Office of International Trade Policy, told J.R. Murray of the Canadian Embassy in Washington that while Canada's efforts to aid Europe had been laudable, the government had discovered the consequences "of what happened when the ability of our home production ... to satisfy the huge additional demands created by the marked inflationary increase in our purchasing power began to decline rapidly ... this demand spilled over our borders into the United States ... Our reserves began to disappear rapidly ..." Nitze went on to say that the United States would shortly be making up the entire deficit of Europe with the hemisphere "and if, therefore, Canada does not take measures to make itself a net contributor to meeting a part of this deficit, and receives substantial amounts of US dollars and gold from the UK [the British having received this money in aid from the US], it is, in fact, getting them from the United States ..." Thus, in Nitze's view, Canada's economy "to the extent that it now constitutes a net drain on the United States economy [has to be] very considerably dampened" (PAC, C.D. Howe Papers, vol. 87, file S48-10-6, Memos att. to Wrong to Pearson, 25 Nov. 47. See on this Queen's University, Grant Dexter Papers, Memo, 30 Apr. 49).
34 State Department Records, 842.5151/10-147, Memo, "Canadian Dollar Problem," October 1, 1947.
35 External Affairs Records, file 265(s), Wrong to Clark, October 2, 1947.
36 Douglas Library, Queen's University, Grant Dexter Papers, "Telephone call from Maxie [Freedman]," October 15, 1947.
37 External Affairs Records, file 264(s), Wrong to Robertson, October 14, 1947.
38 Ibid.; cf. *Foreign Relations of the United States, 1947*, vol. Ill, pp. 126–7.
39 State Department Records, 842.5151/11-147, "Memorandum for the Files," November 1, 1947; External Affairs Records, TS 265(s), Tel. Canadian Ambassador to SSEA, November 1, 1947 and "Summary of US–Canadian Financial Discussions. November 1, 1947"; *Foreign Relations of the United States 1947*, III, pp. 129ff.
40 Department of Finance Records, Deutsch files, vol. 3617, file ITO, "Note of Meeting ... November 6, 1947." Cf. State Department Records, FW 611:422-10/2649, "Memo of Conversation," Dec. 47, by Willoughby in Ottawa.
41 Cited in Spencer, pp. 231–2; External Affairs Records, file 264(s), Wrong to SSEA, November 10, 1947.
42 Department of Finance Records, Deutsch files, vol. 3617, file ITO, "Note of Meeting ... November 6, 1947"; *Financial Post*, November 15, 1947.
43 Ibid.
44 See on the restrictions, *Financial Post*, November 22, 1947; *Foreign Relations of the United States 1947*, III, p. 130ff.

45 *Financial Post*, November 15, 1947.
46 Carlyle, pp. 52, 60, 66; External Affairs Records, file 264(s), Wrong to SSEA, December 15, 1947.
47 John F. Kennedy Library, John Kenneth Galbraith Papers, Box 26, ECA History Project files, Interview with George C. Marshall, October 30, 1952.
48 *Hearings Held in Executive Session* ... : "Memorandum to Senator Vanderburg and Senator Connolly," November 17, 1947, pp. 349–51 and "Report on European Interim Aid Act of 1947," p. 384.
49 John W. Holmes, "Impact of Domestic Political Factors on Canadian-American Relations: Canada," in Fox, et al., p. 22, n. 4.
50 External Affairs Records, file 264(s), Wrong to Pearson, April 15, 1948.

Chapter Three

The Rise and Fall of Canadian-American Free Trade, 1947–1948

J.L. GRANATSTEIN AND R.D. CUFF

"I confess I get alarmed beyond measure," an exasperated Mackenzie King wrote in his diary, "at the casual way in which a few officials take it into their hands to try and settle the great national policies; force the hands of the Government, etc. without the least knowledge of the political side of matters of the kind or the least kind of political judgment."[1] It was 6 May 1948 and the prime minister, with only a few months of power remaining to him, had effectively and finally squelched a move for a free trade arrangement between Canada and the United States, under discussion since the previous fall.

Mackenzie King's testy ruminations about his officials were justified only in part. Canadian politicians had been involved in the planning and in the discussions with American officials, and the prime minister himself had initially seemed enthusiastic about the economic prospects opened up by free trade, a traditional Liberal party policy. The story was much more complicated than King's diary allowed, moreover, for it emerged within the context of an established community of interest among Canadian and American officials who believed in freer trade as a major economic solution to the threatening chaos of the postwar world.

At the end of the Second World War, Canada was forced to negotiate a remarkable change in her international economic relations. "The battlefields of the second war," Harold Macmillan dolefully observed in his memoirs, "mark the end of the heroic age of the British Empire,"[2] a true enough statement and one that only lightly masks the vast liquidation of capital and political investment abroad that the costs of the war had forced on London. But if Britain was strapped by the conflict, the United States had emerged wealthy and powerful, stepping forward to its place as an imperial power second to none. How could Canada deal with this changed condition of affairs?

One way – a method embraced with some eagerness by Canadian officials and political leaders – was multilateral trade relations. A concept popular among American officials, one preached by Secretary of State Cordell Hull and his successors and directed in negotiation by Assistant Secretary of State William Clayton, multilateralism seemed the orderly and world-wide method by which Canada could dispose of its export surpluses and prosper while at the same time creating a freer system of trade that would prevent the re-establishment of tariff barriers of the kind that had helped lead to the world war. Canada was concerned not only with the level of its own trade, King told the House of Commons, "but we have also a fundamental concern for the level of external trade of other countries. The character of our trade, with surpluses of exports to certain countries and excesses of imports from other countries, requires a condition in which surpluses on one account can be converted to offset deficiences on another account. This means that a bilateral approach to trade is not enough."[3] That was a good enough statement of Canada's commitment to a multilateral trading world.

With vastly more power than Canada, the United States had tried to use its leverage during the war to force multilateralism on Britain and its system of preferential tariffs throughout the empire. The weapon employed was Article VII of the Lend-Lease Agreement, and the weapon was a powerful one. No such bludgeons had been necessary with Canada, for although the dominion took no lend-lease aid it had readily agreed in 1942 in an exchange of notes to work toward a reduction in tariffs in a similar fashion to that required by Article VII. As early as 1943 Norman Robertson, the undersecretary of state for external affairs, had signalled to Jack Hickerson, probably the leading Canadian expert in the Department of State, "that the Canadian Government is prepared to move out on a broad front in association with the United Kingdom and the United States in making postwar commercial arrangements under Article 7. He has indicated to me," Hickerson reported, "that Canada is prepared to go the whole distance as far as abolition of preference is concerned, provided the United States and the United Kingdom are willing to make compensatory tariff reductions."[4]

But the road to free trade was not to be smooth. Canada had hoped that the United States would make "multilateral horizontal" tariff reductions, major across-the-board cuts in the protective rates. But Congressional pressures were such, the Canadians were informed at meetings in July 1945, that only selective cuts would be possible. This "deeply disappointed and dismayed" the Ottawa officials present, but after a lengthy discussion of the ways in which the selective tariff cuts could be made, the Canadians had come to believe, or so the counsellor of the embassy in Ottawa reported to Washington, "that it was far more important to get the program under way than to be unduly concerned with the detailed mechanics of the program."[5] Any tariff alterations in a lower direction were apparently better than none.

Nor did the British seem any more eager than the United States to dismantle their tariff barriers. The British continued, to American annoyance, to link their willingness to remove imperial preferences to sweeping American tariff cuts, and Congress was unwilling to accept this. The Canadians were similarly exasperated by British attitudes, and at least one official, Hector McKinnon, president of the Commodity Prices Stabilization Corporation, a crown corporation, "thought that if the present administration in London should not be prepared to take fairly prompt action in the trade barrier field, it might be desirable for the United States and Canada to consider together whether these two countries might not go ahead on a program of their own."[6] There in essence was an indication of the Canadian direction: if a relationship could be worked out to preserve the North Atlantic Triangle in a multilateral context, well and good; if not then Canada should seek to maximize trade with the United States.

These attitudes underlay the Canadian efforts to cope with the rush of events in the immediate postwar years. The dominion's negotiators were active in the discussions leading up to the Geneva conference on the International Trade Organization in 1947 and played a substantial role in working out the General Agreement on Tariffs and Trade. This was a step toward multilateralism, a very important step indeed.[7] Equally Canada concerned itself with the necessity to keep up its export markets abroad. The parlous British economic condition was recognized, and Canada agreed in 1946 to provide a loan of $1.25 billion, a huge sum for Canada – more than 10 per cent of the 1946 Gross National Product, and one-third the size of the American loan. Additional loans to other Western European states raised the total Canadian commitment to the $2 billion mark.[8] This was an investment in domestic full employment, in maintaining the productive capacity that the war had created. And when Canada in July 1946 raised its dollar to parity with the American dollar, this too seemed a sign of confidence and of a willingness to take bold economic measures to control inflation in Canada.[9]

The structure of postwar Canadian prosperity, however, required fulfilment of one major condition. The nation had to export to live, to earn enough American dollars to pay for the huge expansion of imports from the United States that was being fuelled by the purchases of well-off Canadians, hungry for consumer goods after six years of war, shortages, and controls. Any interference with this delicate balance could disrupt Canada's postwar stability.

The disruption was not long in coming. The decision to raise the Canadian dollar to parity stopped the influx of speculative American capital into Canada at the same time that it increased the costs for Canadian exports and encouraged Canadian debtors to pay their bills in the United States.[10] The first half of 1947 saw imports from the United States total $981 million while exports amounted only to $493 million. This deficit of $488 million was balanced by the Canadian merchandise surplus with Britain and other countries, but much of the surplus abroad was financed with Canadian loans. And when in August 1947 Britain was forced by a run on the pound sterling to move away from convertibility, Canada's problems were compounded.[11] Sterling balances would build up in London, almost unuseable, while the deficit with the United States mounted inexorably. The effect of these multiple calamities on Canada's US dollar reserves was striking: over the eighteen-month period from May 1946 to November 1947 Canada's exchange reserves dropped from $1667 million to $480 million, an average loss of more than $65 million a month.[12] As A.F.W. Plumptre noted at the time, "the breakdown of our hopes for selling to England ... for cash was part of a wider breakdown."[13]

What were the trade options open to the Canadian government in this building collapse? Autarky was one, but few could take this seriously. Another was to become part of the sterling area. This was, as Norman Robertson reported from his post as high commissioner in London, the "orthodox" course, but it was not completely satisfactory to everyone because Britain was struggling to keep its head above water itself, spending the Canadian and American loans faster and faster.[14] Still, there were powerful emotive ties to Britain, and the Progressive Conservative party, the official opposition in Parliament, could always be counted upon to fly the Union Jack. More important, the minister of agriculture, James G. Gardiner, desperately needed the United Kingdom market to satisfy Prairie farmers, and indeed in July 1946 he had negotiated a Wheat Agreement providing for large sales to Britain over the next four years.[15] Despite such support, however, the deck was loaded against Canada joining the sterling bloc. Grant Dexter, the *Winnipeg Free Press* editor with extraordinary Ottawa contacts, read through Robertson's despatches from London and dismissed this idea out of hand. To Dexter – and to Robertson – it was clear: Britain was on the verge of disaster, and in the event of her economic collapse there "would be but one course open to Canada – to strive for a customs union with the United States."[16] Robertson said as much in a telegram to his friend and successor as undersecretary, Lester Pearson, when he wondered "whether we should not more or less simultaneously be thinking of a real reciprocity agreement with the United States, which would strengthen our dollar position in the short turn, and in the long run, ensure us against too great a dependence, relative to the United States, on the European market. It might be possible to work out a scheme for a graduated approach to reciprocal free trade in a good many commodities on a continental basis, with the steps selected and their depth determined largely by the requirements of our dollar position ...."[17] Again the continuity in thought is striking, and coming from Robertson, widely recognized as the ablest civil servant of his time and himself an expert in trade negotiations with the Americans, particularly forceful.

By early spring 1947, therefore, the outlines of the problem were distressingly clear. Britain – and all of Western Europe – were short of American exchange, a state of affairs that only the United States could resolve.[18] A British collapse would create great difficulties for Canada's American dollar reserves, force unpleasant short-run measures, and the only solution possible in the long term might be to seek a closer relationship with the United States. There were, perhaps, undertones of this in Mackenzie King's meeting with President Truman in Washington in April 1947. The prime minister spoke of the necessity for "a policy on the part of the States which would help to relieve Europe in a way to enable some of the countries there to purchase our goods with American dollars." That would be important because, as the Department of State's Stanley Woodward wrote in a summary of the meeting, "Canada was very much interested in its trade relations with the world in general and with the United States in particular, and there was a growing shortage of American dollars in Canada, which he hoped might be corrected. What [King] feared," Woodward recorded, "was restrictive action on the part of Canada with respect to imports from the United States."[19]

Mr. King was not alone in fearing such action. To restrict consumer spending would surely endanger the popularity of his government, and the Liberal majority in Parliament was a slender one. Restrictions would also run against all the Canadian preachings for multilateralism and fly in the face of the efforts Canadian negotiators were making to create the International Trade Organization. But what else could be done? The counsellor at the Ottawa embassy reported to Washington that he had talked with Clifford Clark, the deputy minister of finance. "Obviously," he said, "the Canadians are groping pretty much in the dark for a remedy to their financial woes. They may even hope secretly to themselves that we will come forward with some sort of 'Hyde Park' arrangement."[20]

If the government was at a loss, it put on a brave face in public. The budget, presented in April 1947 by Finance Minister Douglas Abbott, was an optimistic document that deliberately aimed to counter the "unfounded rumours" of a dollar drain and painted an optimistic portrait of the future trade benefits that Canada would win as a result of the ITO talks.[21] Opposition critics, however, were fooled not at all. Colonel Alan Cockeram, a Toronto Conservative MP, characterized the King government as "men sitting in a poker game which has got beyond their limits, watching their stakes constantly being whittled away, without having the courage to quit and admit the game is too steep for them, thus protecting their remaining cash." The Liberals, he said, were "like Micawber ... waiting for something to turn up."[22]

Cockeram was right, and the Liberals knew it. Abbott later told a reporter confidentially that "At the time of the budget he knew how serious the situation was. Had he admitted it, and had a big debate started, the shock to business would have been profound and there would have been a mad scramble for US imports."[23] The minister himself had been seeking for ways to earn more exchange, even approaching Washington to try to persuade the Americans to buy Canadian uranium.[24] Graham Towers, the head of the Bank of Canada, had been in Washington as early as February to seek for solutions, and by the spring he was on his way to London to persuade the British to stop drawing on the Canadian loan, thus saving a few more dollars.[25] And in Washington, the State Department had agreed to the Canadian request to set up an informal study group "to explore ways and means of possibly increasing Canadian receipts of United States dollars ..."[26]

There were many suggestions on ways to get Canada more US dollars. Raw materials could be sold to the United States for stockpiling or supplies could be procured in Canada to meet United States military requirements for military and civilian aid for Greece and Turkey, under the American wing since the proclamation of the Truman Doctrine.[27] But there always seemed to be some legal or political or economic reason why these plans fell through, and Louis Rasminsky of the Bank of Canada and the Foreign Exchange Control Board felt obliged to remind the Department of State that this was no time for "an academic investigation of the balance of payments situation."[28] The idea of the Marshall Plan, floated by Secretary of State George C. Marshall on 5 June 1947, seemed another potential source of relief, and one that led Hume Wrong, the Canadian ambassador in Washington, to tell his good friend Dean Acheson, the retiring undersecretary of state, that unless she received benefits from Marshall Plan aid or "unless some new device could be discovered on a large-scale for dealing with our exchange problem on a bilateral basis," Canada would have to impose import restrictions.[29]

Inexplicably, however, the Americans did not seem much concerned with the prospect. Canadian feelers for a large dollar loan were coolly received, and George Kennan of the Department of State told Wrong that Canada could not realistically expect any benefits from the Marshall Plan in time to help the situation. Even when the ambassador said that trade restrictions would be directly discriminatory against American goods, Kennan was unmoved: in his view "there should be no objection in [the United States] to the imposition by Canada of import restrictions to conserve dollars."[30] The sole consolation was a comment by Robert Lovett, Acheson's successor, that the Canadian dollar shortage and its ramifications were "the most insoluble problem he had ever encountered." Wrong could only report that the undersecretary "said finally that if we had any good ideas of what might be done, he would be delighted to hear from us."[31] That was cold comfort indeed.

American officials clearly considered that the blame for the Canadian dollar problems lay squarely on Ottawa. Ray Atherton, the ambassador in Canada, reported late in the summer that "Canada's foreign fiscal policies rather than United States tariffs must bear the responsibility …"[32] That was probably correct, but it did little for a Canadian government that had begun to pine desperately for something, anything, that could prevent the inevitable. The deputy minister of finance, visiting Washington in mid-September, was still hoping for results from the ITO negotiations and banking on future considerations under the Marshall Plan to cut the current losses of US dollars from their present $100 million a month loss rate. But Washington officials held out little hope. "[We] made clear to the Canadians that there is no magic cure in Washington," a State Department summary of a meeting that month noted. "It is the impression of the writer that they have been drifting from bad to worse while wishfully thinking that when the time came we would step in and rescue them by means of a loan or procurement devices or the ITO or the Marshall Plan. We cannot, of course, let them go under," the writer of the memorandum added, in the only note of bleak hope that he permitted himself, "but it was time that we explained to them the difficulties on our side."[33]

The Americans had difficulties enough with Congress, but for Hume Wrong and others the delays in dealing with the Canadian problem were becoming exasperating. Officials in the Department of State, he reported at the end of September, consistently refused to commit themselves on the prospects of Marshall Plan aid and regarded the prospects of Canadian restrictions with benign indifference. "More than once ... during the course of the meeting," Wrong fumed, "I had to discourage the State Department officials from the pace at which they were approaching the restrictive action which we might have to take."[34] Other countries' bureaucracies always seemed to function too slowly.

The Marshall Plan seemed to hold the key to the crisis. In the long run a generous application of American money could resolve Europe's dollar shortage and help Canada balance her books. But as Wrong and other Canadian officials explained in late September, there could be significant short-term advantages and implications as well. In the Canadian view, the extent and the timing of the proposed restrictions would be determined in part by the prospect of the dominion's being given access to Marshall Plan purchasing. If nothing was forthcoming, they indicated, Canada might be forced to take outright discriminatory action against American imports on a long-term basis; if there was the prospect of help, the restrictions could be short-term and not formally discriminatory. This tougher talk at least roused a response in the State Department, its officers arguing strenuously against discriminatory restrictions. As of October, however, they could not promise action favourable to Canada under the Marshall Plan, though they thought it might be possible to indicate the Truman administration's intentions by 15 November. In the meantime, both sides agreed to co-operate in drafting an exchange of notes and an explanatory press release that would minimize friction when the restrictions were imposed. Their hands were tied on the Marshall Plan question, the Americans indicated, but they remained sympathetic and concerned, and they agreed not to invoke the retaliatory measures available to them under the 1938 Trade Agreement.[35]

It was in this context that the Canadians first approached the Department of State on 29 October 1947 with the idea of a comprehensive trade agreement. Hector McKinnon, chairman of the Canadian Tariff Board, and John Deutsch, director of the International Economic Relations Division of the Department of Finance, represented the dominion at this informal meeting; from the State Department were Clair

Wilcox, director of the Office of International Trade Policy, his deputy, Paul Nitze, Andrew Foster, head of the Canadian desk in the British Commonwealth Division, and Woodbury Willoughby of the Commercial Policy Division. According to the American summary, McKinnon had said that "The Canadian Cabinet authorized him to explore with United States officials the possibility of concluding a comprehensive agreement involving, wherever possible, the complete elimination of duties."

> It would be necessary to obtain Congressional approval. Mr. McKinnon indicated that the Canadian government would be willing to enter into an agreement even if it necessitated a major readjustment and reorientation of Canada's international economic relations. They feel that Canada must either integrate her economy more closely with that of the United States or be forced into discriminatory restrictive policies involving greater self sufficiency, bilateral trade bargaining and an orientation toward Europe with corresponding danger of friction with the United States, if not economic warfare.
>
> Mr. Wilcox explained some of the difficulties of obtaining at the coming regular session of Congress approval for tariff cuts beyond those authorized by the Trade Agreement Act but said that he did not want to close the door to the possibility of negotiating a new comprehensive agreement. He said that he would take the matter up with the higher officers of the Department.[36]

Wilcox would do so, and the significance of the Canadian suggestion would soon become apparent. In their desperation the Canadians had indicated their willingness to shift direction substantially, and it would be in response to this that the State Department's technicians would ultimately fashion an alternative proposal designed, they hoped, to overcome anticipated objections to further tariff reductions within both Administration and Congress. It was a proposal, moreover, that would generate crucial discussions even after the Canadians won their long-sought promise of dollar-aid under the Marshall Plan.

As State Department officials had indicated, the Truman administration had reached its decision in mid-November. In testimony before Congressional committees, Secretary Marshall had outlined his intention to permit recovery funds to be expended outside the United States. Whether Congress would permit these "off-shore" purchases remained uncertain, but at least the prospect of Canada getting benefits from them was now at hand. Had there been no hint of relief here, Kenneth Wilson of the *Financial Post* noted on 15 November, "it is more than likely that the measures which Canada would have to take to curb US imports would have been far more drastic and more lasting in their import than those which are to be shortly announced."[37]

A first-rate reporter with pipelines into the cabinet and the bureaucracy, Wilson was correct. The Canadian government's dollar-saving restrictions were promulgated on 17 November, ironically the same day that the prime minister announced Canada's signing of the General Agreement on Trade and Tariffs. A limit of $150 per year was imposed on pleasure travel in the United States, a special excise tax of 25 per cent was slapped on a number of specified consumer goods, and quota restrictions were instituted. In addition, a stand-by credit of $300 million was arranged with the Export-Import Bank in Washington.[38]

Such restrictions were the antithesis of the overriding goal of multilateral trade to which both Canadian and American officials subscribed. They clashed as well with the personal sentiments of Mackenzie King, who believed that "Great care will have to be taken to see that they are not regarded as and do not become protectionist measures."[39] And indeed throughout the discussions of late October and early November Canadian spokesmen made their distaste for such measures crystal clear; they had made their approach to Washington on 29 October for a new and more comprehensive trade agreement in just this spirit. Nor was it any coincidence that the two Canadian spokesmen on the issue, McKinnon and Deutsch, had negotiated the GATT agreement for Canada. They carried the enthusiasm of Geneva to Washington and with King's blessing. Despite the inevitable restrictions, then, the Canadians had emphasized throughout that they "would be very anxious, at the time of the announcement of the restrictions, to be able to announce that we had entered into conversations with the US Government, looking toward a long-term agreement to increase the flow of the trade between the two countries."[40] The Americans, for their part, "were very receptive to the ideas put forward by McKinnon and Deutsch on seeking a special trade agreement with Canada which would go far beyond the Geneva Agreement ..."[41]

As it turned out, no announcement of the trade talks with the United States was made after 17 November, both parties preferring to maintain secrecy. Part of the reason, perhaps, was best expressed in a report by Julian Harrington, the counsellor at the embassy in Ottawa. He had talked with Douglas Abbott, the minister of finance, he said, and "the Finance Minister went out of his way to express appreciation of the assistance given him by our people in Washington. The success of his plan is very largely dependent upon still further assistance from the US. He admitted to me that Canada is part and parcel of our economic orbit and hoped that we would continue to be helpful. In so saying he was thinking less of possible Marshall plan benefits than of the expanded use of American branch plants to export to dollar areas ..."[42] We have long recognized the inevitability of Canada becoming closely integrated into the American economic sphere, but it was encouraging to hear Abbott's frank admission of it."[43] Frank admissions of that sort would be political dynamite, and it would be best for politicians in both countries if as little as possible were said.

In the days immediately following news of the expected Marshall Plan aid and Canada's imposition of the restrictions, McKinnon and Deutsch, in informal conversations with their American counterparts in the State Department, began to pass on data on items which might be included in a prospective tariff agreement,[44] taking advantage in part of the real enthusiasm Clair Wilcox had had for the idea from the beginning.[45] But if Wilcox, like Will Clayton, his former chief in the State Department, represented the Hullian tradition in American foreign policy, then John Deutsch brought an intriguing Western Canadian twist in his enthusiasm for free trade to the common orientation. Deutsch saw the world divided into two basic areas. In his view one area, comprised largely of North America, was a free economy with a high standard of living. In the other, the economy of the various nations was more or less completely controlled, and this second group included the sterling bloc. For Deutsch the idea was to avoid a controlled economy of a kind implicit in import restrictions. A bilateral free trade agreement for Canada and the United States was a continental analogue of GATT and ITO. "We have the choice between two kinds of worlds," Deutsch said: "– a relative free enterprize [sic] world with the highest existing standard of living and a government controlled world with a lower standard of living. Which we do not want. Obviously the first. This means meshing our economy as much as possible with that of the United States." Deutsch viewed with alarm the prospect that Canada would quietly and without conscious intention end up as a high-cost country by restricting US imports, and he believed the pressures in this direction, already very great, would increase the longer that vested interests had time to grow up under import restrictions.[46]

The proposal that Deutsch and McKinnon had brought to Washington on 29 October had set off a round of brainstorming in the State Department. At its conclusion, support had solidified behind the idea of a modified customs union for North America, with Woodbury Willoughby, a career officer, free trade enthusiast, and director of the Commercial Policy Division, its central champion.[47] In the view of American officials, an agreement to lower further US duties of a kind the Canadians proposed would not pass Congress. Some other approach was required. They first broached the idea of a customs union, an idea already gaining some support within Scandinavian countries and among prospective members of the International Trade Organization, then negotiating in Havana.[48] But a customs union by strict definition required the complete elimination of all tariffs between members and uniform tariffs on imports from countries outside the union, and the Canadians regarded neither condition as politically acceptable. Such an agreement would involve raising tariffs against the UK, abandoning the empire in effect, as well as having Canada, the unequal partner, adjusting her tariff in response to American moves. At the same time it would be open to attack in Canada as an important step, whether calculated or not, toward political absorption by the United States.

To obviate such political difficulties Willoughby and Nitze, with the support of State's British Commonwealth Division, proposed a modified form of customs union "under which there would be substantially free trade between the two countries but each would retain its separate tariff vis-à-vis third countries." They anticipated additional variations to the pure form as well, including quotas to protect subsidized agricultural products and a special balance of payments arrangement. Such exceptions would hopefully satisfy the Canadians, while the customs union idea was "sufficiently bold and striking to fire the imagination of the (American) people and force favorable action by Congress."[49]

In forwarding Willoughby's proposal to Clair Wilcox, acting as chairman of the US delegation at the ITO conference in Havana, Nitze recognized its departure not only from the general American stand on the most-favoured-nation principal, but also its deviation from the orthodox customs unions currently allowed under GATT. Consideration of the Canadian case among others, he said, had led department staff members to "wonder if some formula could not be devised in the orientation of the ITO which would effectively control the traditional abuses in preferential systems and at the same time permit the achievement of the obvious economic benefits of regional economic unity." From Nitze's point of view, the Canadian case illustrated the utility of exceptions to the most-favoured-nation principle of a kind that might be extended to other areas, including Western Europe or the Arab nations. But it was a proposal that would require an amendment to the charter's provisions on special customs unions.[50]

Willoughby put the modified customs union proposal to John Deutsch and James Murray, second secretary at the Canadian embassy, at a private dinner party in Washington on 31 Dec., and did so "on a strictly confidential and personal basis," explaining that the idea had not been cleared with top officials. According to Willoughby, Deutsch thought the subject would be "political dynamite" in Ottawa and urged the utmost secrecy.[51] For Deutsch personally, of course, the idea held great appeal. It might force inefficient central Canadian manufacturing firms to adapt or die, and thus increase the overall competitive quality of Canadian business and offer a promising opportunity to divert Canadian exports from the collapsing UK market.[52]

Back in Ottawa Deutsch found opinion divided among the few in whom he confided. Graham Towers of the Bank of Canada was skeptical; some officials in Trade and Commerce were opposed. But C.D. Howe, the minister of trade and commerce, and Finance Minister Abbott were very interested indeed.[53] Abbott's own soundings on the proposal, for example, convinced him that it provided a way out of the present import restrictions and offered a substitute for the uncertainty of European markets. But most important of all and much to Deutsch's surprise, Mackenzie King indicated strong approval, noting that "It is clear to me that the Americans are losing no opportunity to make their relations as close as possible with our country."[54]

With the green light from Ottawa, Willoughby and Deutsch put their staffs to work. As part of their campaign, they won support from Wilcox to have the ITO Charter amended so as to leave open the door for a modified custom union.[55] Within the State Department itself, Willoughby's activity generated a wide variety of papers on aspects of the projected union during January and February. Studies emerged on the mechanics of proposed escape clauses for safeguarding balances of payments, on the ways US and Canadian exchange rates would function, and how specifically to plan for the reorientation of the Canadian economy under a union. Lists of questions and answers were compiled for a potential public relations campaign and analyses made on the political dimensions of passage of a trade agreement through the Senate Finance and Foreign Relations Committees.[56]

Deutsch and McKinnon engaged in a continuous series of discussions with Willoughby and the technical staffs of the State Department throughout January and February. But whereas the Canadians seem to have reported directly to the prime minister, the American side of the negotiations remained, until March at least, at the level of the assistant secretary of state. For his part, Mackenzie King remained as committed to the idea in early March as he had been in late December,[57] and Deutsch and McKinnon were eager to press this advantage. Willoughby believed the Canadians wanted to act quickly because "(1) Mackenzie King, who [is] likely to retire in August, would be more apt to obtain approval of the proposal in Canada than would anyone likely to succeed him, (2) the import restrictions are unpopular and the government would like to conclude as soon as possible trade arrangements that would facilitate their removal, (3) they are fearful that the rigid import restrictions will in time build up vested interests that will make difficult their removal."[58] And Willoughby, though recognizing difficulties in obtaining Congressional approval in the current session, suggested having the proposal signed before the elections to ensure a favourable plank in both the Democratic and Republican party platforms for the 1948 presidential election.[59]

Agricultural quotas, balance-of-payments exceptions, likely product competition, potential political import, interest group responses, branch plant complications, the effects on third countries (particularly Great Britain), the implications for GATT and Havana, the tactics of timing – all these considerations and more confronted Deutsch, McKinnon, Willoughby, and their colleagues during early 1948, but by mid-March they had settled on the basis for a general agreement. Their overall plan envisaged among its central points the immediate removal of all duties by both countries, the prohibition of all qualitative restrictions on imports after five years with important exceptions on both sides, the inclusion of the right of both sides to impose absolute transitional quotas on certain products during the five-year period, and joint consultation on agricultural marketing.[60]

The proposal was now ready to move formally up the line at the State Department to the undersecretary of state, Robert Lovett. And in keeping with his sentiments throughout the negotiations, Woodbury Willoughby emphasized to his superior that in his view "There has never been a time when conditions in Canada, both economic and political, were more favorable." In the United States, too, the public would favour the customs union "on both economic and strategic grounds."[61] Subsequent analyses emphasized both these points. On the economic side, it was argued, both American agriculture and industry would be less affected by competition at the moment, given the great domestic and foreign demand for American goods, than under more normal conditions. In addition, recession was forecast for 1949. More than that, in Willoughby's view "the psychological factors favor immediate action. The widespread popular concern over Russian policy will undoubtedly lead to an acceptance of the international political and strategic implications which will override the supposed economic difficulties in the minds of many people."[62]

In March, as before, Willoughby had the full support of Deutsch and McKinnon, and by extension, Clark and Abbott, in pressing Washington for action on free trade. Thus on 9 March, after consultations in

Ottawa, Deutsch indicated his hope that the treaty would be ratified or at least inserted in the Democratic and Republican party platforms as a prerequisite for a Canadian election on the issue.[63] Were the plan not adopted, Deutsch feared among other things that "it will be necessary to continue the import restrictions indefinitely and that this will force Canada into a program of increasing self-sufficiency and progressively [sic] reduction of its dependence on the US."[64] Delay also involved the likelihood of opposition arising in a series of provincial elections expected in the summer.[65]

By late March, the timing rather than the nature of the plan itself had become the central issue for the technicians in both Ottawa and Washington. At this point there was still no assurance that Lovett, the senior American official involved, would press for action on the treaty. And although Willoughby's staff had projected plans for a public relations campaign in search of bipartisan support, no systematic attempt had yet been made to build support for the proposal in Congress. The need for secrecy precluded this step in any case. Moreover, as Willoughby had said more than once, it was unlikely Congress would even take up the proposal before the session ended, and the State Department was completely unable to predict how Congressional leaders would regard the pact. It was possible too that a fight would have erupted with the United States Agriculture Department, antipathetic to the multilateral sentiments of the State Department and jealously guarding the protected, subsidized interests of US agriculture.[66]

In Ottawa Mackenzie King similarly had begun to ponder the questions of timing involved in a free trade proposal, and the ramifications now began to give him pause. The political calculus of such a decision, one so pregnant with change and one that had historical antecedents threatening to the Liberal party, was frightening, and King's well-developed intuition preached caution. The opposition, he believed, would be sure to cry "that it was commercial union that we were after." The Luce publications in the United States had already began to predict such a course, much to King's alarm. And for the prime minister "to be placed in the position of being the spearhead of furthering a commercial union as the last act of my career would be," in his own view, "to absolutely destroy the significance of the whole of it."[67] Nor could he be certain to carry all of Ottawa officialdom with him on the matter. The Department of Finance strongly supported the move, to be sure, and Howe remained intrigued. But James Gardiner's Department of Agriculture would likely oppose it, and more important still, Louis S. St. Laurent, the secretary of state for external affairs and heir-apparent, was distinctly cool.[68] King's sentiments, evolving toward a negative conclusion through March, were not immediately translated into policy, however. On a flying visit to Washington on 25 March John Deutsch still held out substantial hope, and Woodbury Willoughby was still pressing State Department officials on the matter five days later.[69]

By 29 March, however, as he prepared to leave for a visit to Washington and Williamsburg, Va., the prime minister had made up his mind. Mackenzie King explained his reasons to Hume Wrong at the embassy in Washington the next day. First there was simply not enough time available to permit such a momentous decision. Then there were the political risks involved in the issue, risks dangerous enough to involve the defeat of the government. And, finally, the customs union proposals could lead toward the fulfilment of "the long objective of the Americans ... to control this Continent."[70]

Though bitterly disappointed at the outcome, Wrong informed the State Department that the Canadian government "was not in a position to take immediately a favourable decision on the economic proposals" and considered that "the official talks should be suspended for the time being." Timing, not the substance of the proposals themselves, predominated in Wrong's explanation. "There is no disposition to underestimate the importance of the United States market for Canada and the desirability of removing as fully as possible barriers in the way of trade between Canada and the United States," he explained. "Indeed, fullest development of this trade may be the only sound foundation for Canadian economic stability and prosperity." But Wrong went on to say that an issue of such importance required "preparatory educational work."[71]

Though it might have appeared that the customs union proposal was officially dead, Mackenzie King had not finally shut the door completely. On 21 April, therefore, Abbott, Howe, St. Laurent, Lester Pearson, the undersecretary of state for external affairs, and McKinnon had met with the prime minister. "The two latter," King wrote in his diary, "were anxious to get final word from the Government as to whether they could proceed ... The time they thought had come when matters should be brought to the attention of the President." Abbott and St. Laurent were concerned about the constraints of time, while Howe, "more inclined to urge very strongly going ahead ... [finally] conceded that it would perhaps be impossible in so short a time to effect a satisfactory result."[72] In the end only Pearson and McKinnon pressed King to move forward, and the prime minister flatly refused: "I stressed strongly that regardless of what the economic facts might be, the issue would turn on union with the States and separation from Britain ... Pointed out, too, that the fact that it was proposed both political parties in the States would join, would be a detriment rather than an advantage in getting acceptance of the treaty in Canada ... That to get an agreement between now and the time of the general election in the States, was simply out of the question. All were finally agreed that this would have to be made known to the Americans, and that, at once."[73]

And so the proposal to bind Canada and the United States together in a modified customs union, the subject of months of discussion and investigation by Willoughby and Deutsch and their staffs, became one of the might-have-beens of history. It is true, however, that the search for ways to lower tariff barriers between Canada and the United States did not cease. On 27 April, for instance, C.D. Howe suggested to American officials that the Liberals should "put a plank in the party platform advocating not merely the reduction, but the complete removal of import duties on trade with other countries, provided this could be accomplished on a reciprocal basis in each case." If public opinion proved favourable, Howe said, then the plan could later be pursued after Mackenzie King's retirement.[74] Although Howe explicitly disavowed the customs union idea in this conversation, he was nonetheless called before the prime minister when he returned to Ottawa to explain himself. "My own opinion," Mackenzie King grumbled in his diary, "is that in matters of the kind, Howe is almost an innocent abroad."[75] Within a few days Ambassador Wrong, presumably pressed by Ottawa, had sought and received explicit assurances from the State Department that Howe's visit in no way implied "any commitment on either side to pursue the proposal at a later date."[76] Certainly Mackenzie King remained adamant on the issue: "I told Pearson that while I might miss to be the head of the Government," the Prime Minister wrote in his diary on 6 May, "I would never cease to be a Liberal or a British citizen and if I thought there was a danger of Canada being placed at the mercy of powerful financial interests in the United States, and if that was being done by my own party, I would get out and oppose them openly."[77]

That effectively settled the question, and the Canadian government continued to beat a steady retreat from the high ground of March 1948. C.D. Howe, for one, seemingly abandoned his enthusiasm for free trade and turned to preaching for a new Hyde Park agreement to cover defence materiel. Mackenzie King convinced himself that he had saved Canada once again, and Louis St. Laurent, after August his successor as Liberal leader and prime minister, showed no more enthusiasm. As a French Canadian, moreover, and particularly as one facing a general election in 1949, St. Laurent could not afford to leave himself open to the charge that he had sold Canada to the Americans by scuttling imperial preferences and ties.[78] There would be a few brief flurries of interest in free trade among the politicians in 1949,[79] and men like Deutsch remained enthusiastic supporters of it,[80] but after May 1948 it would never again come close to capturing the government.

Nor did there seem as much economic sense in it once the dollar shortage was resolved. And to the surprise of everyone, the crisis of November 1947 had disappeared with some speed. From a loss of $743 million in 1947 and after a slow start in 1948, Canada's American dollar holdings recovered to a gain of $496 million in 1948, and with Marshall Plan off-shore purchases holding out promise for the future there was every expectation that further improvements would follow. The restrictions of November 1947, moreover, had reduced American imports while exports, mainly of raw materials, increased in 1948 from $1,061 million to $1,508 million.[81] The statistical changes in the indicators signalled the end of the problem to all but men like Deutsch and Willoughby.

Thus reciprocity, and specifically the idea of a customs union, was dead. Can we say that a genuine opportunity had passed? Had reciprocity been a realistic proposal even if Mackenzie King had not vetoed it? Some believed it had. Bruce Hutchison, a distinguished Canadian journalist with good connections in both Ottawa and Washington, had gone to the American capital in February 1949. Here, he wrote in a confidential memorandum, "it is recognized that we failed to strike the reciprocity iron when it was hot last year and it is cooling rapidly. We may have lost our chance in practical American politics which strikes me as [the] most serious thing I have found here."[82] Woodbury Willoughby, one of Hutchison's sources, shared his view. As the chief architect of the American proposal, Willoughby remained convinced that the customs union proposal would have cleared Congress. He had been optimistic in early 1948, and he had been bitterly disappointed by the Canadian decision not to proceed.[83] And John Deutsch, Willoughby's Canadian counterpart, emerged from the whole affair, according to Hutchison, "very, very bitter."[84] Like Willoughby, Deutsch believed until his death in 1976 that a great opportunity to rationalize the North American economy and to show a model liberal capitalism at work had been lost. This seemed especially the case in 1949 when the recession-weakened American economy slowed and Congressional leaders and interest groups became even more ill-disposed to tariff cuts. Canada had had leverage in 1948 of a kind it was never to possess again, Deutsch said.[85] A great chance had been squandered.

This affirmative view finds a contemporary echo in the recent Canadian resurgence of interest in free trade among political scientists and economists, some of whom have associated themselves with the Economic Council of Canada and its advocacy of greater liberalization of trade.[86] From this present-day perspective, Mackenzie King's intervention had scotched a promising opportunity.[87]

And yet some had been unpersuaded in 1948. Andrew Foster of the British Commonwealth Division of the State Department had regarded the difficulties as "insuperable."[88] St. Laurent had been cautious and Abbott worried. Mackenzie King's political antennae, remarkably sensitive to the currents of political opinion, had warned him off the question, and Lester Pearson eventually concluded that King was correct when he ended the discussions. Moreover, as he wrote in his memoirs, "I have always believed that if the question had even reached higher political levels on the American side, it would also have been rejected."[89] It may just be that the customs union of 1948 had been too much too soon.

NOTES

1 J.W. Pickersgill and D. Forster, *The Mackenzie King Record*, IV: *1947–48* (Toronto 1970), 270–1.
2 Harold Macmillan, *Tides of Fortune 1945–55* (London 1969), xv.
3 King in House of Commons, *Debates*, 9 Dec. 1947, 99. For public calls for multilateralism, see J.F. Parkinson, "Problems of International Economic Reconstruction," in Alex Brady and F.R. Scott, eds., *Canada after the War* (Toronto 1943), 199ff; Grant Dexter, *Canada and the Building of Peace* (Toronto 1944), 72ff; W.M. Drummond, "Trade for Prosperity," *Behind the Headlines*, V, 1945; K.R. Wilson, "Dollar Famine," ibid., VII, 15 Jan. 1948. On general similarity of Canadian and US goals, see Louis St. Laurent, *The Foundations of Canadian Policy in World Affairs* (Toronto 1947), esp. 29–31. See also D.G. Creighton, *The Forked Road: Canada 1939–57* (Toronto 1976), 125–7.
4 US National Archives, RG 59, Records of the Department of State, Hickerson Files, box 8, J.D. Hickerson to Atherton, 30 June 1943, "Memorandum, Commercial Arrangements between Canada and the United States." Polls by the Canadian Institute of Public Opinion generally found heavy support for free trade with the United States and overwhelming internationalist sentiment during the war. A June 1943 poll reported that 67 per cent supported free trade with heaviest support in the West, among labour and farmers, and in middle income groups. The same question in February 1944 drew 70 per cent in support, more than a

quarter of whom wanted free trade even if it meant that Canadian industries were driven out of business. In October 1944 54 per cent of Canadians indicated that they would be the same or better off if world free trade prevailed. Polls reproduced in *Public Opinion Quarterly*, VII, fall 1943, 504; VIII, spring 1944, 160; VIII, winter 1944–5, 601–2.

5 *Foreign Relations of the United Slates* 1945, VI (Washington 1969), 61–74; RG 59, 611.4231/8-645, Lewis Clark to Secretary of State, 6 Aug. 1945; ibid., 611.4231/7-1845, H. Marks to Acheson, 18 July 1945. See also K.R. Wilson, "Geneva and the I.T.O.," *International Journal*, II, summer 1947, 246.

6 RG 59, 611.4231/8-645, Clark to Secretary of State, 6 Aug. 1945. Lord Keynes had told the House of Lords in London that "primary emphasis on past services and past sacrifices would not be fruitful" in dealing with North America. Robert Lekachman, *The Age of Keynes* (New York 1966), 187. See J.S. Duncan, *Not a One-Way Street* (Toronto 1971), 132 for one early indication of the UK attitude. On Canada-UK war finance see J.L. Granatstein, "Settling the Accounts: Anglo-Canadian War Finance 1943–5," *Queen's Quarterly*, LXXXIII, summer 1976, 234ff.

7 There is a brief account of the ITO and GATT negotiations in Dana Wilgress, *Memoirs* (Toronto 1967), 150ff. Canada had only two alternatives, Wilgress, Canada's chief negotiator at Geneva, said: multilateralism or "chaos and the law of the economic jungle." Public Archives of Canada [PAC], Department of Finance Records, J.J. Deutsch files, vol 3609, file ITO-24, Wilgress to Secretary of State for External Affairs, 28 Nov. 1947, text of address.

8 On the loans, see Finance Minister Ilsley in House of Commons, *Debates*, 3 Dec. 1945, 2844–7 and 11 April 1946, 762–9. There is a good account in Robert Spencer, *Canada in World Affairs 1946–49* (Toronto 1959), 197ff.

9 See J.D. Gibson, "Post-war Economic Direction and Policy in Canada," *Canadian Journal of Economics and Political Science*, XX, Nov. 1954, 445–6; Gerard Curzon, "GATT and the Golden Age of Trade Cooperation," in M.G. Fry, ed., *Freedom and Change* (Toronto 1975), 190ff; C.L. Barber, "Canada's Post-war Monetary Policy 1945–54," *Canadian Journal of Economics and Political Science*, XXIII, Aug. 1957, 357–8; J.W. Pickersgill and D. Forster, *The Mackenzie King Record*, III: 1945–46 (Toronto 1970), 160ff. For a US view on parity, see Harry Truman Library, John W. Snyder Papers, Haas to Snyder, n.d. [August 1946]. For a key Canadian view, see Department of Finance Records, vol. 1, "Prices and Exchange Rate," n.d., by J. Coyne.

10 Gibson, "Post-war Economic Direction," 446; A.F.W. Plumptre, "Detour into Controls," *International Journal*, III, winter 1947–8, 6. A good overview of the Canadian dollar problem is in Queen's University, W.A. Mackintosh Papers, box 4, "A Note on the Canadian Dollar," n.d.

11 On convertibility, see Richard Gardner, *Sterling-Dollar Diplomacy* (New York 1969); Thomas Balogh, *The Dollar Crisis* (Oxford 1949), passim, and his "Keynes and the IMF," *Times Literary Supplement*, 10 Oct. 1975; Plumptre, "Detour into Controls," 3; PAC, W.L.M. King Diary, 31 July 1947.
12 A convenient summary is "Canada's Exchange Reserves," *Bank of Nova Scotia Monthly Letter*, Aug. 1948, or Foreign Exchange Control Board, *Annual Report 1948* (Ottawa 1948). Monthly summaries prepared by FECB are in Department of Finance Records, vol. 3973, file B-2-8-11.
13 Plumptre, "Detour into Controls," 3. One of the best accounts is Maurice Lamontagne, "Some Political Aspects of Canada's Trade Problem," in J.D. Gibson, ed., *Canada's Economy in a Changing World* (Toronto 1948), 31ff.
14 On Newfoundland's problems in this period, see David Alexander, "The Collapse of the Saltfish Trade and Newfoundland's Integration into the North American Economy," a paper presented to the Canadian Historical Association, 1976.
15 Details on the wheat agreement can be found in Department of External Affairs, External Affairs Records, file 8425–40C, and in R. Bothwell and J. English, "Anglo-Canadian Relations in the Age of American Dominance," a paper presented to the American Historical Association, Dec. 1976. Cf., Queen's University, J.M. Macdonnell Papers, G.A. Drew to Macdonnell, 3 Feb. 1948.
16 Queen's University, Grant Dexter Papers, Memos, 6, 22 Feb. 1947.
17 External Affairs Records, file 264(s), Robertson to Pearson, 19 June 1947; John Deutsch interview, 22 Aug. 1975.
18 An American governmental estimate put the total European balance of payments deficit for 1947 at $7.5 billion. Cited in K.R. Wilson, "The External Background of Canada's Economic Problems," in Gibson, ed., *Canada's Economy*, 11. The best US revisionist account of the period and problem is Joyce and Gabriel Kolko, *The Limits of Power* (New York 1972), passim. See also Department of Finance Records, Clark files, vol. 3440, "Foreign Exchange Prospects and Problems," 26 Feb. 1947.
19 Pickersgill and Forster, *King Record*, IV, 31–2; Stanley Woodward "Memorandum," 23 April 1947, enclosed with Stone to Pearson, 29 April 1947, in External Affairs Records, file 127(s). See also ibid., Pearson to Wrong, 21 April 1947 and reply, 23 April 1947.
20 RG 59, 842.5151/4-2547. Harrington to Foster, 25 April 1947 and PAC, C.D. Howe Papers, vol. 87, E.P. Taylor to Howe, 24 Oct. 1947. On Hyde Park see J.L. Granatstein and R.D. Cuff, "The Hyde Park Agreement 1941: Origins and Significance," *Canadian Historical Review*, LV, March 1974, 59ff.
21 House of Commons, *Debates*, 29 April 1947, 2546–7.

22 Ibid., 13 May 1947, 3059. Cf. 14 May 1947, 3086. Note as well Cockeram's references to the Swedish situation, considered analogous to Canada's by many US officials. Cf. *Financial Post*, 15 March, 21 June 1947.
23 Dexter Papers, Max Freedman to Dexter, 23 Nov. 1947.
24 Howe Papers, vol. 87, Abbott to Howe, 30 June 1947, and reply, 5 July 1947.
25 Pickersgill and Forster, *King Record*, IV, 83.
26 External Affairs Records, file 265(s), Wrong to Pearson, 3 June 1947. See also RG 59, 842.5151/6-2347, Marshall to American embassy, London, 23 June 1947.
27 Documents on RG 59, 842.5151/6-2547 and External Affairs Records, file 265(s).
28 External Affairs Records, file 265(s). Stone to Pearson, 7 June 1947.
29 Ibid., Wrong to Pearson, 20 June 1947; ibid., memo, Pearson to Prime Minister, 28 June 1947; ibid., Clark to Pearson, 20 May 1947. See Acheson's memorial tribute to Wrong in his *Grapes from Thorns* (New York 1972), 223–5.
30 External Affairs Records, file 265(s), Wrong to Pearson, 17 July 1947. Cf. ibid., memo for Prime Minister, 2 June 1947; Department of Finance Records, Clark files, vol. 3438, Wrong to Pearson, 31 May 1947; PAC, External Affairs Records, Washington Embassy files, vol. 2158, memo re discussions at State, 11 June 1947.
31 External Affairs Records, file 265(s), Wrong to Pearson, 30 July 1947. Undersecretary Lovett was equally restrained when discussing the possibilities of British economic collapse. See Walter Millis, ed., *The Forrestal Diaries* (New York 1951), 311–12. For Acheson's "old-boyish" description of Lovett, see his *Present at the Creation* (New York 1969), 236.
32 RG 59, 842.5151/9-1147, Atherton to Secretary of State, 11 Sept. 1947. A Canadian economist reached a similar conclusion some years later: "The cause of the 1947 crisis in foreign exchange was that Canada overreached herself." Harry C. Eastman, "A Comment on Canadian Post-War Monetary Policy," *CJEPS*, XXI, Aug. 1955, 364. Cf. Clifford Clark's similar analysis in Department of Finance Records, Clark files, vol. 3440, "Memorandum on the Exchange Position ...," 1 May 1947
33 RG 59, 842.5151/9-1847, Andrew B. Foster to C. Tyler Wood et al., 18 Sept. 1947.
34 External Affairs Records, file 265(s), Wrong to Clark, 2 Oct. 1947. For a State Department summary of his meeting see RG 59, 842.5151/9-3047, Andrew B. Foster, "The Canadian Dollar Problem," 30 Sept. 1947.
35 RG 59, 842.5151/11-147, Andrew B. Foster, "Memorandum for the Files," 1 Nov. 1947; External Affairs, file 265(s), Wrong to Clark, 2 Oct. 1947. See also RG 59, 842.5151/10-1447, Lovett to Brown, 14 Oct. 1947, and

842.5151/10-2747, Foster to Wood, 27 Oct. 1947; External Affairs Records, Washington Embassy files, vol. 2158, memo of conversations, 18 and 25 Sept. 1947; ibid., minute, 7 Oct. 1947. We might note in passing the extraordinary contrast the Canadian response to the Marshall Plan offers to the skeptical view of Norwegian officials who in the beginning, at least, sought to have as little to do with the idea as possible. The Canadians, in contrast, pressed the Americans to take up the burdens of world responsibility and show their financial largesse towards Canada and the rest of the world. See Helge Ø. Pharo, "Bridgebuilding and Reconstruction: Norway Faces the Marshall Plan," *Scandinavian Journal of History*, I, 1976, 1 25–53. Canadian policy to the Marshall Plan is developed further in J.L. Granatstein and R.D. Cuff, "Canada and the Marshall Plan, 1947," a paper presented to the Canadian Historical Association, June 1977.

36 RG 59, FW 611.422/10–2649, Willoughby, "United States-Canada Trade Relations," 29 Oct. 1947; External Affairs Records, Washington Embassy files, vol. 2158, minute sheets, 31 Oct. 1947; Queen's University, John Deutsch Papers, folder 5, Deutsch to Wilgress, 23 Dec. 1947.

37 Kenneth R. Wilson, "Will Marshall Plan Speed Crisis End?," *Financial Post*, 15 Nov. 1947, 1. Cf. Wilson, "Dollar Famine."

38 Spencer, *Canada in World Affairs 1946–49*, 221ff; and Wilson, "The External Background of Canada's Economic Problems,' in Gibson, ed., *Canada's Economy*, 16–19, 24–25. Pickersgill and Forster, *King Record*, IV, 89–90.

39 Pickersgill and Forster, *King Record*, IV, 89.

40 On Deutsch, see Department of Finance Records, Deutsch files, vol. 3609, file ITO-24, Wilgress to Pearson, 14 Nov. 1947. External Affairs, file 265(s), "Summary of US-Canadian Financial discussions, October 28th to 31st," enclosed Wrong to Clark, 1 Nov. 1947.

41 "Summary of US-Canadian Financial discussions." For the immediate follow-up, see Department of Finance Records, Deutsch Papers, vol. 3606, file U-04, Canadian Ambassador to Secretary of State for External Affairs, 5, 11, 13 Nov. 1947.

42 This was a question that troubled many observers – and still does. G.C. Bateman, a wartime and postwar expert adviser to the Canadian government on mineral and raw material production, wrote to the editor of the *Financial Post* to say that part of the dollar problem "arises from the fact that parent companies in the United States dictate the export policies of their Canadian branch plants ... The Canadian government will have to regulate, and if necessary, apply some form of compulsion to see that Canadian companies obtain a fair proportion of the dollar export market." Kenneth Wilson Papers (Toronto), folder E, Bateman to Ron McEachern, 4 June 1947. We are grateful to Professor Robert Bothwell for drawing this to our attention.

43 RG 59, 842.5151/11-2047, Julian Harrington to Andrew B. Foster, 20 Nov. 1947. For Bruce Hutchison's report of a similar American expansionist sentiment in Adolph Berle's thought, see Bruce Hutchison, memorandum 12 June 1940, in King Papers, vol. 19 (Black Binders).

44 See External Affairs, file 265-B(s)(1), Wrong to Moran, 24 Nov. 1947; Moran to Wrong, 29 Nov. 1947; Wrong to Moran, 1 Dec. 1947; Moran to Wrong, 4 Dec. 1947; Clark to Wrong, 5 Dec. 1947. Among the illustrations of what Canada might seek which Deutsch and McKinnon passed along were a free listing of all important fish, of cattle, eggs, hay, and straw, of lumber, shingles, and plywood, and certain heavy chemicals and fertilizer materials. See ibid., Moran to Wrong, 24 Dec. 1947. See also RG 59, 611.4231/11-2147, W.T.M. Beale to W.G. Brown et al., 21 Nov. 1947; Department of Finance Records, Deutsch Papers, vol. 3606, file U-04, Deutsch to Moran, 16 Dec. 1947.

45 "Wilcox was definitely in favour of the idea of going to Congress with a special US-Canadian Trade Agreement. He promised to take up this question at once with his superiors, with a view to sounding out Congressional leaders on a bipartisan basis, at a later date." Cited in External Affairs, file TS 265(s), "summary of US-Canadian Financial discussions, October 28th to 31st," attached Wrong to Clark, 1 Nov. 1947. For a comprehensive introduction to Wilcox's views on economic policy see his *A Charter for World Trade* (New York 1949), which he dedicates to "The Veterans of London Geneva Havana."

46 Dexter Papers, memo, 4 Dec. 1948. See also ibid., 31 Jan. 1950. There seems to have been two competing points of view on these issues within the Canadian government, and Deutsch represented the more historic free trade orientation of Canadian Liberalism. James Coyne and James Gardiner, on the other hand, represented a view more sympathetic towards the sterling bloc, and towards the idea of bilateral arrangements with the British. As a corollary to this they indicated far greater skepticism towards the capacity and stability of the United States market to absorb Canadian goods. From Deutsch's perspective, of course, men like Coyne and Gardiner were motivated by "a perverted nationalism which now expresses itself by hating the US and trying to kick it in the teeth." The Coyne school, in contrast, regarded Deutsch, by his own account at least, "as a poor dupe for the Americans." See ibid., 4 Feb. 1950, and Feb. 1949.

47 In a confidential interview with Bruce Hutchison in 1949 Willoughby is quoted as saying "that Canada and US alone are left in the world of free enterprise and more or less free-trading non-discriminatory nations. They should join together in total free trade and, in the resulting prosperity, demonstrate the validity of trade to the world." Dexter Papers, memo, Feb. 1949.

48 RG 59, 842.5151/12-1847, Nitze to Wilcox, 18 Dec. 1947. For a description and analysis of the customs union and related forms of trade organization see Jacob Viner, *The Customs Union Issue* (New York 1950), passim. See also John S. Lambrinidis, *The Structure, Function, and Law of a Free Trade Association* (New York, Washington 1965), Ch. 1, and Franz Wendt, *The Nordic Council and Cooperation in Scandinavia* (Copenhagen 1949), 97ff.

49 RG 59, 842.5151/12-1847, Nitze to Wilcox, 18 Dec. 1947. For an example of the Canadian critique of a pure custom union see Wilson, "Dollar Famine," 16–18.

50 RG 59, 842.5151/12-1847, Nitze to Wilcox, 18 Dec. 1947, and see FW 611.422/10-2649, Andrew B. Foster, "Memorandum for the Files," 23 Dec. 1947.

51 Ibid., FW 611.422/10-2649, Willoughby, "Memorandum of conversation," 31 Dec. 1947, and Willoughby to Wilcox and Leddy, 7 Jan. 1948

52 Deutsch interview. See also RG 59, 611.4231/12-3147, "Current Problems in US-Canadian Economic Relationships," December 31, 1947.

53 Deutsch interview; Department of Finance Records, Deutsch Papers, vol, 3606, file U-04, Wrong to Deutsch, 7 Jan. 1948.

54 Pickersgill and Forster, *King Record*, IV, 261. In contrast to Deutsch's account, King placed Graham Towers with the pro-agreement group. Ibid., 260. For additional Canadian reasoning on this point see RG 59, FW 611.422/10-2649, Willoughby, "Proposed Tariff Reciprocity with Canada," 22 Jan. 1948. See also Deutsch to A.F.W. Plumptre, 11 Oct. 1973. We are much indebted to Professor T.J. Fay for permitting us to see this letter and other material.

55 Recognizing the inevitable public relations problem if either the United States or Canada introduced an amendment contradicting their general stand on multilateralism, Willoughby and Wilcox, with Deutsch's support, planted the amendment with France. For the regional trade pact idea from Arab countries, see RG 59, FW 611.422/10-2649, Willoughby to Wilcox and Leddy, 7 Jan. 1948; Wilcox to Willoughby, 8 Jan. 1948; C. Southworth, "Memorandum of Conversation," 31 Jan. 1948; and Queen's University, Deutsch Papers, documents on folder 560. Cf. Wilcox, *A Charter for World Trade*, 70–2, and Viner, *The Customs Union Issue*, Ch. 6.

56 See the technical working papers in RG 59, 611.422, as well as the relevant documents in ibid., 611.422/10-2649, including R.F. Mikesell, "Preliminary Thoughts on US-Canadian Customs Union," 23 Jan. 1948, and "Escape Clauses for Safeguarding the Balance of Payments ..."; and A. Rosenon, "US-Canadian Rate of Exchange under a Customs Union," 16 Feb. 1948, and "Reorientation of Canada's Economy under a Customs Union," 16 Feb. 1948.

57 Pickersgill and Forster, *King Record*, IV, 261.

58 RG 59, FW 611.422/10-2649, Willoughby, "Proposed Tariff Reciprocity Arrangement with Canada," 22 Jan. 1948.
59 Ibid.
60 Ibid., FW 611.422/10-2649, Willoughby to Thorp, [n.d.] attached to Thorp to Lovett, 8 March 1948. Printed in *Foreign Relations of the United States 1948* (Washington 1972), IX, 407ff. For the particular details thought important by Abbott and King, see Pickersgill and Forster, *King Record*, IV, 261–2.
61 RG 59, FW 611.422/10-2649, Willoughby to Hickerson, 30 March 1948. For another expression of this view see ibid., C. Tyler Wood to Lovett, 1 April 1948.
62 Ibid., Willoughby to Hickerson, 30 March 1948.
63 Ibid., C. Southworth, "United States-Canada Trade Relations," 9 March 1948.
64 Ibid., C. Southworth, "United States-Canada Trade Relations," 10 March 1948. On the issue of restrictions, W.C. Clark noted in a speech shortly before his death that "the incidental protection which they afforded was having the effect of stimulating high-cost, uneconomic production of some of the goods subject to import control and introducing distortions in the Canadian economy. Vested interests were being created and doubts began to be expressed concerning the merits of trying to follow liberal trading policies in a world of widespread restrictionism ..." W.C. Clark, "Canada's Post-war Finance," *Canadian Tax Journal*, I, Jan.–Feb. 1953, 106.
65 RG 59, FW 611.422/10-2649, C. Southworth, "United States-Canada Trade Relations," to March 1948. See Macdonnell Papers, Jackson to Macdonnell, 20 March 1948.
66 For an example of friction between State and Agriculture on the tariff question see their fight over an import quota for wool in the summer of 1947. Susan M. Hartmann, *Truman and the 80th Congress* (Columbia, Mo. 1971), 91–2. Also, J.D. Hickerson interview, 29 Sept. 1977.
67 Pickersgill and Forster, *King Record*, IV, 267; *Life*, 15 March 1948, 40.
68 Pickersgill and Forster, *King Record*, IV, 268.
69 RG 59, FW 611.422/10-2649, Willoughby, "Proposed Pact with Canada," 25 March 1948 and ibid., Willoughby to Hickerson, 30 March 1948.
70 Pickersgill and Forster, *King Record*, IV, 269.
71 RG 59, FW 611.422/10-2649, Wrong to Hickerson, 1 April 1948.
72 According to Frederick Weihs, "Canadian Trade Policy, 1945–53" (MA thesis, University of British Columbia, 1976), 77ff, an account based on the Pearson and King Papers for this period, Abbott, St. Laurent, and Howe were all strongly in favour of the scheme, as was Clifford Clark. Weihs, citing a letter from Pearson to Norman Robertson, 22 April 48, in Pearson Papers, vol. 13, has King arguing that "from the economic point of view, there was everything to be said for the proposal and little against

it." But King was emphatic "that the Conservatives would seize on this issue ... in order to force an early election. They would distort and misrepresent the proposal as an effort on the part of the Liberals to sell Canada to the United States for a mess of pottage. All the old British flag-waving would be resurrected by the Conservatives ..." The cabinet ministers, Weihs goes on, did not share King's fears, and Howe, in particular, felt "an election issue of this kind would be a magnificent one for the Liberals, and would sweep the country." The ministers went along with the prime minister but, according to Pearson's letter, felt "particular regret at the necessity of coming to this conclusion."

73 Pickersgill and Forster, *King Record*, IV, 270.
74 RG 59, 611.4231/4-2748, C. Tyler Wood, "Removal of Trade Barriers between the United States and Canada," 27 April 1948; Cf. Queen's University, T.A. Crerar Papers, box 88, "Resolutions of the NLF; Meeting of the Advisory Council, Jan. 20–1, 1948."
75 Pickersgill and Forster, *King Record*, IV, 272.
76 RG 59, FW 611.422/10-2649, Wrong, "Memorandum," 10 May 1948.
77 Pickersgill and Forster, *King Record*, IV, 273.
78 Dexter Papers, memo, 6 Dec. 1948; memo, 28 Dec. 1948; and Dexter to Hutchison, 26 Jan. 1949; Deutsch interview.
79 RG 59, 611.4231/2-1149, W. Willoughby, "US-Canadian Trade Relations," 11 Feb. 1949; 4231/30549, C.S. Southworth, "New Trade Agreement with Canada," 5 March 1949. For Truman's Congressional battle over the reciprocal trade program see Hartmann, *Truman and the 80th Congress*, 179–84. A good indication of protectionist sentiment can be found in Senate Foreign Relations Committee reaction to Article 2 of NATO, which was seen as a device to lower tariffs by subterfuge. See United States Senate, *Foreign Relations Hearings held in Executive Session ... S. Res. 239* (Historical Series, Washington 1973), 97–8, 130–1. External Affairs Records, Washington Embassy files, vol. 2163, St. Laurent file, memo of talk with Truman, 12 Feb. 1949; RG 59, 511.421/2-1349, Acheson, "Memorandum of Conversation," 13 Feb. 1949; *Foreign Relations of the United States 1949* (Washington 1975), 11, 393ff; Queen's University, Deutsch Papers, folder 471, Wrong to Heeney, 25 May 1949.
80 Deutsch interview.
81 Department of Finance Records, vol. 3987, file P-2-11, telegram to Wrong, 21 Feb. 1948, and reply, 27 Feb. 1948; F.A. Knox, "Editorial," *Canadian Banker*, LVI, spring 1949, 7ff; Spencer, *Canada in World Affairs 1946–49*, 225–6; FECB, *Annual Report 1948*, 1.
82 Dexter Papers, Hutchison to Dexter, 18 Feb. 1949.
83 Ibid., memo, 3 Feb. 1950.
84 Ibid., memo, 4 Aug. 1949.

85 Deutsch interview.
86 André Raynauld [Economic Council chairman], "Traditional Goals and Contemporary Challenges: A Canadian Commercial Policy for the 1980s and 1990s," presentation to the Standing Senate Committee on Foreign Affairs, 11 July 1975; and Economic Council of Canada, *Looking Outward: A New Trade Strategy for Canada* (Ottawa 1975), passim.
87 See, for example, H. Edward English, "The Political Economy of International Economic Integration: A Brief Analysis," in *Continental Community? Independence and Integration in North America*, Andrew Axline, et al., eds. (Toronto 1974), 39. And for an example of the general ideology characteristic of this position see Peyton V. Lyon, *Canada-United States Free Trade and Canadian Independence* (Economic Council of Canada, Ottawa, 1975), passim. From a contemporary nationalist perspective, of course, a free trade agreement in 1948 was an opportunity better missed. See Peter Newman, *The Canadian Establishment* (Toronto 1975), 325.
88 RG 59, 842.00/12-2347, Foster to Hickerson, 23 Dec. 1947. He added, however: "I am the fellow who would have told Columbus the earth was flat."
89 Lester Pearson, *Mike: The Memoirs of the Right Honourable Lester B. Pearson*, I: *1897–1948* (Toronto 1972), 292. For Pearson's view at the time see Pickersgill and Forster, *King Record*, IV, 269.

Chapter Four

Too Close for Comfort: John Diefenbaker and the Political Uses of Anti-Americanism

In 1958 and 1959, movie theatres around the world still showed newsreels each week. In the months after the Soviet Union put up *Sputnik*, the first satellite launched into an earth orbit, the newsreels featured the United States' effort to develop the huge missiles necessary to duplicate the Russians' feat. The American missiles, however, blew up with amazing frequency, collapsing back to earth in showers of smoke, flames, and explosions. For a time, as Nikita Khrushchev gloated and postured, the Western alliance seemed to be in genuine danger from the Russians' intercontinental ballistic missiles.

The newsreels of these disasters played in Canadian movie houses to a startling response. When the huge missiles strained off their launch pads only to collapse in ruination, audiences all across Canada, and certainly in Toronto, as I cannot forget, clapped, laughed, and cheered, revelling in the Americans' humiliation and failure. Canadian anti-Americanism was alive and well at the end of the 1950s, even though the Soviets' missile successes posed a threat to Canada.

No one could suggest that John Diefenbaker singlehandedly created this mood in Canada. Anti-Americanism existed long before Diefenbaker, and it survived his departure from the prime ministership. But there can be no doubt that Diefenbaker's prickly nationalism had fed Canadian concerns about the Americans, and that those cheering audiences believed their government had major differences with the United States administration. They were right.

The Conservative Party had stagnated in opposition since 1935. Its leadership lacklustre, its policies musty, the party had slipped irretrievably into irrelevance. Tory policies still reeked of imperial sentimentality when the British Empire was on the cusp of history. The African and Asian colonies and territories were grasping for independence, the dominions were at last becoming truly independent nations, and Britain's economic and military power, wasted by war, had collapsed everywhere. The Progressive Conservative Party's rhetoric had a permanent tinge of anti-Americanism at a time when the United States was the leader of the Free World and the magnet that attracted the best and the brightest from all over the world, not least from Canada. Tory support, battered by successive defeats in the elections of 1935, 1940, 1945, 1949, and 1953, seemed on the verge of disappearing as Canada urbanized and modernized. The Liberals under Mackenzie King and Louis St. Laurent had ridden the wave of the future.

Suddenly, almost inexplicably, everything changed. John Diefenbaker, chosen leader of the Progressive Conservative Party at a national convention in December 1956, won a stunning minority election victory in June of the next year over St. Laurent and became Prime Minister. A spell-binding orator, an experienced parliamentarian, and a fervent believer in the British connection, Canadian nationalism, and the Western alliance against the Soviet Union, Diefenbaker personified those Canadians who clung to past imperial glories and looked with increasing desperation for the twentieth century to belong to Canada.

Diefenbaker was born in rural Ontario in 1895, but raised in the western province of Saskatchewan. His mother's maiden name was Campbell, Scottish to the core, but his father's Baden ancestors had come to Canada early in the nineteenth century. Germans laboured under no discrimination in Canada until the outbreak of the Great War in 1914, but then the lash of public opinion fell heavily on those whose language or names suddenly attracted attention. John Diefenbaker, in 1914 a university student, suffered along with his family. From that point on he opposed the hyphenated Canadianism that characterized everyone by their "old country" origins and supported "one Canada," his later descriptive phrase for pan-Canadian nationalism. The young Diefenbaker enlisted in the Canadian Expeditionary Force and served briefly as an officer in Canada and Britain. Either injured in a training accident or suffering from psychological problems, as his most recent biographer suggests, he was demobilized by the Canadian Expeditionary Force before he saw any action in the trenches.[1]

Countless Canadians like Diefenbaker had resented the way the republican United States, always loud in its protestations of virtue, remained neutral in the Great War until 1917. He was even more offended by the Americans' postwar bragging that they alone had won the war.

On the Prairies, where large numbers of Americans had settled in the years around the turn of the century, these attitudes would be hardened by the United States' delay in entering the Second World War.

Thus, John Diefenbaker was a bundle of contradictions. His Scottish forebears gave him a burning interest in Britain and British forms of government and law. A fervent monarchist, he believed that the Crown had a mediatory effect on politics and that the British connection was good for Canada, not least because it provided a counterweight to the sometimes overpowering influence of the United States. At the same time, sensitized by his Germanic surname, he wanted to see a country where foreign elements subsumed their ethnicity in a common Canadian nationalism. As a pro-British pan-Canadian nationalist with anti-American attitudes, he typified many Canadians. At the same time, as a westerner, he resented the financial and political dominance exerted by central Canada over his region. The control exercised by Toronto and its paymasters on New York's Wall Street, along with the weight the federal government gave to French Canada's attitudes and sensitivities, rankled in him and his region.

Diefenbaker took his hardening attitudes into politics. He failed to win election to Parliament in the 1920s, he lost out as a municipal candidate in his home town of Prince Albert in the 1930s, and he failed as a provincial Conservative in the last years of the Great Depression. But in the general election of 1940, an election in which Mackenzie King and his Liberal Party swept back into power with a huge majority, he finally won a place in the House of Commons as a Conservative. His party was in ruins, reduced to a mere forty seats, all but leaderless. Diefenbaker tried to become House leader in 1940 but failed, and two years later he sought the national leadership, running poorly at a convention. In 1944 he was one of only two Tory MPs to argue in favour of family allowances, an indication that he leant towards social welfare – and away from the free enterprise rhetoric still espoused by the Ontario group that controlled the Progressive Conservative Party. In 1948, by now reasonably well known across the country as a compelling speaker with firm views on domestic and foreign policy, he tried for the gold ring again, losing this time to Ontario's Premier George Drew, a man with strong backing from Toronto's financial circles. Not until 1956, his party still becalmed in the political doldrums it had occupied since 1935, did he finally struggle to the top of the greasy pole. The leadership of the Progressive Conservative Party did not seem much of a prize.

At the beginning of 1957, Diefenbaker's attitudes were much as they had been since his youth. The Suez humiliation of the previous year notwithstanding, he continued to believe in Britain's greatness and in the majesty of the Crown, and the highlight of his accession to the prime ministership was his almost immediate flight to Britain for a Commonwealth Prime Ministers' conference and a meeting with the Queen. Diefenbaker remained suspicious of the United States and its policies, deeply resentful of the way Washington had turned its back on Britain in the Suez Canal crisis and of the way the Liberal government had cooperated with the Americans in humiliating London and Paris by forcing them to withdraw their armies from Egypt. At the same time, as American investment increased to some 76 per cent of all foreign investment in Canada in 1957 and dominated crucial areas of the national economy, he fumed at what he saw as a too-close link between the Liberals and American high finance. He worried about the inevitable loss of control over Canada's economic destiny. Moreover, his dislike for the central Canadian nexus within his own party had not been appeased by his convention victory. Suspicion was John Diefenbaker's middle name.

In the general election campaign of 1957, Diefenbaker, his extraordinary eyes flashing, his arms waving, his voice full of seemingly genuine passion, had appeared meteor-like on the political scene. His stock in trade was Canadian nationalism, which equalled a large dose of understated anti-Americanism. Canada ought to have stood by Britain at Suez, not followed Washington's lead. American investment was too large and threatened a loss of control to the south: "If the St. Laurent government is re-elected," Diefenbaker proclaimed, "Canada will become a virtual 49th state of the American union." Canada's great future was yet to come, and it would be based on an unhyphenated nationalism that would create a wholly independent nation on the northern half of the continent. That attitude guaranteed that there would be flareups in relations with the United States – and there were.

Yet when he became Prime Minister, Diefenbaker was quick to sign Canada on to the North American Air Defense Agreement, an alliance that joined the Royal Canadian Air Force's home defence squadrons and radar lines and the United States Air Force under a single command headquartered in Colorado Springs. He was so quick in this decision that he failed to consult his Cabinet, his Cabinet Defence Committee (which had not yet even been formed), or the Department of External Affairs, which learned about the agreement's signature from the Americans. Diefenbaker had not acted wisely, though he was not playing at anti-Americanism. It was present, however. When NORAD finally came before the House of Commons, the CCF voted against the agreement, the first major break in the widespread support Cold War Canadian foreign and defence policy had commanded.

Diefenbaker soon demonstrated that he was an admirer of President Dwight D. Eisenhower, then in the early part of his second term in the White House. A centrist Republican with a Germanic name (exactly as Diefenbaker was a middle-of-the-road Conservative with a Germanic name), Ike was a war hero, the leader of the great military coalition that had won the Second World War. Now he was the leader of the free world in the conflict with Soviet Communism. Eisenhower was older, a genuinely pleasant and courteous man, and he had the innate good sense to treat Diefenbaker well, to call him "John" in their correspondence, and to flatter the Canadian leader politely. As Diefenbaker wrote in his memoirs: "Unlike his successor, [Eisenhower] did not regard the United States presidency as a glittering jewel; he saw it as a job to be done. I found Eisenhower a warm and engaging person, and we became the best of friends. He had an appreciation of Canada and Canadians ... Eisenhower was a man that one could talk to ... he was prepared to listen to my point of view."

Eisenhower, in other words, played Diefenbaker shrewdly and well, offering him invitations to visit Washington and sending warm telegrams to mark significant events, political and personal. He appeared to understand Diefenbaker's concerns about US influence over Canada, and he went out of his way to relieve them, something he accomplished with remarkable success. The President was also well informed. As a briefing paper prepared in the Department of State for a ministerial meeting put it: "Canadian sensitivity to the actions and policies of the United States is a political reality in handling the problems inherent in the close relations between our two countries ... A complicating factor in dealing with the Canadian Government is that relations with the United States inevitably play an important role in Canadian domestic politics ... the Government feeling itself impelled to outdo the Opposition in defense of Canadian interests."[2]

The public mood fed this attitude in Ottawa. "There was still affection for Americans and a general, if very soft, confidence in the world leadership of the United States, though this trust co-existed uneasily with a widespread and hardening anti-Americanism on the part of all those who had been outraged by the hounding of Herbert Norman and who worried about the aggressive anti-Communism that characterized Washington's foreign policy. Diefenbaker himself professed to worry about this attitude. In an interview with Arnold Heeney, the Canadian Ambassador in Washington in 1960, the Prime Minister pronounced "anti-American sentiment ... now worse than at any time in his lifetime." It was growing into an "avalanche." Heeney characterized the mood as "not ill will but combined asperity and cockiness," and he described the Americans of that era as "generous, charming and often frightening."[3] It was the "frightening" part that troubled Canadians, who were worried about nuclear war, American pressure on the dominion, and the cultural tide sweeping across the border.

Robert Thomas Allen, a popular journalist, wrote in *Maclean's* on September 24, 1960, that his countrymen had "gone slightly out of their minds on the subject of the United States. "They've become the victims of a fixed idea – the idea that the first step toward being right is to establish that the United States is wrong. It's turning them," Allen argued, "into a spectator nation, a breed of carping Monday-morning quarterbacks ... They can't speak intelligently about Americans, or civilly about Americans, or calmly about Americans, or get their mind off Americans."

Matters were destined only to worsen. One of the bestsellers in Canadian publishing in 1960 was a slender book by James M. Minifie, the CBC correspondent in Washington. *Peacemaker or Powder-Monkey: Canada's Role in a Revolutionary World* called on Canada to cut itself loose from the Americans' chariot wheels and to proclaim its neutrality proudly. A Canadian-born, Oxford-educated, American citizen, Minifie seemed to believe that Canada and the United States existed in isolation, that there was no Soviet Union with missiles and bombers poised to strike over the North Pole, and scarcely any need for Canadian defence. His little book sold thousands of copies and stirred debate on the apparent loss of Canadian sovereignty set in train by the Cold War. He did not persuade John Diefenbaker, whose anti-Communism coexisted with his anti-Americanism.

The degree of understanding, the concern for Diefenbaker's sensitivities that the Eisenhower administration had shown, had welded the Prime Minister solidly into the Canadian-American alliance, however much he might bridle on occasion. When John F. Kennedy won election to the presidency in November 1960, however, the new administration proved much more impatient with Canada. In his early forties, good-looking, forceful in speech, Kennedy's attractiveness drew the world's interest, and Canadians were captivated by him every bit as much as Americans.[4]

Diefenbaker had preferred Richard Nixon, Eisenhower's Vice-President whom he had come to know, to Kennedy. He nonetheless paid an early visit to the new American leader on February 20, 1961, and seemed to believe that he had established a good working relationship with the much younger, charismatic Kennedy. The President, however, had been briefed in ways which painted Canada as a potential trouble spot and which suggested that the major problem might be the Prime Minister:

> Canadian support cannot be taken for granted and there will most probably be a variety of Canadian initiatives, some of which will be most annoying to the US ... [Diefenbaker] is not believed to have any basic prejudice against the United States. He has appeared, however, to seek on occasion to assert Canadian independence by seizing opportunities for Canada to adopt policies which deviate somewhat from those of the United States, but he has done so only when it has been possible without overwhelmingly serious consequences to US–Canadian relations.[5]

When Kennedy repaid Diefenbaker's visit by coming north to receive a rapturous welcome in Ottawa in May 1961 (and to injure his back seriously in an unfortunate tree-planting ceremony at Government House), his briefing book again was tart – but completely correct in capturing Diefenbaker's typically Canadian attitudes. Indeed, the briefer's shrewd assessment of Canadian feelings towards the United States in 1961 could likely have been mirrored at most points in the half century after 1945: "The projection of the United States image in Canada during the Presidential visit should take into account the long-standing tendency of some Canadians to believe that we are dominated by a trigger-happy military, that we are not regardful of cultural values, that we are harsh and discriminatory in our attitudes toward minorities, that we are inept and lacking in perception in our handling of relations with under-developed countries in both diplomacy and aid, and that we tend to be absent-minded and neglectful of the interests of Canada."[6]

Difficulties quickly arose at this meeting in Ottawa. A memorandum prepared for the President was apparently left between the cushions of a sofa, and Diefenbaker, who found it and failed to return it as protocol demanded, apparently (and wrongly) interpreted some penned scratches written on the paper as referring to him as an "SOB." As important, there were sharp disputes about Canada's continuing trade with Fidel Castro's Cuba, while the United States, just a month after its humiliating failure in supporting a Cuban exiles' invasion at the Bay of Pigs, was becoming increasingly hard-line in its approach to Cuban Communism and all who lent it aid. There were also continuing differences over Canada's acquisition from the United States of nuclear warheads for the weapons systems Diefenbaker's government had purchased in the late 1950s for use in NORAD and in Europe with the forces of the North Atlantic Treaty Organization. There was no doubt that Canada in 1959 had agreed to go nuclear, but while construction of

Bomarc missile sites in Canada went ahead, the negotiations to lay out the agreed terms under which warheads for the surface-to-air missiles would come to Canada made no progress whatsoever. Howard Green, Diefenbaker's Secretary of State for External Affairs, was pressing hard for nuclear disarmament at the United Nations and in Allied councils, and the delay, as Diefenbaker wavered uneasily and watched his pro-nuclear Defence Minister, Douglas Harkness, had begun to be very noticeable. It wasn't that Diefenbaker was not anti-Communist – not at all. The luxury his government had of sheltering under the Americans' nuclear umbrella made the Chief complacent. The government felt free to carp and complain at Washington, secure in the belief that the Yanks would protect them if the Cold War turned hotter.

Complacency could turn to spitefulness. At their May 1961 meeting in Ottawa, Diefenbaker persuaded himself that Kennedy was too cocky for such a young man and too inclined to use American muscle to push him and Canada around. The Prime Minister developed a sharp and growing dislike for the President, a nostalgic yearning for the camaraderie and respect that Eisenhower had shown him, and a stiff-necked attitude to burgeoning American power that did not bode well for the future of Canada's relations with the new American administration.

Relations grew worse. In early May 1962, with an election campaign in its early stages, the Prime Minister was furious after Kennedy gave a forty-five-minute private interview to Liberal leader Lester Pearson before a dinner to honour Nobel Prize winners. Diefenbaker ranted to US Ambassador Livingston Merchant that the Americans were out to get him and that he might feel obliged to reveal the "SOB" memorandum to the voters. Basil Robinson of the Department of External Affairs, Diefenbaker's foreign policy aide in the Prime Minister's Office, later observed that the Ambassador "had clearly been staggered by the vehemence of the prime minister's tirade against President Kennedy."[7] But Diefenbaker, cautioned by Merchant in a subsequent meeting and obviously having second thoughts of his own, did not make the 1961 memorandum public.

While relations deteriorated during the campaign, Diefenbaker's Cabinet continued to avoid a decision on accepting the nuclear warheads, without which the Bomarcs were only useless, expensive metal. The government was in trouble, its popularity sagging under the strains of a major downturn in the economy, and facing a run on the Canadian dollar that required it to fix the dollar's value at 92.5 cents US. There were increasing doubts about the Prime Minister's leadership capacity and even his mental health. The election results on June 18 reduced the Tories to minority status, leaving Diefenbaker clinging to power.

The United States, asked immediately after the election to help bolster Canadian dollar reserves, gave its assistance, but this renewed evidence of his country's dependency on American largesse did little to improve the Prime Minister's humour. Depressed by his political misfortunes and in pain from a broken ankle, Diefenbaker brooded over the summer. When American reconnaissance aircraft revealed that the Soviet Union was installing intermediate-range nuclear missiles in Cuba, a crisis that brought the world to the brink of war erupted with startling suddenness in October 1962. A political storm along the Canada–US border was almost inevitable.

Canadian intelligence officials had brought word of the Cuban crisis to Ottawa a day or two before Kennedy's envoy flew north to brief Diefenbaker. Although he listened to the briefing calmly, the Prime Minister quickly came to believe that he and his country had been excluded, despite the NORAD treaty's provisions that should have guaranteed Canada a privileged place and early consultation. That fed his belief in Kennedy's impetuousness and, on the advice of and with the support of senior officials in the Department of External Affairs, the Prime Minister gave a speech in Parliament calling for neutral members of the United Nations Disarmament Committee to investigate the situation on the ground in Cuba. An infuriated Washington interpreted the Canadian suggestion as casting doubt on Kennedy's honesty, which, of course, it had. More important, Diefenbaker refused to permit Canadian interceptor squadrons in NORAD to move to a heightened state of alert, and preparatory measures for ground and naval forces also were officially placed on hold. The Americans were properly outraged. *Maclean's* reported from Washington in March 1963: "What Canadians don't always realize is that, if there is anti-Americanism in Canada, there is anti-Canadianism in the US. The Americans, constantly bombarded by the propaganda of the military-industrial complex and the hysteria of John Birchers and other right-wing extremists, are highly emotional about Cuba ... many Americans regard us as traitors to the cause of freedom."

So too did many Canadians. "The Red Scare had reached its zenith," Pierre Berton wrote in his memoirs of the atmosphere in 1962. "Almost every organization slightly to the left of centre was smeared with the Red tag." Berton was well aware of the mood because he had asked Liberal leader Lester Pearson on television in June 1962 if he would rather be Red than dead, and Pearson's reply – that he would rather live under the Communists and work to throw them out of power – had led Conservatives to smear Pearson as soft on Communism. Now Diefenbaker would find the charges thrown at him. Canadians evidently believed it was important to back their ally.

The refusal to bring the Canadian components of NORAD to alert status apparently left the centre of the continent open to a Soviet air attack. In fact, the danger was never there. The Minister of National Defence, acting in defiance of the Prime Minister and on his own authority, placed the RCAF on "Defcon 3," a high-alert status, and turned a blind eye when the Royal Canadian Navy's commander on the East Coast put his ships to sea to track Soviet submarines.[8] The Kennedy administration said nothing officially about Ottawa's dilatoriness – its tolerance can only be described as remarkable – but its extreme displeasure was made clear to Canadian officials and, inevitably, quickly leaked into the press.

While some Canadians that October scrambled to dig fallout shelters in their backyards or basements and stockpiled water and canned goods to help them survive the coming nuclear war, their government did next to nothing. Diefenbaker and several of his key ministers were blinded by their anti-Americanism, their dislike for Kennedy, and their stiff-necked insistence on the right NORAD gave them to be consulted in the greatest crisis of the Cold War. Once the story became public, the impact on Diefenbaker's credibility was devastating. The Cuban crisis eased when the Soviets, eyeball to eyeball with Kennedy, blinked and agreed to pull their missiles out. In this first great Cold War confrontation in which television brought events into people's living rooms, Canadians all across the nation looked to President John F. Kennedy as their leader, not to the ineffectual, indecisive Diefenbaker. The Prime Minister's authority crumbled.

Canada's own crisis was about to begin, helped by the fact that a clear majority of Canadians in a poll on December 22 wanted the Canadian military to be armed with nuclear weapons. The US administration felt no need to hold back in its attack on the Canadian leader. When the retiring NATO Supreme Commander, US General Lauris Norstad, paid a farewell visit to Ottawa on January 3, 1963, he told a press conference that Canada had not lived up to its alliance commitments because of its failure to arm Canada's CF-104 fighter-bombers, stationed in Europe and intended for a strike role against eastern European targets, with nuclear weapons. Norstad's remarks still further undermined the Diefenbaker administration, already weakened by the critical public response to the Prime Minister's inaction during the Cuban crisis and by a Cabinet that was increasingly polarized over the nuclear question. Diefenbaker desperately tried to explain and justify his government's defence policy in a major speech in Parliament on January 25, 1963. His "on the one hand/on the other hand" tone momentarily satisfied some of his critical Cabinet colleagues, but his remarks about American–British nuclear negotiations twisted facts and broke Allied confidences. The State Department in Washington issued a blistering press release on January 30, declaring Diefenbaker a liar, a man whose government "has not as yet proposed any arrangement sufficiently practical to contribute effectively to North American defense." The damning press release did the trick: within days the Conservative Cabinet fell apart, the government suffered defeat in a confidence motion in the House of Commons, and an election was duly called for April 8. Historian Donald Creighton exaggerated dramatically, "About the only manifestation of American power which was spared Canada in the crisis was the sight of American tanks rumbling up Parliament Hill in Ottawa." The Americans, he went on, had indicated to Canadians where their best interests lay, and Pearson's Liberal Party readied itself to seize power from Diefenbaker's faltering grasp.

The Department of State press release had been suggested by the US Ambassador to Canada, Walton W. Butterworth, who had arrived to take up his post in December 1962. An experienced diplomat, a vigorous defender of his nation's positions, Butterworth could be very rough in his advocacy. His acquaintances in Canada included Pearson, whom he had known since their prewar service in London and with whom he was on first-name terms, but Butterworth was not especially admired by his Canadian counterparts. Diefenbaker, who quickly came to despise the Ambassador, called him "Butterballs" or "Butterfingers." Still, his job was to advance American interests, and Butterworth was unrepentant that his press release had caused a storm in Canada. Even opponents of the Diefenbaker government denounced the Kennedy administration for its interference in the country's domestic affairs, but Butterworth's view was that no apology was necessary: "He feels the statement was very useful," Vice-President Lyndon Johnson was told, "and will be highly beneficial in advancing US interests by introducing realism into a government which has made anti-Americanism and indecision practically its entire stock in trade." To the Ambassador, the Diefenbaker government had been characterized by nothing so much as "neurotic political leadership," an "essentially neurotic Canadian view of the world." It was prey to the "traditional psychopathic accusations of unwarranted US interference in domestic Canadian affairs."[9]

Diefenbaker's instant response to the American intervention was to believe he could secure a dissolution of Parliament on the issue. He was convinced, Justice Minister Donald Fleming wrote that "we've got our issue now." His disillusioned Defence Minister, Douglas Harkness, later noted that the Chief believed "he could win an election on an anti-US appeal and this, to him, was all that mattered." Such a possible campaign approach appalled many Cabinet members, and Finance Minister George Nowlan bluntly told the Halifax *Chronicle-Herald* that he had served notice he would quit the Cabinet immediately if an anti-American program was presented by his party and his leader. Richard Bell, the Minister of Citizenship and Immigration, was another minister who told the Prime Minister he would not be party to an anti-American campaign. In response, Diefenbaker raged at Bell: "I will do whatever I bloody-well like and I don't care whether I have your resignation or not." For their part, the traditionally Tory-supporting *Globe and Mail* and the Montreal *Gazette* warned against "the extravagant use of anti-Americanism," which could "shatter our relations with the United States."

The complaints of the newspapers and his colleagues notwithstanding, Diefenbaker's election campaign in the winter of 1963 featured a strong anti-American thrust. Deserted in the large cities by influential supporters and the media, the Chief travelled by train to the small towns, drawing large and enthusiastic crowds. "It's me against the Americans," he told crowds sporting "Vote Canadian, Vote Conservative" buttons, "fighting for the little guy." "We are a power, not a puppet," he said on another occasion, and he frequently referred to the "great interests" against him, "national and international." "Canadians have the right to decide what is right for Canada," he said in Winnipeg. "We make our policy in Canada – not generated by special interests or even by visits across the border." His Agriculture Minister, Alvin Hamilton, told a Montreal audience that the Yanks "think we're a Guatemala or something ... In fact, this country is larger and has immensely more natural resources than the US, so don't push us around, chum!" (The Guatemalan Ambassador reportedly was not amused and protested to the Department of External Affairs.)

Diefenbaker's anti-Americanism was frequently overt. When he blasted the State Department press release as an attempt to treat Canada as if it were a satrapy, he was in full cry. More often, however, he resorted to innuendo: the Americans, preaching the needs of defence to Canadians, had been slow to enter the two world wars, unlike Canada. "When some nations start to point out to us what we should do, let me tell you this. Canada was in both wars a long time before some other nations were ... We don't need any lessons as to what Canada should do after that record of service in two world wars."[10] There were slurs at President Kennedy's youth and inexperience, assaults against

American investment in Canada, and attacks on the American media, most notably on the February 18 issue of *Newsweek*, which had featured a cover photograph of Diefenbaker looking positively Satanic and a story that made his actions appear similarly motivated.

When Congress released secret testimony by US Defence Secretary Robert MacNamara that the primary military worth of the Bomarc anti-aircraft missiles was their ability to draw Soviet ICBM salvoes away from the United States and towards Canada, Diefenbaker was quick to seize on the issue as a virtual American plot to have Canada destroyed in a nuclear war. "Are they going to make Canada into a burnt sacrifice?" he shouted to voters at Dorion, Quebec. The Liberals, who had come out in support of nuclear warheads for the Bomarcs and Canada's defence commitments only on January 12, 1963, when party leader Pearson reversed his long-standing position, clearly were in league with the United States. The proof, for Diefenbaker, was that Pearson had attended the dinner Kennedy had thrown in early May 1962 for Nobel Prize winners, a dinner at which, by clear implication, he had received his orders in a private conversation with the President to take on the nuclear weapons issue and destroy John Diefenbaker. The Prime Minister neglected to mention to voters that it was his government that had signed the NORAD agreement and had purchased the Bomarc missiles, but his brilliantly unscrupulous attacks kept the Liberals on the defensive. At one Vancouver Liberal Party campaign meeting, Pearson's address was disrupted by protesters calling him a "Yankee stooge" and burning American flags. In Hamilton, picketers carried signs labelling the Liberal leader a "Pentagon Pet" and "the All-American." The opinion polls, initially showing very positive trends for the Liberals, began to turn around under the lash of Diefenbaker's extraordinary campaign energy and anti-American rhetoric.

Late in the campaign, the Prime Minister's staff began to drop hints about the so-called SOB memo of May 1961 and about a mysterious letter that, they suggested, would prove that the Liberals were in league with the Kennedy administration. This letter, copies of which had arrived early in April at newspaper offices across Canada, purported to be a private communication dated January 14, 1963, from Ambassador Butterworth to Pearson congratulating him for reversing his party's policy on nuclear warheads two days before. "I was delighted with the timing," the letter said,

> which I considered perfect. It will be quite evident to the electorate that the policy of the Conservatives is narrow minded and that they are unfit to continue governing the country.

At the first opportune moment, I would like to discuss with you how we could be useful to you in the future. You can always count on our support.[11]

"How we could be useful to you in the future." It is only fair to note that the Kennedy administration kept itself completely aware of the mood in Canada, one of the few times in this century that the White House watched Canadian anti-Americanism with concern. The President allowed the Democratic Party's polling expert, Oliver Quayle, to work for the Liberals (just as in 1962 he had agreed that Lou Harris, another Democratic pollster, could assist the Pearson campaign), and he offered additional aid in a telephone call from a White House intermediary to Pearson during the election. The horrified Liberal leader was quick to turn down that offer, which was not yet known to Diefenbaker. "This was a narrow escape," Pearson said later, "since I knew there were people abroad in the land who would insist ... that [the offer] was a deep dark American plot to take over the country ... To my relief [the call] was never reported."

The Butterworth letter, however, was in the Prime Minister's pocket late in March. While Diefenbaker campaigned across the country, Donald Fleming, whose decision not to run again for personal and family reasons had already been announced, was minding the store in Ottawa. On March 26, Diefenbaker sent him the Butterworth letter and asked his opinion. "I said I approached the matter with great caution," Fleming wrote. "I did not believe that the ambassador could be so stupid as to confide such thoughts to paper, that I did not think he could be so crude and inept as even to express such thoughts in any form, that the whole letter was so 'pat' as to suggest it was carefully planted, that the timing alone raised the most serious suspicion, that I had concluded it was a carefully baited trap laid for Dief and in my opinion it could have disastrous and very far-reaching effects for him to be enticed by the bait without full proof of authorship."[12]

Fleming's sound prudence must have been discouraging to the overeager Diefenbaker. Nonetheless, there were veiled hints about the letter in his speeches. On April 6, two days before the election, the letter was printed in the Vancouver *Province*, which had not troubled to check with the United States Embassy or Pearson before printing the text. The *Winnipeg Tribune*, one of the four or five major urban newspapers supporting Diefenbaker which had been couriered the letter by the Diefenbaker campaign, did check. Butterworth repeatedly and flatly denied writing such a letter, while Pearson adamantly denied receiving it. As a result, the *Tribune* did not print it, nor did any other of the mainstream media that were openly opposing Diefenbaker's anti-Americanism and his nuclear weapons policy, along with his government's drifting economic stewardship. The result, as Butterworth said, was that the letter did not hit the presses "at a moment when denials could not catch up with or neutralize the allegation."[13]

The American Embassy had heard rumours of the letter several days before it appeared in the *Province* and had raised it with the Secretary to the Cabinet, R.B. Bryce. "Obviously taken aback" by the letter's contents and its sudden surfacing during the campaign, Bryce said that the letter "must have come from someone in PM's [campaign] party. He could imagine no other way."[14]

In fact, all or almost all the copies of the Butterworth letter distributed to the Canadian media, including a covering letter over an undecipherable signature, had been mailed from Great Britain on March 24 in air-mail envelopes. Unfortunately for those who hoped to benefit by the letter's release, insufficient postage had been applied, and (mail moving faster then than three decades later) the letters reached Canada by sea mail early in April. Diefenbaker's copy, without the covering letter, had been brought to him by Conservative Senator Gratton O'Leary, the former publisher of the *Ottawa Journal*, who had received a message from Britain indicating that "an important person" – journalist Knowlton Nash says it was George Drew, the Canadian High Commissioner in Britain – had a vital communication for Diefenbaker that he "must get to him urgently." O'Leary later told Butterworth that Diefenbaker checked other letters with the Ambassador's signature and decided, because they were the same, that the letter was genuine and that he would use it in a speech. Presumably unaware of Fleming's advice, O'Leary claimed that he persuaded the Prime Minister to hold off because this would worsen Canada–US relations. The Senator also said that Diefenbaker wanted to send for Butterworth and confront him with the letter, but O'Leary reasoned that the Ambassador was certain to ask where the letter had come from and would insist it was a forgery.[15] When Diefenbaker asked him if he should use the letter in a speech, O'Leary told the Prime Minister, "No, it looks too good to me."[16] Cautioned by Fleming and by an influential journalist for whom he had substantial regard – O'Leary was widely credited with stopping a mushrooming caucus revolt in February 1963 with an emotional speech – the Prime Minister refrained from any direct references to the Butterworth letter, contenting himself only with innuendo.

Thus, because of an error in mailing and because one key newspaper was professional enough to check, the Butterworth letter did not become a major issue in the election. Diefenbaker lost, but the Liberals won enough seats to form only a minority government. The political survival of the Progressive Conservative Party and its leader was attributable, partly if not largely, to Diefenbaker's vigorous campaign and its skilful, if unscrupulous, use of anti-Americanism. He had appealed to the innate Canadian mistrust of the United States, and there was more than enough evidence, even without the Butterworth letter, to stoke the country's emotions.

The election had turned out just the way the Kennedy administration had hoped. Pearson quickly met with the President to restore amicable Canadian-American relations and to accept the nuclear warheads for the Bomarcs and the Canadian forces in NATO. The Department of State wanted to drop the matter of the forged letter, but a furious Butterworth argued that it would be a serious error for the United States to revert "to its old ways of treating Canada like a problem child for whom there was always at the ready a cheek for the turning." At the same time, the Ambassador took full credit for offering the advice that led to "the defeat and destruction of the Diefenbaker Government and the ensuing favorable change in the formation of a government headed by Pearson. In the process," he said in a cable to the State Department, "a somewhat more mature Canada has emerged from the electoral crucible and a measure of its neuroses has been exorcized."[17] There was some truth in Butterworth's claims to have played a decisive role. He had suggested the idea of a frontal attack on Diefenbaker to the Department of State and, as Canadians belatedly learned, Butterworth had also held secret briefings on the flaws in Canadian nuclear policy for journalists in the cellar of the embassy. Not until years later did journalist Charles Lynch reveal the American Ambassador's activities.

Butterworth had not written the letter, though the signature was genuine. Embassy staff concluded after close examination that the letter had not been typed on one of their typewriters but had been put together in three parts by photography: the embossed letterhead, the body of the letter, and the signature. Moreover, the type size did not correspond proportionately to the standard official paper on which the letter appeared. Later investigation found the paper to be of British origin. The letter was a forgery – a fact that ought to have been immediately apparent whatever the result of the technical assessment. No ambassador, and especially not one with Butterworth's long experience, would have made the mistake of writing such a letter when its contents could have been conveyed safely in conversation. Moreover, Butterworth's bread-and-butter correspondence with Pearson was on a first-name basis, and the forged letter reeked of formality.

The issue soon moved to the House of Commons where Diefenbaker, now Leader of the Opposition, continued his anti-American attacks. In an address on May 21, 1963, referring to Pearson's January reversal of Liberal Party nuclear policy, he said darkly: "Possibly it will not be very long before we know some of the things that took place, some of the words of deep approval that were given to the Prime Minister for giving this remarkable calisthenic performance." No one had very long to wait. Six days later, Gordon Churchill, latterly Diefenbaker's Minister of Trade and Commerce and then of National Defence, read the text of the forged letter into Hansard.

If the press had restrained itself and withheld publication during the election, now the lid was off. Every major newspaper featured the story, with Butterworth's brief statement that the letter was "a complete forgery." Editorials generally denounced the Conservatives for what was widely viewed as a malicious smear campaign, and the *Montreal Star* said, rather prematurely, that "strident anti-Americanism no longer has political currency in Canada." Other papers played variations on the same tune, burying the idea of anti-Americanism as a factor in Canadian public and intellectual life.

The criticism had no effect on Conservatives in and out of Parliament. Until his death, Churchill continued to believe the letter to be genuine, and he had his own technical analysis done of it in 1965, predictably confirming him in his opinion. No evidence, however, was presented for public scrutiny. Similarly, Diefenbaker proclaimed in his memoirs, published in 1977, that he had "confidential knowledge which will be revealed in due course that it was a true copy"; such evidence, two decades after Diefenbaker's death, has yet to be made public. The Chief added, in one of his very rare confessions of error, that he had made a major mistake in not using the Butterworth letter to the fullest in the 1963 campaign.

Was this extraordinary little episode nothing more than a reflection of John Diefenbaker's unreasoning dislike for John F. Kennedy? Or was it a symptom of a deeper-seated, irrational, and paranoiac anti-Americanism in the Canadian psyche? That Diefenbaker disliked Kennedy is beyond doubt, as even a casual reading of his memoirs makes clear. He resented Kennedy's youthful style and popularity, his good looks, and his attractive wife. Canadian women tried to dress as much like Jackie Kennedy as they could, adopting her hats and trying to emulate her style; none tried to pattern themselves after Olive Diefenbaker, a matronly, even dowdy, woman with a vicious disposition hidden behind a cold smile. Diefenbaker fumed at what he saw as the way the United States took Canada and its leader for granted. The assumption in Washington seemed to be that the Kennedy administration decided and Canada obeyed, and sometimes, it must be admitted, Diefenbaker was justified in this belief. His anger had existed when the Republicans were in office, but Eisenhower jollied Diefenbaker along and most overt manifestations of prime ministerial rage were suppressed; when Kennedy came to power and the efforts to appeal to Diefenbaker as a colleague and friend largely ceased, the rage became visible. By January 1963, beset by enemies foreign and domestic, Diefenbaker was ready to clutch at any straw, and the State Department's press release guaranteed that anti-Americanism played a major role in his election campaign. Significantly, key members of the Progressive Conservative Party were embarrassed, not to say humiliated, by their government's inaction first during the Cuban crisis and then on nuclear weapons. They refused to go along with their leader, and warned against an overt assault on the United States. For the first time in its history, the Conservative Party was not united in the anti-American cause; for the first time, the Ontario members turned away from the issue that had been their bread and butter since John A. Macdonald's time. The United States was the leader of the Western alliance, the economic mecca, the investor of choice, and Tory ministers and members, sensitive to the arguments of their friends in business and finance, had no stomach for a fight against the Yanks – especially when their government was so clearly in the wrong.

Diefenbaker's own decaying fortunes let the dissidents get away with their disobedience. The Prime Minister's almost uncanny hold over his party had weakened by the beginning of 1963 and Diefenbaker, realizing his predicament, understood that he had to keep as much of his party as possible on his side during the campaign. Despite his contemptuous rejection of his critics on an individual basis, therefore, he never let himself go against the Americans completely, and he hesitated to do anything more than make oblique references to the SOB memo and the Butterworth letter.

Only a psychiatrist can adequately explain Diefenbaker's mental state. To this historian, he appears to have been a paranoid personality whose world divided almost automatically into "us" versus "them." By the time of the election of 1963, the "us" side comprised only a few loyal party supporters of a pro-British bent and the "little guys" in small town and rural Canada. By contrast, the "them" side was massive – big business, the cities, the Canadian and American media, the Conservative defectors, the Kennedy administration, and the Pentagon. The campaign might have been expected to be a disaster, given the government's appalling record of indecision and confusion and the manner of its collapse, but the extraordinarily resilient Diefenbaker thrived in the face of the challenge and won 97 seats to Pearson's 131, making the election far closer than anyone would have believed when Diefenbaker's government collapsed in disarray early in February.[18] There can be no doubt that the anti-American tenor of his campaign contributed substantially to this result.

But in many ways, Diefenbaker was a typical Canadian. He reflected the usual Canadian dislike of Americans: the antipathy towards the more powerful neighbour; the dislike of America's crass style, popular culture, and greedy big business; and the fear of Washington's big stick, the stick that had been used against Cuba in October 1962 and against him and his country in the press release of January 30. But Diefenbaker's paranoia reinforced these dislikes, and his rampant anti-Americanism was much like Canada's at its worst and most juvenile. Historically, the nation's weak identity had demanded that anti-Americanism form a large component of Canadian nationalism. People such as Diefenbaker who had long relied on the link with Great Britain as a counterweight to the overwhelming presence of the United States found themselves with nothing to hold onto once Britain lost its power and began to move towards the European Community, as it was trying to do in the early 1960s. Diefenbaker-style imperial and monarchical loyalism was no longer sufficient or relevant in a world and a continent dominated by the brash and confident superpower to the south.

The 1963 election was the first in which a campaign motivated by anti-Americanism had not triumphed. The tide had turned in Canada, and political leaders such as John Diefenbaker had lost their trump card. Anti-Americanism was still strong, but it could not prevail over the forces of continentalism, especially when they were combined, as in 1963, with the attractive force of President Kennedy and the potent anti-Communism that made Canadians believe their country had to work in concert with the United States in defending North America.

The forged Butterworth letter was a minor issue in political terms, but it had substantial significance as an indicator of the paranoid style in Canadian and Progressive Conservative politics. In truth, the Prime Minister and his loyal Conservative ministers had to believe that the letter was genuine, for it offered a ready explanation for their political difficulties. So fierce were they in their resentment of the United States and so angry at the Kennedy administration's actions against them and their defence policy (or non-policy) that the letter gave them both solace and justification. After all, how could they have won the 1963 election once the Americans trained their big guns on them? The Americans, their patience tested to the limit, had finally lashed out against Diefenbaker, thereby confirming their demonic status.

The Butterworth letter, when added to the State Department press release and the other private American attempts to influence the 1963 election, all contributed to the assiduously cultivated legend that the Americans had done in the Chief. Novelist and journalist Heather Robertson encapsulated the continuing force of this myth when she wrote in 1989 of Diefenbaker's "political assassination." The Canadian leader "had not gone to Harvard. When President John F. Kennedy, who had gone to Harvard, suggested that the American missiles on Canadian territory (what the hell were they doing there anyway?) should be armed with nuclear warheads, John Diefenbaker raised his eyebrows and shook his jowls. No." Robertson's parenthetical question was the critical point, even if she, like other proponents of the myth, did not realize it. The American missiles had, of course, been bought and paid for by Diefenbaker's government, which understood and accepted that they required nuclear warheads. Thwarted, Robertson continued, Kennedy then turned nasty: "Who was this guy?" As the 1963 election neared, Kennedy issued an ultimatum: "If nuclear warheads were not accepted, the Americans would see to it that the Canadian government was defeated. And it was."[19] The legend, propped up as always by a few facts and much pop psychological mythologizing, lives on, and not only in bad novels. The true believers evidently cannot accept that Diefenbaker's dithering incompetence brought down the Tory government.

The key point was missed by the mythologizers. In 1891 the anti-American cry had helped to hold power for John A. Macdonald. In 1911 it had propelled Robert Borden into power, his party bound hand and foot to Canadian businessmen who resented reciprocity's challenge to their Canadian markets. But in 1963, even if Diefenbaker's attack on the United States was not as full-throated or as uninhibited as Macdonald's or Borden's,[20] anti-Americanism could not have swept all before it. Indeed, so sharp was the opposition within his own party to Diefenbaker's planned use of anti-Americanism that the Chief had to hold back. As it was, there remained more than enough anti-Americanism in the Tory campaign to discredit it. For all practical purposes, Progressive Conservative anti-Americanism died with John Diefenbaker's leadership of the party.

Canada was evidently in the throes of change. The forces on the right of the political spectrum no longer feared the Americans the way they had a half-century before. Business interests were now much more responsive to the imperatives of Wall Street than they were during the free trade elections of 1891 and 1911. The military and its domestic clients looked to Uncle Sam as the great power which they, like every little brother, wanted to emulate. Sophisticated urbanites, watching American TV and reading American books and magazines, saw Diefenbaker as a Prairie rube whose anachronistic anti-Americanism was crudeness personified and whose government was inefficient and unsuccessful. The forces against the Chief could not be overcome, though his wresting a majority from the Liberals demonstrated that the remnants of the old Canada were stronger than the proponents of change had realized.

The United States, as novelist Graeme Gibson wrote in his *Gentleman Death* in 1993, "embodies the times we must live in. The times to come." Society is imploding and a terrible exhaustion has set in. "It must be true," Gibson says, "that what passes for anti-Americanism, apart from simple envy, is little more or less than a fear and loathing of the future, a despair at the loss of our collective pasts."[21] Diefenbaker was not a reflective man, but somehow he must have sensed that, with the help of the powerful in Canadian society, the American future was destined to wash away the collective past that Canadians had constructed with so much struggle and difficulty. His visceral anti-Americanism reeked of his despair at "the times to come."

NOTES

1 See Denis Smith, *Rogue Tory: The Life and Legend of John G. Diefenbaker* (Toronto 1995), 20ff.
2 United States Treasury Department, Washington, Accession 68A5918, box 87, file Can/9/30, Scope and Objectives Paper for Meeting of United States–Canada Ministerial Committee on Joint Defense, November 8–9, 1959.
3 NA, Arnold Heeney Papers, vol. 2, Memoirs 1959 file, Diary, March 29, 1959; vol. 1, Memoranda of Conversations, August 30, 31, 1960.
4 The Canadian Institute of Public Opinion reported on January 18, 1961, that Canadians, by a five-to-one majority, believed Kennedy would improve US–Canada relations. On December 26, 1962, Canadians ranked Kennedy as the person they admired most, 21 per cent naming him first. Diefenbaker ranked fifth, the choice of only 3 per cent.
5 J.F. Kennedy Library, POP, box 113, Canada Security 1961 file, Memorandum for the President, February 17, 1961.
6 Ibid., Canada Security – Trip to Ottawa (B) file, Scope Paper, May 2, 1961.
7 H. Basil Robinson, *Diefenbaker's World* (Toronto 1989), 268–9.

8 The most recent account, especially useful on naval questions, is Peter Haydon, *The 1962 Cuban Missile Crisis: Canadian Involvement Reconsidered* (Toronto 1993).
9 United States Declassified Documents, (78)301E, Colonel Burris to the Vice-President, February 6, 1963; Smith, *Rogue Tory*, 496–7.
10 When Cuban fighters shot down two small American aircraft in early 1996, the US Congress took tough action against President Castro's regime and countries like Canada that traded with it. North Carolina Senator Jesse Helms was especially scornful of Canada as an "appeaser," treating with Castro much like Neville Chamberlain had dealt with Hitler. The *Globe and Mail* was quick off the mark on March 7, 1996, in phrases that sounded much like Diefenbaker's: "If Mr. Helms wants to talk about the Second World War, may we remind him that Canadians were fighting Hitler for a good two years before the Americans showed up? Three years, in the First World War. Next time the senator from North Carolina goes hunting for appeasers, he should take a look in his own backyard." Some attitudes evidently die hard.
11 George C. Marshall Library, Virginia Military Institute, W.W. Butterworth Papers, box 2, file 25, letter of January 14, 1963, and attached envelope addressed to *Ottawa Journal*.
12 Donald Fleming, *So Very Near: The Political Memoirs of the Honourable Donald M. Fleming*, vol. 2: *The Summit Years* (Toronto 1985), 627–8.
13 Butterworth Papers, box 2, file 25, telegram, Butterworth to State Department, April 23, 1963.
14 Ibid., R.Z. Smith Memorandum of Conversation, April 6, 1963.
15 Ibid., Butterworth to State Department, May 24, 1963.
16 Ibid., Vought memo, June 30, 1967. Dalton Camp, effectively running the Conservative campaign, has been quoted as saying, "We all knew it was a forgery. We all said 'Don't use it!'" Knowlton Nash, *Kennedy and Diefenbaker* (Toronto 1990), 286.
17 Butterworth Papers, box 2, file 25, Butterworth to Department of State, April 15, 1963. Butterworth's line was not uncommon in Canada. See, for example, John Saywell in *Financial Times*, March 11, 1963: "It will be interesting to see if [anti-Americanism as an electoral device] works. Its failure will be one measure of our maturity. Its success could be soul destroying."
18 The opinion polls demonstrated that Diefenbaker's anti-American campaign hurt the Liberals and helped the third parties more than it improved his own position. In January 1963 the Canadian Institute of Public Opinion showed the Liberals with 47 per cent and the Conservatives with 32 per cent. Two months later the Liberals were down 6 per cent, the Conservatives were holding, and the minor parties were gaining strength. The election on April 8 gave the Liberals 41.7 per cent, the Conservatives 32.8, the NDP 13.1,

and the Social Credit 11.9. In Quebec, the anti-nuclear Créditistes drew 27 per cent of the vote and twenty seats; nationally the anti-nuclear NDP won seventeen seats. In essence, the Diefenbaker campaign held the Tory vote intact and drove voters away from the pro-nuclear and – in the public eye – pro-American Liberals.

19 Heather Robertson, *Igor: A Novel of Intrigue*, vol. 3: *The King Years* (Toronto 1989), 11–12.
20 In his *Right Honourable Men: The Descent of Canadian Politics from Macdonald to Mulroney* (Toronto 1994), 211, historian Michael Bliss argues that Diefenbaker wallowed "in a crude anti-Americanism that would have seemed demagogic even in the days of Macdonald and Borden." But there was nothing like the vehemence of 1891 and 1911 in Diefenbaker, who generally pulled his punches in the face of a less receptive public.
21 Graeme Gibson, *Gentleman Death* (Toronto 1993), 216–17.

Chapter Five

When Push Came to Shove: Canada and the United States

"I never realized they resented us as much as they do." After serving as the United States chair of the International Joint Commission that adjudicated Canadian-American boundary questions, Teno Roncalio thought that he had learned something about Canadians in the early 1960s. "I didn't realize that they felt we were a monstrous, mammoth obliteration of their own identity and of their own arts and ... culture."[1] That was a slight overstatement of the reality, perhaps, but Roncalio captured the essence of the Canadian mood that prevailed during the presidency of John F. Kennedy.

Beginning in the mid-1950s, Canadians, as so often in their past, had begun to be concerned once more with the impact that the United States was having on them and their country. Canada's historic defence relationship with Great Britain had largely disappeared in the postwar years, replaced by ever-tightening links with the Pentagon. This process toward military cooperation with the United States had commenced with the creation of the Permanent Joint Board on Defence in 1940 and had then proceeded without check through a variety of agreements and arrangements to the creation of the North American Air Defense (NORAD) Command in 1957 and the Defence Production Sharing Agreement of 1959. Particularly shattering to national pride was the cancellation in 1959 of the Canadian-designed CF-105 Arrow supersonic fighter,[2] a victim of spiraling costs. Instead of building the Arrow, the Canadian government purchased American-produced Bomarc surface-to-air missiles, intended to carry atomic warheads, and in 1961 struck a complicated deal with the United States for American Voodoo interceptors, capable of carrying MB-1 nuclear missiles. Canadian forces on duty with the North Atlantic Treaty Organization (NATO) in Europe also used American-designed equipment and assumed roles that required nuclear weapons. To many, Canadian military independence seemed to be disappearing, and the close connections with the United States disturbed all who anguished over John Foster Dulles's alarmist Cold War rhetoric and policies, massive retaliation, and military expansionists in the Pentagon.[3]

The American economic presence in Canada had become equally worrisome and pervasive. The Royal Commission on Canada's Economic Prospects reported in 1957 that the massive American investment that had fueled Canada's postwar boom had also resulted in American ownership of huge percentages of the oil and gas (73 per cent in 1955), manufacturing (42 per cent), and mining and smelting (55 per cent) sectors of the economy. At the same time, Canada's trade was overwhelmingly linked to the United States. In 1955, 60 per cent of Canada's exports went south while 73 per cent of its imports came from the United States. The apparent loss of economic independence involved in such reliance on one country for foreign investment and trade alarmed nationalists in all political parties, in the universities, and in the trade unions.[4]

Cultural influence from the south had become more pervasive still. American movies held total dominance in the profitable Canadian market, leaving only documentaries, produced by the government's National Film Board, to Canadian talent. *Saturday Evening Post, Life, Time,* and *Reader's Digest* claimed hundreds of thousands of Canadian readers, far more than the struggling Canadian periodicals. And the American television networks, reaching the large Canadian markets from Burlington, Buffalo, Fargo, and Seattle, brought American news, views, and sitcoms to audiences that seemed eager for something other than the often staid television programming provided by the government-owned Canadian Broadcasting Corporation. The question of national identity and cultural independence was much the same in all areas of the arts, and not even the creation in 1957 of the Canada Council, a government effort to spark creativity and foster excellence in the arts and sciences, seemed to hold out much hope for a reversal of the longstanding trends in this area of Canadian life.[5]

Canada's identity, it seemed to many, was in jeopardy. That was one of the reasons commentators offered for the stunning, narrow electoral victory of John G. Diefenbaker, the leader of the Progressive Conservative party, in the general elections of June 1957.[6] Diefenbaker, a sixty-one-year-old Saskatchewan populist with a messianic gaze and pulpit-style oratory who had been a Member of Parliament since 1940 and had won his party's leadership in December 1956 after previous rebuffs in 1942 and 1948, had played on the theme of Canadian nationalism in his campaign. That powerful theme, implicitly (and sometimes explicitly) connoting anti-Americanism, had proved very useful in toppling Prime Minister Louis St. Laurent, the leader of the entrenched Liberal party which had held power continuously since 1935. In 1958, after a successful session of Parliament that had seen Diefenbaker mesmerize the country with his vigor and implementation of progressive change, the Conservatives crushed Lester Pearson, the Liberals' new leader, almost wiped out the democratic socialists of the Cooperative Commonwealth Federation, and captured the largest parliamentary majority to that time. Political pundits soon wrote expansively of the Conservative century, and Diefenbaker acquired an almost mythic stature within his own party.[7]

But by the time of the presidential elections in November 1960, the bloom had fallen from the Tory rose. The Canadian economy had begun a serious recession in 1958 and unemployment was rising almost as fast as the government's deficits. Diefenbaker himself repeatedly maintained that all was well, but stories of his indecisiveness became widespread. Some cabinet ministers grew increasingly disturbed by this trait, especially in the area of the government's budget, where disputes had become embittered among the Minister of Finance, a tight-fisted and orthodox thinker, and a substantial number of ministers who hoped to spend the country out of recession.[8]

The Prime Minister's indecision was also especially evident in the area of defence, where the Secretary of State for External Affairs, Howard Green, a Vancouver Member of Parliament, had become engaged in a Cabinet and interdepartmental struggle with the Minister of National Defence, the blunt and straightforward Colonel Douglas Harkness of Calgary. The Diefenbaker government had signed the NORAD agreement with the United States in its first month in office. Harkness assumed that the Bomarc missiles the government had purchased to meet Canada's commitments to NORAD would be equipped with their nuclear warheads as soon as the two installations in Canada were complete and negotiations with the United States for a "two-key" system of control were concluded. Similarly, Harkness expected the Honest John surface-to-surface missiles with the Canadian brigade group in Europe to receive their nuclear payloads, and he wanted the Royal Canadian Air Force's CF-104 aircraft on NATO "strike-reconnaissance" duties to get their nuclear armament, too. Why, after all, had Diefenbaker's government signed the agreements, purchased the weapons, and accepted the roles if it did not intend to take the nuclear warheads?[9]

But Green opposed the arming of the Canadian forces with nuclear arms. A well-meaning and sincere man who had not traveled to Europe since his service in France during the Great War, Green had become convinced that Canada must play its fullest possible part in pressing the great powers toward nuclear disarmament and halting the spread of nuclear weapons. The world was in peril, he believed – a reasonable perception, to be sure, and one that had been urged upon him by his extraordinarily able and experienced under secretary, Norman Robertson.[10] And if disarmament had become a priority,[11] one avidly sought by peace groups across Canada, then how could Canada convincingly encourage the Americans and Russians toward sanity if its troops and airmen were armed with nuclear weapons? "We were advocating in the United Nations that there should be control of the spread of nuclear weapons," Green said many years later, "... and then to turn around and take them ourselves just made us look foolish."[12]

The two ministers and their departments became locked in a struggle for the soul and mind of John Diefenbaker – a confused mind and a troubled soul. Leery of the Canadian military, the Prime Minister grew angry that the Chairman of the Chief of Staffs Committee in 1957, General Charles Foulkes, had hustled him into accepting the NORAD agreement to honor commitments made to the American Chiefs of Staff. "We stampeded the incoming government ...," Foulkes later admitted.[13] Diefenbaker became understandably appalled at the costs and destructiveness of modern weaponry, and he had been badly burned politically when A.V. Roe Ltd., the manufacturer of the CF-105, had shut down the production line and laid off fourteen thousand workers the very instant the government announced the aircraft's cancellation. Diefenbaker was also acutely sensitive to the hundreds of letters he received from Canadians who called for peace and disarmament; almost none demanded bigger and better defences. On the other hand, Diefenbaker believed in the reality of the Soviet threat. He had agreed to purchase the nuclear equipment, and, as he had told the House of Commons on February 20, 1959, the day the decision to scrap the Arrow and purchase the Bomarc had been announced: "The full potential of these defensive weapons is achieved only when they are armed with nuclear warheads."[14] President Dwight D. Eisenhower, whom the Canadian Prime Minister held in high regard, was obviously and necessarily concerned with the defence of the North American continent and the strategic deterrent, the task the Bomarcs were designed to meet. No Canadian prime minister would lightly pick a fight with Washington on such a sensitive topic as the defence of the continental heartland.[15]

Still, Diefenbaker was torn. Green urged disarmament upon him while Harkness counseled the conclusion of agreements with the United States so that warheads could be readied for use just as soon as the Bomarcs, Honest Johns, and CF-104s became operational. With some time before that eventuality arose, the Prime Minister told an Ottawa audience in November 1960 that Canada would make no decision on nuclear weapons so long as progress toward disarmament continued.[16] That heartened Green and his Department of External Affairs; Norman Robertson told his minister that "it would seem reasonable ... to hold to the view that a decision to acquire weapons at this time is premature."[17]

Eisenhower had seemed content to allow Canada to move at its own pace toward the nuclear decision, but his successor, John F. Kennedy, proved less patient. Diefenbaker, born in 1895, was much older than the young and vigorous President and slightly alarmed by the militant rhetoric that sometimes seemed to mark his speeches. During the American presidential campaign, in fact, the Prime Minister had told Arnold Heeney, his Ambassador in Washington, of his "distaste for Kennedy." The Democratic candidate was outrageously rash and predisposed to a policy of action and Diefenbaker had a much more "favourable opinion of Nixon."[18] Worse, Kennedy had failed to respond to a telegram of congratulations after his election victory. But when Diefenbaker, accompanied by Green, flew to Washington on February 20 for his first meeting with the American leader, a meeting hastily arranged at the beginning of February by Heeney at the Prime Minister's request, his attitude apparently changed. The meeting had been "excellent," he remarked to Heeney. In fact, "it could not have been better."[19] And Livingston Merchant, the American Ambassador in Ottawa, agreed: "I had the feeling that Mr. Diefenbaker and President Kennedy got along extremely well together ..." At Merchant's first meeting with Diefenbaker after his return to Ottawa, the Prime Minister "referred with admiration to the President and expressed his satisfaction with the personal relationship which he felt had been established ..."[20]

Whether Kennedy shared this view remains uncertain. His briefing papers, prepared in the Department of State, noted that, while Diefenbaker was "not believed to have any basic prejudice against the United States," he had "appeared ... to seek on occasion to assert Canadian independence by seizing opportunities for Canada to adopt policies which deviate somewhat from those of the United States ..." The briefing notes described the Canadian government as marked by "general indecisiveness" on economic matters and noted it had "contributed substantially" to the growing debate in defence policy "by indecisiveness and failure to take the initiative by developing a clear and concise policy and rallying public support. This situation," the brief said darkly, "has promoted an undesirable introspection in Canada regarding the country's present and future defense role, particularly with reference to the United States."[21]

As might have been expected, the defence question dominated the discussion between the Prime Minister and the President. Diefenbaker, as he reported to his Cabinet, had told Kennedy that, so long as serious disarmament negotiations continued, "Canada did not propose to determine whether or not to accept nuclear weapons for the Bomarc base or for the Canadian interceptors; but that, if such weapons were accepted by Canada, this country would require joint custody and joint control, and use would be determined in the same manner as on US bases." But Canada would decide quickly on the acquisition of the warheads if war should occur, Diefenbaker added, stating that he did not want a mere policy of "bird-watching" for his country. Kennedy asked if "the same sort of 'two key' arrangement as the United Kingdom had would be satisfactory" and Diefenbaker said it would. Such a system would see two officers, one American and one Canadian, simultaneously arming the weapon. In short, both countries had to agree on the use of nuclear weapons before they could be launched. Kennedy could not have been entirely pleased with that exposition of the Canadian position, leaning, as it so obviously did, toward the views of Secretary of State for External Affairs Howard Green. Those views had been conveyed forcefully to Diefenbaker on the trip to Washington.

Another topic left Diefenbaker, a prickly protector of Canadian sovereignty, uncomfortable. The two men had discussed an application by Imperial Oil of Canada, a subsidiary of Standard Oil of New Jersey, to provide bunker oil to Canadian ships under charter to carry Canadian wheat to China. Kennedy had pointed out that Standard's American directors could be liable for prosecution under American law if they allowed Imperial to provide the fuel because of the United States embargo on trade with the People's Republic. Diefenbaker bristled: Canada would never accept such a restriction. What, he asked, would the American reaction be if the shoe was on the other foot? Believing that Beijing was deeply hostile toward Washington, Kennedy argued that to permit this breach in the economic wall around Communist China could throw open the door to possibilities dangerous to United States security. Then he asked an aide to fetch a memorandum on the subject for him. This statement, "far from helpful," Diefenbaker said, simply re-stated American law. Kennedy then replied that, if Canada applied to the United States government for an exemption for this specific transaction, it would be granted. But again Diefenbaker demurred. He could not concede the right of the United States to apply its laws extraterritorially, nor did he wish his government to become a participant in a private commercial arrangement. After further discussion, Kennedy finally conceded that Imperial could supply the bunker fuel in the expectation that the United States government would not bring pressure to bear on Standard Oil.[22]

Diefenbaker had won a small victory, but Kennedy's apparent inability to recognize the importance of the issue to Canadian sovereignty must have been disturbing to him. For Kennedy, the Prime Minister's attitude throughout the one-day visit confirmed the remarks in the State Department briefing paper that the Diefenbaker government has "tended to attach less weight than we have to the need for ostensible military strength ... [and] has more readily accepted as sincere Communist protestations of good faith ..."[23] Canadian-American relations, despite the cordiality of the Diefenbaker-Kennedy talks, remained troubled.

When Kennedy, battered the month before by the failure at the Bay of Pigs, came to Ottawa in May 1961 for a full state visit, he was armed with yet another blunt briefing paper, this one prepared by the Central Intelligence Agency. Diefenbaker showed "disappointing indecisiveness on important issues, such as the defense program, as well as a lack of political courage and undue sensitivity to public opinion," it read.[24] The tensions between the two countries inevitably became exacerbated despite the popular acclaim the youthful President and his attractive wife received from a fawning Canadian people. Troubles sprang up everywhere. First, Kennedy hurt his back turning the sod at a tree planting at the Governor-General's residence. Then, Diefenbaker, whose confidence in the President had been shaken by the Bay of Pigs fiasco, seemed even more negative on the nuclear weapons issue than he had been in February. As External Affairs informed its delegation in Geneva, "Prime Minister said that in view of public opinion in Canada, it would be impossible politically at moment for Canada to accept nuclear weapons." Nor would Canada accept Voodoo aircraft from the United States so long as arming them with nuclear missiles was required.[25] Kennedy also angered his host by urging Canada in his address to Parliament to join the Organization of American States, a prospect that had long alarmed many Canadians who had no desire to be whipped into line like the Latins on world issues and never more so than in the light of strained Cuban-American relations.

But the key incident occurred after one private meeting in Ottawa. Diefenbaker found a memorandum left behind in the folds of a couch. On it Walt W. Rostow, the President's deputy adviser on national security questions, had listed points like membership in the OAS and a decision on nuclear weapons on which Kennedy should "push" the Prime Minister.[26] Diefenbaker fumed at the document's tone, and, contrary to protocol, did not return it to its authors. "The P.M.," an appalled Arnold

Heeney recorded in his diary later, "said he had not so far made use of this paper but 'when the proper time came,' he would not hesitate to do so ..."[27]

The rancor of May had replaced the good relations of February 1961. From admiring the President, Diefenbaker had come to see him as rash and aggressive, not one who would pay attention either to Canadian national sensitivities or to the *amour propre* of the older Prime Minister. The stubborn Diefenbaker was not about to let Kennedy or his aides "push" Canada into anything.

On the other hand, when Berlin again became a flash point in the summer of 1961, Diefenbaker and his Cabinet were firm in supporting the Kennedy Administration's stance against the Soviet Union. The Canadian government in August decided on a major buildup of the country's armed forces (from 120,000 to 135,000 men) and the dispatch of an additional 1,100 soldiers to Europe to strengthen the forces assigned to NATO. In addition (and partly as a measure to ease unemployment), the government decided to recruit 100,000 men in Canada for training in civil defence duties.[28] And in Vietnam, Canadian representatives on the International Control Commission tried hard to get their Indian and Polish co-commissioners to recognize and condemn the intrusions from the North, at the same time as the Canadians tried to close their eyes to American and South Vietnamese violations of the 1954 Geneva accords. Howard Green told Parliament that the United States could not be singled out for blame in Vietnam. "There have been troops infiltrating from North Vietnam," he stated, "and *I am certain* that the Communists have been at the root of most of the trouble in South Vietnam ... Any action the United States has taken has been in a measure of defence against Communist action."[29] In keeping with that view, Canadian officers and diplomats on the ICC shared information with the Americans in Saigon and Washington, as they had done before Kennedy took power and as they would continue to do under his successor.[30]

But it was a quite different matter to support United States policy toward Fidel Castro's Cuba. Canadian and American officials had exchanged sharp opinions before Kennedy look office, particularly at a summer 1960 meeting of the Canada–United States Ministerial Committee on Joint Defence at Montebello, Quebec. The Americans had indicated that they were moving toward economic sanctions as a way of bringing home to the Cuban people the costs of supporting Castro. As one senior Canadian wrote afterwards, they hoped "to avoid the use of armed forces." Howard Green was horrified, telling the meeting that "this was a grave and disturbing communication with very serious implications for Canada," adding, as the Canadian record put it, that "he was very doubtful of the wisdom of attempting to deal with the Cuban situation by external economic pressure ..."[31] In the Canadian view, such measures would surely force Havana into an ever-tighter embrace with Moscow. Whatever the government in power, Ottawa was almost always less hawkish than Washington.

That posture disturbed the Kennedy Administration, tougher and probably less aware of the limitations of American power than was its predecessor. Ambassador Heeney discovered this when he sat beside Dean Rusk, the Secretary of State, at the Gridiron dinner in Washington on March 11, 1961.[32] Rusk told his old friend of new measures to curb trade with Castro. American subsidiaries in Canada would be exempted from the new regulations, but, the Secretary said, "he hoped that we would agree to prevent shipment of mill & refining parts & I think vehicle replacements." Heeney replied that "this move would not be well received in Canada ... We doubted the wisdom of such action for the purpose for which it was intended – to prevent Cuba going completely Communist." Rusk, Heeney noted,

> got quite hot in his response. The US were simply not going to have a Communist base established in Cuba ... and would do whatever had to be done to prevent it including if necessary sending in troops. This was primarily a matter of the Monroe Doctrine for protection of the hemisphere. Further US policy was not going to be altered because Canada didn't like it.[33]

Such ardent American attitudes soon manifested themselves in the disaster at the Bay of Pigs. In the fall of 1962, the Administration's fixation with Cuba – and the extraordinarily risky gamble of Soviet Premier Khrushchev in placing missiles on the island – would bring the world close to the brink of general war and profoundly embitter Canadian-American relations in the process.

The Diefenbaker government was *in extremis* by the fall of 1962. The great majority of 1958 had been wiped out in the election of June 18, 1962, when a disenchanted Canadian people gave Diefenbaker's Progressive Conservatives 116 seats in a House of Commons of 265, enough for only the most tenuous minority government. Worse yet, a pre-election run on the dollar had threatened Canada's economy while a post-election austerity program jeopardized what remained of the government's popularity, and the balance of power in the new Parliament rested in the hands of the Social Credit Party, a group with only the haziest grasp on economic reality. Diefenbaker, moreover, continued to temporize on the nuclear question. He had also been forced by the economic crisis to slap temporary tariff surcharges on American exports to Canada. However necessary they were, the import-reducing duties seemed like scant thanks for Washington's ready assistance in propping up the shaky Canadian dollar.[34]

Such was the setting on October 21 when two Canadian intelligence specialists who had been at a meeting in Washington returned to Ottawa with the first word of impending crisis. The next day, Assistant Secretary of State Livingston Merchant, a popular former Ambassador to Canada, flew to Ottawa to brief Diefenbaker and deliver a letter from Kennedy. As the President wrote to the Prime Minister, "we are now in possession of clear evidence ... that the Soviets have secretly installed offensive nuclear weapons in Cuba and that some of them may already be operational."[35] Merchant showed Diefenbaker photographs of the installations, explained forthcoming American actions, and read Kennedy's speech, to be delivered on television two hours later to announce the imposition of a blockade around Cuba. Some questions arose, but, as Defence Minister Harkness later wrote, "the Prime Minister stated that in the event of a missile attack on the United States from Cuba, Canada would live up to its responsibilities under the NATO and NORAD agreements."[36]

No one doubted Canada's response in time of war. The question now was what Canada would do in the immediate crisis. As soon as Kennedy's television broadcast ended, the NORAD Command went to Defense Condition (DEFCON) 3, the middle of the five alert statuses. The Canadian contribution to NORAD was expected to follow suit within a few hours at most,[37] but when Harkness asked the Prime Minister for the necessary authority, he found Diefenbaker "loath," arguing that "it should be a Cabinet decision." The next morning, October 23, Harkness explained to his ministerial colleagues the reasons why an alert had become necessary. "I believe all the cabinet would have agreed to this," Harkness said, almost certainly underestimating the resentment of many of his colleagues at Kennedy's late notice of his blockade to Canada, "but the Prime Minister argued against it on the ground that an alert would unduly alarm the people, that we should wait and see what happened etc. He and I finally came to fairly hot words, but he refused to agree ..." The Cabinet agreed only to consider the matter once more, after the reactions of other countries and especially Britain had been ascertained. When Harkness returned to the Department of National Defence, however, he ordered on his own the Chiefs of Staff to put an alert into effect "in as quiet and unobtrusive a way as possible." That made the Canadian forces as ready as they could be, given the unarmed nature of much of their weaponry, but it did not "reassure the United States and our other allies ... that we were prepared to fight," or so Harkness noted.[38] Not until October 24 did Diefenbaker finally agree to authorize the NORAD forces alert, and then he acted only because NORAD headquarters in Colorado Springs had moved to DEFCON 2 and because Harkness shouted at him until he agreed to act.[39]

What lay behind Diefenbaker's extraordinary immobility? Part was unquestionably his congenital inability to make difficult decisions. Part was his dislike for the brash young President and his conviction that Kennedy's Cuban policy was dangerously unsound. Part was his resentment that, in his view, the United States had not met its obligation under the NORAD agreement to consult Canada.[40] And part also was his call, announced in the House of Commons on October 22, for a United Nations–sponsored mission to Cuba to give the peoples of the world "a full and complete understanding of what is taking place in Cuba." That idea had emerged from the Department of External Affairs essentially as a way to cool the crisis or, as some suggested, to secure Diefenbaker's ultimate support for the American demand for the withdrawal of the Soviet missiles when their existence could be confirmed.[41] Whatever its motive, the proposal for a United Nations role landed as an immediate dud in Washington, for it implied that the government of Canada did not believe Kennedy or the evidence in the reconnaissance photographs.

If the Americans became angry, so too did Canadian public opinion, which overwhelmingly supported American actions during the crisis. As important, several of Diefenbaker's Cabinet colleagues, their faith in "The Chief" already shaken by the 1962 election results and Diefenbaker's indecisiveness on a plethora of issues, had their worries reinforced mightily.[42]

These doubts about Diefenbaker's judgment mattered because his government was clearly faltering, about to be laid low by the festering nuclear arms controversy with the United States. Through 1961 and 1962, negotiations with Washington on the Bomarcs, Honest Johns, CF-104s, and Voodoos had proceeded at a glacial pace. Diefenbaker at times sounded determined to move ahead on the question and at others determined only to go slow.[43] But after the Cuban missile crisis, Harkness demanded that negotiations be concluded without delay. The ministers decided on October 30, 1962, to take the "nuclear ammunition" for the Honest Johns and CF-104s in NATO on the same terms as other alliance members had accepted, although no announcement was made because Diefenbaker vowed to delay informing the public until the whole nuclear package was resolved. For the Bomarcs and Voodoos in Canada, Harkness wrote, "we were to try to get an agreement under which the nuclear warheads, or essential parts of them, would be held in the United States, but could be put on the weapons in Canada in a matter of minutes or hours."[44] The Cabinet named a committee of three ministers to negotiate this arrangement with the Americans, and it did not take long before Harkness, at least, convinced himself of the essential impracticality of the scheme. What if there were a heavy fog or a snowstorm (the Bomarc bases were in northern Canada, after all) on the day of a crisis and the aircraft with the missing parts could not get to Canada? Howard Green, also on the negotiation committee, typically did not see this as an obstacle, and the Americans quickly became convinced that there was little prospect for any agreement with Diefenbaker.[45] Again, matters had stalled.

But events intervened. On January 3, 1963, General Lauris Norstad, the retiring NATO Supreme Commander and a United States Air Force officer, told an Ottawa press conference that Canada had committed itself to accept a nuclear role in Europe[46] – a question that Diefenbaker had fuzzified enough to have created doubts. Then on January 12, Lester Pearson, the leader of the Liberal party, reversed his and his party's position and announced that Canada "should end at once its evasion of responsibility by discharging the commitments it has already accepted ... It can only do this by accepting nuclear warheads ..."[47]

For the next three weeks, turmoil rocked the Cabinet and the country. Harkness fought the issue daily in Cabinet while Diefenbaker, now certain that he should oppose the Liberals on the defence issue by delaying the nuclear decision still further, resisted. Finally, on January 25, Diefenbaker delivered an equivocal address to the House of Commons and the nation. He revealed the secret negotiations with the United States over the "missing part" approach, but then he cast doubt on the utility of a nuclear role for Canada.[48]

Diefenbaker's speech infuriated the United States government. At 6:15 p.m. on January 30, the Department of State issued a press release. The document detailed the weapons Canada had purchased, noted the inconclusive nature of the negotiations, corrected some of Diefenbaker's errors in his House address, and then noted with devastating force that "the Canadian Government has not as yet proposed any arrangement sufficiently practical to contribute effectively to North American defense."[49] The Americans had called the Prime Minister a liar, and Dean Rusk, briefing the media the next day, removed none of the sting: "... we regret it if our statement was phrased in any way to give offense. The need for this statement, however, arose not of our making but because of statements which were made in the defense debate in Ottawa ..."[50]

Theodore Sorensen, White House aide, later noted that the President "did not like and did not respect Diefenbaker, and had no desire to see him continue in office,"[51] a comment that could be read to mean that Kennedy intended the press release to hurt Diefenbaker politically. McGeorge Bundy, however, told the Canadian Ambassador that Kennedy had known nothing about the statement in advance.[52] Washington's new ambassador in Ottawa, Walton Butterworth, reported his unsurprising view that no apology was needed, a comment that was entirely predictable because his embassy had drafted the release. It was "very useful" and "will be highly beneficial in advancing US interests by introducing realism into a government which had made anti-Americanism and indecision practically its entire stock in trade." Butterworth also referred to Canada's "neurotic" political leadership.[53] According to the ambassador, the release had been sent from the embassy to the State Department where it was reviewed by George McGhee, George Ball, and Secretary Rusk; then it had gone to the White House where Bundy gave it his approval.[54] Weeping crocodile tears, Bundy soon took the blame (or credit) himself: it was "a case of stupidity and the stupidity was mine."[55]

Stupid or deliberate, the press release finished the Diefenbaker government. Within days Harkness and two other ministers resigned and the government, defeated on a vote of no-confidence in the House of Commons, had to call an election. Cabals of rebels and clutches of loyalists, Cabinet revolts and caucus battles soon rocked Ottawa. Diefenbaker hung on to the prime ministership, however, and led his party into the election. But virtually every observer was pronouncing the Conservative century at its end.[56]

The Canadian electorate, however much it may have distrusted Diefenbaker, was still sorely torn. No one, whatever his or her political coloration, tolerated the American intervention into Canadian politics, and noisy statements of anti-Americanism abounded. The nuclear issue continued to trouble many, and Diefenbaker, conveniently forgetting that he had purchased the weapons, now denounced nuclear warheads with fervor. His new stance was greatly aided by the badly timed release of secret congressional testimony by Secretary of Defense Robert McNamara that suggested the Bomarcs in Canada were useful only because they might draw Soviet fire toward Canada.[57] In this atmosphere, many Canadians believed the story, leaked during the campaign, that Butterworth had written Liberal leader Pearson with assurances of American support.[58] The letter was actually forged, but it reinforced the Conservatives' anti-Americanism. In these circumstances, the Liberals won by only a small margin. Pearson won 129 seats while Diefenbaker held 95, many more than anyone had expected. The balance of power remained with the anti-nuclear New Democratic Party and the divided Social Crediters.

Pearson's victory produced great sighs of relief in the American embassy in Ottawa (and in the Department of External Affairs and its posts abroad). Ambassador Butterworth, his strategy vindicated, wrote to Walter Lippmann, the distinguished columnist, that the outcome of the election had turned on fundamental questions. "That is why the facing up to them was so very serious and why the Pearson victory in the April 8 election was so significant." Canada's place in world affairs and particularly its relations with the United States had been the key issue. He added confidently that "at any rate, the outcome holds salutary lessons which will not be overlooked by future aspirants to political office in Canada."[59]

If Butterworth expected relations between Canada and the United States to be smooth now that Diefenbaker had been disposed of, he was mistaken. The Liberal government had pledged to honor the nuclear commitments made to the United States, but it was a nationalist government nonetheless, committed to reducing the Canadian economy's dependence on foreign, and especially American, investment. The new Minister of Finance, Walter Gordon, had been the chair of the 1956 Royal Commission on Canada's Economic Prospects, which had pointed to foreign investment as a major problem, and he was also an old friend of Lester Pearson, the architect of his leadership convention victory in 1957, and the man who had organized the Liberal party for its election victory in 1963. When Walter Gordon spoke, in other words, Mike Pearson listened.

Pearson himself was no anti-American. A phenomenally successful diplomat since the late 1920s, he had served in Ottawa, London, and Washington, and in 1944 he had become Canada's first Ambassador to the United States. In 1948 he had entered politics at the top, becoming Secretary of State for External Affairs in the St. Laurent government. He won the Nobel Peace Prize in 1957 for his role in creating the United Nations Emergency Force, which allowed Britain and France to extricate themselves from their incompetently managed war against Egypt, and he had become the public's very embodiment of enlightened Canadianism – a man of great personal charm who combined the reserved attitudes of the British and the open friendliness of Americans into something uniquely Canadian.

The new Prime Minister and the President met at Hyannis Port on Cape Cod for an extraordinarily cordial two-day discussion within three weeks of the change of government in Canada.[60] Kennedy had already sent a genuinely warm message to Pearson saying that the "early establishment of close relations between your administration and ours is a matter of great importance to me."[61] But the serious problems between the two countries could not be resolved by good intentions alone.

The nuclear question, however, *could* be settled. Pearson told the President that "he was sorry that the previous Canadian Government had undertaken nuclear commitments," but in the circumstances his government "was prepared to stand or fall in Parliament on its intention to conclude the bilateral agreement" with Washington for the acquisition of the warheads. The House of Commons on May 20 narrowly accepted the Pearson government's decision to arm the Bomarcs, CF-104s, and Honest Johns. That festering issue was effectively concluded.

But the seeds of future difficulty were sown when the two talked about American investment, apparently a subject on which Kennedy had not been briefed.[62] His government, Pearson said, "did not wish to discourage the inflow of United States capital, but nonetheless it had to be recognized that the effect of United States investment in Canada constituted a political problem." The Prime Minister added that "it was the intention of the Government to take steps not to penalize United States interests but to encourage Canadians to invest more in Canadian companies." Kennedy asked how Pearson intended to proceed and was told

> that there were means of encouraging Canadian control by informal methods, e.g., by persuading United States companies of the importance of putting Canadians in management positions and also by resisting any tendency to make United States regulations and laws apply to Canadian companies in Canada. The Government also intended to establish a Canadian development corporation, one purpose of which would be to help Canadians to buy into industrial companies in such a way as not to invite legitimate United States criticism.

The Canadian note on the meeting added that "the president listened attentively but did not comment."[63] Once Ottawa's proposals were on the table, however, that silence would be broken.

The Pearson government's plans to control foreign investment formed a critical part of Walter Gordon's hurriedly prepared budget – the Liberals had campaigned with the promise that they would deliver "Sixty Days of Decision" so the budget, delivered on June 14, had to come within that two-month time frame – and it drew instant and devastating criticism at home and abroad. The central points were a 30 per cent takeover tax on sales of shares in Canadian companies to nonresidents and a reduction in the withholding tax on dividends paid to non-residents by 5 per cent for companies that were at least one-quarter Canadian-owned and an increase of 5 per cent for companies with a lower proportion of domestic control. Companies with more than 25 per cent Canadian ownership also received benefits in calculating their depreciation allowance.[64]

Gordon might have expected criticism. The Governor of the Bank of Canada had warned that the withholding tax could produce "massive attempts at liquidation" of foreign investment, but Gordon had gone ahead nonetheless.[65] Canadian businessmen, directly hooked into the continental economy, were furious, and the talk in the clubs of Toronto and Montreal, to say nothing of the business pages of the newspapers, became poisonous. By June 19, Gordon had withdrawn the takeover tax, and the next day, the battered minister offered his resignation to Pearson. The gesture was not accepted.

The Kennedy Administration was similarly agitated, the retreat of June 19 notwithstanding. Part of the anger arose because Pearson had not informed Kennedy of the extent or nature of the discriminatory actions.[66] As Assistant Secretary of State Griffith Johnson told the Canadian Chargé in Washington:

> Frankly these features had come as a real surprise. While Prime Minister Pearson had indicated at Hyannisport that consideration was being given to some measures regarding investment, we were not under the impression that any measures were contemplated which would affect United States investment so directly.[67]

American resentment surfaced strongly the next month when the Kennedy Administration proposed that restrictive measures be applied to Canadian and other foreign borrowing in the United States – measures designed to grapple with the emerging American balance of payments deficit. There was some pleasure on the American side as the Canadians scrambled to deal with a policy that threatened to choke their economy. With a straight face, for example, the Under Secretary of State offered the Canadian Ambassador

> [his] categoric assurance that there was no element of retaliation or discrimination in the development of these measures. Rather they were the consequence of the need to meet an urgent situation.
>
> The Under Secretary also observed that the United States had shown much restraint in reacting to the Canadian budget measures ... In addition, United States assistance to the Canadian government during the 1962 balance of payments crisis was mentioned.[68]

On July 21, after Canadian appeals for an exemption, a deal was struck.[69] The Kennedy Administration had demonstrated very effectively that Canada – and its Minister of Finance – needed the United States. And none in Canada failed to draw the appropriate lesson. The Assistant Deputy Minister of Finance, for example, told a meeting of Canadian and American officials that "Canadians [were] seriously disturbed by this reminder of dependence on USA."[70]

Pressure within the Liberal party for Canada to create a nationalistic economic policy did not disappear after the July humiliation. Similarly, the widespread Canadian desire for a foreign and defence policy that was not dragged behind Washington's chariot wheels also persisted. But it proved much easier to move in those directions after Kennedy, both very popular in Canada and tough in his actions toward it, was assassinated. Indeed, just before November 22, McGeorge Bundy had sent a memorandum to key Cabinet members and others noting that "all aspects of Canadian-American relations are of intense interest and concern to the President himself." For that reason, "the President desires that the White House be fully informed of all significant negotiations or plans for negotiation with the Government of Canada ..."[71] The Bostonian's charm had only lightly masked his interest in and his toughness toward his North American ally, and John Diefenbaker, no less than Walter Gordon, had reason to remember clashes with the President.

Did Kennedy leave a lasting imprint on Canadian-American relations? For the United States, his legacy was likely a realization that Canada could be a difficult, hesitant partner, but one that could be made to do the "right" thing. For Canada, Kennedy was the first President in the postwar era to use American muscle to achieve his ends, and that left a lingering caution, a certainty that the United States could not be pushed too far. But that caution should not be overstated. Pearson essayed economic nationalist gestures, and his successor, Pierre Trudeau, at various points reduced Canadian defences, set up an agency to screen foreign investment, and implemented a strongly nationalist oil policy. Canadian nationalism, in other words, survived the clash between Kennedy and Diefenbaker intact and alive. Indeed, the clash probably induced a greater sense of nationalism in Canadians. Yet the defence and economic aims of Kennedy's America have not been truly checked by this nationalism. In the 1980s, American investment was more dominant in Canada than it had been a quarter century before, Canada's trade had become even more concentrated on the market to the south, and the two countries' defences had become, if anything, even more closely integrated. The Americans, as one Canadian politician of the 1960s put it with unintended meaning, are Canadians' best friends whether they like it or not.

NOTES

1 Teno Roncalio OH [Oral History] Interview, JFKL.
2 On NORAD and the Arrow cancellation, see J.L. Granatstein, *Canada 1957–1967: The Years of Uncertainty and Innovation* (Toronto, 1986), 101–38; James Dow, *The Arrow* (Toronto, 1979).
3 See James M. Minifie, *Peacemaker or Powder-Monkey?* (Toronto, 1960.)
4 For one statement of economic nationalism, by the chair of the Royal Commission on Canada's Economic Prospects, see Walter Gordon, *Troubled Canada* (Toronto, 1961). The statistics are from F.H. Leacy, ed., *Historical Statistics of Canada* (Ottawa, 1983), G291–302, G401–14.
5 See especially the *Report of the Royal Commission on National Development in the Arts, Letters and Sciences* (Ottawa, 1951). For the formation of the Canada Council, see J.L. Granatstein, "Culture and Scholarship: The First Ten Years of the Canada Council," *Canadian Historical Review* LXV (December 1984), 441–74.
6 The best analysis remains John Meisel, *The Canadian General Election of 1957* (Toronto, 1962).
7 On 1958, see Granatstein, *Canada 1957–67*, pp. 35–8. On Diefenbaker after the victory, Peter Newman, *Renegade in Power* (Toronto, 1963), remains valuable.
8 On Diefenbaker's troubles, see Granatstein, *Canada 1957–1967*, pp. 62–100, and Robert Bothwell, et al., *Canada Since 1945: Power, Politics, and Provincialism* (Toronto, 1981), 197–9.
9 Still useful on defence procurement decisions is Jon B. McLin, *Canada's Changing Defense Policy, 1957–1963* (Baltimore, 1967).
10 See on Robertson and Green, J.L. Granatstein, *A Man of Influence: Norman A. Robertson and Canadian Statecraft, 1929–1968* (Ottawa, 1981), 322–63.
11 See Lt.-Gen. E.L.M. Burns, *A Seat at the Table: The Struggle for Disarmament* (Toronto, 1972). Burns led Canadian disarmament delegations from 1960 to 1968.
12 Howard Green OH Interview, York University Archives, Toronto.
13 Canada, House of Commons, Special Committee on Defence, *Minutes*, May 13, 1963, p. 510.
14 Canada, House of Commons *Debates*, February 20, 1959, p. 1223.
15 This was especially so because one of the main factors in the Eisenhower Administration's decision to continue Bomarc development had been Canada's choice of the SAM system. "Memo of Conversation with the President," June 10, 1959, Staff Notes, Whitman Files, DDEP, DDEL.
16 John G. Diefenbaker, *One Canada: The Memoirs of the Rt. Hon. John G. Diefenbaker* (Toronto, 1975–7; 3 vols.), III, 71.
17 Norman Robertson to Howard Green, February 14, 1961, vol. 3, Howard Green Papers, Public Archives of Canada, Ottawa (hereafter PAC).

18 Diary, August 30, 1960, vol. 2, Arnold Heeney Papers, PAC.
19 Heeney to Diefenbaker, February 20, 1961, vol. 15, US Ambassador file, ibid.
20 Livingston Merchant OH Interview, JFKL.
21 Memorandum for the President, February 17, 1961, and attachments, Box 113, Canada Security 1961 file, POF, JFKP, JFKL. Howard Green in these notes was characterized much more harshly: "naive and almost parochial approach ... self-righteousness and stubbornness ... less flexible ... almost pacifist attitude ..."
22 R.B. Bryce to Harkness, March 2, 1961, envelope 1, vol. 84, Douglas Harkness Papers, PAC; Memorandum, H.B. Robinson to Under Secretary, February 21,1961, H.B. Robinson Papers, Historical Division, Department of External Affairs, Ottawa; Merchant OH Interview; Fred Dutton Memorandum for President, February 20,1961, Canada 1961 file, Box 113, POF, JFKP.
23 Memorandum for Meeting with Prime Minister Diefenbaker, att. to Memorandum for the President, February 17, 1961, Canada Security 1961 file, ibid. On the February 1961 visit I have benefited from H. Basil Robinson's as yet unpublished "From Eisenhower to Kennedy." Robinson was External Affairs aide in the Prime Minister's Office.
24 "Trends in Canadian Foreign Policy," May 2, 1961, Canada Security 1961, box 113, Trip to Ottawa (D) file, POF, JFKP.
25 Telegram, External to Geneva, May 18, 1961, NATO and Nuclear Weapons file, vol. 8, Green Papers.
26 Donald M. Fleming, *So Very Near: The Political Memoirs of Donald M. Fleming*, Vol. II: *The Summit Years* (Toronto, 1985; 2 vols.), 586 reprints the memorandum.
27 Diary, March 18, 1962, vol. 2, Heeney Papers.
28 Fleming, *So Very Near*, II, 371–3. Fleming was Finance Minister in Diefenbaker's government.
29 House of Commons *Debates*, March 8, 1962, p. 1602. See also Ramesh Thakur, *Peacekeeping in Vietnam* (Edmonton, 1984); James Eayrs, *In Defence of Canada*, Vol. V: *Indochina: Roots of Complicity* (Toronto, 1983), and especially Douglas Ross, *In the Interests of Peace* (Toronto, 1984).
30 See Victor Levant, *Quiet Complicity: Canadian Involvement in the Vietnam War* (Toronto, 1986), chaps. X–XII.
31 "The Cuban Situation," July 13, 1960, John Starnes Papers, Historical Division, Department of External Affairs, Ottawa; "Record of meeting on July 12–13, 1960," ibid.
32 March 12, 1961, ibid.
33 Ibid.
34 See H.H. Fowler to McG. Bundy, February 28, 1963, Treasury 2/63 file, Box 90, POF, JFKP.

35 Telegram, American Embassy, Ottawa, October 22, 1962, Box 20, NSF, JFKP.
36 "The Nuclear Arms Question and the Political Crisis Which Arose from It in January and February, 1963," August 19–27, 1963, file 2, vol. 14, Harkness Papers. A version of this document was printed in a number of Canadian newspapers. See *Ottawa Citizen*, October 22, 1977. See also Jocelyn Ghent, "Canada, the United States, and the Cuban Missile Crisis," *Pacific Historical Review* XVIII (May 1979), 159–84.
37 Air Marshal Slemon to Foulkes, March 3, 1965, NORAD Consultation file, Gen. Charles Foulkes Papers, Directorate of History, Department of National Defence, Ottawa.
38 "The Nuclear Arms Question," Harkness Papers. See also Jeffry V. Brock, *The Thunder and the Sunshine*, Vol. II: *With Many Voices* (Toronto, 1983; 2 vols.), 110, which attests to the Royal Canadian Navy's actions without authority from Ottawa.
39 Cabinet Conclusions, October 24, 1962, Cabinet Records, Privy Council Office, Ottawa; "Nuclear Arms Question," Harkness Papers.
40 See Robertson to Green, November 7, 1962, file 50309-40, Historical Division, Department of External Affairs.
41 Granatstein, *Man of Influence*, 352; Diefenbaker, *One Canada*, III, 83; Washington to External, October 23, 1962, file 2444-40, Historical Division, Department of External Affairs; House of Commons *Debates*, October 22, 1962.
42 See Peyton Lyon, *Canada in World Affairs 1961–1963* (Toronto, 1968), 52–4; Pierre Sevigny, *This Game of Politics* (Toronto, 1965), 253, 257.
43 See Granatstein, *Canada 1957–1967*, pp. 122–3.
44 Cabinet Conclusions, October 30, 1962, Cabinet Records; "Nuclear Arms Question," Harkness Papers; Jocelyn Ghent, "Did He Fall or Was He Pushed? The Kennedy Administration and the Fall of the Diefenbaker Government," *International History Review* I (April 1979), 246–70.
45 Canadian Joint Staff Washington to Chairman, Chiefs of Staff, February 14, 1963 (re talk with Paul Nitze), Defence Policy – Canada-US Relations file, Office of the Chief of the Defence Staff Records, Directorate of History, Department of National Defence.
46 Lyon, *World Affairs*, 130–6.
47 See J.T. Saywell, ed., *The Canadian Annual Review, 1963* (Toronto, 1964), 287. The most famous critique of Pearson's switch is Pierre-E. Trudeau, "Pearson où l'abdication de l'esprit," *Cité Libre* (avril 1963), 7.
48 House of Commons *Debates*, January 25, 1963, pp. 3125–8.
49 Lyon, *World Affairs*, 157–8.
50 Documents attached to Memorandum for Minister, February 1, 1963, and Robertson to Prime Minister, January 30, 1963, vol. 9, Green Papers.

51 Sorenson OH Interview.
52 Confidential interview.
53 Col. Burris to Vice-President Lyndon B. Johnson, February 6, 1963, No. (78)301E, DDRS.
54 Ghent, "Did He Fall?," 262.
55 Memorandum for Minister, February 7, 1963, file 50309-40, Historical Division, Department of External Affairs.
56 See Granatstein, *Canada 1957–1967*, pp. 130–3.
57 Memorandum for Rusk, March 29, 1963, Canada Security 1963 file, Box 113, POF, JFKP; Lyon, *World Affairs*, 203–4.
58 Election 1963-Butterworth file, vol. 105, Gordon Churchill Papers, PAC; Churchill's ms. "Recollections," chap. XII, which remained, before his death, in Churchill's possession; House of Commons *Debates*, May 27, 1963, pp. 319–22.
59 Butterworth to Lippmann, May 20, 1963, File 351, Box 59, Sec. III, Walter Lippmann Papers, Yale University Library, New Haven, CT.
60 See memorandum for Under Secretary, May 12, 1963, file 60, vol. 232, Paul Martin Papers, PAC.
61 Telegram, President to Prime Minister, April 22, 1963, Canada Security 1963 file, Box 113, POF, JFKP.
62 Nos. (78) 261C; (76) 54G; (76) 265D; (76) 54E; and (76) 54F, DDRS originally from LBJL, constitute the US briefing papers.
63 "Meeting Between the Prime Minister of Canada and the President of the United States, Hyannisport, Mass., May 10–11, 1963," vol. 232, Martin Papers.
64 Granatstein, *Canada 1957–1967*, pp. 276–9.
65 "Some Comments on the Budget," May 31,1963, file LR76-549, Louis Rasminsky Papers, Bank of Canada Archives, Ottawa.
66 See memorandum for Mr. Pearson, May 7, 1963, file U-10, Walter Gordon Papers, Toronto (private collection).
67 "Discriminatory Measures in Canadian Budget," June 28, 1963, Box 19, NSF, JFKP; Butterworth Memo to McG. Bundy, July 16, 1963, ibid.
68 "Canadian Reaction to Proposed US Balance of Payments Measures," July 19, 1963, Canada General file, Box 17, NSF, ibid. See also Paul Martin to Prime Minister, July 19, 1963, file 852.2 Conf., vol. 284, L.B. Pearson Papers, PAC.
69 Press Release, July 21, 1963, Office of the Minister of Finance, Ottawa.
70 "Meeting of Canadian and United States Officials ... Washington, D.C., August 18, 1963," file LR76-5360-1, Rasminsky Papers.
71 Bundy to Secretary of State et al., November 11, 1963, Canada General file, Box 19, NSF, JFKP.

Chapter Six

The Importance of Being Less Earnest: Promoting Canada's National Interests through Tighter Ties with the US

The prime minister and the president did not get on well. The younger president, his election tarnished by voting irregularities, did not show the deference the older and more experienced prime minister expected – and had, in fact, usually received from the president's predecessor. All this played to the Canadian's strong anti-Americanism, his reluctance to be pushed around by the superpower, and fed into the older man's conviction that his own judgement remained sound and that his nation's moral standing soared over that of the neighbour's. Even the gravest of threats to the security of North America failed to move him very far or very fast, and the Americans grew ever more furious.

The wires between Washington and the embassy in Ottawa hummed until the ambassador, his patience finally at the breaking point over what he described as Canada's "neurotic" political leadership that "has made anti-Americanism and indecision practically its entire stock in trade," received the go-ahead. Now he could strike at the government's weak spot: a Canadian public that wanted to be independent of the US but also fretted continually about getting out of step with the southern giant.

It was January 1963. John Diefenbaker's Progressive Conservative government was on the verge of implosion, its road to the Opposition benches and the dustbin of history helped mightily by a US State Department press release, drafted in the embassy, that slammed the prime minister for his failure to propose "any arrangement sufficiently practical to contribute effectively to North American defence."[1]

In the context of modem history, the angry remarks by Ambassador Paul Cellucci in the aftermath of the Jean Chrétien government's refusal to support the United States in its war against Iraq were not a unique event. The 1962–3 crisis over nuclear weapons that led the

John F. Kennedy Administration into a heavy-handed intervention in Canadian politics and brought Lester Pearson's Liberals to power was not dissimilar to the events that would roil Canada-US relations 40 years later. For his part, Pearson had serious difficulties of his own with Lyndon Johnson's government over Vietnam, while Pierre Trudeau faced substantial scorn from Ronald Reagan's government for the so-called peace initiative of 1983–4. Even Brian Mulroney, often painted by nationalists as a puppet of Washington for his efforts to establish and maintain what he referred to as "super relations" with the US, moved very cautiously before committing Canadian ships, aircraft, and some troops to the Gulf War in 1991.

In other words, Canada is not the United States. Canada has less power, wealth, and population. It also has a different history, different institutions, different ties to nations overseas, and, as a result, its national interests and values are not necessarily the same as those of its great neighbour. Anti-Americanism has been and, to a substantial degree, remains Canada's state religion, the very bedrock of Canadian nationalism, its strength rising and falling with events. Our present leaders still use it knowingly to manipulate public opinion.[2] Yet Canada has to live beside the United States, and the ever-increasing interconnectedness of the two nations makes the fostering of a satisfactory relationship more important with each day. This demands that Canada at last begin to define its national interests and values in a realistic manner. For a nation that is as old as Canada, the fact that we think we know our values but fail to understand our interests is unsettling. We have failed to determine what is truly critical to us, we fall back on our self-professed values, greatly overrating their importance, and, as a result, we fail to base policy on our national interests. In the new world of the 21st century, this self-indulgence can be sustained only at a high price.

Looking at the Facts

First, a few truisms need to be stated. Canada is part of the world community, and it has and will continue to have multilateral interests and obligations. But Canada is inescapably part of North America, and, however much some Canadians may wish they could alter this fact, they cannot. We are joined to the United States hip and thigh, and this will not change. The Americans may make major alterations in their strategic dispositions around the world, but our location along the US's northern border guarantees that the United States must take an interest in Canada for pressing US strategic reasons. President Franklin D.

Roosevelt in 1938 put it succinctly: "I give to you assurance that the people of the United States will not stand idly by if domination of Canadian soil is threatened."[3] A few days later, Prime Minister Mackenzie King offered Canada's reciprocal pledge: "We, too, have our obligations as a good friendly neighbour, and one of them is to see that ... our country is made as immune from attack or possible invasion as we can reasonably be expected to make it, and that ... enemy forces should not be able to pursue their way, either by land, sea or air, to the United States, across Canadian territory."[4]

Both nations were serving their own – and each other's – interests with these promises. Sensible Canadians then (as now) understood that their nation's defence ultimately was provided by the United States. They also recognized that Canada could never allow its defences to decay so much that the United States believed itself in danger because of Canadian weakness, obliging the US to take over the complete defence of the northern half of the continent whatever Canadians might say about it. The impact of any such action on Canadian sovereignty should be obvious. As Mackenzie King put it in 1936, it would be humiliating "to rely on the United States without being willing to at least protect our neutrality." If Canada were independent, the nation would have "an enormous cost to meet in the way of defence."[5] Nothing today differs from the King years. Indeed, the terror attacks of September 11, 2001, have guaranteed that the US interest in Canadian geography remains as focussed as it has ever been in the last century.

Canada's economic prosperity similarly depends on the US market. The British trade and investment market was once critical for Canada, but this has not been so for more than three-quarters of a century. Efforts to switch trade from the United States back to Britain or to Europe and Japan have been tried (John Diefenbaker's impromptu 1957 call for a 15-per cent diversion from the US to Britain was one; Pierre Trudeau's Third Option in the 1970s was another) and roundly failed. Canada-US trade has doubled in dollar volume since 1994, with some $2 billion in trade crossing the border each day, 85 per cent of Canadian merchandise exports going to or through the United States, 23 per cent of American exports coming north, and the US buying almost 40 per cent of Canada's gross domestic product (GDP). Canada's dependence on the US market for its economic success is a demonstrable fact.[6]

Canadian Ambivalence

Still, Canadians' ambivalent attitude toward their US neighbour remains stubbornly unchanged. Canadians like to think that they understand the Americans better than any others, though there is little evidence of this in, for example, the way Ottawa misunderstood the US reaction to the attacks of September 11, 2001. We want to enjoy all the benefits of the North American standard of living, and we consider it our right to trade with and visit the US, all the while reading US books and magazines and watching US television. At the same time, Canadians sneer at America, bemoan its flag-waving patriotism and aggressive bumptiousness on the world stage, and have half-persuaded themselves that they could really run the world better.

The endemic anti-Americanism in Canada, a product of history, proximity, and a different institutional culture, does Canadians no credit. This attitude will not change, however, without leadership from the same political and cultural elites who regrettably continue to use anti-Americanism for their own purposes. It should be obvious to everyone that anti-Americanism hurts, rather than helps, Canada in dealing with the superpower with which it shares the continent. Unfortunately, too many Canadians are oblivious, or deliberately blind, to this basic truth. Restoring Canadians' sight on this issue should be a priority. The nation now must take the essential steps to rethink its policies, restore its defences, and restructure its cabinet machinery and the bureaucracy that the government maintains in Ottawa and in the US to reflect the overwhelming importance the United States has for us.

A Delicate Dance of Interests and Values

Canada is a nation that rarely discusses its national interests. A colony of France and Britain for centuries – indeed, a historical anomaly in some senses – Canada assumed that its interests were identical with those of the metropolis. Canadians even went into the world wars in 1914 and 1939, to cite the two most important examples, with scarcely anyone asking whether such actions served this country's interests; it was enough that Britain was threatened.[7]

The first real attempt to state Canada's interests in foreign policy did not come until two years after the end of the Second World War. Louis St. Laurent, the secretary of state for external affairs, delivered a lecture in Toronto, in 1947, defining the principles upon which Canadian foreign policy rested: "national unity, political liberty, the rule of law, the values of Christian civilization, and a willingness to accept international responsibilities."[8] That was as close as any senior minister came to stating national interests for years. Then in 1969, the Trudeau government fixed the nation's defence priorities as sovereignty, North America, the North Atlantic Treaty Organisation (NATO), and peacekeeping, in that order. The next year it issued *Foreign Policy for Canadians*. The series contained six booklets, as Allan Gotlieb says, with "hexagons, goals, values, objectives, and many prescriptions" but, incredibly, nothing on Canadian strategies for dealing with the United States, the core of Canadian national interests. The study is less than useful as a result and offers no hard assessment of Canadian imperatives, other than to call for social justice, quality of life, and economic growth.[9] *Canada in the World*, the Chrétien government's foreign policy white paper of 1995, did little better and indeed shoved the projection of values abroad to the fore.[10] The idea of national interests seems to have drifted away almost totally, while the nation endlessly prattles about superior values.

What Are Those Values?

Minister of Foreign Affairs and International Trade Bill Graham invited Canadians in January 2003 to engage in an online dialogue on Canada's foreign policy, and a paper set out his department's baseline position. Despite some brief discussion of Canadian foreign policy goals, there is scarcely any mention of Canada's national interests in a paper intended to point the way to a review of foreign policy. The minister and his department either do not think in such terms, or they regard interests as so obvious that they need no elaboration. Or, perhaps, there is a concern that many earnest Canadians might think it abhorrent even to suggest that a country as idealistic and moral as ours has national interests.[11] The unspoken belief may be that Canada thinks and acts only in terms of multilateral processes and its concomitant, the global good.

On the other hand, Graham's truly vapid, preachy paper has not the slightest hesitation in raising "values" to prominence:

> Canada's foreign policy agenda must reflect the nation we are: a multicultural, bilingual society that is free, open, prosperous and democratic. The experiences of immigrants from around the world and the cultures of our Aboriginal peoples are woven into the fabric of our national identity. Respect for equality and diversity runs through the religious, racial, cultural and linguistic strands forming our communities.[12]

The paper goes on to suggest that Canada use its position to "promote our values" abroad and so advance its humanitarian and human rights concerns. "One of the most internationally respected elements of Canada's foreign policy," it says, "is our long-standing advocacy of human rights, the rule of law, democracy, respect for diversity, gender equality and good governance." It then notes Canada's flexible federalism, its respect for cultural differences, and its core values of democracy, human rights, diversity, and civility.[13]

But is multiculturalism really a Canadian value? Is gender equality? Flexible federalism? Civility? We might hope they are, but, even if so, should Canada try to export such values to all societies, including those theocratic ones that believe in patriarchy and stress religious purity or those that believe civility to be a Western conceit? There is a danger here that we will sound overbearing and patronizing, implicitly suggesting that our values are universal, rather than merely postmodernist and politically correct. The Department of Foreign Affairs and International Trade comes perilously close to claiming a status for Canada as a moral superpower (or to a parody of the Indigo and Chapters bookstores' slogan "The World Needs More Canada") when it says "A better world might look like a better Canada."[14] If only the Palestinians and Israelis and the Indians and Pakistanis would settle their differences in the prescribed Canadian manner!

If Canada actually put up sufficient funds to help it live up to its self-professed image as a caring, sharing nation, we might legitimately be able to press our values on the world.[15] Perhaps. But very few of the values the ministry's paper trumpets are truly entrenched in Canadian society. Multiculturalism has been government policy for only three decades, hardly long enough to be pronounced immutably Canadian. The yet-to-be-achieved goal of gender equality has been in place for even less time, flexible federalism is a swear word to some Canadians, and Canada's good governance is not quite the model for the world we might wish it to be. Values that are not long-lived and widely cherished by the Canadian people may be seen more as government propaganda than as expressions of the popular will.

On the other hand, most Canadians agree that their country is secular, democratic, liberal, and pluralist, the last a less politically contentious word than multiculturalism. No one would take issue with the fact that freedom is a core value we share. If the foreign minister truly feels compelled to press our values on the world, these indisputable ones, the basis of our national life and the foundation of our success, are those that we ought to be encouraging. Unfortunately, very little in Bill Graham's on-line dialogue refers to these harder-edged values.

The fundamental truth is that these few but important Canadian traits aside, values or principles are for individuals, while nations have *interests* above all. Canadians need to know what their government considers to be Canada's national interests. They must be spelled out, and policy must be based on a clear conception of what truly matters, not on perpetually calling for multilateral processes in the tiresome

Ottawa way or on some vague and shifting sense of what Canada and Canadians might be or stand for.

Things That Matter

National interests are not difficult to detail for most nations, and Canada's, in fact, are very clear:

1 Canada must protect its territory, the security of its people, and its unity.
2 It must strive to protect and enhance its independence.
3 It must promote the economic growth of the nation to support the prosperity and welfare of its people.
4 It must work with like-minded states, in and outside international forums, for the protection and enhancement of democracy and freedom.

This statement of interests is deliberately blunt, omits many subtleties, and includes both ultimate goals and instruments (or ends and means). The first, second, and third of these interests are unquestionably Canada's domestic goals, and they threaten no other nation or people. They state simply and clearly what any nation must do in its own interests.

The foremost national interest is that Canada must keep its territory secure and protect its people, the basic task of government. The question of unity is more difficult, given the nation's history of linguistic and regional factionalism. All that needs to be said in this paper is that it is a mistake to act against the will of any large region of the country. Surely, as Louis St. Laurent said in 1947, "Our external policies shall not destroy our unity." At the same time, it is an error not to act abroad if most of Canada wishes to do so. Squaring the circle might be easier, but managing this national interest carefully and properly is absolutely critical for any government, "the ultimate litmus test," says one scholar, "for any international or domestic policy."[16]

The second national interest could be interpreted by some as being directed against the United States, the only state that can jeopardize Canadian sovereignty in the foreseeable future. The US does not pose a military challenge to Canada and has not for more than a century, but it is nonetheless a benign threat. Its powerful magnetic pull, the vigour of its corporations, culture, and institutions could put Canadian independence in question. It is in Canada's clear interest that this not occur, and we must seek out the ways to ensure Canada's survival as an independent nation.

The third national interest, however, all but forces Canada's government to promote beneficial trade with the huge market to the south. The tension between the two interests, the two national goals, will always be present, but, like the conundrum of unity, it must be managed. As with unity, getting the balance right between these interests is a test of a government's capability.

The fourth statement of national interest, a means toward the furtherance of Canadian security, may be more contentious to some of today's Canadians than it was to our forefathers, but it is neither messianic nor a call for a manifest destiny. It merely reflects our own history, the global record of the last century, and the troubling way the 21st century has begun. Cooperation with our friends and allies has been the means through which we have survived and prospered. Canada has been threatened in the past by the rise of dictatorships and oligarchies, and the spread of liberty, democracy, and economic freedom remains the best guarantor against future threats to us. We have a genuine interest in working with our friends to help protect and encourage the spread of political and economic freedom around the world.

Balances

A sensible foreign policy should be based on established national values and the country's clear national interests, with the two categories properly weighed and balanced. Interests, always important and always permanent (though the priority of one over another and the ways of achieving them will certainly change over the long term), must be at the fore. Often more transitory, ordinarily subject to interpretation, and, in Canada, usually dripping with self-congratulatory moralistic rhetoric, our values are important to us, but they must be subordinated to interests. Canada needs to re-balance its understanding of national interests and values as it moves through the difficult and dangerous times of the present era. Our values will count for nothing if the nation does not survive and for very little if we fail to prosper.

This does not mean that Canada should play only hardball realpolitik in its foreign and defence policy. The Canadian people almost certainly want their idealism to have an important place in their nation's dealings with the world. But our governments must always act to protect the nation's interests first and foremost, carefully weighing the hard-headed achievement of them with the more idealistic promotion of Canadians' values. Practicality has ordinarily been in the forefront of Canada's trade policy, where we have worked hard and with substantial success to create organizations such as the General Agreement on Tariffs and Trade (GATT), the World Trade Organization (WTO), the Free Trade Agreement (FTA), and the North American Free Trade Agreement (NAFTA) that have rules-based regimes. But sometimes practicality has been in short supply in Canadian foreign and defence policy, occasionally being sacrificed to the earnest promotion of values that do not always serve the country's core interests. What the nation needs is a foreign policy of realism tempered by the application of its values. More realism, in other words, and less moral earnestness.

The Multilateralist Impulse

James H. Taylor was undersecretary of state for external affairs from 1985 to 1989 and is a man with a reputation for thoughtfulness. In a paper written in 1999, he notes:

> Canada is overwhelmingly dependent on the United States as an export market and very heavily dependent on it as a source of imports, whether of goods, ideas, technology or capital ... To have unhindered, trouble-free access to the world's closest, richest and most open market is a vital Canadian interest.

And he goes on to observe: "Happily, such access is, broadly speaking, available most of the time. Many Canadians, however, have viewed this dependence with alarm, as a factor of national weakness and vulnerability."[17]

Taylor states the public's response to the nation's dependence on the US market succinctly. But it is also abundantly clear that the presence of the United States dominates virtually all aspects of Canadian foreign and defence policy. And this dominance, too, is viewed with alarm by many Canadians.

Cold-War Realities

By the end of the Second World War and the beginning of the Cold War, Canada was tightly tied into the continental economy, a process of integration that continues still. The Soviet military threat guaranteed that the cooperation of the militaries of the two nations, begun in the war, would continue apace. The story is too well-known to need reiteration beyond pointing to a few of the highlights: the creation of the North Atlantic Alliance and Canada's decision to dispatch troops to Western Europe, the Korean War, and the North American Air Defense Agreement. Canadian governments properly assessed the national interest in keeping democratic Europe free, aggressive communism in check, and North America defended and went willingly into an American-dominated world.

In truth, our leaders decided that the benefits of taking the American road far exceeded those of striving for expensive neutrality or a penurious independence. Geography could let the Swedes be neutral – at a high cost in defence spending. Island status could permit Cuba a kind of psychologically impoverished independence. Canada was no island and its geography made cooperation with the United States essential. Neutrality that was inoffensive to the Americans would have required a huge Canadian defence budget, and few were prepared to pay this price, even if it had been – and it was not – in the national interest.

Not all Canadians accepted this as a fact, and endemic anti-Americanism flared up repeatedly. John Diefenbaker's attacks on the Kennedy Administration for what he described as ramming nuclear weapons down Canada's throat, for example, almost obscured the fact that he had willingly agreed to take the weaponry. His miraculous semi-survival in the 1962 election, the most anti-American campaign since that over reciprocity in 1911, was proof of the potency of playing to the suspicions Canadians still harboured about their neighbours.

However, if the American road was not the preferred one for many, where else could Canada go? The Commonwealth was one possibility, but with Britain dissolving its empire and creating a weak, fractious organization in its place, this was never a realistic political or economic choice. NATO was a second possibility; the Treaty's Article 2 conceivably pointed the alliance toward political and economic integration. This did not happen, and, although Canada sought to use the multilateral nature of NATO as a counterweight to its bilateral relationship with the US, the alliance itself was dominated by the Americans.

That left the United Nations. Canadians had been present at the creation of the UN but, initially at least, had little faith in it. The Cold War atmosphere pervaded and paralysed the UN, and although the organization resisted North Korea's invasion of South Korea in 1950, this was possible only because the Soviet Union was absent, its representatives fortuitously boycotting the Security Council at the time. What made the United Nations a Canadian icon was the Suez Crisis of 1956, when Lester Pearson, then external affairs minister, conjured an emergency force out of war, fear, and confusion. Pearson won the Nobel Peace Prize for interposing the first large peacekeeping force between the British, French and Israelis on one side and the Egyptians on the other.

Even though his efforts held the Western alliance together, Pearson's achievement at the UN was not unanimously hailed by Canadians.

Once he received the Nobel Prize, however, peacekeeping became Canada's *métier*. Canadians fell in love with the idea of keeping the peace, almost literally forcing their government to take a major part in every peacekeeping operation even when participation made little military or political sense. Canadians had to serve in Lebanon, Yemen, Western New Guinea, the Congo, and dozens of other troubled states and regions. Sometimes, these roles were hazardous, as when Ottawa threw lightly armed soldiers into combat in Cyprus in 1974 and into serious danger in the Congo in 1960. Prime ministers and foreign ministers tried to emulate Pearson's diplomatic coup, sometimes with success (Paul Martin and Cyprus in 1964) and sometimes with failure (Jean Chrétien and the Congo in 1995). If Canada were a middle power locked into a bilateral relationship with the United States, it could nonetheless work at the multilateral UN and do things the superpower US could not do. Canadians revelled in the belief that they were the keepers of the world's peace and in the thought that somehow the world recognized their nation's high moral standing.[18] The Americans might be a military superpower, but Canada was the moral superpower, its values supreme, or so we told ourselves at every opportunity. Americans made war, the mantra ran, but we kept the peace.

While the Cold War was underway, this made some sense. Canada was acceptable in parts of the world where other alliance nations were not. The country carried no colonial baggage and its bonafides were usually recognized. At the same time, Canada knowingly and deliberately did its peacekeeping to serve Western and NATO interests.[19] It agreed to join the International Control Commission in 1954 in the former Indochina for this reason; it went into the Congo in 1960 because the area was then a theatre in the Cold War, and it took the lead in creating the UN Force in Cyprus in 1964 because the possibility of war between Greece and Turkey, NATO allies, was unthinkable.

The Post–Cold War Chill

Once the Cold War ended, however, Canada's indispensability disappeared. The demands on the UN increased as the dead hand of Moscow fell away from Eastern Europe, Africa, and the Middle East. The barrier to US participation in peacekeeping disappeared at the same time as peacekeeping – usually involving small groups of observers or buffer forces between combatants – began to be transformed into peace support or peacemaking, both of which soon became synonymous with war. Backed by substantial public support, the Canadian Forces (CF) continued to take part in such operations, paradoxically at the same time as the capabilities of the military began to collapse. The end of the Soviet threat, the subsequent elimination of Canada's European role in NATO, and the federal deficit that forced major defence spending cuts combined to weaken the CF dramatically throughout the 1990s. So bad had things become that Lloyd Axworthy, then foreign minister, preached a moralistic, soft-power human-security policy to the world, in effect making Canada's weakness-is-strength into an Orwellian virtue.[20] Moreover, "Canadians are moved by humanitarian impulse, not by the cold-blooded or rational calculations of realpolitik," says UN Ambassador Paul Heinbecker, with extraordinary force and precision. "Principles are often more important than power to Canadians."[21]

If power has not mattered to Canadians, neither have their armed forces. By the beginning of the 21st Century, the Canadian Forces had lost their ability to serve Canadian interests in a sustained, effective way in peacekeeping, peacemaking, or war. Shortages of equipment and personnel all but eliminated Canada's military capacity,[22] and an all-singing, all-dancing military, a CF able to do everything with relatively little, was gone. What, if anything, is to replace it remains very unclear as Canadians await a new prime minister. The one certainty is that the Canadian public will demand that Canada's peacekeeping role continue, even if peacekeeping as it exists in the public mind[23] no longer has any relevance in the new world disorder of civil wars and terrorism in which we live.

The Fantasy of the UN

Peacekeeping's extraordinary longevity and popularity in the Canadian imagination has also led to the UN's major role in Canadian governmental and public discourse. This is extremely puzzling, for the UN's failings are manifold, not least in peace operations where Canadian military planners had to learn to work around UN headquarters' ceilings on equipment when, as was often the case in the former Yugoslavia, the situation on the ground exposed Canadian troops to danger. The UN old-boys' club of incompetent officials and its inability to reinforce adequately its small peacekeeping force in Rwanda, to cite another example, left the Canadian force commander, Major-General Roméo Dallaire, completely unable to prevent a horrific genocide. The United Nations has proven to be a weak reed, most especially when it confronts the peace and security issues it was created to address.

Yet Canadians profess to love the UN and the idea of multilateral security. Sheila Copps, a candidate for the Liberal leadership, attacked her front-running rival Paul Martin because, as she put it, he has made "very clear that the United States trumps the United Nations." Said Ms. Copps: "In my books, the United Nations trumps any individual country and I think the strength of Canada is going to be in building ... multilateral relationships, especially and including the United Nations."[24] This type of UN-centric attitude, very widespread during the long Security Council debates in 2002 and 2003 prior to the Iraq war, led to the government's quite incredible decision to support the United States in the war only if the Council gave its assent to military force. France and its friends on the Security Council guaranteed this would not happen, and Canada, flying in the face of its national interests, chose to refuse its neighbour political and military support.

The Iraqi crisis revealed in boldface the fundamental truth: the United Nations is dysfunctional. Paul Martin stated it well in a major address on foreign policy: "With Iraq, we witnessed a failure in the capacity of the international community to forge a shared consensus on how to proceed."[25] An organization created at the end of the Second World War, the UN today is a relic of that era, perfectly preserved in amber. How can it be anything else if France has a Security Council veto? Rather than simply bleating that the UN's processes should be supreme, a responsible Canadian role would be to press strongly for ways to remake the UN to fit the needs of a new century and a very different world. The UN is important for the services provided by its agencies, which range from the World Health Organization to the International Refugee Organization, the UN Educational, Scientific and Cultural Organization (UNESCO), and a host of other bodies. As a political forum, regrettably, it has been, and is, much less successful. Canada might usefully try to galvanize efforts to change the organization.[26] If it cannot be reformed, Canada would be most unwise to hang its multilateral hat on such a wobbly structure.

NATO and a G-20

The North Atlantic Treaty Organization is much more important to Canada's national interests than the UN, even if it cannot counterbalance the United States' weight in North American defence. NATO brings together the Western European democracies and, more recently, the liberated nations of Eastern Europe with North America. The alliance peacefully won the Cold War and still plays a critical role in keeping Europe at peace. NATO mans the stabilization forces in the former Yugoslavia and fought a successful humanitarian war in Kosovo against Slobodan Milosevic's regime. (Canada participated in the war with fighter aircraft and troops for the Kosovo Implementation Force – which had no UN sanction, something that seemed to have been forgotten in the debate over Iraq.)

NATO has provided the bulk of the present peacekeeping force for Afghanistan, a very dangerous and major out-of-area deployment and one of interest to Canada. When the Chrétien government surprised the Canadian Forces with its announcement of a major deployment to the Central Asian nation on February 12, 2003, a task essentially beyond the military's capabilities (and supply lines!),[27] NATO took Canada off the hook two months later by agreeing to command and coordinate the International Security Assistance Force in Kabul. In effect, NATO would provide medical, engineering, and support units of the kind that Canada could not. Thus the alliance still matters to Canada, Europe, and the world, and membership continues to accord with Canadian interests and values. Moreover, NATO has demonstrated that it, unlike the UN, can adapt to new realities.[28]

But if the UN cannot be changed, and that is probably the case, then Canada will have to choose its policy course when the next crisis occurs. Is the choice for Ottawa again to be bound by the Security Council? Or should Canada be guided by the principle that Martin suggests: "In appropriate circumstances, and consistent with our values, when full consensus on the right steps is not possible, we should be prepared to use the means necessary to achieve our international goals."[29] It was this phrase that led Ms. Copps to her attack on Martin and, as Martin is very likely to become prime minister, it is this phrase, heavily qualified as it is, that suggests Canadian foreign policy might break free from the hypocritical UN-multilateralist-anti-American box that Jean Chrétien has constructed. Martin's suggestion was for the leaders of the 20 most important states "to help set the global agenda and to get working on important issues of global concern." This new G-20 might work and might point the way to "a world where nations, not multilateral institutions, set the agenda."[30] A new G-20 sounds suspiciously like yet another multilateral institution, but, even if it does work, the United States, the G-l of the world, will unquestionably continue to set the agenda within which Canadians must operate.

For or Against: There's Little In-Between

Certainly for the foreseeable future, the aftershocks of 9/11 are shaping Americans' view of the world and their relationship with Canada. A war against terror and the states that sponsor it is at the top of the US agenda, sharing space with homeland security. To the US administration, righteous in its determination to smash the Islamic terrorists and their state sponsors, nations are either with Washington or against it, the United States' own borders cannot be porous, and security trumps trade and everything else. The vengeful single-mindedness with which the Bush administration approaches its tasks worries many.

Perhaps that helps explain why in Canada, the horror of 9/11 quickly dissipated. Many Canadians, including the prime minister and others in government, apportioned some of the blame for the attacks on the gap between rich and poor nations or on US policies. A few academics and journalists did not even wait for a week to pass. The unholy glee at US casualties and discomfiture did not go unnoticed in the United States; neither did the stupid comments of the prime minister's press secretary, at least one of his ministers, and far too many members of his parliamentary caucus as the US began to mobilize support for the war against Saddam Hussein's Iraq.[31] These Canadians and their friends did very serious damage to Canada's relations with the White House and State Department, and the prime minister's belated, insincere efforts to discipline them worsened the problem, as did his gratuitous comments at the end of May 2003 on President Bush's budget deficit. This problem of loose lips was manageable; that it caused the harm it did provides an example of the quality of leadership the prime minister delivered and the wretched example he set.

Thus, when Canada chose to elevate the processes of multilateralism to the status of a national interest by declaring that its position on war in Iraq would be determined by the Security Council's decision, whatever it might be, the Americans were furious. The French and the Russians shaped their position of opposition to the US on the basis of their own definitions of national interests. Canada, however, decided its stand on the basis of process in a bogged-down Security Council and refused to participate in, or lend political support to, the war. Foreign Minister Bill Graham put it this way on April 15, 2003:

> We would have preferred being able to agree with our close friends and allies [the US and UK]. However ... the decision ... must always be consistent with Canada's long-standing values and principles: in this case the recognition that the use of force must always be the last resort of states and our commitment to working through multilateral institutions to resolve questions of peace and security.[32]

Significantly, only values and process, not national interests, figured in his and his government's thinking.

Relations between the Chrétien government and the Bush administration soon reached a low point that had not been equalled since the Kennedy-Diefenbaker era four decades before. The government bobbed and weaved in its policy toward the coming war; while the prime minister seemed to be exquisitely concerned with opinion polls. In Quebec, public opinion was very cool toward supporting the war, with the numbers opposed running at least 20 per cent higher than in English Canada. This mattered, in particular, because of the coincidence of the provincial election campaign in Quebec. Voters there (and viewers at 24 Sussex Drive) saw all three party leaders sport antiwar ribbons during their televised debate. The way Quebec attitudes appeared to determine Canada's course disturbed many. Alberta's Ted Morton notes: "As the Iraqi war reminded us, Canadian foreign policy is set by public opinion in Quebec, which has meant abandoning our historical allies."[33]

Former prime minister Brian Mulroney pointed out in 2002 that in the US, "The president energizes the process, so when word goes out that the president ... likes and admires [the prime minister] and wants a file to be given the highest priority – that goes right through the system."[34] The reverse is presumably also true, and President Bush has been turning visits to his Texas ranch into public declarations of his pleasure – and displeasure.[35] Prime Minister Chrétien was noticeably not invited.

Curiously, Canada did not seem to have been seriously punished for its refusal to follow Washington's lead on Iraq, probably because the Americans recognized that Chrétien would soon be gone and a new regime likely had to be interested in restoring relations.[36] Also Canada was not on the UN Security Council during the Iraq war debates, and thus its opposition was somewhat less visible than that of the French, Germans, Mexicans, and others. President Bush cancelled a visit to Ottawa scheduled for May 2003 and pointedly refused to reschedule it, the US ambassador spoke out about his government's disappointment, and industry leaders in Canada gave vent to their fears for the future of the economic relationship.

Special Treatment

What the Iraq crisis highlighted was the question of whether Canada would continue to receive the special treatment from the US administration that Canadians have long taken for granted. Allan Gotlieb, former ambassador to Washington, noted that there are "101 ways we ask the Americans to take into account our special situation as their largest trading partner, chief energy exporter, reliable defence partner and so on." After the Iraq war, would such consideration continue from the administration of a US president not known for his forgiving nature? Would the "absence of goodwill ... affect the willingness in Washington to make a special effort to take Canada's unique circumstances into account?"[37]

If it does, Canadians are in trouble because Canada needs that special effort. After 9/11, the long delays in clearing traffic through border points had a brief but substantial impact on Canadian manufacturers. If there are future terrorist attacks (or even the threat of attacks), the impact next time might not be so manageable, particularly for vulnerable industries dependent on just-in-time inventory management or perishable goods. Canada fortunately has secured exemptions for Canadian citizens from the pending tough American immigration and customs procedures, but it could not get similar treatment for landed immigrants, a matter of substantial concern for many corporations and tens of thousands of individuals. With some 220 million border crossings each year, with airline security lineups increasing, and with border controls tightening for both goods and people, doing business in North America, on which Canada's economy depends, becomes riskier every. Yet, the Canadian government gambled and allowed the Iraq war to threaten the relationship, a decision that made no sense on any calculation of the national interest. A top priority for Canada must be to protect its economic links with the US and that is the case no matter who fills the presidency. That the US fought the war in Iraq to topple a monstrous dictatorship and liberate a people similarly suggests that participation would have served Canada's national interests in protecting freedom and democracy.

Canadians also should remind themselves of the US's present conviction that security is more important than trade. After 9/11, no American government could survive without placing the country's homeland and global security interests first. This has led the US into wars in Afghanistan and Iraq and into major strategic reassessments. The Pentagon is shifting bases, transforming the military into a lighter, faster host, reevaluating alliances, and spending vast sums to ensure that the United States can be as secure as possible in an era of terrorism. Canada has been obliged in its own interest and in the interest of its relations with Washington to step up security. The immigration and refugee systems have been tightened at last, the Canadian Security Intelligence Service has received a major increase in funding and personnel, and the government has put much time into creating a smart, secure border. All this is to the good, and Canadians now must consider if their interests dictate that they go further. A security perimeter around North America – with Canada inside the tent – will likely become essential if terrorism is not smashed soon. Those who argue for the Big Idea, a major and comprehensive economic and security package with the US, make precisely this point and push it even further. Canada faces hard choices, and the decisions must be based on Canada's interests.

Defence Spending in Self-Defence

The one area since 9/11 where Canada has still done far too little is defence.[38] The Canadian Forces received an $800 million increase in the February 2003 budget, but the CF's needs for new equipment and more personnel are staggering. Much more money will be necessary to rebuild the military to a level that meets Canadian requirements. Canadians want to play a role in the world, and they want their soldiers to be able to make and keep the peace. Increasingly, they also seem to recognize that rebuilding the CF is essential. On a high-tech battlefield, in a world of smart bombs and global positioning systems (GPS), however, the budgetary demands can be endless. A full-scale defence review, followed by a white paper completed before the end of 2004, is vitally necessary to point to the areas where Canada wants to play its part. That review must recognize that what we now call peacemaking is, in fact, what used to be called war. A robust military is a necessity, and ideally it would to be structured to operate abroad on a variety of missions (with or without the participation of the United States), as well as at home. To maximize Canada's military resources, the CF must be made as interoperable as possible with the forces of the US and other friendly nations.[39] The Canadian navy, for example, built its frigates in the 1980s and 1990s to work seamlessly with the ships of the United States navy in the antisubmarine warfare that was then one of the navy's main roles. As it turned out, the Soviet submarine threat largely disappeared with the end of the Cold War, but the frigates' interoperability enabled the Canadian navy to work with its US counterpart around the world and, indeed, participate in and command task forces. Interoperability expands the nation's ability to project power and lets Canada enhance its military capacities, not least because the necessary and expensive research and development have often been done elsewhere. The CF's ability to work with friendly states, however, is threatened by the government's failure to acquire up-to-date equipment for the armed forces and its continuing reluctance to solidify and deepen the military relationship with the US.

This is evident in the continuing debate over Canadian participation with the United States in its ballistic missile defence (BMD) system.

The Bush administration is pressing ahead with this program, which is not yet functioning effectively. It is designed to protect North America against small-scale missile attacks from rogue states like North Korea or against accidental missile launches from states like China or Russia. Although the odds of such attacks are long today, they might not be tomorrow, and Canada has as much to gain from a moderate, land-based missile defence system as the US. For this reason, the government announced on May 29, 2003, its decision to begin discussions with the US on possible Canadian participation in BMD.

There is, however, continuing opposition to BMD in the government and in the Liberal caucus and much fear of the so-called weaponization of space and of an escalation in American preemptive attacks and aggressiveness if the US is protected against incoming missiles. This is a short-sighted position that once again threatens the national interest in maintaining a close defence relationship with the United States. It is, in fact, a classic instance of anti-Americanism affecting policy. Many elected Liberals, government officials, and media commentators view the world through anti-American lenses and see cooperation as a diminution of Canada's sovereignty, overlooking the fact that cooperation can serve the national interest and, by getting Canada a share, however small, in the decision making, enhance sovereignty.[40] Certainly, the government's early reluctance to work with the US on BMD guaranteed that Canadian interests were not considered in working out the basing and command-and-control arrangements. "Indecision about participation in the program," says Dwight Mason, a former US chair of the Permanent Joint Board on Defence, "has deprived Canada of influence on the system's design and architecture especially as it may or could affect the defence of Canada."[41] BMD will affect Canada whatever we do, and a refusal to participate can only diminish the country's sovereignty.

The impact of a rejection of wholehearted cooperation in BMD could also lead to the complete marginalization or even the winding-up of the North American Aerospace Defense Command (NORAD), the Canada-US military arrangement that has given Canada its present disproportionate voice in continental defence for almost a half-century.[42] The present NORAD agreement expires in 2006. At a minimum, non-participation in BMD would mean that Canadians in NORAD could no longer participate in much of the warning-and-threat assessment process. It might also cut off the flow of space surveillance data Canada now receives. This would diminish Canadian influence in continental defence and increase Canadian difficulties in defending our airspace. But if Canada joins in BMD and if NORAD controls this – to be fair, something less than likely – Canada's influence actually stands to increase as it expands its right to consultation, participation, and decision-making. This is one decision that demands the application of a national interest calculus.[43]

In addition, as one Canadian expert, James Fergusson, puts it: "Missile defence is designed to protect a nation's citizens, and the fundamental role of a democratic government is to provide protection to its citizens."[44] Long-serving diplomat David Malone added: "If Canada wishes to engage seriously with the US on geo-strategic matters, it will need to come to grips with the reality of American attachment to ballistic missile defence as the future cornerstone to continental defence." It makes no sense, he writes, "for Canada to define its defence policy in out-dated and increasingly irrelevant terms."[45] Canada must cease moralizing over things it cannot change and buy into BMD as quickly and completely as possible. The nation's interests demand nothing less.

Getting to Win

Pollster Michael Marzolini recently observed that Canada has a "strange" relationship with the US.

> Unqualified support for everything [the US does] diminishes us in our own eyes. Yet we are their friends, and we owe much of our standard of living, as well as our safety, to our proximity and relationship.[46]

Opinion polls, he added correctly, demonstrate that Canadians realize this. Still, anti-Americanism is as strong today in Canadian public life, academe, and the media as it has been in the last half-century, so much so that it sometimes seems to have become a core value for many politicians and commentators. Anti-Americanism, however, is mean-spirited and openly based on an unhealthy mix of fear and envy. Moreover, it is clearly against the national interest.

It is time for Canadians to recognize that there is no shame in agreeing with the United States when its actions accord with our national interests and in working to advance those interests with Americans. Sovereignty is not necessarily lost by cooperation, and it can even be advanced by it. Nor is there any reason to resist US policies for the sake of opposition. We can disagree with George W. Bush's Washington, but we must pick our spots. On most issues, Canada can be as vocal as it chooses, slanging the Americans upside and down. Americans argue among themselves, too, and they will not be offended. Canadians can also posit their distinct views on global issues, and Deputy Prime Minister John Manley is correct in saying:

> The world needs a middle power like Canada that brings a point of view to the world that is rooted in North America, but which is independent from the United States.[47]

Since the terrorist attacks of September 11, 2001, Americans believe that their vital interests are at stake and their security is gravely threatened. Canadians should have sense enough to be very cautious in challenging Washington on global or continental security questions. Ottawa must recognize that Washington is both a target for the world's resentments and a superpower with global concerns vastly different from those of our small, weak nation. The events of 9/11 changed the US. The Canadian government and people have not yet grasped the fact that security now supersedes every other issue in Washington. This new reality obliges us to improve the ways in which we deal with the US. Canadian governments simply must recognize that their American policies, particularly those involving security, require much greater coordination.

Other issues come into play along the border as well. Decriminalizing marijuana use, for example, may well be sensible policy if looked at on its own, an easy way to differentiate Canada from the US. But does it make any sense if it angers the White House and the US drug czar? Or if it leads to serious consequences along the border that affect the trade on which we depend and the flow of business and individual travel? This does not mean that Canada should refrain from moving on marijuana, nor does it mean that Canada must slavishly harmonize all its policies with those of the United States. It does, however, suggest that prioritizing issues is essential. And if the Canadian government decides to proceed with a particular measure that it knows will anger Washington, it should do so only with a full understanding of the consequences and a willingness to pay the costs involved. Hope is not a policy.

Whether the nation chooses to move toward the Big Idea, the Canadian government desperately needs to come to grips with Canada's US problem. In the first days of his tenure, the incoming prime minister must make the relationship his major foreign policy priority, work to repair the harm done by the Chrétien government, and ensure that his ministers and backbenchers stay on message. He must also push departments to overcome their turf concerns and to cooperate in managing the Canada-US file, at least on the most critical issues. As well, he has to consider whether Canada requires a homeland security department to be able to cooperate more closely with Homeland Security Chief Tom Ridge's huge new department in Washington. He should consider naming a deputy-minister-level ambassador to the US, with full access to the prime minister and cabinet. Also needed are a powerful cabinet committee on relations with the US, chaired by the prime minister or the deputy prime minister,[48] and a mirror committee of deputy ministers, chaired by a deputy secretary to the cabinet, responsible for foreign and defence policy. Such steps can be taken in the first month a new leader is in office.

The government also needs a small national security council, operating under the privy council office and with close links to experts outside government, to deliver advice on security, broadly framed and interpreted, to the prime minister and cabinet. The creation of such a council should be a goal of the new prime minister's first year in office. At the same time, the Department of Foreign Affairs and International Trade should assign an associate deputy minister to manage the US relationship.

Also, the government must provide the funds needed to increase staff at the Embassy in Washington, where the present Canadian complement of 50 is insufficient. We must have our ablest diplomats in Washington lobbying Congress and the administration and working to further the country's vital interests. After budget cuts in the 1990s, Canadian consulates and offices in the US dropped from 19 in 1994 to a paltry 14 today, and Canadian staff in the US dropped from 146 to 108. This was false economy. Canada has to raise its representation in the US (particularly in the south, southwest, and west where population and power are shifting), so that it has early-warning eyes and ears and trade promotion offices in every major city, region, and sub-region of the country. The budget of February 2003 allocated just $11 million over two years for five to seven new consulates in the US and in September, the government announced it would create seven, a good start. A useful stop-gap measure would be to name honorary consuls from expatriate, well-connected Canadians where Ottawa has no representation. Mexico, by comparison, has 63 consulates and offices in the US. By the time the new prime minister is ready to call an election, these changes should be in place.

Moreover, Canadians should realize that the United States is so huge and diverse that the one hand in Washington does not always know what the other five fingers in Iowa, Maine, Pennsylvania, Oregon, and North Dakota are doing. If the US puts a higher tariff on wheat or softwood lumber, the White House may not be directly involved. Under the US system, interest groups like North Dakota's wheat farmers or the Pacific northwest's timber producers can raise trade issues, garner congressional support, and all but oblige the US trade representative and the commerce department to take action. This will always cause Canada problems, no matter how close the bilateral relationship becomes.

When the White House takes an active part in a trade dispute, as it may when the administration wants to send a shot across Canada's bow, then we can be in for trouble. However, if Ottawa can get its substantially smaller act together and properly coordinate its dealings with the US, we might be able to take fuller advantage of the cracks and fissures in the American body politic. Proper planning on how best to deal with the US should be a Canadian core value; certainly it is in our national interest. It is also inescapably true that broader strategic interests – the war in Iraq, for example – can affect trade. Canadians need to keep that fact in mind and, moreover, understand that it is up to them, not the Americans, to maintain good relations.

Small states have always formed coalitions of the weak to try to hobble great powers. "Let's be honest with ourselves," says Gordon Smith, a former deputy minister in Foreign Affairs. Canada's interest in multilateralism

> may have something to do with the fact that our neighbour to the south is much more powerful than us, with the knowledge that Canada is off the screen of political elites in the US and with the belief we do better in negotiations where more players are involved.[49]

Multilateralism can usefully be employed to help constrain the tendency toward unilateral action and protectionism in the United States, and it is in the Canadian interest – and in accord with Canadian values – to work with our friends in international organizations to this end. But Canadians cannot ever again allow their government to put them in the position of opposing for the sake of opposition, as the Chrétien government did over the Iraq war. The multilateral process may be a good in itself, but a close bilateral relationship is an absolute necessity, critical to the national interest. If the choice is between feeling good or eating regularly, Canada must be for nutrition.

Ideally, Canadians ought to be able to feel good and eat regularly, for multilateralism and bilateralism can usually exist in something close to harmony. This will certainly be true on most international issues, and Canadians must work to keep the tracks running parallel. When divergences occur, as they certainly will, Canada has to choose, and on major security issues the choice must be for bilateralism. The nation mistook its loudly professed values for its interests and kicked sand in President Bush's face over Iraq. In response, Ambassador Cellucci sent a message, and Canadians, their economy dependent on the colossus to the south, should listen to it. Perhaps we did, thus explaining the government's eager willingness to assist in the rebuilding of Saddam's destroyed state and to negotiate on President Bush's plan for BMD – a "full grovel," as columnist Richard Gwyn calls it.[50] Even so, it would have been better if we had not tried to have our bilateral cake while supping so intemperately at the multilateralists' table.

If Canada carefully assesses its national interests and weighs them in relation to its values, the nation should be able to chart its course for the future. We have muddled through long enough, too often neglecting our interests, too frequently mistaking transitory values for permanent national goals. The United States will always be with us and getting on with the Americans must be on our minds at all times.[51] If we wish to survive and prosper as a nation, we must come to terms with this inescapable fact. If a comprehensive economic and security arrangement is required as a means to the goals of survival and prosperity, then so be it.

Above all, Canada must have a plan, a long-range foreign policy strategy, and it must be based on what matters most to Canadians – their national interests. Allan Gotlieb, one of the few Canadian practitioners to speak and write in this vein, describes the need clearly: "If the foreign policy of a state is not based on its national interest, it can become arbitrary, quixotic or even a personal indulgence of its leader."[52] Canada has had too much of that type of unplanned, ill-thought out policy, so much so that today we verge on becoming a noncountry with a nonmilitary and a non-foreign policy – "invisible" and "irrelevant," as the *Toronto Star's* Gwyn writes.[53]

Canadians sometimes act as if they believe they are immune from the ills of the world. Some Americans may believe they constitute a new Rome, but most now realize that there are still barbarians out there who may yet sweep down on the imperium. Even Margaret Atwood, a true-believing nationalist always deeply skeptical of the Americans, says: "We know perfectly well that if [the US] goes down the plug-hole, we're going with you."[54]

We share a continent, most values, many traditions, and much history. Ultimately, we share our bed with the Americans. After all, we Canadians helped make this bed, we lie in it, and we need to face up at last to the reality of our situation. Moral earnestness and the loud preaching of our values will not suffice to protect us in this new century. We have to put interests ahead of values, hard-headedness before wishful thinking. The alternative is too self-destructive to contemplate.

The Importance of Being Less Earnest 147

NOTES

1 J.L. Granatstein, *Yankee Go Home? Canadians and Anti-Americanism* (Toronto: Harper Collins), 132–3.
2 "I make it my policy [not to do what the Americans want]," Prime Minister Chrétien was overheard saying to other leaders at a summit of the North Atlantic Treaty Organisation (NATO) in Madrid in July 1997. "It's popular." Hampson and Molot call the comment "ill- publicized." See Fen O. Hampson and Maureen Molot, "The New 'Can-Do' Foreign Policy," in *Leadership and Dialogue: Canada among Nations 1998*, ed. Fen O. Hampson and Maureen Molot (Don Mills, Ont.: Oxford University Press, 1998), 12.
3 Franklin D. Roosevelt and William Lyon Mackenzie King, *The United States and Canada: Reciprocity in Defence: Declaration by the President of the United States at Queen's University, Kingston, Ontario, August 18, 1938, and Acknowledgment and Reply by the Prime Minister of Canada, in a Speech at Woodbridge, Ontario, August 20, 1938* (Ottawa: King's Printer, 1939), 4.
4 Ibid., 7.
5 Norman Hillmer and J.L. Granatstein, *Empire to Umpire: Canada and the World to the 1990s* (Toronto: Copp Clark Longman, 1994), 134.
6 It is worth noting, in addition, that 82 per cent of Canadian goods and services exports go south and that Canada receives 72 per cent of its merchandise imports and 70 per cent of its goods and services imports from the US. Canada, Department of Foreign Affairs and International Trade, "A Dialogue on Foreign Policy," January 22, 2003 (accessed May 2003), table 1c.
7 Sir Robert Borden said that "the 'national' interests of Canada and the 'imperial' interests of Canada during the Great War were demonstrably the same." Quoted in Robert Craig Brown, "Sir Robert Borden, the Great War, and Anglo-Canadian Relations," in *Towards a New World*, ed. J.L. Granatstein (Toronto: Copp Clark, 1992), 44. I am indebted to Norman Hillmer for reminding me of this remark.
8 Robert Bothwell et al., *Canada since 1945: Power, Politics and Provincialism* (Toronto: University of Toronto Press, 1981), 105–6.
9 See Allan Gotlieb, "Foremost Partner: The Conduct of Canada-US Relations," in *Coping with the American Colossus: Canada among Nations 2003*, ed. David Carment et al. (Don Mills, Ont.: Oxford University Press).
10 *Canada in the World* named three objectives: prosperity, protection of security, and projection of values and culture abroad. Canada, Department of Foreign Affairs and International Trade, *Canada in the World* (accessed May 2003).
11 Paul Martin, whom Graham supported for Liberal leader and prime minister, also places Canadian values – freedom, tolerance, mutual respect,

democracy, and pluralism – first. But in his opening leadership campaign address on foreign policy, he did say, unlike Graham: "We have our interests, too." Paul Martin, "Canada's Role in a Complex World" (address to the Canadian Newspaper Association, Toronto, April 30, 2003). Curiously, as I discovered after drafting this address, both Kim Nossal and Denis Stairs, Canada's two leading foreign policy scholars, have articles on the need for clarity in Canadian interests appearing in late 2003. That senior scholars have such articles coming out surely indicates a switch in attention toward Canadian interests.

12 Canada, *A Dialogue on Foreign Policy* (Ottawa: Department of Foreign Affairs and International Trade, 2003), 13.
13 Ibid., 14.
14 Ibid., 3.
15 We don't provide such support, suggests one recent and authoritative US study. In 2003, the Center for Global Development in Washington and the journal *Foreign Policy* ranked the 21 richest nations on how their aid, trade, migration, investment, peacekeeping, and environmental policies help or hurt poor nations. Canada ranked 18th, well down in every category except trade and migration.
16 Hector Mackenzie, "Canada's Vital Interests in International Affairs," *bout de papier* 19 (2003): 6.
17 James H. Taylor, "Canadian Foreign Policy and National Interests" (discussion paper for Canadian Institute of International Affairs Foreign Policy Consultations, Ottawa, April 14–15, 1999), 7.
18 Support for peacekeeping – and peacemaking – in public opinion generally remained high even through the military difficulties of the 1990s. See Pierre Martin and Michel Fortmann, "Support for International Involvement in Canadian Public Opinion after the Cold War," *Canadian Military Journal* 2 (Autumn 2001): 46ff.
19 This is the main argument in Sean Maloney, *Canada and UN Peacekeeping: Cold War by Other Means, 1945–1970* (St. Catharines, Ont.: Vanwell, 2002).
20 See Fen O. Hampson and Dean Oliver, "Pulpit Diplomacy," *International Journal* 53 (Summer 1998).
21 Paul Heinbecker, "Human Security: The Hard Edge," *Canadian Military Journal* 1 (Spring 2000): 12.
22 Prime Minister Chrétien did not grasp this point. At the end of May 2003, he pledged troops for any new peacekeeping force set up to protect a Palestine-Israel peace. "We will be able to help if we are needed," he said. "There is no doubt about it." Chrétien added: "Peacekeeping has always been the No. 1 priority for Canada. We are able to send troops at short notice and can move faster than others." The very same day, however, the incoming Chief of the Land Staff, General Rick Hillier, said he doubted

troops could be found for such an operation. The troops, the general said, were stressed and "at the top end of our capability." Hillier was right, Chrétien wrong. Robert Fife, "PM Offers to Send Troops to Mideast," *National Post*, May 31, 2003. By mid-June, Foreign Minister Bill Graham had concluded Canada should not despatch troops to the region.

23 Awareness of the specifics of Canadian peacekeeping, however, is not high. In the Canada Day poll taken by Dominion Institute/Ipsos Reid on July 1, 2003, three in 10 Canadians could not name a single operation Canada participated in during the 1990s, and another three in 10 could name only one.

24 Shawn McCarthy, "Copps Rips Martin on Star Wars," *Globe and Mail*, May 5, 2003.

25 Martin, "Canada's Role in a Complex World."

26 When John Manley was a candidate for the Liberal Party leadership, he made UN reform a central part of his foreign policy proposals. "This is no time to shirk our global responsibilities," he titled an article in the *Ottawa Citizen* (May 27, 2003).

27 The 12-month CF commitment to Afghanistan in 2003–4 has been estimated by the Conference of Defence Associations to cost "upwards of $900 million" – or more than the budget increase of $800 million given the military in February 2003 (e-mail from executive director, CDA, June 16, 2003).

28 The European Union sent its EUFOR military force on its first mission to Macedonia on March 31, 2003, significantly replacing a NATO force. The implications of an EU rapid-reaction force could make NATO redundant or, at a minimum, significantly affect what remains of Canada's position in NATO.

29 Martin, "Canada's Role in a Complex World."

30 Ibid.

31 "Canadians should remember that, presumably to their surprise, there are many in the US government who carefully register their words and the messages and attitudes behind them. It is a brutish political reality that systematic, open disrespect by a small weak state for a large and powerful state rarely ends to the benefit of the former." David T. Jones, "Yo, Canada! A Wake-Up Call for Y'all Up There," *Policy Options* 24 (February 2003): 48. Jones was political minister-counsellor at the US embassy in Ottawa from 1992 to 1996. For an informed (if self-serving) Canadian view, see Brian Mulroney, "Smile When You Say No to the US," *Globe and Mail*, May 15, 2003.

32 William Graham, "Notes for an Address by the Hon. Bill Graham, Minister of Foreign Affairs, to the Canadian Club on Sovereignty, Interdependence and Canada-US Relations," Vancouver, April 15, 2003.

33 Ted Morton, "Triple-E – or Else," *National Post*, May 22, 2003. In some polls before the start of fighting, more than 83 per cent of Canadians opposed

war with Iraq without UN approval and 23.5 per cent opposed Canadian military action in any circumstances. In Quebec, where all the leaders fighting a provincial election were antiwar, 50 per cent of the population opposed war with or without a UN vote. Joseph Brean, "UN Approval Key to Canadian Support for War," *National Post*, March 10, 2003. When asked in an Ipsos-Reid poll in June 2003 if Canada was justified in not supporting the US in the Iraq War, 11 per cent of respondents in Quebec, but 52 per cent in Alberta, said no, a huge and almost unparalleled difference. Kim Lunman, "Majority Supports Chrétien on Iraq, Poll Finds," *Globe and Mail*, June 16, 2003.

34 Robert Fife, "Former PM Deflects Pressure to Lead Tories," *National Post*, November 19, 2002.
35 British Prime Minister Tony Blair said that he genuinely trusted President Bush and that was "important." He added, "When you go through something like [the Iraq war], you really find out whether you can or can't trust somebody. Don't ask me to go through all the world leaders and rate them on scores of 1-to-10." David Margolick, "Blair's Big Gamble," *Vanity Fair* 514 (June 2003), 227. How Canada's leader is rated by Blair or Bush would be interesting to discover.
36 Defence Minister John McCallum did talk of a chill in the North American Air Defense Command (NORAD) and in the provision of intelligence from US sources. Daniel Leblanc, "McCallum Tells of Chill from NORAD," *Globe and Mail*, May 31, 2003.
37 Allan Gotlieb, "The Chrétien Doctrine," *Maclean's*, March 31, 2003, 43.
38 Dan Middlemiss's assessment is particularly bleak: "Canada has long abandoned any pretence of robust self-defence, and has given but token acknowledgement to the military defence of its sovereignty at home ... Canada is wholly dependent on the United States for its physical protection, and has largely taken on the trappings of a vassal state." Dan Middlemiss, "A Military in Support of Canadian Foreign Policy: Some Fundamental Considerations" (paper prepared for the Canadian Defence and Foreign Affairs Institute, May 2003).
39 The best source on this subject is Ann L. Griffiths, ed., *The Canadian Forces and Interoperability: Panacea or Perdition* (Halifax: Centre for Foreign Policy Studies, Dalhousie University, 2002). For a perfect example of confusing values with national interests, see Byers' arguments against closer military relations with the US because, among other things, Canadian service personnel's rights might be affected if they are francophone, gay or lesbian, or female because the US military regulations differ from the Canadian. Whether it is in Canada's interest to have closer military relations or not, our values in these areas should not affect the decision. Michael Byers,

"Canadian Armed Forces under United States Command," *International Journal* 58 (Winter 2003): 101ff.

40 "The new missile program is part of a dream long-nurtured in far-right Republican circles – the dream of fighting and winning a nuclear war," or so said Linda McQuaig, in one of the most foolish comments during the debate on BMD. Linda McQuaig, "Why Help the US Create a System That Will Eventually Lead to the Unthinkable: A Nuclear Attack on a 'Rogue' Country," *Toronto Star*, May 11, 2003. Delay in joining in on BMD will ensure that no contracts for development are let in Canada. See Simon Tuck, "Missile Defence Decision Urged Soon," *Globe and Mail*, May 12, 2003.

41 Dwight Mason, "Canada and Missile Defense," *Hemisphere Focus* 11 (June 2003): 2.

42 Fergusson notes that NORAD operational costs are 90 per cent borne by the US and that capital costs in the US were 100 per cent carried by the US; in Canada, historically two-thirds were paid by the US. James Fergusson, "Canadian Defence and the Canada-US Strategic Partnership: The Aerospace Dimension" (paper presented to Canadian Defence and Foreign Affairs Institute seminar, Ottawa, September 2002).

43 See the most recent Department of Foreign Affairs and International Trade paper: "Canada and Ballistic Missile Defence," May 8, 2003 (accessed May 2003), as well as W.D. Macnamara and Ann Fitz-Gerald, "A National Security Framework for Canada," *Policy Matters* (Institute for Research on Public Policy) 3 (October 2002): esp. 10ff. Brian Mulroney suggested in May 2003 that it was too late for Canada to matter on BMD: "I don't think the Americans much care ... They're going to do this anyway. Canada's role is now peripheral." Quoted in John Ibbitson, "It's Time for Healing," *Globe and Mail*, May 12, 2003.

44 Fergusson, "Canadian Defence and the Canada-US Strategic Partnership," 7. Defence Minister John McCallum echoed this comment in announcing the Canadian decision to negotiate participation in BMD: "A sovereign government should not wash its hands of the protection of its own citizens." Quoted in Jonathan Fowlie, "Canada to Start Missile Defence Talks with US," *Globe and Mail*, May 29, 2003.

45 David Malone, "Canadian Foreign Policy Post-9/11: Institutional and Other Challenges" (paper prepared for the Canadian Defence and Foreign Affairs Institute, May 2003), 15.

46 Michael Marzolini, "Canadian-US Relations" (address delivered to the Economic Club, Toronto, March 25, 2003).

47 Steven Edwards, "US View Not Only One, Manley Tells Americans," *National Post*, June 27, 2003.

48 This idea has been endorsed by Paul Martin and by Allan Gotlieb. See especially Allan Gotlieb, "The Paramountcy of Canada-US relations," *National Post*, May 22, 2003.
49 Gordon S. Smith, "The New World Order: Staking Out Canada's Interests" (address to APEX, Ottawa, June 5, 2002).
50 Richard Gwyn, "Get Ready for the Full Grovel," *Toronto Star*, April 6, 2003.
51 And when Canada disagrees with the US? I have come to favour the "quiet diplomacy" approach advocated in 1965 by long-time bureaucrat and diplomat Arnold Heeney. "It is in the abiding interest of both [Canada and the US] that, wherever possible, divergent views ... should be expressed and if possible resolved in private, through diplomatic channels." Arnold Heeney, *The Things That Are Caesar's: The Memoirs of a Canadian Public Servant* (Toronto: University of Toronto Press, 1972), 189ff.
52 Gotlieb, "The Chrétien Doctrine," 42.
53 Richard Gwyn, "Our Foreign Policy Making Us Invisible," *Toronto Star*, February 23, 2003.
54 Margaret Atwood, "A Letter to America," *Globe and Mail*, March 28, 2003.

SECTION TWO

Canada and Britain

Chapter Seven

The Anglocentrism of Canadian Diplomacy

In a book published in 1948, one of Canada's most honoured and senior diplomats and citizens expatiated on the ties that bound Canada and Great Britain and on the ways that being part of the British Commonwealth and Empire enhanced Canadian status and power.

> There are good reasons why the Commonwealth is of importance to us in our national life; important both in our relations abroad and in our domestic affairs. For one thing, we have greater influence in the world as a member of the British family than would otherwise be ours. Membership gives us in a sense a double status. It provides one of the rare instances in which one can "eat one's cake and have it too." I feel sure from my own experience that the fact that Canada appears on the international scene, not only as an important country on her own account, but also as a member of a great world association, lends her enhanced prestige. In the international world, prestige means influence.

And at home? Surely there the British and Commonwealth connection weakened the chances for the development of a distinctive Canadian nationalism. Not so, said the diplomat.

> In Canada we have certain institutions and traditions and characteristics which give us, whatever language we speak, our meaning as a separate country. Without the British connection these things would steadily evaporate and we should have less and less significance as an individual state. How long would a Canadian republic maintain its individuality here in North America? The forms of our sovereignty might be retained, but we should be caught inexorably by the southward undertow and completely assimilated to American life. It is thus true to say that the British connection is essential to Canadian independence; we are the more Canadian for being British.

What then of Britain's role as an imperial power? Did this not tarnish Canada's good name by association? Again, our diplomat argued that this was spurious reasoning.

> The British Commonwealth and Empire today represents the most impressive effort to extend personal liberty and promote human welfare in the world. This may sound like a rhetorical exaggeration; it is nothing but the truth ...
>
> The march towards self government is Empire-wide. It is important to think about the subject in *contemporary* terms. No empire ever showed less "imperialism" than does the British Empire today ...
>
> It is, for instance, a sad fact that a country which above all others has always shown hospitality and tolerance to persons of Jewish race, and does so today on a generous scale, should as a result of her commitments in Palestine be bitterly attacked as hostile to the cause of Jewry.

Finally, our diplomat noted that "Our links with Great Britain are imponderable. They belong to the realm of things of the spirit; those subtle habits of mind we have in common and which elude definition. It is commonly said that such bonds are stronger than material ties; so they are ..."[1]

Vincent Massey, the author of those sentiments, had been the first Canadian minister to the United States and high commissioner in Great Britain from 1935 to 1946. It did not matter that he was almost a caricature of the Canadian anglophile, a man who made even the British elite feel unspeakably colonial. Nor did it matter if Massey's conception was of a Canada so weak and unsure of itself – notwithstanding a massive war effort from 1939 to 1945 and billions of dollars in aid to Britain during and after the war – that only the British connection, even then palpably weakening, could keep Canadians from the American maw (into which, arguably, they had by 1948 already slipped). Massey believed that Canada's Britishness was a positive and attractive force to French Canadians and to those others who had made Canada their home and native land. Even though jails in Asia and Africa were filled with political dissidents, he believed that the British empire was everywhere a force for liberty and freedom. There was a wilful blindness in Massey and those who thought like him, an inability and an unwillingness to recognize both what Canada was and the costs imposed on it by its British links. Oh, if only everyone could have attended Upper Canada College!

We can now look back at the Vincent Masseys of those days with a somewhat amused tolerance. The sentiments, not to say sentimentality, of 1948 are so foreign to us thirty-seven years later that they might have been uttered in 1898 (and almost certainly were). But in that postwar period and for a good many years afterward, Massey's sentiments were not dated. That was the way a great many Canadians acted and believed and talked in the clubs of Halifax, Anglo-Montreal, Toronto, and Vancouver. More to the point for this paper, that was what many senior figures in government and diplomacy in Ottawa and abroad believed.

To a substantial extent, such attitudes had been inculcated in Canadian leaders at birth and in the course of schooling. The key English-speaking figures in Canadian government in the years following the Second World War were all men – none was a woman – born in the Victorian or Edwardian eras. They had been raised on Henty stories, had thrilled to tales of the British square and "fuzzy-wuzzies," and had accepted as an article of faith that the sun never set on the British empire. Their schooling had stuffed their heads with British history and offered them very little of that of their own country. And, to single out only the senior figures in the Department of External Affairs from 1948, most had received some university education in England. Lester Pearson and Hume Wrong attended Oxford after their service in the Great War. Norman Robertson, Escott Reid, and Arnold Heeney were Rhodes Scholars and hence, as Reid described it in a 1930 speech to a Rhodes Trust dinner in Oxford, were made up of "smugness, two parts, of brutality, one part, of tact, one part, unctuous rectitude, one part."[2] Outside the foreign service, men such as Louis Rasminsky, A.F.W. Plumptre, R.B. Bryce, and J.W. Pickersgill, all of whom had substantial influence on Canadian foreign policy, were educated at Cambridge, Oxford, or the London School of Economics.

Now it is true that almost all these men returned to Canada far more nationalist in their attitudes than when they had left their native shores.[3] A few years in England seemed to persuade them that, after all, they were not English, that British policy was as selfish as or more so than that of any other nation, and that British chauvinism matched that of any other nation in its virulence. They were not English, they were Canadian. But their attitudes and mannerisms, their style and sensibilities, had been unalterably affected by the experience of living in college. None of them (except, perhaps Plumptre and, to a lesser extent, Reid) retained any trace of a British accent, but all were indelibly marked by their experience abroad.

And when they joined the public service in the years from the late 1920s through the opening years of the Second World War, they joined as scholar-diplomats, men cast in the mould of the imperial service. This showed in their ability to write splendid memoranda, their delight in being able to scribble a witty piece of poesy or an epigram that could poke fun at the foibles of their colleagues, allies, and countrymen, and their inability to administer their department's affairs in an efficient fashion. After their retirement this activity was evident in the production of graceful memoirs that are beautifully crafted but much less critical of their colleagues and less illuminating than they could and should have been.[4]

But like many scholars, the Ottawa men had their blind spots. The men in External Affairs, Finance, the Privy Council and the Prime Minister's Office, and the Bank of Canada somehow forgot about the make-up of the country they were serving so well. Very few among the mandarins were French Canadians – indeed not a single key figure, Jules Léger excepted, in the period to 1957 in the Departments of External Affairs, National Defence, Finance, Trade and Commerce, the Bank of Canada, the Privy Council Office, and the Prime Minister's Office was a Québécois – and there was, in addition, only one Roman Catholic, John Deutsch, whose career included service in the Bank, External Affairs, and Finance, and only one Jew, Louis Rasminsky of the Bank of Canada. Not surprisingly, those two were the only members of the key mandarin group whose ancestry was other than Anglo-Saxon.[5]

The bureaucrats cannot be blamed for their ethnicity (although their political masters might be judged harshly for their shortsightedness). But they can be faulted for failing to consider seriously enough the domestic problems of their country. For example, once the Second World War had been won and the question of conscription had been successfully finessed by Mackenzie King, the problem of Quebec and of French-English relations scarcely crossed an Ottawa mind. Certainly Premier Duplessis was a troublesome figure, and Quebec constantly frustrated efforts to move federal-provincial relations in the desired direction, but Quebec was quiescent, relatively satisfied, and safely under the thumb of the Union Nationale provincially and the Liberals federally. There was no real trouble there, and hence virtually no need to give Quebec and its francophone citizens their proper share of the senior posts in the bureaucracy or a chance to operate in their own language in the public service or in Canada at large. When the Quiet Revolution began in the late 1950s the storm would break and the federal governments of John Diefenbaker, Lester Pearson, and Pierre Trudeau would have to scramble to undo the wrongs of generations. The politicians deserve the lion's share of the blame, but the bureaucracy cannot escape part of it.

The multicultural aspect of Canada was, if possible, even more ignored than the French Canadian. At least many Canadians recognized the dual nature of the country, even if English Canadians were still too prone to state that "we beat them on the Plains of Abraham in 1759" as an answer to every attempt by Quebec to improve its lot. But ethnic Canadians were expected to know and keep their place even more than Quebeckers – after all, they were here on sufferance. The immigration officers plotted how to keep immigrants and refugees out; the bureaucrats worried about communism among Finns, Jews, and Ukrainians, Nazism among Germans, and Fascism among Italians; and the politicians calculated how best to deal with the *padrones* to get the bloc vote. The rest of the time ethnic Canadians were ignored.

Certainly they were ignored in the symbols that were employed by government in Canada. The Union Jack and the Red Ensign had nothing for immigrants and the latter flag had only a few tiny fleur-de-lys for Quebec. "God Save the King" was foreign. "O Canada" – in French or English – had little for newcomers, except reference to "our home and native land" or "terre de nos aieux" which made many feel left out, and endless repetitions of "we stand on guard for thee" which made Canada sound far more warlike and threatened than it was. The monarchy was no more welcoming. In 1961 Vincent Massey told the audience for the Romanes Lecture at the Sheldonian Theatre in Oxford that "new-comers quickly learn to appreciate the meaning of the Monarchy in our national life. On the occasion of royal tours in Canada, touching tributes are always paid to the visitors by members of what are rather inelegantly called ethnic groups."[6] That was Massey's opinion. Mine would be different. For most members of ethnic groups, the monarchy was yet another symbol of not belonging; for the great majority of French Canadians it was a symbol of conquest, for some of oppression, and for almost all of the economic control held by the Anglo-Saxon establishment. Whatever else it was, the monarchy was no symbol of unity for a majority of Canadians; rather it and other "Canadian" symbols were seen as evidence that they did not truly belong in God's Anglo-Saxon country.

Symbols, education, and attitudes are important for they shape the way peoples and governments react. The power of symbols had taken Canada into two world wars in this century, wars in which its territory was not threatened, at least not at the outset of the wars. The potency of symbols had led English Canadians to impose conscription and enforce it, even though French Canadians and many, perhaps most, members of immigrant groups opposed it bitterly. And the strength of symbols to English Canada in two wars and in the opening years of the Cold War almost obliged us to give the British government substantial financial and material aid.

This last point is worth some expansion, if only because of the consequences of this policy for Canada. At the outset of the Great War, the United Kingdom was the richest power in the world, and the mother country had neither hesitation nor difficulty in financing much of Canada's war effort in 1914. But a year later, Britain was beginning to reel under the fiscal strain, and Canada was turned loose to fend for itself. The result was that for the first time federal and provincial governments separately went to the New York market for loans. All Canadians recognize 1867 as a crucial date, and most consider 1931 and the Statute of Westminster vital as well. In a real sense, however, 1915 is more important, for in that first year of war Canada began the route to financial dependence on the United States.

A roughly similar situation soon came to prevail in the area of munitions production. The Imperial Munitions Board, an imperial agency operating in Canada to purchase munitions, had created an impressive industrial capacity. But by 1917 Britain was running out of money to pay for munitions, so huge were the war's expenditures. For some time London had been pressing Canada to pay a greater share of the war costs, but the government of Sir Robert Borden was reluctant. Now in the spring of 1917, the British told Ottawa that they could no longer afford to pay for Canadian goods, including munitions, wheat, and cheese. In effect, the British were saying that if Canada wanted to export to Britain, the Canadian government would have to pay the shot; if not, unemployment and unrest were certain to rise and 1917 was an election year. The only alternatives, as Prime Minister Lloyd George told Borden, "are that we should largely diminish orders placed in Canada or that Canada should make itself mainly responsible for financing these orders. We should be most reluctant to adopt the former course."[7]

In its dire necessity, Britain was blackmailing Canada, and Ottawa had no option but to cave in. But the Borden government insisted that Britain secure for it $15 million a month in American dollars. Why? Because the more Canada exerted itself to help Britain, the greater its trade deficit with the United States. Every shell, every engine, every truck produced in Canada for Britain had its American components, and the effect of the war on the balance of payments was calamitous. The British eventually agreed to try to secure the American dollars. But even that did not resolve all Canada's problems. With the entry of the United States into the war in April 1917, the Wilson government forbade foreign governments to borrow on the New York markets; all the allies, including Canada, had to borrow only from the United States government. Fearing the effect of this on municipal, federal, and provincial governments, Finance Minister Sir Thomas White went to Washington on a pilgrimage to seek exemption from United States rules, and, by pleading the special relationship, he won his point. He also secured the Treasury's agreement to the provision of $15 million each month on the British account – in effect an indirect form of American aid to Canada.

But even this was not the end of American generosity. The Imperial Munitions Board, fearing that the still-strapped British might cut orders in Canada in any case, began to seek contracts in the United States. The IMB, a British agency, began to lobby for American orders for Canadian firms, an arrangement that was formalized by agreement in November 1918. Thus orders stayed up, employment continued, and profits grew. And in February 1918, after he had seen President Wilson, the newly re-elected Robert Borden wrote that Wilson's view was that "the resources of the two countries should be pooled in the most effective co-operation and that the boundary line had little or no significance in considering or dealing with these vital questions."[8]

The point is that Canada – and the Borden government that had fought the 1911 election on the slogan of "No truck or trade with the Yankees" – was forced south by British weakness. And that point was to be repeated again in the Second World War when the Mackenzie King government, finding the deficit with the United States increasing as components and materiel were imported for incorporation into munitions, tanks, and trucks for Britain, was forced to seek aid from the Roosevelt administration The Hyde Park Declaration of April 1941 resolved the problem when the president agreed to purchase increased amounts of raw materials in Canada, thus effectively welding Canada more tightly into the American economic system. A few months earlier, in response to the Allied defeat in France, the defences of the two nations had been combined. Yet again, British military and economic weakness drove Canada south.[9]

And to demonstrate that history does repeat itself (and perhaps also to show that Canadians are incapable of learning from history), in the immediate postwar years Canada again had to seek succour from the United States. This time, with great good will and some calculation, Canada had given Britain credits of $1.25 billion so that it could continue to purchase Canadian goods during the reconstruction period. But with the peace, Canadians were buying substantial quantities of American luxury goods, and the result by late 1947 was another dollar crisis. As in the 1939–45 war, Canada's substantial trade surplus with the United Kingdom could not be used to pay off the United States for the pound sterling remained inconvertible. And the Canadian problem was compounded by the huge loan to Britain.

The only answer was to go to Washington yet again to persuade a reluctant Truman administration to permit funds from the European Recovery Program – the Marshall Plan – to be spent in Canada. In effect, the American taxpayers' dollars would pay Canada for the wheat it shipped to Liverpool. Again the Americans agreed and bailed out Ottawa.[10]

Why was this bailout necessary? Because on three occasions from the Great War to the Cold War Canada had allowed its sentimental anglo-centrism to determine its policy. Each time, the British *in extremis* had shown no reciprocal sentimentality. They were fighting for their lives, and Canada had bloody well better go to Washington for help. And each time Ottawa did so. The irony of Canadian history is that those three major turns to the south effectively bound the Canadian and American economies together, creating by 1950 virtually a single continental market, and one that was not directed from Ottawa. Perhaps there was no alternative. In 1914 Canada was a colony, one with no option other than to go to war when Britain did. In 1939, though nominally independent, Canada again went to war when Britain did and because Britain did, and for no other reason. The postwar aid to Britain was at least based on a conception of Canadian self-interest, a desire to keep employment high in the reconstruction period and a desire to keep a foothold in the British market for Canadian goods. Nonetheless, Anglo-sentimentality had played a major part in turning Canada from a British to an American nation.

Canada's new situation had to change the way the nation tried to operate in the world of the Cold War era. The United States was the world power, immensely rich and strong, occasionally aggressive and rambunctious. The conflict with the Soviet Union affected all of America's allies, and not least Canada, unfortunately situated as it was directly between the two superpowers. And American defence concerns would lead to the creation of the North American Air Defense Command (NORAD) in 1957, an alliance that integrated the air defence systems of the two countries.

But many Canadians seemed slow to realize that Washington was the new locus of action for Canada. This was immediately obvious during the Suez crisis of 1956 when Britain and France slowly and hesitantly mounted an invasion of Egypt in collusion with Israel. The details of the invasion and of the Anglo-French-Israeli discussions that preceded it need not concern us here. Nor does the unfortunate fact that the invasion occurred at precisely the same time as the Soviet Union was brutally suppressing the Hungarian revolution, thus permitting the USSR to escape the full weight of world opinion. What is of interest is the way the Canadian government reacted to the crisis and the way its action was judged by the electorate and the Opposition.

There is no doubt that the Canadian government knew through military channels that Britain had determined on a resort to force, and it knew this as early as August 1956.[11] There is similarly no doubt that the Canadian government was not consulted by Britain before the Anglo-French ultimata, air attack, and seaborne invasion that took place at the end of October and the beginning of November 1956. Neither was the American government, then in the last days of a presidential election campaign.

But what was the response of Prime Minister Louis St. Laurent, Secretary of State for External Affairs L.B. Pearson, and the foreign service? The initial Canadian reaction came in a trans-Atlantic message from Pearson to Norman Robertson, the high commissioner in London. Pearson told his friend that he was "to express to the United Kingdom Government our feeling of bewilderment and dismay at the decision which they may have taken ..."[12] That was conveyed and, after Eden had sent a dissembling telegram to St. Laurent justifying Britain's course of action, so was a chilling message from the Canadian prime minister. Without more information, St. Laurent said, "we cannot come to the conclusion that the penetration of its [Israel's] troops into Egypt was justified or that the probable resistance of the Egyptians necessitated the decision of the UK and France to post forces in the canal zone." Canadians, St. Laurent added, "will endeavour to shape our course in conformity with what we regard as our obligations under the Charter of and our membership in the United Nations."[13] If Eden anticipated a "ready, aye ready" response from Ottawa, he was sorely mistaken. But cold as it was, St. Laurent's message was not as harsh as it might have been. Even so, the tone of the telegram caused substantial difficulties in the cabinet, particularly with ministers from southwestern Ontario who were worried about the reaction of their constituents. Similarly, when the question was how Canada should vote on a relatively mild resolution at the United Nations, moved by the United States, that called for a ceasefire and withdrawal of forces, the cabinet was divided. The prime minister reportedly felt that to do anything other than to support the resolution would be cowardly, but, after consultation with Pearson in New York, Canada ended by registering an abstention, one of only six countries to do so.[14] The anglocentrism of Canadian diplomacy was asserting itself yet again, and on an issue where there were no doubts whatsoever about rights and wrongs.[15]

Pearson himself noted that his initial idea was to attempt to transform the invading Anglo-French forces into a United Nations force, "not to give United Nations respectability to the Anglo-French intervention but to change its character and make it serve different ends." That idea, given the mood at New York, was a non-starter, he quickly realized. Pearson then raised the idea of a United Nations emergency force, again largely as a device to extricate the British and French from their dangerous and untenable position.[16] This proposal, as we all know, succeeded brilliantly and won Pearson his well-deserved Nobel Peace Prize. (It was unfortunate that the Department of National Defence selected the Queen's Own Rifles as Canada's contribution to the United Nations force, a battalion – like all others in the Canadian Army – with an unfortunate name, weapons and equipment similar to those of the British invaders, and a flag that made prominent use of the Union Jack. President Nasser's complaint that his people could not tell the difference between Canadians and Britons was by no means foolish.)

Now there can be no doubt that Pearson was realistic and extremely clever in his actions at the United Nations. He acted with great skill in a period of tension, and he brought great credit to Canadian diplomacy with his efforts to restore peace to the Middle East, to repair the North Atlantic alliance, and to keep the Commonwealth together.[17] Whether what he did was right or not may be another question. Certainly, morality in international politics would have been better served if Canada had joined the United States and most of the other members of the United Nations in condemning the Anglo-French-Israeli aggression for what it was; instead, Canada abstained. There was little in American policy in this period, shaped as it was by the stern moralism of John Foster Dulles, that can compel admiration. Still, the Americans had been betrayed by their closest allies who had acted stupidly in the midst of Eisenhower's re-election campaign and, besides, negated the greatest Western propaganda coup since 1945. As a result, the Americans straight-forwardly condemned their friends for their actions, and as Arnold Heeney, the Canadian ambassador in Washington, later recalled, "The coldness between the British and Americans ... over this was the worst I've ever encountered between two allied countries."[18] The implications were most serious for NATO and the West. But if the American reaction was brutal, it was also honest, perhaps more so than the Canadian response that sought to rescue the aggressors from the consequences of their ineffectual stupidity.

Curiously, the net effect of the whole Suez affair in Canada, notwithstanding the government's efforts to rescue the British, was undoubtedly harmful to the St. Laurent Liberals.[19] In English Canada, as newspaper editorials and opinion polls made clear, the British were seen as working to prevent another world war by stomping a Hitler–Nasser of

Egypt – at an early and appropriate stage. There was much flag-waving, much affirming that Downing Street knew what it was about, and fierce resentment over St. Laurent's extemporaneous remark in Parliament that the days of the supermen of Europe were over.[20] It was the truth, but the truth did not sit well with those who ached for the days when the empire ruled the waves and the "wogs" and the Commonwealth acted as a unit. In the election of 1957, most studies agree, the Pearson initiative at the United Nations did not help a struggling government. Ironically, the Canadian efforts to save Britain, the efforts to avoid condemnation, availed the Liberals not at all. John Diefenbaker and his Progressive Conservatives painted the Liberals as having sold Britain short, stabbing the mother country in the back in its hour of need.[21] To no one's surprise, the anglocentrism of the Canadian electorate, or of substantial parts of it, exceeded that of the St. Laurent government.

The anglocentrism of the new Diefenbaker government was certainly real enough. Despite his Germanic surname, John Diefenbaker was half-British by birth and one-hundred-per-cent British by allegiance. To him, and to many of his ministers, the Commonwealth was a real and living force. This could be seen almost as soon as the new government took office, for one of the prime minister's first acts was to fly to Britain for a Commonwealth conference and to propose that Canada divert 15 per cent of its trade from the United States to Britain – over the warnings of officials that this would be virtually impossible to accomplish.[22] And soon after, a Canadian trade delegation was en route to the United Kingdom and a reciprocal delegation was touring Canada. The rhetoric of blood brotherhood was very potent, and in the heyday of the government it may even have been believed. Certainly Diefenbaker's efforts to tighten the ties with Britain did not hurt the government at the polls in the 1958 election.

But it was not very long before the British themselves were looking elsewhere. The European Common Market beckoned, and, after a few years outside the Six, Britain determined to seek admission. But what of the Commonwealth? What of empire preferences? What of Canada? With characteristic concern for their own interests, the British clearly decided that the Commonwealth would be protected to the extent they could persuade Europe to agree, but if sufficient protection could not be secured, then the Commonwealth's trade – and Canada's – would be set adrift.

The details of the bargaining over Common Market tariffs on sugar and wheat and minerals and manufactured goods need not distract us. What must, however, is the extraordinary response that the British move to Europe provoked within the Diefenbaker government.

Certainly Canada had substantial trade with Britain, even if Diefenbaker's diversion scheme had not worked. In 1956 Canada had exported $812.7 million in goods to the British Isles; in 1959 the total was only $785.8 million. Imports over the same period had risen from $484.7 million to $588.6 million, a more substantial showing. But there could be no doubt that the British market was far less important than the American, as had been the case since the late nineteenth century. In 1945, American imports exceeded British by just over $1 billion; in 1959, the difference was $3.2 billion. The same story applied to exports: in 1945 Canada had exported $230 million more to the United States than to Britain (and that was a year in which munitions made up a substantial part of exports to the United Kingdom); in 1959, exports to the United States exceeded those to the United Kingdom by $2.3 billion. In other words, Britain's share of the Canadian market was shrinking and continued to do so.[23]

Moreover, as one of Diefenbaker's senior ministers involved in the shaping of Canadian policy on this issue noted in a memo for the prime minister, at least one-third of Canada's exports to the United Kingdom would be completely unaffected by British entry into the Common Market, no matter what that entry did to tariff rates. Another third would be only partially affected. No more than 10 per cent of Canadian world trade would be affected in any way, and only 5 per cent would be hurt seriously. This would cause difficulties, of course, but the overall effect was not a catastrophe. Was it worthwhile to fight to the death if those were the stakes?[24]

But rationality had little place in the calculations that shaped policy. The offer to divert trade had been made in the face of calculations that such a course was impossible. The resistance to British entry similarly flew in the face of the facts.

In September 1961, for example, Donald Fleming, the minister of finance, and George Hees, the minister of trade and commerce, represented Canada at a Commonwealth economic conference at Accra, Ghana. There the two alarmed the British – and their own prime minister – with the vehemence of their assaults on the British desire to join Europe. As Fleming told Parliament after his return: "... if the United Kingdom accedes to the community on the basis of the treaty of Rome ... there would be [a] changed political relationship involving the United Kingdom."[25] A British reporter covering the conference phrased it more bluntly: the Accra communiqué represented a "deliberate attempt to sabotage British entry altogether ... this is the policy only of the Canadians, whose eloquent Finance Minister, Mr. Fleming, drafted the document. Mr. Fleming ... is well aware of the value of appealing over the head of the British government to the profound fund of Commonwealth sentiment that exists in this country."[26] Diefenbaker shared this view, fuming privately that his two ministers had demonstrated "excessive belligerence" and were "going a long distance in endeavouring to destroy the British Commonwealth ..."[27]

Still and all, the Canadians did have grounds for concern. The British had made pledges to protect Commonwealth trade, but those were dismissed by some observers. Gratton O'Leary, the dean of Ottawa Tory journalists, wrote privately that "What I fear, alas – it may only be my Fenian youth coming back on me – is that you will discover what the Irish learned through four centuries, namely: that when it comes to their own advantage the English will sell you down the river every time, assuring you that it is God's will and for your own gain."[28]

Eventually even John Diefenbaker seemed to accept that diagnosis. At the 1962 Commonwealth conference in London, the Chief unloaded. As the *Observer*'s diplomatic correspondent reported, "Diefenbaker, it was confidently expected, should be speaking" at the opening session only "for the benefit of yokels back on the prairies." Instead,

> as [Prime Minister Harold] Macmillan watched and Diefenbaker adjusted the microphone on Tuesday morning, it was at once plain that something was badly wrong. Diefenbaker was obviously in a highly emotional state. It was worse, far worse, than the most pessimistic forecast. He was rejecting the whole tenor of Macmillan's speech. He was quoting again and again the 1959 speeches of the present Chancellor of the Exchequer, Mr. Maudling ...
>
> "We must recognize," Maudling had said, "that to sign the Treaty of Rome would mean having common external tariffs which, in turn, would mean the end of Commonwealth free entry, and I cannot conceive that any government of this country would put forward [such] a proposition ..." This wasn't aimed at the yokels. This was a direct assault on the British government.
>
> Still worse was to come. [Diefenbaker] was attacking not only the British position, but the very idea of the Common Market. Macmillan had hoisted the flag of Europe; Diefenbaker was shooting down the flag. As he went on the British became more and more anxious, more and more annoyed. Must he go on forever about Maudling? Would he have anything positive to offer ...?
>
> By the time Diefenbaker sat down, the damage was done. A fuse had been lit ... the reception accorded "Dief" was an ovation. One of the Ghanaians, as he told the Queen a few nights later, "was so moved that I thought I was going to cry."[29]

As we all know, President de Gaulle of France, much to the relief of the Diefenbaker Conservatives, prevented the British from joining the European Common Market on their first try. But what can account for the extraordinary Canadian response? What other than a sense of betrayal? Britain had let down Canada, jeopardized the whole structure of the Commonwealth, and denied the high purpose of the English-speaking world by seeking to throw its lot in with the Germans, French, and Italians. This was betrayal to anglocentric Canadians. It was much more than the loss of some exports, and it had about it a strong sense of *déjà vu*. Had the British not sold out Canada in negotiating the Treaty of Washington in 1871? Had they not given away the Alaska Panhandle in a vain search for American friendship? Canada had created the modern Commonwealth, and now the perfidious English were sacrificing it for mere economic gain.

Perhaps that appeal to the Common Market had some part in killing most of what was left of Canadian anglocentrism for within a few years it was all but gone. Probably it was the adoption of the Canadian flag that applied the *coup de grace* (even if John Diefenbaker pulled out every last anglo-stop in a vain effort to roll back the tide of history). Whatever it was, by 1967 when Britain again was applying for admission to the Common Market there was scarcely a whimper from Canada. The times had changed, and Canadians, seriously concerned with the chances of survival of their own country, suddenly seemed to realize that the anglocentrism of their political and opinion leaders had distinctly negative effects on large sections of the population. If Quebec and English Canada were to survive together, no one any longer could apply tests of Britishness to public questions, no one could impose foreign symbols on the nation, and no one could ever again expect Canadians to fight "British wars," if such a phrase had much meaning in an atomic age. The Falklands War *was* a British war and although the Argentinians were perhaps the nation least deserving of sympathy, no one offered to go off to fight the Argies "at Britain's side whate'er betide." The times had changed, and Canada for better or worse was on its own. And high time, too.

NOTES

1 Vincent Massey, *On Being Canadian* (Toronto: J.M. Dent 1948), 100ff.
2 Public Archives of Canada, Escott Reid Papers, Speech at Rhodes Trust Dinner, 15 June 1930.
3 J.W. Holmes, *The Better Part of Valour: Essays on Canadian Diplomacy* (Toronto: McClelland and Stewart 1970), 105.

The Anglocentrism of Canadian Diplomacy 169

4 One exception is the two-volume *Memoirs of Hugh L. Keenleyside* (Toronto: McClelland and Stewart 1981, 1982) which is often critical. Of course, Keenleyside did his graduate work in the United States, not Oxford.
5 The "key figures" designations here are those employed in J.L. Granatstein, *The Ottawa Men: The Civil Service Mandarins, 1935–57* (Toronto: Oxford University Press 1982). See also John Porter, *The Vertical Mosaic* (Toronto: University of Toronto Press 1965), 441ff. For detail on the composition of the Department of External Affairs, see Gilles Lalande, *The Department of External Affairs and Biculturalism* (Ottawa: Information Canada 1970), 27.
6 Vincent Massey, *Canadians and their Commonwealth*, Romanes Lecture, 1 June 1961 (Oxford: Oxford University Press 1961), 18–19.
7 Cited in Robert Cuff and J.L. Granatstein, *Ties that Bind* (Toronto: Samuel-Stevens 1977), 30.
8 Ibid., 37.
9 See J.L. Granatstein, *Canada's War: The Polities of the Mackenzie King Government, 1939–45* (Toronto: Oxford University Press 1975), chap 4.
10 See Robert Cuff and J.L. Granatstein, *American Dollars/Canadian Prosperity: Canadian-American Economic Relations 1945–50* (Toronto: Samuel-Stevens 1978), chaps. 2–5.
11 Directorate of History, National Defence Headquarters, Office of Chief of Defence Staff Records, Suez file, tel. Col. Cook, CJS(L.) to Gen Foulkes, 2–3 August 1956; Foulkes to J. Watkins, 3 August 1956.
12 Department of External Affairs, file 50134-40, 30 October 1956.
13 L.B. Pearson, *Mike: The Memoirs of the Right Honourable Lester B. Pearson, 2: 1948–1957* (Toronto: University of Toronto Press 1973), 238–9.
14 Confidential source. Escott Reid noted that he was sharply criticized by Indian diplomats for this vote. *Envoy to Nehru* (Delhi: Oxford University Press 1981), 151.
15 On the crisis generally, see Pearson, *Mike* II, 240ff; J.L. Granatstein, *A Man of Influence: Norman A. Robertson and Canadian Statecraft, 1929–68* (Ottawa: Deneau 1981), 300ff; A. Taylor, et al., *Peacekeeping: International Challenge and Canadian Response* (Toronto: Canadian Institute of International Affairs 1968), 118ff.
16 See Holmes, *The Better Part of Valour*, 107; C.S.A. Ritchie, *Diplomatic Passport* (Toronto: Macmillan 1981), 122. Pearson later told Parliament that "I do not for one minute criticize the motives of the United Kingdom and France in intervening in Egypt at this time. I may have thought that their intervention was not wise, but I do not criticize their purposes." Canada, House of Commons, *Debates*, 29 November 1956, 168.
17 John Holmes said that "after 1956, the Commonwealth was never quite the same at the United Nations." He should have added "or anywhere else." Holmes, *The Better Part of Valour*, 93.

18 Public Archives of Canada, A.D.P. Heeney Papers, vol. 3, oral history transcript, 8 September 1965.
19 Ritchie recorded a British friend as saying "What if we *are* wrong? If one of my friends made a mistake ... I would back them up." Another said, "Don't desert England – how can you?" Ritchie, *Diplomatic Passport*, 120. Many in Canada said the same.
20 Canada, House of Commons, *Debates*, 26 November 1956, 20. The best account of public opinion is James Eayrs, *Canada and World Affairs 1955–57* (Toronto: Oxford University Press 1959), 186ff.
21 "Not far beneath their reasoning," Eayrs wrote of a similar but earlier situation, "lay a crude emotional appeal, manipulating the images of Empire: King and Queen, Royal Family, Union Jack, Mother Country, Land of Hope and Glory – were not these potent symbols on the hustings still?" *In Defence of Canada*, 3: *Peacemaking and Deterrence* (Toronto: University of Toronto Press 1972), 208.
22 Confidential source, memorandum of 9 August 1957.
23 M.C. Urquhart and K. Buckley, eds., *Historical Statistics of Canada* (Toronto: Macmillan 1965), 181–2.
24 Confidential source, memorandum of 4 September 1962.
25 *Debates*, 28 September 1961, 9054–5.
26 Nigel Lawson in *Sunday Telegraph*, 24 September 1961.
27 Confidential source, memorandum of 15 September 1961.
28 Confidential source, letter of 22 November 1961.
29 "Commonwealth's longest week," *Observer*, 16 September 1962.

Chapter Eight

Dealing with London

The concern for national unity that had been demonstrated by Canada's separate declaration of war on September 10, 1939 would continue to dominate Canadian policy. Nowhere was it more prominent than in the first few months of the war when Canada engaged in a series of difficult negotiations with London on military and economic matters.

To Mackenzie King and the Canadian government, national unity meant the relations between French and English Canadians above all. To keep harmony at home the war effort would have to be moderate in all things, particularly in contributions of manpower, or casualties overseas might lead to demands for conscription. But national unity was more than simply the relations between English and French. The economic war effort was important too, and the interests of the farmer and the manufacturer had to be protected and enhanced. Prairie wheat had to be sold at good prices, and orders for war materiel were necessary if the Canadian economy was going to recover at last from the lingering effects of the Great Depression. National unity meant getting a good price abroad for Nova Scotia apples just as much as it meant securing British orders for aircraft parts for Toronto heavy industry.

This sounded like self-interest, and it was. Canada was in the war out of a sense of duty, not because her own national interests were directly threatened. This being so, why shouldn't the war produce some benefits for Canadians, a people still suffering from heavy unemployment and depressed national productivity? This was selfish, but this Canadian attitude was matched, and more than matched, by the British attitude to Canada. Few orders would find their way to the Dominion until the fall of France relaxed the British government's insistence on steering contracts to British firms, and the financial and military relations between the two countries would be characterized by tough, difficult bargaining. Canadian national unity and Canadian self-interest demanded no less.

I

While the Quebec election was progressing towards its conclusion, the King government was beginning negotiations with the United Kingdom on a proposed Empire air-training scheme. The scheme, eventually to be known as the British Commonwealth Air Training Plan (BCATP), would become the major Canadian military contribution to the Allied war effort, training tens of thousands of air crew from Canada, Australia, New Zealand, and Britain and her colonies. But as with other war programs involving money, prestige, and concepts of Imperial relations, the genesis of the BCATP was troubled.

The BCATP's origins probably go back at least to 1926 when, at the Imperial Conference of that year, Mackenzie King himself had suggested in general terms the possibility that Canada and the United Kingdom might co-operate on bases, on the provision of helium for dirigibles, and on the creation of a reserve of airmen.[1] Nothing appears to have come of this suggestion, and nothing further was heard on the subject of air training until 1936 when the German threat was already looming. The Baldwin government began pressing the King government in that year to facilitate the recruiting of men in Canada for service in the Royal Air Force, but these suggestions foundered on the rock of autonomist objections from within the Department of External Affairs.[2] The British continued their interest despite the unenthusiastic response to their initial suggestion, changing their aim to securing a training school in Canada. The Cabinet was cool to this idea too.[3]

Pressure then subsided for two years, but in May 1938 the Chamberlain government returned to the charge with a new proposal that the Royal Canadian Air Force should conduct training for RAF candidates at one or more Flying Training Schools in Canada.[4] Unfortunately the High Commissioner and the Prime Minister became involved in a dispute over who had said what to whom during these negotiations, the result being substantial acrimony between London and Ottawa and yet another cool Canadian response.[5] Mackenzie King's primary objection, as he told the House of Commons, was to having "a military station to be put down in Canada, owned, maintained and operated by the Imperial Government for Imperial purposes."[6] This was very different in King's view from having British pilots train in Canada in Canadian establishments that were under Canadian control.

London clearly believed that King's House of Commons statement marked a change of position from opposition to any air-training scheme whatsoever, and the Air Ministry quickly sent a mission to Canada to explore the new state of affairs.[7] The British visitors, however, still found Canadian-made difficulties in their way, and after months of negotiations the British discouragingly noted that it seemed "extremely dubious whether there is any possibility of persuading the Canadian Government to operate any scheme which involves financial contribution on their part."[8] Further negotiations led to an agreement in April 1939; under its terms, fifty RAF pilots a year would receive medium and advanced flying training in Canada. The new scheme, an expensive one by the standards of the Air Ministry, cost £1,500 per pilot more than training in Britain, but presumably the involvement of Canada in Empire air training was considered worth the money.[9] No pilots had arrived in Canada for training by September 1939.

The initial British plans had foundered on London's persistence in ignoring Mackenzie King's clearly expressed views that only British pilots could be trained for the RAF in Canada and only in training stations under Canadian control. Given King's long insistence on autonomy, the British were beating their heads against a stone wall on this issue, as on others. An onlooker could admire their persistence, not their tactics. The same mistakes would be repeated again and again in the course of the air-training negotiations in the fall of 1939.

Understandably, on the outbreak of war the Air Ministry had no major plans for air training in Canada. The first suggestions were for the training of 2,000 pilots a year and as many air crew as possible.[10] Within a few days, however, RAF studies raised the number of pilots desired to 8,000 per year. The RAF view was that the RCAF should control this training scheme and make it the major role for the Canadian air force in the war. Naturally other Dominions were making proposals to London as well, and the need for a rationalized scheme was becoming clear. According to Vincent Massey, the Canadian High Commissioner in London, the idea for a giant British Commonwealth Air Training Plan originated with him, was discussed with his Australian counterpart in London, and then presented to Anthony Eden, the Secretary of State for Dominion Affairs on September 16.[11] At no time apparently did Massey tell Ottawa of his part in this affair, a curious but understandable lapse of responsibility on the part of the Canadian government's representative in Britain. Massey's reputation with Mackenzie King and with the Department of External Affairs was not very high at this point;[12] had his superiors known of his role in the birth of the Air Training Plan their anger might have been very great.

The Air Training Plan idea won ready acceptance in London and by September 26 official telegrams were sent off by Prime Minister Chamberlain to the Dominion Prime Ministers. The message to Mackenzie

King, partly drafted by Massey who knew his master well,[13] was carefully phrased:

> I am sure that you will agree that the scheme outlined is of first importance. For this reason, and because it invites co-operation with Canada to a very special degree, I want to make a special personal appeal to you about it. I feel that so far-reaching a project will strike your imagination particularly as it concerns an all important field of war activity in which Canada has already made so striking and gallant an individual contribution. May I therefore ask that the matter should receive very urgent attention?[14]

The British scheme was based on the need for "not less than 20,000 pilots and 30,000 personnel of air crews annually for maintenance of [an] enlarged force. To provide for these, it is estimated that about ninety elementary and advanced flying training schools ... would be necessary." The British expected that elementary training would be carried out largely by each individual Dominion, but that since "Canada has special advantages of nearness to the United Kingdom, greater potentialities for Manufacture of service type of aircraft and proximity to the vast resources of the United States of America ... advanced training for trainees from elementary training schools should be centred in Canada." London also suggested a meeting of experts to discuss the plan and indicated that this should take place in Canada. The telegram noted the "immense influence" such a scheme could have on the course of the war – "it might even prove decisive."[15]

The careful wording of Chamberlain's telegram made its mark on Mackenzie King: "It is felt that we might in this way render as great a service in bringing the war to a close as was rendered in the late war by the US coming in at the end. This is the most important despatch so far."[16] But the next day when he told Cabinet of the British proposal, he was somewhat less enthusiastic. "It shows how quite unprepared the British ... were in their plans that until now they have not been able to tell us definitely what really is the best of all plans, and which would have saved us having anything to do with an expeditionary force at the start."[17] That was the key in King's view. The delay in suggesting the giant scheme had forced Canada to plan an expeditionary force, something that might otherwise have been avoided. Still, the reaction in Cabinet was extremely favourable to the suggestion. Cost was the major worry, along with the possibility that Canadian planning in other areas, already based on the maximum financial contribution of which Canada was believed capable, might have to be altered.[18] The Cabinet agreed that a telegram should be despatched to London accepting the scheme in principle, but raising certain questions: Where would the aircraft come from? Where would instructors be found? How would costs be shared? Those were the Cabinet's main questions, but Mackenzie King also had to redraft personally the telegram prepared by Dr. Skelton.[19] "The truth is he, at heart, is against much in the way of co-operation," King wrote. "Quite rightly feels the British are very selfish but fails to see the larger significance of the fight for freedom that is being waged."[20] The pot was calling the kettle black.

Before the public announcement of the air-training plan could be made, there was a small but not insignificant *contretemps* between London and Ottawa over its wording. Skelton and the Prime Minister wanted London's announcement to make clear that this was the most important Canadian contribution to the war, an effort that was clearly doomed to failure. King was disappointed but not surprised by the British attitude for he had "felt they would stick at that in a public pronouncement. They were prepared, however, to use it to get us into the scheme."[21] The announcement, unsatisfactory as it may have been to Canada, was made on October 10.

The British Air Training Mission, headed by Lord Riverdale, a bluff and undiplomatic Sheffield industrialist, was already at sea and hard at work preparing the British plans. Riverdale aimed at an equitable sharing of the burden and its distribution in a manner that would cause the least difficulties with foreign exchange, already becoming critical in England. In the Air Ministry's view equity could best be achieved by dividing the costs on the basis of the numbers of trained personnel allocated to each of the several forces. That prospect, however, might lead the Dominions to reduce their share to keep costs down and that would weaken the British foreign-exchange position. The smaller the size of the RCAF, the Air Ministry noted, "the smaller will be, not only the share of the total cost which Canada would bear, but also the amount of Canadian dollars which we would receive in respect of aeroplanes, bombs, stores, etc., manufactured in this country, and issued to the Canadian squadrons which come to Europe." If possible Riverdale should attempt to have the Canadians "fix the number of squadrons at which they propose ultimately to aim for despatch overseas, before the Mission becomes involved in discussing the division of costs ..."[22] Money was clearly going to be a vital component of Riverdale's talks, and it seems clear that Riverdale approached the question as a cost-conscious industrialist, not as a negotiator skilled in dealing with sometimes balky Canadians. At the first meeting of the Mission staff he told his colleagues of the serious British dollar position, "and it was not possible as yet to indicate what solution could be found. We had not yet promised to buy Canadian wheat," he said, "and it might well be that we could eventually make such a promise in order to facilitate the acceptance of the proposed training scheme by Canada."[23] Riverdale was no fool, however, and he worried whether Canada had the financial resources necessary to support such a costly plan.[24]

The result of the Mission's work during the sea voyage to Canada was passed to Canadian officials in the form of a memorandum on October 14th. The British envisaged an intake of 2,910 aircrew trainees every four weeks, not including the British contribution. Canada was to raise 1,396 aircrew each four weeks, the remainder being found in Australia and New Zealand. Thirty-seven flying schools would be necessary in Canada plus thirty-five aircrew schools and an array of supply and record depots. No cost estimates were indicated.[25]

Mackenzie King received the British delegation on October 17. Riverdale began the interview badly both by referring to the plan as "your scheme" and by creating in King's mind the impression that London was dictating to Canada. It was never hard to do this, of course, and King felt compelled to respond. It was very kind of Riverdale "to speak of the scheme as ours," he began, "but it was really theirs, and how far we could go in developing it would depend very largely on what Britain herself would do." King added in his diary that he "was rather amused at the sort of railroading, taking for granted style which Riverdale adopted." It was "amazing how these people ... from the Old Country ... seem to think that all they have to do is tell us what is to be done. No wonder they get the backs of people up on this side."[26] A Canadian officer who was present at this meeting remarked that he was impressed that King "did not show any sign of surprise or give any indication that what was happening was anything out of the ordinary" although the Riverdale proposal was "so far ahead of anything that we had thought of that everyone ... was quite taken aback at its magnitude ..."[27]

So, in his own way, was Riverdale. In conversation with W.D. Euler, King's Minister of Trade and Commerce, he learned that Canada contemplated an eventual expenditure of $300 million per year on defence. If there was added to this even $250 million for the air-training scheme, that would be more "than the Canadian Government could face."[28] As Riverdale wrote to Kingsley Wood, the Secretary of State for Air, in a letter on October 19, "It is doubtful whether even if they doubled their taxation the Canadian Government would be able to find the money for our training scheme as well as the help which they are giving to the Navy and the Army ..."[29]

It is strikingly clear from all this that the British had come to Canada with only a rough draft of a scheme, with little idea of the numbers of aircraft required or their source, and with only the scantiest idea of Canadian financial resources. All the financial calculations of the scheme were carried out in Canada by the RCAF, rushed and harried to produce the data that should have come from London.[30] In essence the British had found an idea and they brought it to Ottawa looking for someone else to put up the cash.

By October 31, when senior Canadian Cabinet ministers met formally with the British Mission, some of the cost data were ready. Capital expenditure was put at $400 million and maintenance for a three and one-half year period was set at $508.5 million. After a deduction for a cost differential, the cost of the Air Training Plan was fixed at $888.5 million.[31] In the British view this scheme was a good one for the Canadians, for "a large part of the capital expenditure incurred ... will go to provide employment in Canada and also that a large amount of employment in Canada is being provided by the orders which the British Government has placed and contemplates placing ..."[32] The Canadians, having met earlier to consider the estimates,[33] were not impressed. Riverdale read his statement and then announced Britain's decision to make a contribution – a "free contribution" – of $140 million in kind to the cost of the scheme. Of the remaining $748.5 million, he hoped that Canada would bear half the cost. Colonel Ralston, the Minister of Finance (called by one of the British negotiators "a lawyer who was maddeningly pernickety"),[34] interjected at this point that this was the first time that any proportionate sharing had been suggested, a clear implication that the minister felt the Canadian proportion was out of line.

After Riverdale had concluded and after Captain Balfour, the British Parliamentary Under Secretary for Air, had added a few words, the Prime Minister took the floor:

> The Prime Minister in reply [the British note of the meeting records] said that when the war broke out Canada lost no time in ranging herself on the side of Great Britain and France and declaring war on Germany, but it was not Canada's war in the same sense as it was Great Britain's, and it would do more harm than good if they were pressed to do more than they felt they were able to do; he was afraid there could be no question of taking on responsibility for the scheme in the proportion which Lord Riverdale had suggested today ... he ... was afraid that the Canadian Government could not take the line that money would be found somewhere. They must only undertake what they were sure that they would be in a financial position to do ... He felt he must speak plainly on this question right at the beginning so that there should be no misunderstanding. He and his Ministers appreciated Great Britain's difficulties and they wished to cooperate in

overcoming them, but they did not want to have the spirit of cooperation which animated them crushed at the outset by excessive demands. Lord Riverdale had talked about Great Britain making a contribution under the scheme as if it were a contribution to Canada but [it was] only a contribution to the cost of a scheme suggested by the British Government, and for which the British Government must be mainly responsible.

Mackenzie King concluded by observing that this "was the kind of scheme in which they were happy to join and he wished that they had more money to put into it."[35]

Ralston then spoke and expressed the view that while Canada hoped to do her utmost, it would simply not be possible to come within "shooting distance" of the Riverdale estimates. The British, he argued, "had made a point of the fact that the pilots and crews trained in these Canadian Schools would be maintained in the field by the United Kingdom; in his view it was quite right that they should be so maintained; these were schools for training crews for the British Air Force. They were being located in Canada simply because Canada was situated in a convenient position geographically ... the United Kingdom should pay for these men." He did not want to put a damper on the scheme, Ralston said, effectively doing just that, but he "had to look at it as a businessman."[36]

The only agreement to emerge from this meeting was that the British would meet with Ralston and with C.D. Howe, the Minister of Transport, and continue the talks. Before these meetings could begin on November 3, however, Sir Gerald Campbell felt compelled to register his disapproval of Mackenzie King's remarks at the October 31 meeting. He had been shocked, he told Dr. Skelton, to hear King say "this is not our war." That phrase had been conveyed to London and he didn't know what they would make of it there. One member of the Mission had wondered if the Prime Minister would dare to make such a comment in Parliament. Skelton's diplomatic reply gave nothing away: "It certainly was not Canada's war in the sense that the war did not originate in any German threat against Canada or in any Canadian pledge in Eastern Europe. This of course did not mean that Canada had not made Great Britain's and France's cause her own." As for any statement in Parliament, Skelton indicated, that might safely be left to Mackenzie King.[37]

When he learned of this, Mackenzie King was furious. Riverdale, he wrote, wanted to load the whole scheme onto the Dominions and he had given his hand away when he talked about free gifts from Britain to Canada. To King the British tack was "to extricate themselves from the wrong position they were in by giving a wholly false interpretation to my remark that this was not our war, which was made in reply to Riverdale's statement 'we are making this contribution to you.' I had said in reply that so far as there were contributions, it was the other way, and that what we were doing was for the common cause." King was disturbed enough about this imputation of near-disloyalty to see the Governor General and to urge him to call in Sir Gerald Campbell. Tweedsmuir agreed to do this.[38]

More important to the Prime Minister, however, was the very great cost of the British air-training scheme, and on November 3, the day detailed negotiations were to begin with the British Mission, King telegraphed to Chamberlain. The scope of the plan was staggering, King said, and for reasons that were well known in Britain Canada could not afford as great a proportion of her national income for war as could Britain. Moreover it was clear that Canada had not been successful in conveying a full understanding to the United Kingdom "and particularly to its various agencies concerned with the purchase of Canadian products or with making arrangements in regard to the various aspects of our military contribution. I may instance the fact," King stated baldly, "that While the British Air Mission are pressing us in regard to their air training proposals which would involve a substantial increase in Canada's direct military expenditures, we on our part have for many weeks been pressing without satisfactory result for a decision in regard to wheat purchases which is the biggest single item in our whole economic programme and the most far-reaching in its public consequences. In our opinion," the Prime Minister added, "the questions of military and economic participation in the war effort are inextricably intertwined and cannot be dealt with separately."[39] The Canadian Prime Minister was clearly interested in bargaining, but he was also right. Canada could not pump millions more into guns unless and until some of its butter – and wheat – were sold abroad.

King's ministers bargained equally hard. The Mission met with Ralston, Howe, Ian Mackenzie, now the Minister of Pensions and Health, and Norman Rogers, the Minister of National Defence, on November 3. The Canadians hammered away at the outset at the British contribution of $140 million in kind. "It was explained," the British notes of the meeting record, "that this sum represented the cost of all material to be manufactured in the United Kingdom which would be required as the first equipment of each school. The Canadian ministers felt that there was no logic in a proposal of that nature and that it would be necessary to devise a more rational method of dividing the costs." The amount Canada was expected to shoulder in any case was too much. Ralston presented data showing that Canada was spending $190 million for defence in 1939–40 and planning to spend $352 million, $330 million, and $300 million in each successive fiscal year. The Finance Minister indicated that the national income was $3,575 million and an increase of 15 per cent in that figure might be expected as a result of war orders. Nonetheless government expenditures amounted to $1,490 million or 36.3 per cent of National Income. If this was raised to 42 per cent, adding a further $237 million to defence spending, Canada could not possibly carry the costs of the training scheme to anything like the extent envisaged by the British. C.D. Howe, in suggesting that the plan was too grandiose, added that Canada had made proposals early in September "as to the form which the Canadian war effort was to take, and they had understood that these proposals had been welcomed by the United Kingdom Government. The United Kingdom Air Mission then arrived with proposals for the financing of an Air Training Scheme which apparently took no account of the defence commitments into which the Canadian Government had already entered."[40]

Meanwhile the Australians and New Zealanders had arrived in Ottawa for discussions on their role in the Air Training Plan. They were friendly, but the Antipodean Dominions hoped to do as much air training as possible on their own territory, an attitude that forced new cost estimates to be made.[41] These figures were presented to the Canadian ministers on November 9. The capital and maintenance costs now were put at $686 million, a figure that was shortly lowered again to $650 million. Towards that cost Britain now offered $175 million. That left $475 million to be divided among the three Dominions, and the shares were expected to be Canada – $335 million, Australia – $115 million, and New Zealand – $25 million.

In the Canadian view this was better, but still too much. If this estimate were accepted, the Canadians argued, they would be unable to afford to send a second division overseas; Britain would have to pay more. The ministers insisted that Britain should pay for $23 million in air frames and engines already ordered as well as the freight charges on the additional aircraft she was providing, a further $20 million. This would bring the British share up to $218 million, leaving $432 million to be split among the Dominions. On November 13 it seemed that agreement was readied on this arrangement, with Canada bearing 72.5 per cent of the cost ($313 million), Australia 22.5 per cent ($97.4 million), and New Zealand 5 per cent ($21.6 million). [42]

The Cabinet War Committee considered this scheme and accepted it on the following day. King believed that the government was "going much further than we intended" but that it was right "so that the

British Government might feel that we had acted generously." Graham Towers of the Bank of Canada took this view, telling the ministers that British government purchasing officials "would likely go much further with us if we were not niggardly with them." King reassured himself by noting that the heavy costs did not fall at the beginning of the Plan and "If war lasts two years or more, people ... will be ready to stand the higher outlays."[43] But there were two conditions laid down by the War Committee. The British would have to agree that the Plan took priority over all other forms that a Canadian contribution to the war effort could take, and there would have to be a satisfactory result to the economic discussions then underway in London.[44]

The British War Cabinet jibbed at everything. Kingsley Wood wrote to Riverdale that "Just as the Canadian Government feel unable to give the all-clear pending the outcome of the discussions here on economic relations generally, so we for our part cannot commit ourselves in regard to the scheme until we know where we stand in the same respect."[45] There were also some severe doubts about granting the Canadians the assurance on priority they sought. "It is troublesome of Mr Mackenzie King ...," Kingsley Wood's memorandum to the War Cabinet on November 18 said, but he did urge that approval be granted.[46] But when the matter was discussed a week later the Secretary of State for Dominion Affairs, Anthony Eden, balked and said "we should probably have to take a firm line. The matter was a purely domestic one ..."[47]

Of course it was, and that was why King was so adamant about it. He told the British High Commissioner that Canada would not sign the agreement unless Britain conceded these points, and both Sir Gerald Campbell and Lord Riverdale felt obliged to urge that the conditions be accepted.[48] On one point, at least, all parties agreed when on November 25 the British signified a willingness to meet the costs discussed on November 13.[49] Regrettably those figures were already out of date. The Australians had decided to reduce the amount of time their trainees would spend in Canada and the Canadians insisted that the British raise their contribution to meet any increased costs. The new cost of the scheme was set at $607 million, of which Britain was to contribute $185 million, Australia $39.9 million, and New Zealand $28.6 million. The Canadian contribution was now $68 million for schools that would be used only for the training of Canadians plus $285.4 million to the joint scheme or a total of $353.4 million, an increase of more than $40 million over the November 13 figures and an amount that substantially exceeded the estimates the Canadians had rejected as too much a few weeks earlier. But this new estimate had been cleared comma by comma with the Canadian negotiators and the British hoped for quick acceptance.

They were to be disappointed. On King's recommendation the Cabinet War Committee delayed, deciding that a "dissembling" telegram from Chamberlain was not satisfactory in its assurances on the two Canadian conditions.[50] Chamberlain had said only that "I have no hesitation in giving this assurance as I entirely agree that it is for Canada to decide on the priority of her effort and therefore I should not think of interfering in it whatever our own opinions might be. I should explain that we ourselves have attached the highest priority to this Training Scheme ... which we believe may be a decisive factor in the war. If the Canadian Government decided to contribute to the scheme on the scale contemplated, their policy will be in the closest correspondence with our own. But," Chamberlain said at the sticking point, "we should not have liked to emphasise the priority of the Air Training Scheme lest it should have embarrassing effects on our relations with the French who are pressing us strongly to increase our effort on land."[51] This reply did dissemble, for as King wrote on the telegram what he wanted was an assurance "That in Br. Govt. view the scheme will be considered as having priority to anything that may subsequently be put forward by Br. Govt."[52] In these circumstances King would go no further than permitting a press release on November 27 stating that "a basis of agreement" had been reached and referred to the various governments for decision.[53]

By this date Canada was insisting on five conditions before it would accept the Air Training Plan. The RCAF would have to administer the scheme. This was accepted. The British would have to help Australia and New Zealand raise the Canadian dollars needed to pay their costs. This was agreed. The financial discussions in London would have to be resolved satisfactorily. This eventually took place. The desired statement on the priority of the Training Plan would have to be issued. This was ultimately offered on December 7.[54] Surprisingly the final, crucial difficulty hinged on the Canadian insistence that aircrew be identified with Canada to the maximum extent possible once their training was completed.

From the first proposal on September 26 it had always been assumed that separate Canadian squadrons would be formed in the field. But not until December 7 were steps begun to arrange for this, and almost immediately there were problems.[55] On December 8 Norman Rogers wrote to Riverdale, setting out his understanding of a discussion between the two men that day: "Canadian personnel from the training plan will, on request from the Canadian Government, be organized in Royal Canadian Air Force units and formations in the field."[56] Riverdale's reply – Canadian requests would be met "in all circumstances in which it is feasible"⁵⁷ – infuriated the Canadians who found it totally unacceptable. In King's view the British government was trying to "keep Canadian squadrons at its disposal, merged into British forces, creating all the trouble in the air field that was created on land with the army in the last war. This," he said, "must be avoided at all costs and will be by my standing firm on this matter." The next day he added that it was "really shameful the way in which the British government in these matters seek to evade and undo and to change the meaning of the most definitely understood obligations."⁵⁸

The British viewed this problem very seriously. In the first place the Canadian position that the United Kingdom should pay for RCAF units in Europe understandably bothered the War Cabinet in London, all its members believing firmly in the principle "that a Dominion unit must be paid for by the Dominion concerned." Secondly, if an agreement was made with Canada to segregate Canadians into RCAF units, the other Dominions might demand equal treatment. Up to half the fighting personnel of the RAF could be made up of Dominion squadrons, but since the RAF would have to provide the supporting ground crew, far more than half the total personnel would be British.⁵⁹ The complaints about money were rather more soundly based.

The British offered a new proposal on December 14. If Canada provided the ground crews, the British suggested, then its squadrons could be identified as RCAF and placed under Canadian command. The RCAF favoured this, but Mackenzie King quickly pointed out that the financial provisions for the Training Plan were based on the RAF providing ground support.⁶⁰ For the next three days haggling was intense on this question. At one point on December 15 the parties reached agreement, but Riverdale quickly reneged. New British proposals, financially unacceptable to Mackenzie King, were then produced.⁶¹ Riverdale's note referred to a new condition that "the factor governing the numbers of such pupils to be so incorporated at any one time should be the financial contribution which the Canadian Government have already declared themselves ready to make towards the cost of the Training Scheme." Previous discussion, King noted in his diary, had always been based on questions of feasibility and practicality. "Now the message implied what we have all along thought, that the Air Ministry was trying to exact more in the way of money out of the Government of Canada, or make the position such as to render impossible command by Canadians where service crews were British."⁶² King also overheard one RAF officer with the Air Mission say that "if Canadian squadrons were being serviced by British crews, it would mean that there would be a larger number of Englishmen under the command of Canadians.

I said nothing at the time, but made a very careful note of the remark ... which really ... let the cat out of the bag."[63]

The next day, December 16, King continued to press Riverdale to sign the agreement on terms satisfactory to the Canadian government. The reason for haste was in large part King's intention to make a national broadcast on December 17 in order to announce both the successful conclusion of the agreement and the arrival of the First Canadian Division overseas. The 17th was King's birthday, and for this reason the number 17 was one to which he attached near-mystical properties. Under this pressure the agreement was finally signed and sealed in the early morning hours of December 17, an added fillip for Mackenzie King who could now both announce his agreement and sign it on his birthday. The question of Canadian squadrons – later called "Canadianization" – was left essentially unresolved.[64]

If Mackenzie King was jubilant, the British were not. The Secretary of State for Air felt that everything had turned out well, but the Chancellor of the Exchequer was gloomy, pointing out to the War Cabinet that he had sent no congratulatory telegrams after the signing of the agreement. "He had not agreed that Canada could insist on unlimited units of the RCAF being provided at the expense of the United Kingdom taxpayer."[65] The High Commissioner in Ottawa shared the gloom. His report on the negotiations, sent on December 19, is probably one of the more blistering despatches sent about one Commonwealth government by the representative of another:

> I can best begin by saying bluntly that the United Kingdom delegation ... approached the common problems to be solved from an entirely different angle from that of the Canadian Government ... [We] never forgot that [we] were here to forge a weapon for use against the common enemy. The Canadian Government saw everything in terms of the advantage which might be secured for Canada and for themselves ... When the Empire training scheme was first proposed to them, the Canadian Government considered it and saw that it was good: good, that is, because if they played their cards right, they could employ the essential features of the scheme for the greater honour and glory of Canada. It would, incidentally, be an effective weapon against the enemy, and this fact had its own value, since the Canadian people were pressing for effective measures on the part of their Government. But first things come first, and here was a plan which promised a far better return in the way of political capital than the despatch of a mere division or two to the Western Front. Having thus decided, the Canadian Government, it must be conceded, played their hand remarkably well.

This extraordinary despatch then proceeded to list the concessions squeezed out by the Canadians: control of the administration of the plan; the British statement of the priority of the plan over other forms of contribution to the war; and the assurance that Canadian pupils would be placed into RCAF squadrons. Why such concessions were so difficult for Sir Gerald Campbell to swallow is difficult to conceive, but the blame for it all rested on one man:

> ... the Prime Minister is the Government, and ... a very complex character. On the one hand he goes far beyond the average Canadian in his mystical and idealistic talk of a crusade or holy war against the enemies of civilization and democracy. On the other hand he is the narrowest of narrow Canadian nationalists. It is this twofold outlook which makes him at one moment believe that he is serving humanity by dedicating Canada to the common cause, and at the next moment consider what the common cause can be made to do to help Canada. It is thus that he is able simultaneously to compose his own exalted platitudes and to encourage the pettifogging niceties of the Minister of Finance.[66]

A fairer comment on this difficult negotiation can be found in a memorandum made by Floyd Chalmers of the *Financial Post* after a discussion with Sir Christopher Courtney, a member of the British Air Mission:

> ... he had got the impression, when he was over on the BCATP in 1939 that Canada was inclined to bargain pretty hard. I suggested to him that *neither* Britain nor Canada were in the war with all they had in 1939 and if Canada's financial authorities – then feeling their way – were cautious in their estimate of Canada's financial limitations, the British were pursuing a policy of virtually ignoring Canada as a war workshop.[67]

In these two assessments combined there is probably something close to a reasonable judgement. Excised of its vindictiveness and spleen, Sir Gerald Campbell's despatch was quite shrewd. Mackenzie King was difficult to deal with when he was fighting to protect what he and his colleagues perceived as the Canadian national interest, a commendable objective even in wartime. The British, after all, were demonstrably acting in their own interests in trying to pass as much as possible of the costs of the BCATP onto the Dominions. King was fighting to protect national unity, too, for a successful BCATP seemed to him likely to be the best guarantor against heavy infantry casualties and a consequent demand for conscription. The agreement seemed likely to produce a successful air-training plan, and the alterations that the Canadian negotiators had won went some distance in protecting Canadian sovereignty, although the financial costs were very heavy.

The Prime Minister stressed these costs in his radio address on December 17, and he also put special emphasis on the British statement about the priority status of the British Commonwealth Air Training Plan:

> The United Kingdom Government has ... informed us that, considering present and future requirements, it feels that participation in the Air Training Scheme would provide for more effective assistance towards victory than any other form of military co-operation which Canada can give.[68]

The BCATP was a ten-strike for the Liberal Government. On the one hand it was possible to feature it as Canada's greatest effort to help Britain, a true and reasonable claim. On the other hand it was a form of military effort that likely would not lead to enormous casualties, a positive inducement for French Canada to admire the government's wise management of affairs. The BCATP, therefore, would receive a prominent place in Liberal propaganda in the coming election campaign. And well it might, for the Plan was a great undertaking that would unquestionably rank as Canada's major contribution to the Allied war effort. Still, there can be no doubt that Mackenzie King and his Cabinet fought against the preconceived notions of the British government in the first months of the war with more vigour than either Canada or Britain mustered against Hitler.

II

Money. This was the major basis of the disagreements between British and Canadian negotiators during the course of the BCATP discussions. Who would pay how much and for what was bound to be of great importance in the opening phase of a war of limited liabilities. To the British the important thing was to produce as much as possible of the necessary war materiel in Birmingham, Manchester, and Sheffield, and to import as little as possible at as cheap a price as could be obtained. To the Canadians the goal was to secure orders for manufactured goods and raw materials at as high a price as could be negotiated. There was bound to be conflict, and it was certain to be exacerbated by what Mackenzie King saw as exorbitant demands for Canadian aid on the one hand and an absolute refusal to negotiate seriously on the other.

Clearly Britain began the war expecting very little in a material sense from Canada. "At first," the historian of British war supply says with characteristic understatement, Canada "may not have figured very largely" in British calculations. The country's industrial resources were small, "and in the nature of things Canadian munitions production could never reach sufficient volume, least of all in the crucial categories of tanks and aircraft, to alter the basic assumptions of British war production planning." In addition there were serious "doubts about the ability of Canadian industry to deliver the goods quickly" and a very real "shortage of dollars."[69]

Those assumptions were not entirely incorrect. Mackenzie King had been more than a little dubious throughout the last years of peace about turning Canada into a manufacturer of munitions. To do such a thing would effectively foreclose the Canadian option of choosing neutrality in a British war, and for domestic political reasons that option was one that Mackenzie King never chose to foreclose entirely. Only in mid-1939 did the King government begin to show some interest in seeking arms contracts. The Canadian Manufacturers Association began to demand assistance from Ottawa in negotiating with the British government and its agencies; this was given;[70] and a CMA delegation visited England in August 1939 in an effort to get munitions orders. The reception the delegation received was heartening but by the time it returned to Canada war had broken out[71] and the situation had altered decisively.

From the British point of view the best financial aid Canada could give in the early stages of the war was to help Britain purchase goods in Canada. Chamberlain's telegram to Mackenzie King on September 6 made this very obvious: "As regards supplies, there will undoubtedly be large requirements of Canadian dollars." Canada had a trade surplus in normal years, the telegram went on, and war demands would likely increase it. "For instance, if dollars are available for food defence department would like to increase our normal food imports from Canada by a very large amount, perhaps 100 million dollars."[72] When Mackenzie King read this telegram to Cabinet, he noted that he thought his ministers were "a little stunned at the amounts asked for by way of credits – something like $300,000,000 ..."[73] The key words in Chamberlain's telegram, of course, were "if dollars are available" and the shortage of dollars was soon to cause problems.

As Chamberlain noted, even in peacetime Britain had a large trade deficit with Canada. In 1938, for example, Canada exported $341,424,000 to Britain but imported only $119,292,000 from her, a surplus of $222 million.[74] Of course Canada needed this surplus to balance her large deficit with the United States. The problem for both Canada and the United Kingdom was certain to be compounded by the war and the consequent end of the free convertibility of sterling to dollars.

Thus while Canadian purchases in the United States would eventually increase as a result of war needs, so too would United Kingdom purchases in Canada. The certain result was that both Commonwealth countries would be in difficulty.

The British saw the problem first, and their almost instinctive response was to cut non-essential imports from Canada and the United States to the bone. A Cabinet paper from the President of the Board of Trade on September 19 argued for restrictions "for the purpose of enabling us to concentrate all available resources in dollar exchange on the purchase of commodities which are essential for the prosecution of the war." Already, the minister stated, luxury imports and imports of goods that could be produced in Britain had been stopped. This amounted to about £5.25 million from Canada. Now controls had to be imposed on tobacco and fresh and canned fruit, the value of these Canadian imports being about £2.7 million per year.[75]

However necessary and reasonable these controls, the response from Canada was predictable. The Cabinet considered the question on September 20, and Mackenzie King noted that the restrictions had been made at the same time that Britain "has undertaken to take all of Australia's wool supply and all her surplus agricultural products, and also after she had made equally generous arrangements with New Zealand. Our Government," King fumed, "has been the first to arrange to send an expeditionary force and yet we are the first to be cut off."[76] Dr. Skelton told the High Commissioner that when Canada was trying to make as many dollars as possible available to Britain "it was hardly encouraging to find that two commodities in which Canada was specially interested and of which she is a large supplier should be restricted." Sir Gerald Campbell noted that Skelton "thought it was highly unsatisfactory that the whole question of handling dollar resources should be dealt with in a piecemeal manner." The High Commissioner added that "I confess I do not find this argument easy to meet ..."[77] The official Canadian reply made the same points and urged a delay in any such decision. The breathing space was accorded, aided by a memorandum from the Dominions Secretary, Anthony Eden, to the Cabinet, which coolly noted that "The Canadians will obviously feel that it is wrong that we should be pressing them to supply and even finance purchases in Canada essential to *our* interests while we are taking unilateral action which must damage *their* essential interests."[78] These arguments succeeded in converting a ban on apples into restrictions,[79] a minor victory, perhaps, but one of importance in Nova Scotia and to its representative in the Cabinet, the Minister of National Revenue, J.L. Ilsley.

The apple incident, not of profound significance, did illustrate a certain British insensitivity to Canadian concerns. The High Commissioner, a constant critic of Mackenzie King and his policies, had been favourably impressed in early September by what he reported as "several gratifying instances of a readiness to co-operate."[80] But that willingness was being frittered away, as a memorandum prepared in the Department of Finance showed in October. The British already had indicated that they expected a trade deficit with Canada of about $445 million in the first year of the war,[81] and it was their expectation and hope that Canada would agree to finance all or a large part of this. But what had Canada got from Britain so far? At best, about thirty orders for $10 million;[82] an offer to purchase cheese at a price that was too low; a refusal to buy bacon at the Canadian price; an offer to purchase copper under the going rate. This was no way to win Canadian co-operation.[83]

But what did Ottawa want? Another Finance Department memorandum set out the Canadian position. Canada would supply food, supplies, some equipment and munitions, plus a small expeditionary force for which Canada would pay the costs. Britain and France would be charged for supplies they used, and Britain would ship them overseas. Canada, however, would assist Britain (and possibly France)[84] in financing purchases in Canada and in return the British would repatriate Canadian securities held in the United Kingdom.[85] The Canadian policy on negotiations with London also was stated simply. The program had to be considered as a whole, not piecemeal as had happened with apple imports. Financial assistance would be offered in a package, not with regard to specific commodities, and fair treatment would have to be shown to Canadian producers. In addition, under no circumstances would Canada tie the dollar to the pound sterling,[86] and Ottawa wished to use Canadian credit balances in London to reduce both public and private indebtedness to Britain.[87]

Clearly the Canadian policy was not one of *guerre à l'outrance*.[88] But as Graham Towers of the Bank of Canada told J.A.C. Osborne (the British Treasury representative in Ottawa and a former Deputy Governor of the Bank of Canada), "the United Kingdom should realize how enthusiastically Canada has come into the war and that they are determined to put forward their maximum effort ... Of course," Osborne observed, "the term 'maximum effort' is elastic and likely to mean different things to different countries according to their needs and the degree of immediate danger they experience, a thing we will not allow the Canadians to forget."[89]

This was the heart of the Canadian argument. R.B. Bryce, the young but exceedingly able student of the great British economist, John

Maynard Keynes, and a key aide to W. Clifford Clark, the Deputy Minister of Finance, laid out the Canadian position in a memorandum that argued persuasively that Canadians could not be expected to devote as large a proportion of their national income to the war as the British. "The War is a European War in which the vital interests of the UK are at stake. Not so with Canadians, who are 3,000 miles from the scene of war, who whether rightly or wrongly appreciate the protection they enjoy from their great southern neighbour, and who enter the war more from a sense of loyalty to the Mother country and in a spirit of a crusade for the protection of our ideals of freedom and democracy." Moreover, Bryce argued, Canada was a sprawling country with "a lesser degree of real national unity behind the prosecution of the war" and much less accustomed than Britain to the controls and regimentation that might make possible a large diversion of the national income to war. Furthermore the Canadian governmental structure was less efficient than the UK's and Canada was "relatively and absolutely ... the greatest *debtor* country in the world."[90] The Prime Minister had said exactly the same thing to the British Air Mission.

The Canadian position on financial questions was taken to London at the beginning of November by T.A. Crerar, the Minister of Mines and Resources. As a Manitoban, Crerar was particularly concerned about wheat sales, and he argued as vigorously as he could that Britain had an obligation to buy wheat from Canada at a price that would give a reasonable return to the Prairie farmer. At Treasury insistence, British policy thus far had been to buy on the world market at the going rate, a price well below the Canadian one.[91] But by November, when Crerar was beginning his negotiations, the British had decided to buy in Canada if the price was right.[92] It wasn't. The British maintained that 70¢ a bushel was fair while the minister said that such a sum "could not be considered."[93] Crerar suggested a Canadian guarantee to supply wheat for twelve months at 93 1/2¢ or until July 1, 1941 at $1.[94] The British were unhappy, and Graham Towers, in London with Crerar, "pointed out that Britain had obtained cheap food for nine years, except for brief periods, and Canadian farmers had had poor prices. It would be impossible to convince the Canadian farmer that he was unreasonable in asking for a better price now." This speech prompted the British Minister of Food, W.S. Morrison, to argue that an increase of 30¢ per bushel would raise the price of bread in Britain by a penny and a half a loaf. "Such an increase in the cost of living would have a very serious effect, not only on the spirit of the workers of this country, but on the whole capacity of the country to exert its maximum war effort." This emotional blackmail failed to move Crerar, and the question remained unresolved, the British evidently preferring to continue to buy and sell on the open market.⁹⁵ London obviously hoped prices would stay low, while in Ottawa Mackenzie King and the Cabinet expected "wheat will rise considerably from now on."⁹⁶ In May 1940, finally, Britain contracted to take fifty million bushels at 82 1/2¢, a price then still above the market price.⁹⁷ Further orders followed in August after the change in the war situation.

Crerar's discussions on the extent of Canadian aid were equally important. The British beyond doubt believed that Canada was acting in a niggardly fashion, and much of the discussion centred on how much of its national income each country was spending on the common cause.⁹⁸ Crerar presented the Canadian position in a paper, "The War Finance of Canada." The Dominion effort would take two forms, he said, military assistance and the provision and financing of supplies. The most that Canada could do during the next year was to spend $320 million for military purposes and about $200 million to finance British purchases in Canada. "It was hoped," Crerar said, holding out the carrot, "that this last sum might possibly be increased if orders from the United Kingdom and other allied countries were placed in Canada promptly enough and on a large enough scale to give an immediate and substantial stimulus to the expansion of Canadian production and Canadian national income." According to Crerar, Canada was already spending 47.3 per cent of national income on government operations and the war, and even if the war pushed the national income up 15 per cent this would still mean that governmental expenditures would be 41.1 per cent of national income. By contrast Britain, a principal power, was spending only 51.1 per cent of her national income on such uses.⁹⁹

The British reaction to this kind of reasoning was amused contempt. "Broadly speaking," a Treasury note argued, "the Canadian Treasury appears to be making elaborate calculations as to the cost of Canada's war effort in the first year and from this there emerges at the finish a figure which they say represents the maximum financial assistance which they could give by loan to the United Kingdom. The whole thing seems to us mildly preposterous." Canada was underestimating its national income, and the calculations were based on "theoretical reasonings and rough estimatings which make it a ridiculous method to choose."¹⁰⁰ Perhaps, but the Canadians held firm in the negotiations. Sir Frederick Phillips of the Treasury met with Graham Towers on December 1, and heard the Bank of Canada governor confirm that the total amount Canada could lend was $237 million less the cost to Canada for financing the first year of the BCATP, some $46 million. This was unfortunate, Phillips said. "Mr Towers said that however unfortunate it might be they could not offer us a sum which they did not honestly believe they could find inside the economic structure of Canada." Towers did add that if the estimates proved too low, Canada would do more. "This," Phillips sighed, "seems to me reasonably satisfactory and I do not think we shall get more out of them."[101] Towers had been at some pains to point out that the Canadian offer was not one that the country could bear with ease, but rather one that would entail considerable sacrifice by the Canadian people.[102]

Canadian generosity had been pushed as hard as it could be in the fall of 1939. More might have been forthcoming had the British demonstrated a willingness to place some orders in Canada, but even the British negotiators' own estimates showed only £7 million in orders as of November 21.[103] This failure, for so it was seen in Canada, provoked Mackenzie King enormously, and in an Ottawa press conference at the end of November he let fly. Grant Dexter of the *Winnipeg Free Press* recorded the Prime Minister's off-the-record remarks in a private memorandum:

> This matter of war orders was admittedly difficult to explain to the public. But in fact the explanation was simple. The British were not in a position to place orders. And when they did decide to place orders it was usually discovered that one of two reasons existed which made action impossible: 1. some essential blueprint or pattern would be missing and would have to be brought out from England, entailing a very long delay; 2. the approval of the British treasury had to be obtained. He had never been able to understand why the British purchasing authorities at home did not get the approval of the treasury before instructing the war mission in Canada to make the purchase. Indeed, he said, there seemed to be very little cooperation between the British treasury and the purchasing authorities and, in consequence, orders in every direction were being held up. He said that no doubt the British treasury was very busy and greatly in arrears. Meantime everybody would have to be patient.[104]

Some people in Canada seemed to believe that the Treasury was determined to stop all orders to the Dominion.[105] That was probably too strong, but there was no doubt that, as Lester Pearson wrote to a friend from London some months later, British officials had been "criminally short-sighted" in ignoring Canada as a base of supplies. The Canadians were not blameless, Pearson added with his usual willingness to see both sides of any problem, but Britain's very existence was at stake and there could be no excuse for not placing orders in Canada "even if it might mean the loss of a few orders by their own manufacturers."[106]

Dealing with London 193

The British, thinking of their own unemployment and profits, unfortunately did not see it this way, and they would not until the fall of France altered their views of the war. Ottawa's fiscal perceptions would change at the same time.

NOTES

1 Public Archives of Canada [PAC], W.L. Mackenzie King Papers, Black Binders, Vol. 14, file 51, exhibit 1; C.P. Stacey, *Arms, Men and Governments: The War Policies of Canada 1939–1945* (Ottawa, 1970), p. 81.
2 PAC, Department of External Affairs Records, Vol. 42, folio 243, Vol. 1, "Recruitment of Canadians for Service in Royal Air Force," 3 Mar. 1936; ibid., Christie to Skelton, 5 May 1936.
3 Ibid., Ian Mackenzie to King, 4 Sept. 1936; King Papers, Memo, 10 Sept. 1936, f. C109341; Fred Hatch, "The British Commonwealth Air Training Plan, 1939–45," Ph.D. thesis, University of Ottawa, 1969, 1983.
4 Public Record Office [PRO], Dominions Office Records, DO 114/85, Secretary of State for Dominion Affairs [SSDA] to High Commissioner, 13 May 1938.
5 External Affairs Records, Vol. 42, folio 243, Vol. 1, "Precis of Conversations ... 12 Aug. 1938"; PRO, Prime Minister's Office Records, Prem 1/397, "Training of R.A.F. Pilots in Canada: Political Note," 11 Nov. 1938; Stacey, *Arms, Men and Governments*, pp. 83–4.
6 House of Commons *Debates*, 1 July 1938, pp. 4525–31.
7 Prem 1/397, "Training of R.A.F. Pilots ..."; PAC, C.D. Howe Papers, Vol. 48, file S-14-i(i), Memo, "R.A.F. Training Scheme," n.d.
8 Prem 1/397, "Training of R.A.F. Pilots ..."
9 Ibid., att. to letter Sandford[?] to Sir H. Wilson, 28 July 1939.
10 PRO, Cabinet Records, Cab 66/1, W.P. (39)4, 4 Sept. 1939; King Papers, Black Binders, Vol. 15, file 53, High Commissioner to Secretary of State for External Affairs [SSEA], 4 Sept. 1939, f. C267860.
11 Vincent Massey, *What's Past Is Prologue* (Toronto, 1963), pp. 304–6. PRO, Air Ministry Records, Air 20/333/11IC/3/4, Note of Meeting ..., 22, 23 Sept. 1939; ibid., Street to Barlow, 24 Sept. 1939; Stacey, *Arms, Men and Governments*, p. 79.
12 Massey's paternity is vigorously denied by the then Australian High Commissioner, Stanley Bruce, and by the Under Secretary of State for Air, Harold Balfour. In his memoirs Balfour goes to some length to award sole credit to the Australian: "The Empire Air Training Scheme ... was born with Stanley Bruce ... as father." Harold Balfour, *Wings Over Westminster* (London, 1973), pp. 112–13. There is ample evidence on this point including Massey's memoirs, the *Mackenzie King Record*, and the recollections of

External Affairs personnel in this period. Interviews with C.S.A. Ritchie, Lester Pearson, and John W. Holmes, 1971.
13. Massey, pp. 304–5; Lester B. Pearson, *Mike: The Memoirs of the Rt. Hon. Lester B. Pearson*, Vol. I: *1897–1948* (Toronto, 1972), p. 151; Prem 1/397, Eden to Chamberlain, 25 Sept. 1939 and atts.
14. King Papers, Tel. Prime Minister [PM] to PM, 26 Sept. 1939, ff. 2247898.
15. Ibid.
16. King Diary, 26 Sept. 1939.
17. Ibid., 27 Sept. 1939.
18. Ibid., 28 Sept. 1939; King Papers, Memo re. Emergency Council of Cabinet, 28 Sept. 1939, ff. C110723ff.
19. Ibid., P.M. to P.M., 28 Sept. 1939, ff. 224801ff.
20. King Diary, 28 Sept. 1939. For Skelton's next shot at the proposal, see King Papers, Memo, Skelton to King, 29 Sept. 1939 and King's reply, 30 Sept. 1939, ff. C109479ff.
21. King Diary, 10 Oct. 1939; King Papers, Memo, Skelton to King, 7 Oct. 1939, ff. C267916–8 and docs on ff. C267928ff.; James Eayrs, *In Defence of Canada*, Vol. II: *Appeasement and Rearmament* (Toronto, 1965), pp. 106–7.
22. Air 19/83, "Memo on the Incidence of Cost of the Air Training Scheme," 5 Oct. 1939. See also docs on Air 46/1, Air 46/2, and PRO, Foreign Office Records, FO 414/272 for further information on the UK side of the negotiations.
23. Air 20/405/11IC/3/13, Note of 1st Meeting ..., 10 Oct. 1939.
24. Ibid., Note of Third Meeting ..., 13 Oct. 1939.
25. King Papers, "Dominion Training Scheme," 13 Oct. 1939. Additional Canadian material can be found in PAC, Ian Mackenzie Papers, file X-41. The Montreal *Gazette* estimated costs at $100 million for the first year. 16 Oct. 1939.
26. King Diary, 17 Oct. 1939.
27. Directorate of History, National Defence Headquarters, Ottawa, Air Vice Marshal E.W. Stedman Papers, Memo, "BCATP," p. 2. The British were relatively optimistic after this meeting. See Air 20/405/111C/3/13, Notes of 6th Meeting ..., 18 Oct. 1939; Air 8/280/1P3/574, Mission to Canada ..., n.d.; Air 20/338/111C/3/14, Riverdale to Wood, 19 Oct. 1939.
28. Air 20/405/11IC/3/13. Notes of 7th Meeting ..., 19 Oct. 1939.
29. Air 20/338/11IC/3/14, Riverdale to Wood, 19 Oct. 1939.
30. Stedman Papers, "BCATP," pp. 2ff.; ibid., folders on Flying Training Scheme, estimates, 23 Oct., 16, 26 Nov. 1939; Hatch, 839.
31. Air 20/338/111C/3/14, Riverdale to Wood, 30 Oct. 1939 and atts.
32. Air 20/404/111C/3/7, "Points for Tuesday's Meeting ... [31 Oct. 1939]."
33. PAC, Privy Council Office Records, Cabinet War Committee Records, Memo re Emergency Council of Cabinet, 31 Oct. 1939.
34. Balfour, *Wings Over Westminster*, p. 115.

35 Queen's University, C.G. Powers Papers, [UK] Notes of Meeting, October 31. The Canadian minutes are not essentially different. Memo re Emergency Council of Cabinet, 31 Oct. 1939. Cf. King Diary, 31 Oct. 1939, and Air 20/338/HIC/3/14, Riverdale to Wood, 6 Nov. 1939.
36 King Diary, 31 Oct. 1939, Power Papers, Notes ... 31 Oct. 1939; Memo re Emergency Council ..., 31 Oct. 1939; Air 8/280/1P3/574, Mission to Canada ... n.d.
37 King Papers, Memo for PM, 1 Nov. 1939, ff. C109539ff. The British version is on PRO, Treasury Records, T160/1340, High Commissioner to SSDA, 1 Nov. 1939.
38 King Diary, 1, 3, 10 Nov. 1939; King Papers, Memo by Skelton, 2 Nov. 1939, ff. C268010ff.; Stacey, *Arms, Men and Governments*, p. 22. In connection with the "free gift," Power noted that Britain at no time revealed details of costs of engines, equipment, etc. "The suggestion has been freely made that at that time the economic planners of Great Britain had no desire to see Canada ... developing an aircraft industry of her own." Norman Ward, ed., *A Party Politician: The Memoirs of Chubby Power* (Toronto, 1966), pp. 200–1.
39 King Papers, PM to PM, 3 Nov. 1939, ff. 224807ff.
40 Air 20/404/1HC/3/7, Notes of Meeting ..., 3 Nov. 1939; Air 20/338/1HC/3/14. Riverdale to Wood, 6 Nov. 1939.
41 Ibid., Air 8/280/1P3/574, "Air Mission to Canada ..."
42 Ibid.; King Papers, "Air Training Scheme Proposals," n.d., ff. C109455-6.
43 King Diary, 14 Nov. 1939.
44 Cabinet War Committee Records, Minutes, 14 Nov. 1939; FO 414/272. Note of a Special Meeting, 15 Nov. 1939; Toronto *Telegram*, 15 Nov. 1939.
45 Air 20/338/1HC/3/14, Wood to Riverdale, 22 Nov. 1939.
46 Cab 67/2, WG (39) 105, 18 Nov. 1939.
47 Cab 65/2, Minutes, 25 Nov. 1939.
48 Cab 67/3, High Commissioner to SSDA, 25 Nov. 1939.
49 See the notes by King on his talk with Campbell on 25 Nov. 1939, which indicate that financial aspects still troubled him most of all. King Papers, "Re: Air Training Scheme," ff. C109614ff.
50 Cabinet War Committee Records, Minutes, 27 Nov. 1939; King Diary, 27 Nov. 1939.
51 Cab 67/3, PM to PM, 27 Nov. 1939; ibid., High Commissioner to SSDA, 27 Nov. 1939; Air 20/338/1110/3/14, Riverdale to Wood, 30 Nov. 1939.
52 Eayrs, II, p. 111; King Papers, Memo, "Priority of Air Training Scheme," 28 Nov. 1939. ff. C268121-5.
53 Ibid., Statement, f. C109624; King Diary, 27 Nov. 1939. For King's views on the UK at this time, see Queen's University, Grant Dexter Papers, Memo, 30 Nov. 1939.

54 See Stacey, *Arms, Men and Governments*, pp. 24–5; Cab 65/2, Minutes, 2 Dec. 1939; King Papers, PM to PM, 1 Dec. 1939, ff. C268144–5; Eayrs, II, p. 111.
55 Hatch, 104ff.; King Papers, Memo for PM, n.d., ff. C268153ff.
56 Power Papers, Rogers to Riverdale, 8 Dec. 1939.
57 King Papers, Riverdale to Rogers, 9 Dec. 1939, f. C268164.
58 King Diary, 9–10 Dec. 1939; Stacey, *Arms, Men and Governments*, p. 26; King Papers, Memo by Heeney, 11 Dec. 1939, ff. C268210ff.
59 Cab 65/2, Minutes, 11, 13 Dec. 1939; Cab 67/3, WG (39) 148, 12 Dec. 1939; King Papers, Memo to PM, 13 Dec. 1939, ff. C268219–21.
60 King Diary, 14 Dec. 1939; Power Papers, [UK] Notes of Meeting ..., 14 Dec. 1939.
61 Proposal in ibid., Riverdale to King, 15 Dec. 1939; King's reply in King Papers, PM to PM, 16 Dec. 1939, ff. C268318ff.
62 King Diary, 15 Dec. 1939.
63 Ibid.
64 Air 8/264/1P3/575, Notes of Transatlantic Conversations ..., 17 Dec. 1939; King Papers, Black Binders, Vol. 1, Comments by Colonel Ralston, 16 Dec. 1939; Power Papers, Riverdale to Rogers, 16 Dec. 1939; King Diary, 16 Dec. 1939, and press reaction in King Papers, ff. C268247ff.
65 Cab 65/2, Minutes, 18 Dec. 1939; Prem 1/397, Memo for Prime Minister [Chamberlain], 26 Dec. 1939.
66 Ibid., High Commissioner to SSDA, 19 Dec. 1939. By way of contrast, see Campbell's bland comments in his memoir, *Of True Experience* (New York, 1947), p. 101.
67 Floyd Chalmers Papers (Toronto), "Re Canada–UK War Financing Arrangements," November–December, 1941.
68 "The British Commonwealth Air Training Plan" (Ottawa, 1939). This is a pamphlet version of King's address on 17 Dec. 1939.
69 M.M. Postan, *British War Production* (London, 1952), pp. 229, 235. See also H.D. Hall and G.C. Wrigley, *Studies of Overseas Supply* (London, 1956), pp. 52–3; H.D. Hall, *North American Supply* (London, 1955), pp. 3ff.; J. Hurstfield, *The Control of Raw Materials* (London, 1953), p. 177.
70 E.g., King Papers, Skelton to Campbell, 15 May 1939, ff. 23698711.
71 On the mission, see PAC, A.G.L. McNaughton Papers, Vol. 241, CMA Mission files; King Papers, Memo by McNaughton, n.d., ff. C269932ff. On supply generally before 1939, see Stacey, *Arms, Men and Governments*, pp. 100ff.
72 Department of Finance, Ottawa, W. Clifford Clark Papers, file U-3-2, PM to PM, 6 Sept. 1939.
73 King Diary, 6 Sept. 1939.
74 M.C. Urquhart and J.A.H. Buckley, *Historical Statistics of Canada* (Toronto, 1965), p. 183.
75 Cab 67/1, WP (G) (39) 14, 19 Sept. 1939.

76 King Diary, 20 Sept. 1939.
77 Cab 67/1, WP (G) (39), High Commissioner to SSDA, 21 Sept. 1939.
78 Ibid., (39) 18, 22 Sept. 1939.
79 Ibid., (39) 45, 18 Oct. 1939.
80 FO 371/23966, High Commissioner to SSDA, 20 Sept. 1939.
81 See T160/1141, "Canada's Sterling Balance," 30 July 1941, which indicates that the British estimated the deficit in fall 1939 at between £73–90 million. Cf. Hall, p. 229.
82 Stacey, *Arms, Men and Governments*, p. 30, estimates UK orders at $5 million as of 8 Dec. 1939.
83 Clark Papers, file U-3-3, "Summary," n.d.; Hall, pp. 10ff.
84 Incredibly, discussions with the French did not begin until mid-May 1940. See PAC, Department of Finance Records, Vol. 2691, Towers to Ralston, 17 May 1940.
85 See R.S. Sayers, *Financial Policy, 1939–1945* (London, 1956), pp. 326–7.
86 Ibid., pp. 333–4.
87 Clark Papers, file U-3-3, "Financial Aspects of Negotiations with United Kingdom," n.d. [early Oct. 1939].
88 Stacey, *Arms, Men and Governments*, p. 11 cites Ralston saying on 21 Sept. 1939 that the $100 million war appropriation for the period to 31 Mar. 1940 set "the limits within which expenditures can be made" and efforts should be made to spend less.
89 T160/1141, Osborne to Sir F. Phillips, 6 Oct. 1939. Osborne had been loaned to the Bank of Canada in its formative years by the UK Treasury.
90 Finance Department Records, Vol. 3440, National Income Statistics 1940–42, "What Proportion of the National Income ...," n.d. [Oct. 1939]; Sayers, pp. 330–1.
91 Ibid., p. 328
92 Cab 21/490, DMV (C) (39) 1, 2 Nov. 1939. On the negotiations, see docs on Cab 99/1.
93 Cab 21/490, DMV (C) (39) 12, 22 Nov. 1939.
94 See Pearson, I, p. 145.
95 Clark Papers, file U-3-3, Summary of Minutes of Meeting ..., 1 Dec. 1939; Cab 21/490, DMV (C) (39) 13, 1 Dec. 1939; Dexter Papers, Memos, 12, 29 Dec. 1939.
96 King Diary, 7 Dec. 1939.
97 King Papers, "Canadian Economic Contribution," 1 June 1940, f. C246775. On wheat negotiations and problems, see J.W. Holmes, "Bushels to Burn," *Behind the Headlines*, No. 1 (September, 1940); D.A. MacGibbon, *The Canadian Grain Trade 1931–1951* (Toronto, 1952), pp. 100–1; and esp. G.E. Britnell and V.C. Fowke, *Canadian Agriculture in War and Peace 1935–50* (Stanford, 1962), pp. 200ff.

98 The whole National Income framework was Keynesian, of course. See Robert Lekachman, *The Age of Keynes* (New York, 1966), p. 145.
99 Copy of Crerar Memo on T160/1340; External Affairs Records, Vol. 67, file 388, SSEA to High Commissioner London, 8 Nov. 1939; *Hall*, pp. 12–13; Sayers, p. 330; T160/1140, Osborne to Phillips, 27 Oct. 1939. W.K. Hancock and M.M. Gowing, *British War Economy* (London, 1949), p. 369 provides comparative figures on war spending as a percentage of national income. In Graham Towers' view, the maximum Canada could spend in the first year of the war was 40 per cent of the national income. Finance Department Records, Vol. 777, file 400-16, "Notes on Canada's War Potential," 31 Oct. 1939.
100 T160/1340, Treasury Note, n.d. and "Note on Memo on Canadian War Finance," n.d. By January 1942 the Canadians had come to believe the national-income idea somewhat unsatisfactory. See Finance Department Records, Vol. 3440, National Income Statistics 1940–42, Towers to Clark, 6 June 1942. See also F.H. Brown et al., *War Finance in Canada* (Toronto, 1940), pp. 65, which also seems to feel the Canadian national-income estimates were too low.
101 T160/1340, Note by Phillips, 1 Dec. 1939; External Affairs Records, Vol. 67, file 388, High Commissioner to SSEA, 14 Dec. 1939.
102 Cab 21/490, DMV (C) (39)11, 1 Dec. 1939; Clark Papers, file B-2-8-7-2-3, Towers to Ralston, 23 Jan. 1940; Stacey, *Arms, Men and Governments*, pp. 11–12; Hall, pp. 15, 229; Sayers, pp. 331–2.
103 Cab 21/490, D.MV (C) (39) 13, 21 Nov. 1939. In his memoirs, J.S. Duncan of Massey-Harris records that his firm was the first to get a British war contract – in December 1939. *Not a One-Way Street* (Toronto, 1971), p. 107.
104 Dexter Papers, Memo, 30 Nov. 1939; Sayers, pp. 328–9.
105 British policy at this time was to keep North American purchases "limited to those materials unobtainable elsewhere." Hurstfield, p. 181. Floyd Chalmers, in 1939 editor of the *Financial Post*, recalls conversations with British emissaries to Canada who were worried that orders in Canada would do nothing to solve British unemployment. Interview, 27 Sept. 1973.
106 Dexter Papers, Pearson to Dexter, 21 Aug. 1940.

Chapter Nine

How Britain's Weakness Forced Canada into the Arms of the United States

In the Broadway musical *Pal Joey*, one of the main characters takes off her clothes in a bump-and-grind routine. In her song, the amateur ecdysiast says, "I was reading Schopenhauer last night, and I think that Schopenhauer is right." Well, I was reading Hegel last night, and I think that Hegel is right. Especially when he said, "What experience and history teach is this – that people and governments never have learned anything from history, or acted on principles deduced from it." Regrettably, Hegel was probably correct, and it may be that there is no better example than the efforts of the Canadian government to help its struggling mother country, Great Britain, in the years after the Second World War.

Surely this country's government ought to have learned from experience. In the Great War, the British in their financial desperation and exhaustion had pressed Canada to raise money in the United States and encouraged the forging of economic links across the border so that Canadian industry might better serve the British and Allied war effort. In the Second World War, British military weakness obliged Canada to ensure its national security by striking a military alliance with the United States. British financial weakness similarly demanded that Canada find some way of increasing its exports of raw materials to the United States to cover the trade deficit resulting from the import of munitions components necessary so that Canada could support Great Britain. The Hyde Park Declaration of April 1941 resolved Canada's economic problems, just as the Ogdensburg Agreement of 1940 had solved her military security problems. But the net result was that Canada and the United States emerged from the Second World War more closely linked than ever.

Surely there could not be a third instance in which Britain's weakness would force Canada to the south? In fact, as we shall see, the Mackenzie King government's efforts to help Britain and to keep up Anglo-Canadian trade led to precisely this outcome. Britain's economic weakness drove Canada to Washington yet again, and for a third time in just three decades the United States freely offered the requested assistance. After that happy event, Canada entered a long era of unprecedented prosperity, enjoying a standard of living undreamed of before the start of the 1939 war. All that had been sacrificed to achieve this prolonged boom was Canada's chance of economic and military independence.

When he considered the postwar period in his *The Forked Road: Canada 1939–1957*, Donald Creighton wrote that Liberal prime ministers Mackenzie King and Louis St. Laurent "stubbornly continued to act as if they still cherished the senile delusion that freedom from British control was alone necessary to ensure Canadian autonomy, and that independence in a continent dominated by the United States was an easy and effortless business which had no need of constant attention and protective care."[1] That, I have to say, is a wholly uninformed and inaccurate assessment.

Nor is James Laxer's "Liberal sell-out" interpretation of what happened any more complete. In his most recent book, *Decline of the Superpowers*, Laxer notes that Canada was at a crossroads in 1945. "For the Liberal government of Mackenzie King," he says, "it was natural enough to base post-war economic policy on still closer ties with the United States." Most especially, "it was American investment that would guarantee takeoff. US investment poured into the manufacturing and resource sectors of the Canadian economy."[2] Some of that is true, but Laxer seems completely unaware of the reasons Canada had to choose the American road. The reasons, almost as much as the result, are what matter.

The world in 1945 was in ruins. Britain, Europe, and Asia had been destroyed by six years of war. Their housing stock was bombed into rubble, much of their industrial plant was levelled or just plain worn-out, and their men, women, and children were dead or dying of malnutrition and disease. Only two nations had emerged from the Second World War stronger economically, politically, and militarily than when they entered it, Canada and the United States. Both North American nations were committed and idealistic, Canadians probably more so than Americans, though Canada, of course, had far less strength than its superpower neighbour. Like the Americans, Canada's government and almost all her businessmen wanted to see a world that traded freely on a multilateral basis. Such a situation, replacing the prewar world of high tariffs, was in Canada's interest, one that would allow us to capitalize on our strengths, our ability to produce, and the advantage we had after 1945 of having goods for sale in what was expected to be a seller's market.

But what country could buy what Canada had to sell? The world was starving and impoverished, and few nations had the dollars to pay us for our food and manufactured goods. Unless we found buyers, Canadian workers and farmers might find themselves on the pogey once more. The choice in 1945 seemed to be either to give aid to our traditional trading partners in Britain and Europe or to face massive unemployment at home. The Canadian government sensibly chose to offer aid.

The result was an unprecedented and generous program that saw Canada provide $2.2 billion in loans and credits to Britain and the Western European nations in the years immediately after the war. Our object was twofold: idealistically to help reconstruct and rehabilitate a ravaged world and, out of self-interest, to keep up Canadian exports and prosperity. The United States did much the same although, in proportionate terms, Canada's assistance was greater. But then our dependence on trade was also greater. To cite only a few examples, Britain took almost all of Canada's exports of eggs, bacon, and canned salmon, and a high proportion of exports of wheat, newsprint, and timber. If the British could not pay for these goods, where was Canada to sell them?

The major part of the Canadian aid package was the loan to Britain negotiated early in 1946. If they were to trade with Canada, British negotiators said, if they were not to be forced to fall back on restrictive practices and on commerce only within a sealed-off Sterling Area, they had to borrow dollars.[3] Certainly Britain had suffered economically during the war. Great Britain had lost a quarter of her prewar wealth and had become the world's largest debtor. Capital assets abroad had been sold off to pay for the war, and even the British merchant fleet was 30 per cent smaller than in 1939.[4] The United Kingdom was almost on the ropes.

Contentious negotiations in Washington had finally led to arrangements for a loan from the United States of $3.75 billion in December 1945 – with humiliating conditions.[5] The British demands of Canada were for fewer dollars, but for far more than the usual 17:1 ratio that differentiated the American national income from the Canadian. London needed almost $2 billion all told, part of a complicated arrangement involving the write-off of war debts on both sides as well as a straight dollar loan. The negotiations were argumentative, the British insisting again and again that while they wanted to buy Canadian goods, they could not do so without dollars. The Canadian ministers and officials had fought among themselves over the terms, but Prime Minister Mackenzie King, always a sentimental imperialist and monarchist at heart, Donald Creighton notwithstanding, helped tip the balance in the direction of generosity. As King wrote in his diary, "It certainly will be difficult for my political opponents through generations to come to say that I have been anti-British with what has been done for Britain under my administrations in the war and post-war years."[6] King could not have been more wrong – his political opponents and the historians faced no such difficulty.

Nonetheless, the result was the settlement of all war debts and a loan of $1.25 billion for fifty years at 2 per cent interest – a loan moreover made without humiliating conditions, unless 2 per cent interest could be thought to be humiliating.[7] Incredibly, Canada had given Britain one-third the amount offered by the United States. The loan was also about 10 per cent of the 1946 Gross National Product. That was a testimony to the King government's commitment to the maintenance of Anglo-Canadian trade.

But the loan was not charity to Britain, Finance Minister J.L. Ilsley told the House of Commons: "it is an investment in the future of Canadian trade."[8] Progressive Conservative leader John Bracken agreed: the loan was "essential to the preservation of the Canadian economy as we see it today. Ours is an export economy; we are more than any other country dependent upon foreign nations for a market for our products."[9] The *Financial Post* made the same point, and then added that it was not simply because the loan had to be spent in Canada for Canadian products that Ottawa had offered it: "We could just as well have spent the dollars here ourselves." The loan was made, the business paper said in only slightly hyperbolic terms, to "afford Britain an opportunity of eventually making a greater contribution to world trade ... The loans, in substance, will act as a lever to get trade moving."[10]

And trade was moving. Very soon, the difficulty was that too much was coming from the United States into Canada. After ten years of depression and six years of war, Canadians wanted the good things in life. The war had put money into the pockets of farmers who had sold everything they could produce for high prices, of workers who had had as much overtime as they could handle, and of servicemen and women whose pockets bulged with their service gratuities and re-establishment grants. The imports of refrigerators, automobiles, record players, and radios soared, and winter holidays in the American south again became a possibility for the wealthy. The government compounded the difficulty in July 1946 when it raised the Canadian dollar to parity with the American, thus increasing the cost of Canadian exports and encouraging the payment of debts in the United States.[11] The results became almost immediately apparent in the trade statistics and in Canadian holdings of American dollars. Imports from the United States rose to $1,387 billion in 1946, then the highest peacetime total ever, and the next year they were half as much again. The trade deficit with the United States was $500 million in 1946 and $920 million in 1947.[12] The government's holdings of American dollars, about $1.6 billion in 1946, fell precipitously, sinking to $480 million in November 1947.[13] In the circumstances, every effort to encourage American investment in Canada and sales of metals and minerals to the United States seemed – and was – justified.[14]

This was almost the same situation that had occurred in 1917 and 1941. American dollars, the scarcest commodity in a world of scarcities, were again in short supply. And, as in 1917 and 1941, Canada could not use its surplus in trade with Britain – in 1946, $460 million and in 1947, $560 million – to help redress matters with the United States.[15] The pound sterling, declared convertible for non-residents of the United Kingdom in July 1947 to satisfy the terms of the American loan to Britain, was once more forced into inconvertibility in August when the British government, frightened by a rush of other countries to convert soft sterling into hard dollars, again slapped on controls. Then, the British and the Europeans were using the loan from Canada to pay for the goods they bought in Canada; Canada, in other words, was financing virtually all it sold to Britain and Europe. As A.F.W. Plumptre noted at the time, "the breakdown of our hopes for selling to England ... for cash was part of a wider breakdown."[16] Paradoxically, yet predictably, because the Canadian government had wanted to help Britain and Europe and to keep up trade and employment, Canada was in danger of sliding into financial disaster in its relations with the United States.

What was to be done? One possible option was autarky, but no one took this seriously. Another was to join the Sterling Area, the one sure way of expanding trade with Britain and the remnants of empire. But realism had to prevail – in the circumstances of 1947, any alignment with Britain had all the overtones of handcuffing Canada to a corpse. Britain was stopping its aid to Greece and Turkey, abandoning foreign fields to the United States, and the country was on the verge of economic collapse, the Chancellor of the Exchequer "reaching his wit's end."[17] In the circumstances, there seemed to be only one possible course for

Ottawa: to recognize that Canada was part of the American sphere and to seek a customs union with the United States. Norman Robertson, the wise Canadian high commissioner in Britain, put it best when he asked "whether we should not ... be thinking of a real reciprocity arrangement with the United States, which would strengthen our dollar position in the short turn, and in the long run, ensure us against too great a dependence, relative to the United States, on the European market. It might be possible to work out a scheme for a graduated approach to reciprocal free trade in a good many commodities on a continental basis, with the steps selected and their depth determined largely by the requirements of our dollar position."[18] There it was in a nutshell. Canada's dollar shortage, brought on in substantial part by the effort to assist Britain, forced Canada to consider the prospect of reciprocity with the United States. The British government, it is necessary to note, always tended to take Canada's assistance for granted and failed to realize the difficulties Ottawa now found itself in as a result of its aid. That likely explains London's preference for canned salmon from the Soviet Union, timber from Scandinavia, and bacon from Poland. Those countries cheerfully took sterling for their goods, which helped Britain save hard currency dollars for the products it absolutely had to have from North America.[19]

In the meantime, the dollar shortage from which Britain and Canada suffered was a world-wide problem. Britain and Western Europe were in danger of economic collapse, reconstruction was proceeding at a glacial pace, and the Communists in France, Italy, and elsewhere seemed poised to come to power. Western civilization, or so many in Ottawa and Washington believed, seemed as much in danger as it ever had during the war. America's answer was the Marshall Plan, a proposal to give Britain and Europe the dollars they needed to buy American goods. That would rebuild the Continent, check communism, and sell the products of America's factories and farms. But Secretary of State George C. Marshall's plan was only an idea until Congress accepted it.[20]

Even so, there was an opportunity here for Canada. If the Truman administration could be persuaded to use Marshall Plan dollars to pay for Canadian goods, then Canada's dollar shortage could be resolved. There was in this idea a striking parallel to the situation in 1941 when Britain's Lend-Lease account had been charged for the components Canada had to import from the United States so it could manufacture munitions for Britain.

But it was a long way and a longer time from idea to implementation. First, the United States' attention had to be gained. In mid-September 1947, State Department officials concluded that the Canadians "have been drifting from bad to worse while wishfully thinking that when the time came we would step in and rescue them by means of a loan or procurement devices ... or the Marshall Plan. We cannot, of course, let them go under, but it was time that we explained to them the difficulties on our side."[21] Not until the end of October, by which time Canadian reserves had dwindled to under a half billion US dollars while the trade deficit widened, did the US administration pay attention. A Canadian delegation to Washington, led by the deputy minister of finance, Clifford Clark, presented two plans for consideration: Plan A hinged around brutal import restrictions and the banning of virtually every identifiable consumer item imported from the United States; Plan B also involved quotas but foresaw Canadian participation in the Marshall Plan and the placing of some procurement for the European recovery program in Canada.[22] The Americans, anxious to avoid the shattering effects on Canadian-American trade certain to be produced by Plan A, promised to make "a strong stand to obtain the flexibility which they wish in order to make 'off-shore procurement' possible." As a result of this quasi-promise and of discussions that followed in the next days, Finance Minister Douglas Abbott announced the more moderate restrictions of Plan B on 17 November.[23] Abbott pointed to the prospect of Marshall Plan purchases being made in Canada, and he added that "A program of this kind would resemble in many respects the Hyde Park Agreement that proved so effective and constructive during the war."[24] Indeed, an arrangement similar to Hyde Park was as necessary in 1947 as it had been in 1941.

At the same time as these discussions were under way, Canadian and American negotiators had begun to consider the possibility of a free-trade agreement. The negotiations went on well into the New Year, and the result was a draft agreement that called for the creation of a modified customs union between the two countries, the immediate removal of all tariffs, and a five-year period in which quantitative restrictions on specified imports could be imposed.[25]

But free trade was not to be – at least, not in 1948. Although he had supported the beginning of negotiations, and although he had seemed enthusiastic as late as 6 March 1948, Mackenzie King had become concerned about the idea of free trade. Henry Luce's *Life* magazine coincidentally had called for a customs union between Canada and the United States on 15 March, and support from that advocate of "the American Century" was enough to frighten any sensible Canadian. Coincidentally, on 24 March the prime minister had reached onto his bookshelf and pulled down a copy of Richard Jebb's *Studies in Colonial Nationalism*. The book had fallen open at a chapter entitled "The Soul of Empire." Would free trade destroy the unity of the empire? King asked himself. Would it weaken the regard in which he was held by his people? Would it let the Conservative party paint him as the man who had sold out Canada to the United States as the culmination of his long political career? "I would no more think of at my time of life and at this stage of my career attempting any movement of the kind," King wrote in his diary, "than I would of flying to the South pole."[26]

To the chagrin of the few of King's officials who knew of the secret negotiations with the Americans, free trade was dead. The only concession they could get from the old man, still the dominant figure in the country though he was only a few months away from retirement, was the suggestion that if and when a satisfactory "North Atlantic Security Pact" were reached, then "It would be natural for the trade discussions to be related to the pact, since they are concerned with measures for economic defence against aggression. It might also turn out," Hume Wrong, ambassador to the United States, said, "to be desirable later to add the United Kingdom to such discussions."[27] The officials' disappointment at the scuttling of free trade almost certainly explains the zeal with which the Department of External Affairs fought to get Article 2, a clause encouraging economic collaboration, into the North Atlantic Treaty.[28]

If free trade were dead, the Marshall Plan lived. The great Economic Cooperation Act, the postwar counterpart to Lend-Lease, passed the Congress on 3 April 1948, speeded in its passage by the Communist coup in Czechoslovakia and by inspired telegrams to Washington from American officials in Germany that foresaw war with the Soviet Union just around the corner. In a first-year appropriation of $5.3 billion, the American Congress allowed "off-shore procurement" under the act, and the Canadian government seized the opportunity provided. Every conceivable good that could be shipped to Britain and Europe, including wheat Britain had already contracted to buy, seemed to come under the Marshall Plan. "It will mean no more food for us," British embassy officials in Washington said, "and no more money for Canada, but it does mean that shipments will continue at a steady rate with payment guaranteed."[29]

That was an understatement. The more Marshall Plan aid Britain received, the less strain there would be on the Anglo-Canadian financial relationship. Almost exactly as in 1917 and 1941, the United States gave Britain the dollars it needed to pay for purchases in Canada. The importance of this solution was enormous, exactly as in 1917 and 1941. Now Britain could keep up its contracts with Canada rather than trying to break them in order to get "free" American aid.[30] Moreover, the

Marshall Plan dollars – and Canada received over a billion US dollars over the next two years – meant the resolution of the dollar shortage of November 1947. Canada's success in getting the Truman administration to push for off-shore purchases was a major triumph for Canadian diplomacy – and prairie farmers.

As always, there was a downside to this triumph. Because of Marshall Plan financing of Canadian exports, and because of the high proportion of Canadian exports destined for the United States, an unhealthy part of Canadian eggs were in one, American, basket. An official at the Canadian embassy in Washington who looked at the numbers at the end of 1948 concluded that $2,089 million of Canada's total exports of $3,045 million went to the United States or were paid for with US Marshall Plan funds. What would happen, he asked, if the Americans changed their policy?[31] No one had an answer, but there should be no doubt about the reasons for the Canadian plight. Canada had been forced to the south by the weakness of the United Kingdom – and the slow pace of Western Europe's reconstruction.

The British soon plunged into yet another financial crisis, and again they moved to reduce imports from Canada as a way of saving dollars. A worried Graham Towers, the governor of the Bank of Canada, put the situation very clearly to London's high commissioner in Ottawa in April 1949. If the British continued to reduce imports from Canada, he said, "pressures might be set up which might shift the whole outlook of the country towards the United States as the only remaining economic life-line."[32] Increasingly, Canadian government officials and exporters were obliged to seek trade with the one country able to pay for the goods it imported, the United States; increasingly, the United States was almost Canada's sole paying customer.

That troubled Secretary of State for External Affairs Lester Pearson, for one, although in 1948 he had been an enthusiastic supporter of free trade with the United States. In early 1950 Pearson, a minister for little more than a year and somewhat uncomfortable in criticizing one of the government's giants, told C.D. Howe, the minister of trade and commerce, that "in the turbulent post-war stream, the current seems to be carrying our boat rather far from its accustomed course, rather too close, perhaps to rocks on one side of the channel." There was a risk involved in such dependency, "a rock below the surface," Pearson argued, and Canada ran the risk of being subjected to American political pressure.

The "Minister of Everything" was then at the pinnacle of his enormous power, the virtual co-prime minister to Louis St. Laurent. Howe was not amused by criticism from External Affairs or from Pearson who was, he thought, "a little too frightened of the American bogey and, therefore, just a little too anxious to do everything to help the British."[33] His reply to his junior colleague was brutal in its bluntness. Of course, Canada should try to expand exports to soft currency countries, Howe said, but "Our export policy should be to sell as much as possible wherever possible. The United States has become the healthiest and most receptive market in the world at a time when intense difficulties are being encountered elsewhere." Trade with Europe, despite Canada's best efforts, could not equal trade with the Americans. As Howe argued, in words with their own (unconvincing) echo in our own times, "It is not at all obvious that Canada's sovereignty would be impaired, even by a large increase in the percentage of our exports going to the United States. The surest way to lose our sovereignty," he concluded, "would be to get into financial insolvency ... Selling our goods to the Americans is a much better alternative."[34]

Perhaps Howe was correct – the Gross National Product figures which demonstrated that the United States GNP of $381 billion was more than 500 per cent greater than that of the United Kingdom in 1950 certainly suggested that he was – though the Canadian government made repeated efforts to expand trade with Britain and Europe after 1950.[35] Those efforts, no matter the force with which Canadian negotiators urged the British to make sterling convertible again and to increase imports from Canada, invariably foundered. The United Kingdom, its hard currency reserves in a parlous condition, maintained that it simply could not afford the luxury of imports from a dollar country such as Canada, though, of course, they were willing to export everything possible to this country to earn as many dollars as possible. The problem with expanding sales in Canada was that British export goods too often were badly designed for North America – Vanguard, Austin, and Hillman automobiles that ran poorly in summer and not at all in winter, or apartment-size refrigerators that, unless chained to a steel pipe, moved around the floor every time they were switched on. In any case, as British negotiators baldly told the Canadians, their intention was to decrease imports from Canada even further. They were successful too. British exports to Canada by 1956 were at roughly the same level in constant dollars as in 1913, despite a 450 per cent increase in Canadian imports over the period. Canadian exports to Britain in 1956 were 17 per cent of Canada's total exports; in 1937 they had been 40 per cent. It seemed to be government policy, and also easier for British firms, to import goods from the Sterling Area that Britain, its empire fading away with astonishing rapidity, still dominated economically.[36]

The result on Canada was obvious. Canadian exporters were forced increasingly, inevitably, to the reliable and rich American market.

And Canadian products flooded south while American imports came northwards. Investment funds also came from New York, and American companies established new subsidiaries in Canada. As Bruce Muirhead noted in his able study of Canadian postwar trade policy, "with Western Europe and Great Britain effectively excluded as possible destinations for billions of dollars worth of Canadian exports, only the United States remained as a market willing and able to absorb a significant amount of Canadian production ... Ottawa took the only course open to it at that time, although not without some qualms and reservations. Henceforth, the United States would become the single most important sun in the Canadian economic constellation, dwarfing in importance all other past or future trading partners."[37] Ottawa had not become continentalist in its economic policy by choice, Muirhead concluded, but by necessity. "Ottawa preferred and actively pursued economic multilateralism," but the British and European response was "very disappointing, largely because of British post-war economic problems which persisted well into the reconstruction period" and beyond. Ottawa had been "forced to accept the realities of international trade as it evolved after 1945," he said, "which meant that Canada would increasingly move into the American orbit in order to enhance its economic well-being."[38]

That well-being was most impressive, too, though the Canadian economy had started to falter by the time John Diefenbaker unexpectedly came to power after the election of June 1957. Long disturbed by the increasing American presence in Canada and angered by what he saw as the St. Laurent government's abandonment of Britain during the Suez Crisis of the previous fall, the anglophilic Diefenbaker went to London immediately after he assumed office to visit the Queen and attend a Commonwealth Prime Ministers' Conference. When he returned to Canada on 7 July, the cheers of the British still ringing in his ears, he emotionally proclaimed his government's "planned intention" to divert 15 per cent of Canadian imports from the United States to Britain. Planned intention or not, the prime minister had not consulted the officials in Trade and Commerce or External Affairs before that announcement, and the bureaucrats quickly sent evidence forward that the prime minister's proposal was simply impossible. The British had no capacity to enter half the Canadian import market either because their factories did not produce the goods in question or because their products were inferior to American ones in design, styling, and quality. The General Agreement on Tariffs and Trade also put barriers in the way of any such massive shift. The diversion, in other words, was a policy pronouncement made without any understanding of the facts, and the government backed away from the Chief's unplanned intention very quickly.³⁹

Diefenbaker continued to look to Britain, however, though his attitudes began to alter when London decided in 1960 to open negotiations in an effort to join the European Economic Community. A long series of meetings with the British in bilateral and Commonwealth forums ensued, the Canadian rhetoric getting hotter as London drew closer to an acceptable bargain with the EEC.⁴⁰ Ottawa's position was curious. Official estimates were that 77 per cent of Canadian industrial exports and about half of all exports to Britain would be unaffected by British entry and, as we have seen, those exports were decreasing in percentage terms with great rapidity.⁴¹ Only Canada's wheat sales to Britain appeared seriously threatened, and there were promising prospects of huge sales to China that held out the hope of averting any prairie dislocation. At a Commonwealth Economic Consultative Council meeting at Accra, Ghana, in September 1961, Finance Minister Donald Fleming and Trade and Commerce Minister George Hees told the delegates that Canada viewed the British negotiations with "disappointment and grave apprehension" and feared for the Commonwealth's survival. The choice for Britain, the Canadian message went, was either Europe or the Commonwealth.⁴²

Diefenbaker ordered his ministers home and roasted them royally for their extreme language, but the Chief soon expressed his own views as vehemently. The prime minister told Britain's Harold Macmillan that Commonwealth preferences were vital to Canada "as a means of staving off United States domination" and, he added, the Commonwealth was a vital part of the Canadian identity.⁴³ At a subsequent Commonwealth Prime Ministers' Conference in September 1962, Diefenbaker again denounced the British effort to move into Europe. He argued that the prosperity of every member of the Commonwealth depended on that of Britain, something that was certainly no longer true for Canada. Macmillan had claimed that only the larger market of Europe could let Britain grow but, Diefenbaker said, if that were correct, then it followed that Canada should seek a similar relationship with the United States. Canada, however, had refused to seek economic union with the Americans because that meant a weakening of the ties with Britain and the Commonwealth.⁴⁴ Again that was scarcely true. Nonetheless, the Chief had hoisted the by-now tattered flag of empire economic unity, and he drew the cheers of his fellow Commonwealth prime ministers. The *Sunday Observer* reported that "One of the Ghanaians, as he told the Queen a few nights later, 'was so moved that I thought I was going to cry.'"⁴⁵

John Diefenbaker, perhaps, might not have turned to the United States once Britain rejected his importunate demands. His relations with the Kennedy administration were not so good as to permit any effort to forge closer economic links with the United States. Even so, at the Commonwealth conference Diefenbaker had slid over some unpleasant facts. When, during and immediately after the election of 1962, there had been a run on the dollar, his government had sent its officials to Washington for loans to bolster Canada's reserves. Despite its dislike of the Diefenbaker government, President Kennedy's administration had arranged the requested funds. In hard economic times, Diefenbaker, just as his predecessors had done, turned to the south for help.[46]

In the end, of course, President Charles de Gaulle blocked British entry into the EEC in January 1963, just days before the Canadian prime minister lost a confidence vote in the Commons on his government's defence policy. Diefenbaker had "won" the Common Market fight with Britain because the game had been called off, but what had he preserved? Trade with Britain was already small and growing ever smaller in percentage terms. Essentially, it now seems clear, Diefenbaker had been fighting for the idea of Great Britain as it existed in his mind, for the idea of a British Commonwealth and empire that could protect Canada from Americanization. Whether that was any longer a worthy goal or not is immaterial; certainly it was one that no longer had the remotest prospect of realization, as the British, desperately trying to join the Continent, clearly understood. In the context of this essay, however, what is significant is that Britain turned its back on Canada, no matter how much Diefenbaker pleaded with London to reverse the tides of history and save Canada from the United States. For John Diefenbaker, exactly as for Borden, King, and St. Laurent before him, Britain's fixed concentration on its own future had left Canada no alternative.[47]

Canada made one further, final, and futile effort to summon up Britain and Europe as a counterweight to the United States. In keeping with its "Third Option," the Trudeau government negotiated a contractual link with the European Community in the mid-1970s. The link quite deliberately aimed to increase trade with the EC nations to reduce Canada's increasing reliance on the American market. Though the link was brilliantly negotiated and widely hailed, except in London where the British were noticeably cool to the Canadian plan, unfortunately little resulted from it. Trade with Britain and Europe remained relatively inconsequential in percentage terms thanks to the Common Agricultural Policy, design problems with Canadian goods, and a characteristically lackadaisical effort by Canadian industries to sell their products to the Europeans. Meanwhile, trade with the United States continued to increase in volume. The Europeans might have been to blame for this. Or perhaps Canadian exporters, so accustomed to the relative ease of dealing with the United States, found the difficulties of coping with a multilingual Europe too bothersome to pursue actively. No matter whose fault, the link failed to materialize.[48]

In the area of defence, the close Anglo-Canadian relationship had long since disappeared, to be replaced by what the political scientists call transnational links between the Canadian and American armed forces. After 1945, the British had urged that Ottawa show due caution in joint defence efforts with the United States[49] – a useful warning, but one that lost its force when London tried to persuade the Commonwealth countries to plan for defence together. This was a transparent dodge to have Ottawa, Pretoria, Canberra, and Wellington pay for part of Britain's defence costs or assume some of its shrinking imperial responsibilities. Those attempts went nowhere, Mackenzie King, in particular, scouting the idea as he always had.[50] Nonetheless, Canadian and British troops served together in Korea and cooperated in NATO, though much less so after the Trudeau government's defence cuts of 1969, and a few officers continued to attend staff courses in the United Kingdom. Britain's decline as a world military power had become obvious to everyone after the abortive Suez invasion of 1956.[51] Moreover, the equipment used by the Canadian Armed Forces increasingly was American, as were its tactics and doctrine. Whose fault was this? According to Donald Macdonald, minister of national defence at the beginning of the 1970s, it was Britain's. Macdonald told the *Ottawa Citizen* that the two countries were moving apart "because this is the way the United Kingdom wants it"; in particular, Prime Minister Edward Heath was actively cutting ties across the Atlantic. "There used to be the old club rules related to the Commonwealth but Heath doesn't feel they obtain anymore," Macdonald said. As a result, "it was natural Canada would get into the stream of American military equipment." But, the minister added, "we have to be very wary the Pentagon doesn't pull a snow job on us."[52] Wary or not, there would be snow jobs aplenty.

Thus, the end of this melodrama. The simple truth is that Canada has had little success in its efforts to find markets or links abroad to act as a counterweight to those with the United States. The Mulroney government has resolved this difficulty in its own collective mind by opting for a free-trade arrangement with the United States. This is not the place to argue the merits or demerits of the particular deal that Simon Reisman and Derek Burney negotiated. But this essay should demonstrate how we reached the point where a Canadian government might think it necessary to seek such an arrangement.

In this century, Canadian governments, Conservative and Liberal, repeatedly tried to maintain and strengthen their trade, economic, and defence relationship with Britain. They assisted the mother country with men, loans, and gifts in two world wars and at the onset of the Cold War, and the British were duly grateful; but not so grateful that they would hesitate to press Canada to the south when it served their interests; nor so grateful that they could help Canada resist the inexorable tug of continentalism. Canada's herculean attempts to aid Britain forced this country's sweet surrender to the United States, with London cheering our governments on. The Americans opened their arms to us, and their embrace was a gentle one. It was a close embrace all the same, one that proved indissoluble. Donald Creighton's argument notwithstanding, it was not Mackenzie King and the Liberal party that sold us out and forced Canada into the arms of the United States, but Great Britain's economic and military decline.

Did and do the Americans want us in their arms? Dean Acheson, the son of Canadian parents, was a friendly yet unforgiving critic of Canada – the "stern daughter of the Voice of God," in his words. He once wrote that Canadians were "a tribal society, naive, terribly serious about the wrong things and not at all aware of their real problems ... Their best move would be to ask us to take them over; and our best move would be to say, no."[53] I hope Acheson was right in predicting the best American move, for it looks as if we are now asking to be taken over. It must also be said that it is not the Liberal party that is doing the asking.

I began these essays in a deliberately melodramatic fashion. "You must pay the rent." "I can't pay the rent." The old landlord drove our heroine out into the cold, obliging her to try to fight off the advances of he who had always coveted her. In classic Victorian melodrama, the heroine was always rescued at the end of the last act by the hero, pure, chaste, and noble. But no one can play hero for Canada, I regret to say, as we come to the end of the last act, mine if not yet Canada's. Henceforth, we will all surely pay the rent.

NOTES

1 Donald Creighton, *The Forked Road: Canada 1939–1957* (Toronto 1976), 187. Some contemporary British writers have come to recognize that Britain, bereft of power though it may have been in 1945, still tried to treat Canada as a colonial appendage. See, for example, Hugh Thomas, *Armed Truce* (London 1988), 292–3.

2 James Laxer, *Decline of the Superpowers* (Toronto 1987), 120–1.
3 The British by 1944 were calculating how best to reduce purchases in Canada: "In certain cases the Canadian position should be satisfactorily met by the proposed long-term contracts, tapered off when suitable ... in other cases we are apparently looking to switch pretty completely from Canadian to European sources of supply as soon as we can." PRO, Treasury Records, TI60/1376, Clutterbuck to Robertson, 24 April 1944. Eventually, this policy led the United Kingdom to consider "whether it was right to 'save foreign exchange' by importing bauxite and manufacturing it into aluminum here at a cost far above that of imported Canadian aluminum." Sir Richard Clarke, *Anglo-American Economic Collaboration in War and Peace 1942–1949* (Oxford 1982), 60. On the loan negotiations and the discussions preceding it see the fine memoir by Douglas LePan, *Bright Glass of Memory* (Toronto 1979), chap. 2, and Alec Cairncross, *Years of Recovery: British Economic Policy 1945–51* (London 1985), The official British version of postwar financial relations which, unlike most British studies, actually pays some attention to Canada and the Canadian loan is L.S. Pressnell, *External Economic Policy Since the War*, vol. I (London 1986).
4 Thomas, *Armed Truce*, 316
5 See R.N. Gardner, *Sterling-Dollar Diplomacy* (New York 1969). "Humiliating conditions" is Thomas's phrase; *Armed Truce*, 316.
6 J.W. Pickersgill and D.F. Forster, *The Mackenzie King Record*, vol. III: *1945–46* (Toronto 1970), 175
7 Pressnell, *External Economic Policy*, 343ff; Hector Mackenzie, "The Path to Temptation: The Negotiation of Canada's Reconstruction Loan to Britain in 1946," Canadian Historical Association, *Papers, 1982*, 196ff.
8 House of Commons, *Debates*, 11 April 1946, 772.
9 Ibid., 16 April 1946, 929. The CCF and Social Credit leaders supported the loan as well.
10 *Financial Post*, 22 June 1946. See also A.F.W. Plumptre, *Three Decades of Decision* (Toronto 1977), 74ff.
11 On the dollar see Queen's University Archives, W.A. Mackintosh Papers, box 4, "A Note on the Canadian Dollar," n.d.
12 F.H. Leacy, ed., *Historical Statistics of Canada* (Ottawa 1983), G401–14. There is a breakdown of the components of the balance of payments with the United States in R.D. Cuff and J.L. Granatstein, *American Dollars – Canadian Prosperity* (Toronto 1978), 30–1.
13 See National Archives of Canada (NA), C.D. Howe Papers, vol. 87, file S48-10, "The Canadian Exchange Problem," 18 Aug. 1947; R.C. McIvor and J.H. Panabaker, "Canadian Post-War Monetary Policy 1946–52," *Canadian Journal of Economics and Political Science* (CJEPS) 20 (May 1954),

215; J. Douglas Gibson, "Post-War Economic Developments and Policy in Canada," CJEPS 20 (Nov. 1954), 446–7.
14 See Cuff and Granatstein, *American Dollars*, chap. 5. It is worth noting that even while Canada scrambled for US dollars, quantities of scarce raw materials were reserved for the British market.
15 Leacy, ed., *Historical Statistics*, G401–14.
16 A.F.W. Plumptre, "Detour into Controls," *International Journal* 3 (winter 1947–8), 3. The British Treasury looked at Canada's dire dollar situation in July 1947 and concluded that "Help for Canada is important to us in order to enable the Canadians to continue to let us draw on their Credit, and, indeed, in order to let them lend us more." Clarke, *Anglo-American Economic Collaboration*, 172.
17 David Dilks's phrase in the introduction to his *Retreat from Power*, vol. II: *After 1939* (London 1981), 22.
18 Department of External Affairs (DEA), Records, file 264(s), Robertson to L.B. Pearson, 19 June 1947. See also Denis Smith, *Diplomacy of Fear: Canada and the Cold War 1941–48* (Toronto 1988), 197–8, for Dana Wilgress's views of the situation.
19 Based on Bruce Muirhead, "Canadian Trade Policy, 1949–57," book ms., chap. I, 28.
20 A dispatch from Washington analysing the administration's difficulties is DEA, file 264(S), Hume Wrong to secretary of state for external affairs, 26 Sept. 1947.
21 United States National Archives (USNA), Department of State Records, 842.5151/9-1847, A.B. Foster to C.T. Wood et al., 18 Sept. 47.
22 Ibid., 842.5151/11-147, "Memorandum for the Files," 1 Nov. 1947; DEA, file TS 265(5), Tel., Canadian ambassador to secretary of state for external affairs, 1 Nov. 1947, and "summary of US-Canadian Financial Discussions, November 1, 1947."
23 See, on these negotiations, J.L. Granatstein and R.D. Cuff, "Canada and the Marshall Plan, June–December 1947," *Historical Papers 1977*, 197ff. The restrictions reduced imports from the United States by $153 million in 1948. Leacy, ed., *Historical Statistics*, G408–14. See also Robert Bothwell and William Kilbourn, *C.D. Howe: A Biography* (Toronto 1979), 234–5.
24 NA, D.C. Abbott Papers, vol. 16, file 48, text.
25 See Robert Cuff and J.L. Granatstein, "The Rise and Fall of Canadian-American Free Trade, 1947–8," *Canadian Historical Review* 57 (Dec. 1977), 459ff.
26 NA, W.L.M. King Papers, Diary, 24 March 1948. King was wiser than he knew. Willard Thorp, assistant secretary of state for economic affairs and an American participant in the free-trade talks, told his superiors that the agreement offered "a unique opportunity of promoting the most efficient

utilization of the resources of the North American continent and knitting the two countries together – an objective of US foreign policy since the founding of the republic." Thorp to Lovett, 8 March 1948, *Foreign Relations of the United States 1948* (Washington 1972), IX, 406.
27 State Department Records, PW 611.422/10-2649, Wrong to J. Hickerson, 1 April 1948.
28 See J.L. Granatstein, *A Man of Influence* (Ottawa 1981), 236–7, for the origins of this idea.
29 Montreal *Star*, 6 May 1948. Canada and off-shore purchases go unmentioned in Forrest Pogue's *George C. Marshall: Statesman 1945–59* (New York 1987).
30 See DEA, file 264(5), Memo for Moran, 16 April 1948; ibid., Robertson to Clark, 19 April 1948.
31 DEA, Washington Embassy files, vol. 2158, "Economic Cooperation" file, Murray to Wrong, 20 Dec. 1948
32 Dominions Office Records, Sir A. Clutterbuck's "Note of a Private and Confidential Conversation with Governor and Deputy-Governor of Bank of Canada," 14 April 1949, as quoted in Bruce Muirhead, "Trials and Tribulations: The Decline of Anglo-Canadian Trade, 1945–50," unpublished paper, 14
33 Bank of Canada, Bank of Canada Records, file 5D-450, "Comments by C.D. Howe on Mr. Pearson's Memorandum entitled 'A Review of Measures to Promote Canadian Exports to Soft Currency Countries,'" 21 April 1950. I am indebted to Bruce Muirhead for this reference. Howe, moreover, had come over time to see the British as unreliable partners. "They would, in his view," Robert Bothwell wrote of dealings in atomic energy matters, "take any way out of a deal, and leave the Canadians to pick up the tab ... The Americans, as Howe knew, had more money, and that made it easier to deal with them." *Eldorado* (Toronto 1984), 195–6.
34 Howe Papers, vol. 4, file S4-12, Pearson's "A Review of Measures to Promote Canadian Exports ..." 19 April 1950; ibid., "Comments by C.D. Howe ..." 21 April 1950; Bothwell and Kilbourn, *Howe*, 236–7.
35 Paul Kennedy, *The Rise and Fall of the Great Powers* (New York 1987), 369. UK GNP (in 1964 dollars) in 1950 was $71 billion. British per capital GNP was just above half that of the United States.
36 Based on Bruce Muirhead, "Canadian Trade Policy, 1949–57: The Failure of the Anglo-European Option," PhD thesis, York University, 1986; Urquhart and Buckley, eds., *Historical Statistics*, F334–47.
37 Muirhead, "Canadian Trade Policy," 13
38 Ibid., 16
39 See J.L. Granatstein, *Canada 1957–1967: Indecision and Innovation* (Toronto 1986), 44–5. On the impossibility of the trade diversion see NA, Gordon Churchill Papers, vol. 14, "Diversion of Canadian Imports," 9 Aug. 1957.

40 See, for example, *Globe and Mail*, 14, 21 June 1961, 17 April 1962, 12 Sept. 1962.
41 NA, George Drew Papers, vol. 390, Memos attached to Green to Drew, 17 July 1961.
42 Peyton Lyon, *Canada in World Affairs 1961–63* (Toronto 1968), 448–9. For Donald Fleming's account of the Accra conference and the subsequent flap see *So Very Near: The Political Memoirs of the Hon. Donald M. Fleming*, vol. II: *The Summit Years* (Toronto 1985), 389ff.
43 DEA, file 12447-40, Record of Meeting, 30 April 1962.
44 Green Papers, vol. 7, Minutes of Meeting of Commonwealth Prime Ministers 1962, 11 Sept. 1962
45 *Sunday Observer* [UK], 16 Sept. 1962
46 See Granatstein, *Canada 1957–67*, chap. 4.
47 A few years later, the British complained about what Prime Minister Pearson called the "very strong" Canadian "export performance in the British market" and their own "rather poor showing" in the Canadian market. To Pearson it did "seem inescapable to us that their weakness in trade with Canada reflects a broader weakness in the British economy as a whole." Those complaints, and implied threats of action to curb Canadian export success, inevitably focused Canadian attention southwards. NA, Department of Trade and Commerce Records, vol. 58, UK General file, Pearson to L. Chevier, 14 April 1966 (draft). I am indebted to Dr. Gustav Schmidt for this reference.
48 This paragraph is based on a work in progress by Granatstein and Robert Bothwell on Trudeau's foreign policy, 1968–84.
49 See Smith, *Diplomacy of Fear*, 170.
50 Elisabeth Barker, *The British between the Superpowers 1949–50* (Toronto 1983), 58–60, 137–8.
51 On Suez see John English and Norman Hillmer, "Canada's Alliances," *Revue internationale d'histoire militaire* 54 (1982), 38–9.
52 *Ottawa Citizen*, 23 Feb. 1971.
53 David McClellan and David Acheson, eds., *Among Friends* (New York 1980), 250.

Chapter Ten

From Mother Country to Far Away Relative: The Canadian-British Military Relationship from 1945

Lieutenant-Colonel Ian Hope of the Princess Patricia's Canadian Light Infantry commanded Task Force Orion, the first Canadian battlegroup to operate from Kandahar, for the first seven months of 2006 in Afghanistan. Colonel Hope, who spent time in the British Army, is writing a book on his experiences, and he has published at least one article in which he offers some interesting judgments.[1] Take this one, as he writes about the American soldiers of Devil Company of the 2nd Battalion, Fourth Infantry Regiment, who were under his command: "I was proud of these Devil soldiers. Later, as I reflected upon this, I realized that, at some point in the past decade, we have had a fundamental shift in the culture of the Canadian infantry, making us identify most readily with the American, and not British, soldiers." D Company, he says, was "easy to work with, reliable, and very professional. Perhaps the biggest similarity was that they wanted to fight, unlike the soldiers of other countries who remained very risk-averse ..."

It is unusual for a Canadian officer to heap public praise on the US Army whose leaders, Hope says, "demonstrated decisiveness and tenacity, and [whose] soldiers performed battle drills quickly and with great effect." Hope speaks for himself alone, but I believe him to be correct.

I begin with his quote for two reasons. The first is to tell you where the Canadian army – and also the air force and navy – are today in their relationship with the US and UK. The second is to suggest that Colonel Hope is also right when he notes that the army's very close relationship with the British military had lasted well into the 1990s. The Royal Canadian Air Force had flown south by the mid-1950s and the Royal Canadian Navy had certainly sailed the same way by 1962. Why did the army stay loyal to its traditions for so long? What drove the military relationship apart for the other services?

Canada and Great Britain emerged from World War II as the closest of friends and allies. At least a half-million Canadians served in Britain during the war, and Canadian soldiers, sailors, and airmen fought under overall British command in Northwest Europe, Italy, and Asia. The Canadian government also gave billions of dollars in gifts and Mutual Aid to Britain with the overwhelming support of the Canadian people.

But the war changed everything. Britain's defeat on the Continent in May and June 1940 forced Canada to turn south for protection, the Permanent Joint Board on Defence (PJBD), created in August 1940, being the first North American defence alliance. It was followed by the Hyde Park Agreement in 1941, in effect the first economic alliance. Prime Minister Winston Churchill scorned what he saw as Canada's scurrying for cover under the US umbrella, but though he saw the future, he was wrong in 1940. Without the guarantee of homeland security provided by the US alliance, Canada could not have sent the huge forces to Britain that it did between 1940 and 1945. On the other hand, Canada prepared a division for service in the invasion of Japan, one that was to be organized on American lines and equipped with US weapons. Why? As General A.G.L. McNaughton, the Defence Minister in 1945 and always a cautious man in dealing with the Yanks, said, "One of the primary reasons ... was to obtain experience with the United States system of Army organization and US equipment in view of the obvious necessity for the future to co-ordinate the defence of North America ..."[2] The future was drawing near and it was American.

These strategic military (and economic) changes turned out to be permanent, as Churchill foresaw, just as the commitment to the PJBD was renewed in 1947. The Soviet threat kept Canada and the United States working closely together on continental defence, and the signing of the North Atlantic Treaty in 1949 and the despatch of troops and an air division to Europe in 1951, cemented Canada's reliance on its neighbour. Yes, the Canadian NATO brigade, just as the Korean brigade, served with British troops, but very significantly, the soldiers in Korea refused to eat British or Australian rations and insisted on American. Brigadier J.M. Rockingham "explained that my cooks had been trained to cook American rations and my soldiers had become used to them and liked them very much."[3] The RCN, operating three destroyers in Korean waters, found much the same thing. "The Commonwealth base at Kure [Japan] ... had the right kinds of ammunition and machinery spares for the Canadian ships," Commander Tony German wrote, "but ... British provisions were terrible. Canadian ration scales were much better than RN now, but in Kure they mainly got tough mutton ... From the Americans in Sasebo there was first-rate beef ... ice cream, milk, fresh fruit and vegetables and such magic as frozen French fries ..."[4] Armies (and navies too) march on their stomachs and, whenever they could be secured, the Canadians now simply refused to march with British rations. That was a harbinger of the coming changes.

American equipment too was increasingly coveted. Sometimes this was because US equipment was both more comfortable to wear, better designed for protection, and simply more effective than the Second World War–pattern British material used by the Canadian forces. For example, the steel helmet used by British and Canadian forces offered no cover for the back of the neck, weighed a ton, and was so awkward that it was almost impossible to run while wearing it. "The less said about the present helmet the better," wrote one infantry battalion commander. The American helmet, by contrast, offered better protection and, because it had a liner that was removable, could even be used for cooking over an open fire in a pinch. No Canadian wept when the UK helmet was scrapped in the late-1950s. Even the American mess tins, eating utensils, and cup were better designed than the comparable Canadian equipment issued to soldiers in the field.[5] In advanced weaponry, this American superiority was even more marked and, as the Avro Arrow cancellation in 1959 demonstrated, Canadian industry now was priced out of the market for big ticket items. So too were the British, as the cancellation of the Blue Streak missile in 1960 also showed. Nonetheless, Canada bought British Centurion tanks in the 1950s and used them for more than two decades.

Still there were big differences between the Canadian and US armies. The army commitment to northern Germany under the British Army of the Rhine had been pushed through by the anglophile Chief of the General Staff, Lieutenant-General Guy Simonds, one of the few victories he won over the US-leaning Chairman of the Chiefs of Staff Committee, General Charles Foulkes. Simonds had complained in 1947 that the American "military authorities made plans based entirely on potential enemy capabilities, whereas it was the practice in Canada to take into consideration not only capabilities but probabilities."[6] Simonds tried to maintain the filial links with the British forces and even created a Regular Force regiment of Canadian Guards when he was Chief of the General Staff. The Anglo-Canadian alliance was implicit and informal; Simonds wanted it to be more, but the fact that the RCAF in NATO served under the US and that the RCN served under SACLANT, run out of Norfolk, Virginia, were in retrospect far more significant.

The next key event, of course, was the Suez Crisis of the autumn of 1956. The Eden government had not taken Canada into its confidence as it planned its strike at President Nasser's Egypt, and the sense of shock in Canada and in the St. Laurent government was pronounced when British and French aircraft attacked Egypt, followed belatedly by soldiers. Whatever the rights or wrongs of the case, London and Paris' timing was execrable, the attacks coming in the days just before a US presidential election and during the time when the USSR's iron heel was being applied to Hungary. Ottawa's instinctive response was to try to save Britain from its folly, and Lester Pearson tried to turn the Anglo-French invaders into a United Nations peacekeeping force. It took only a few moments for that to be a non-starter, and Pearson then called for the creation of the first large UN force. That idea worked, gave Britain and France a way out of Egypt, and won Pearson a Nobel Peace Prize.

The military significance of Suez for Canada was real. Pearson offered Canadian troops for the UN Emergency Force, a battalion of the Queen's Own Rifles of Canada. The Egyptians protested – how could their citizens distinguish between the British invaders and the Canadian peacekeepers? The name of the unit reeked of Empire, the uniforms were very similar, and the flag carried by the Canadian soldiers had the Union Jack in the corner. There was much logic in this complaint, and it took a major diplomatic effort to persuade Nasser to let Canadian logistics troops into UNEF.

Pearson learned from this experience. First, the government in which he served lost the 1957 general election to John Diefenbaker who espoused loyalty to the Empire, one sign that much of the Canadian public still looked to London for its lead. Diefenbaker's loyalism was severely shaken by British efforts to join Europe and to abandon the Commonwealth trade relationship, and by the time he left office, Britain scarcely mattered economically to Canada. Second, and more important militarily, when Pearson came back to power in 1963, this time as Prime Minister, he moved to give Canada its own distinctive flag, and his government pushed through the unification of the Canadian Forces with a distinctive uniform worn by all three services.

The lessons of Suez indeed. An unintended effect was that Pearson's Nobel Prize made the Canadian public believe that peacekeeping was their métier, and over time this attitude let governments cut defence budgets because peacekeepers did not need much beyond blue berets. The attitude also affected the soldiers who came to think that they were not meant to fight.

The air force had already changed imperial masters. The Royal Canadian Air Force and the United States Air Force had developed a close relationship after World War II. The Canadians wanted US fighters, and they secured the F-86 Sabre. They recognized that they had to cooperate with the USAF in defending the continent, and both air forces pushed their governments into the North American Air Defense Agreement in 1957-8, a pact that treated air defence as a shared task. Historian Joseph Jockel noted that the "two air forces had every reason to cooperate. They were faced with a common military threat. As airmen, they shared an outlook which created a similar identity and even an emotional bond. They were interested in convincing civilians of the danger to the continent. Both were locked in struggles with their sister services for defence funds. Finally, for the RCAF, the USAF was a source of funding for radar stations and a source of pressure on Ottawa to recognize the importance of air defence."[7] And soon the RCAF wanted nuclear weapons to make its air defence task easier and aircraft like the CF-104 Starfighter and the CP-140 Aurora under schemes that often saw parts built in Canada or offsets for Canadian industry included in the deal. American equipment was not always the very best available, but it was invariably close to it.

Moreover, in contrast to the increasingly impecunious Canadian and British armed services, the United States military had the goods of modern warfare in lavish profusion, and the officers and men of the Canadian Forces inevitably and understandably wanted their small share of it. In effect, this equipment envy was often a driving force for policy. The RCAF desire for Bomarc surface-to-air missiles in fact destroyed the Diefenbaker government with just a little push from the Kennedy administration in early 1963.

The navy similarly had turned south. There had been mutinies on RCN ships in early 1949, and one cause was said to be slavish imitation of Royal Navy style. Canadianization was urged on the sailors, but Americanization was to follow. As one commentator noted, "The coming change was first detected in the new terminology" – the British term "asdic" was superseded by the American word "sonar."[8] The establishment of NATO's Supreme Allied Command Atlantic (SACLANT), with headquarters at Norfolk, VA, also meant that the RCN now had its place with the USN and not the Royal Navy. The RCN worked itself into being a first-rate anti-submarine fleet, and the ties forged with the United States Navy were strong, so much so that in the fall of 1962 during the Cuban missile crisis, the RCN in Halifax put to sea on its commander's orders despite the refusal of the Diefenbaker government to order a full-scale alert. Rear-Admiral Kenneth Dyer's relationship with his US commanders at SACLANT had been formed over the years in countless NATO exercises and was so close and so trusting, his assessment of the Soviet threat so fearful, that he felt obliged to put to sea to assist his ally. "That 'band of brothers,' Nelson's basic way of running things at sea, by mutual understanding and a firm grasp of the basic aim," Commander Tony German wrote, "was alive and well in North America in 1962. The navy ... honoured Canada's duty to stand by her North American ally."[9] Even if the Prime Minister had wished otherwise. The air force did much the same at its air defence bases in Canada, responding to NORAD, not to Ottawa.

Only the army seemed untouched by the southwards attraction. Canadian soldiers tended to sneer at the Americans as too wasteful of lives and equipment, too soft, too American. Brooke Claxton, a Canadian Corps veteran of the Great War and the Minister of National Defence under St. Laurent, visited Korea and returned unimpressed with the American commanders and appalled by the "lying" of staff officers who gave the briefings. He wrote a friend that "American expenditures of lives and ammunition are high according to our standards, higher than our people would be willing to accept."[10] The British model of mustachioed officers with their swagger sticks was the better one, or so soldiers appeared to think. The regimental names, the links to British units, the royals as colonels-in-chief, even uniforms made by British military tailors (on credit) – all such things kept the ties alive for a long time as the world changed.

Unification in 1968 was a major blow to the traditions and links, dealing a killing blow to the Army's system of corps and its distinctive and much loved uniforms, buttons, and badges. The dark green uniform that came with unification homogenized the Canadian military and especially weakened the land forces' psychological defences against Americanization. It was, one officer unhappily said, "an attempt to cleanse the forces of their Britishness," a trait "contrary to the cause of Canadian unity."[11] The 1970 stand down of regiments like the Black Watch, the Queen's Own, and the Guards also sapped army morale – and further diluted Britishness.

But for another three decades the Canadian army still resisted the southward pull. It was still "leftenant" and "kharki," not "lootenant" and "khaki." The ties, like the pronunciation, I think, disappeared under the strain of the 1990s. The Canadian army had been reduced to some 25,000 all ranks by successive cuts, and as the Cold War ended, it was so weak that it could not despatch a fully equipped battalion, let alone a brigade, to participate in the first Gulf War. Then came Somalia and revelations of torture and murder by members of the Canadian Airborne Regiment and failures in command by senior officers. Simultaneously there was the operation in Former Yugoslavia where at least one unit performed very well in action against Croatian regulars, but others, handicapped by post-Somalia rules of engagement, found themselves referring to the Judge Advocate General's branch for permission to smoke, let alone fight. The Canadian units were abbreviated as Canbat I and II, for Canadian battlegroups I and II. They were known to British troops in theatre as the "Can't bats," and it was largely true.

The dismal 1990s turned the Canadian Forces and especially the army inwards, and it determined that it was ill-educated, ill-prepared, ill-trained and, most obviously, ill-equipped. The events of September 11, 2001 made clear that this was no longer adequate, and the Paul Martin and Stephen Harper governments began re-arming the military. The psychological change had already occurred, and I would suggest that looking south for the model and finding it in the US Army that had regenerated and re-educated itself after the disasters of Vietnam was both appropriate and necessary. The names of Canada's historic regiments remain, redolent of Empire, but little else of that British past is still there. We are friends and allies forever, but the Canadian military now look fondly to Britain as a relative living far away. Mama, sometimes feared and occasionally admired, is now right next door.

NOTES

1 In Kevin Patterson and Jane Warren, eds., *Outside the Wire: The War in Afghanistan in the Words of Its Participants* (Toronto, 2007).
2 John Swettenham, *McNaughton, Vol. III: 1944–1966* (Toronto, 1969), p. 171.
3 John Melady, *Korea: Canada's Forgotten War* (Toronto, 1983), p. 82.
4 Tony German, *The Sea Is At Our Gates: The History of the Canadian Navy* (Toronto, 1990), p. 223.
5 Lieutenant-Colonel K.L. Campbell, "Summary of Experiences: Korean Campaign, 25 Mar 53–25 Mar 54." This document was kindly provided by Prof. David Berenson.
6 Quoted in David J. Bercuson, "A People So Ruthless as the Soviets: Canadian Images of the Cold War and the Soviet Union: 1946–1950," a paper presented at the Elora Conference on Canada-USSR relations, 1989, p. 12.
7 J.T. Jockel, *No Boundaries Upstairs: Canada, the United States and the Origins of North American Air Defence, 1945–1958* (Vancouver, 1987), p. 56.
8 John Harbron, "The Royal Canadian Navy at Peace 1945–1955: The Uncertain Heritage," *Queen's Quarterly* (Fall 1966), p. 317.
9 German, pp. 260ff.
10 Library and Archives Canada, Brooke Claxton Papers, vol. 31, Claxton to G.V. Ferguson, 27 May 1953.
11 John Hasek, *The Disarming of Canada* (Toronto, 1987), p. 146.

SECTION THREE

Canada in the World

Chapter Eleven

Canada as an Ally: Always Difficult, Always Divided

Canada's modern-day political and geographic position seems relatively secure, or as secure as any state can be in a world of terrorism and weapons of mass destruction. It is separated from Europe and Asia by great oceans and a sea of (melting!) ice. It borders on the world's only superpower, a state with which it has generally friendly, though sometimes very difficult, relations. And Canada is, in addition, one of the world's great joiners, a member of every international club that will have it, a supporter of multilateralism, and a believer in the worth of the United Nations. Canadians, moreover, believe profoundly in their essential goodness as a people, their multiculturalism and tolerance, and their self-proclaimed status as a moral superpower.[1] "The Americans fight wars," their mantra goes, but "Canadians keep the peace."

Nonetheless, Canada has been and is a member of politico-military alliances. As a British Dominion, a colony in law and fact, it automatically entered the Great War the day the United Kingdom did; as a Dominion, but after the Statute of Westminster of 1931 a colony no more, it went to war almost automatically in September 1939, one week after Britain. During the Second World War, much like Australia, it entered into its first military alliance with the United States, a relationship it continued and deepened with the coming of the Cold War. Canada joined the North Atlantic alliance in 1949, sent troops and ships to fight in Korea the next year, and deployed overseas a brigade group, an air division, and a large anti-submarine navy for collective defence against the Soviet Union. The Cold War may be over, but Canada remains a member of NATO and a partner in military alliances with the United States. The story, however, has never been quite so clear and straightforward, and this paper will look critically at Canada's steadfastness as an ally and the political and demographic reasons that continue to shape national policy.

Canadian national interests are simple and dear. As with any nation, Canada must protect its territory, maintain its unity, and enhance its independence. It must advance its economy to improve the welfare of its people and, as a small country with global interests, it must work with others to advance democracy and freedom.[2] Those interests, usually understood only in vague ways and frequently conflated and confused with values, ultimately have determined Canada's alliances. Security and economic necessity obliged Canada to rely on Britain through the nineteenth century and on the United States in the twentieth century. The requirement for national unity, pitting French Canada against the rest of the country, however, frequently constrained wholehearted support for the nation's allies. So, too, did anti-American attitudes, usually sharpest among the English-speaking, which have waxed and waned in Canada for some three centuries.

The United States to the south, always larger, richer, and sometimes menacing, was a constant that could not be ignored, though it was frequently scorned. Also too large to ignore was the substantial population of French-speaking Canadians. They amounted to never less than a quarter of the population, always sought increasing autonomy for their province of Quebec, were militant in their anti-militarism, and looked on Britain and, very frequently, the United States in different ways from their compatriots. The American and francophone presence determined – and determines – everything in any story of Canada as an ally.

Canada's British alliance was the product of victory in the Seven Years' War and especially of the battle at Quebec in 1759. Canada was British, a status reaffirmed by the failure of the Thirteen Colonies to "liberate" it during the Revolutionary War or the War of 1812. The French-speaking habitants (who had themselves fought a succession of wars against the American colonists and their native allies) accepted their new masters with varying degrees of grace, but the key event in shaping Canada's alliance with Great Britain was the arrival in British North America of the United Empire Loyalists, those Americans who had supported the losing side in the Revolutionary War. These displaced persons harboured long-lasting grievances against the bumptious "mobocracy" to the south, and their anti-American and pro-Empire attitudes shaped subsequent Canadian history.

When Britain went to war in South Africa in 1899, Anglo-Canadians demanded that Canada participate and a hysterical press campaign urged them on. The government, led by Sir Wilfrid Laurier, a francophone, was initially uninterested, but public opinion in English Canada simply forced a commitment. Canada eventually dispatched some 7,000 soldiers, raised and commanded by Canadians but paid by the War Office. The government explicitly declared this not to be a precedent obliging Canada to participate in all British wars, but Joseph Chamberlain, the Colonial Secretary, knew otherwise. So too did *nationaliste* Member of Parliament Henri Bourassa who declared that "the precedent, Sir, is the accomplished fact."[3] To Bourassa, automatic commitments could be no badge of sovereignty.

But English-speaking Canadians by and large wanted to be part of the Empire in arms and, as the German naval threat began to arise, pressure for Canada to create a navy or to give dreadnoughts to Britain began to grow. In fact, Canada did both – after a fashion. A tiny navy was created in 1909 and, after Laurier's government lost the election of 1911 (for trying to secure a free trade agreement with the US), the Conservative government under Robert Borden offered capital ships to the Royal Navy. This proposal died in the Canadian Senate, strongly opposed by francophones and the Liberal Patty.

The divisions in Canada seemed to melt away when Britain went to war in August 1914 – for a brief period. Bourassa had narrowly escaped internment in Germany and patriotic Imperial fervour and unity prevailed until recruiting revealed sharp differences in the country. The first division, dispatched overseas in October 1914, was overwhelmingly composed of British-born, secondarily of English-speaking Canadians, and with only very small numbers of francophones. That trend tended to prevail throughout the war; not until the Armistice did just above half the enlistments in the Canadian Expeditionary Force of 620,000 comprise Canadian-born soldiers; at the very most 50,000 were French-speaking (one-twelfth of the CEF, as opposed to almost four in ten in the population of eight million as a whole), a number swollen by conscripts in the last few months of the war. Other than adventurers and the few Imperial patriots, Québécois wanted nothing to do with the war. Their gaze was focused internally, their loyalty to Quebec and Canada, not to Britain. The English-speaking, by contrast, owed loyalty to Canada and Britain, and the differences were irreconcilable.

The government of Sir Robert Borden nonetheless supported the war effort to the maximum. It won an election in December 1917 on conscription and embittered Quebec voters against the Conservative Party for almost two generations.

At the front Canada proved to be a difficult Dominion. The Canadians refused British requests at the outset of the war to have their battalions serve in British divisions. As soon as officers could be trained, Canadian officers filled all (or almost all) command and staff positions in the Canadian Corps. They resisted British attempts to create an army of two corps and smaller divisions because they did not want to weaken the striking power of the Corps and its divisions. And they insisted on having more artillery, more machine guns, and more trucks in their Corps than the British did in theirs. The Canadians also chafed under British commanders, the Corps commander, Lieutenant-General Sir Arthur Currie, refusing service in one army because he had no confidence in its commander and resisting British GHQ efforts to employ Canadian divisions piecemeal against the Germans' 1918 offensives.[4] Field Marshal Sir Douglas Haig grumbled bitterly that "I could not help feeling that some people in Canada regard themselves rather as 'allies' than fellow citizens in the Empire."[5] Precisely. The war had made Canadians believe they could do great things together – and fight better than the British. That nationalist sentiment will not be unfamiliar to Australians.[6]

Canada's autonomy advanced more than psychologically during the Great War. As a provider of troops, supplies, and money, the Dominion believed it had earned a place at the table and a voice in the decisions. Borden took a prominent part in the Imperial War Conference and argued strenuously for his points of view. He secured Canada a signature on the Treaty of Versailles, albeit slightly indented under that of Britain, and a seat in the League of Nations. The Prime Minister came away convinced that a common foreign and defence policy for the Empire could be made to work.[7] His successor in 1920–1, Arthur Meighen, believed the same but, when he warned Britain not to renew the Anglo-Japanese Alliance, he stressed Canada's vital interest in peace with the United States. The national interests of Australia and New Zealand carried far less weight in Meighen's mind and, as it played out, in Whitehall's as well. The Japanese alliance was duly and truly scuppered.[8]

The new Liberal prime minister, William Lyon Mackenzie King, came to power in December 1921. King enjoyed the pomp of Empire and monarchy, but he did not believe in ideas of a common foreign policy that could commit Canada to war and endanger its fragile unity.

The British government gave him ample opportunity to resist, not least during the Chanak crisis of 1922 when London publicly claimed the support of the Dominions before Canada had been consulted. King's efforts at the 1923 and 1926 Imperial Conferences led to the end of any idea of a common foreign policy and five years later to the Statute of Westminster. At the Imperial Conference of 1937, King's refusal to move toward a common policy toward Nazi Germany, while shortsighted in the extreme, similarly put paid to any idea of a common defence policy in peacetime.[9]

When war with Germany came in September, King's attitude, while he was without question personally determined to take Canada to war, was that "Parliament will decide." And it did – approving the Speech from the Throne that called for war. On 10 September, one week after Britain (and Australia), Canada went to war. This badge of autonomy, however, was vigorously criticized by the media and the Opposition. Nonetheless, Canada's professed independence surely was not helped by the fact that Canada's interests arguably were not directly threatened by the Nazi invasion of Poland, any more than Australia's, and that the only reason Canada declared war was that Britain did. If Chamberlain had stayed out of war, so too would have Canada. Moreover, King's Canada was united in support of the war only because he had pronounced against conscription for overseas service, a gesture to French Canada, and declared Canada's role one of "limited liability," a position designed to stress that Canada would sell munitions and supply food to Britain and would not sustain casualties like the 60,000 dead of 1914–18. Promises to constrain a war effort, made at the onset of hostilities, could not be maintained as the war unfolded differently than British and Canadian planners had expected.

Militarily, the war effort was huge, 10 per cent of the nation's population of eleven million in uniform. Incredibly, Canada generated the third largest air force and fourth largest navy in the world and a full army overseas of two corps. The government, however, remained worried about casualties, and the army's leader in Britain, General A.G.L. McNaughton, wanted to keep his forces together, strenuously resisting efforts until 1943 to detach divisions for service outside the United Kingdom. McNaughton was overridden by Ottawa, which needed some army action for morale purposes at home after the disastrous raid on Dieppe in August 1942, and one infantry division took part in the Sicilian invasion that year (where it served with great distinction). The Italian commitment inevitably grew, so that by 1944 Canada had a corps fighting in the Mediterranean theatre.[10] The First Canadian Army was not reunited until March 1945 in the Netherlands. By and large, the army followed British models and adopted the mother country's tactics; unfortunately, the command flair and the soldiers' distinctive style that had distinguished the Great War's Canadian Corps seemed almost wholly absent, although in this war the nation's soldiers were overwhelmingly Canadian-born.

If the army's service was constrained, members of the air force and many RCAF squadrons served in every theatre, crews mixed in with RAF and British Commonwealth Air Training Plan graduates, more than 130,000 of whom had been trained in Canada. The largest Canadian-commanded formation was No. 6 Bomber Group, based in Yorkshire. The navy also operated as a de facto part of the Royal Navy, most of its service coming in the North Atlantic convoy war. Had the war against Japan continued into 1946, the Royal Canadian Navy would have had large representation; as it was, the cruiser HMCS *Uganda* voted itself out of the war, a majority of its crew refusing to re-volunteer for Pacific War service although every sailor had already volunteered for service anywhere.[11]

As that suggested, Quebec politics, and the Liberal government's base of support in French Canada, drove the requirement to make military service as non-compulsory as possible. French Canadians in all provided some 150,000 servicemen and women, just under 15 per cent of the total, a substantial improvement over Great War enlistment. But English-Canadian opinion, nonetheless, was harshly condemnatory, and the government had to balance on a knife edge throughout the war. "Not necessarily conscription," Prime Minister King stated in 1942 in a wholly accurate description of his temporizing policy, "but conscription if necessary." His government had imposed compulsory service for home defence in 1940 but did not send conscripts (derisively known outside Quebec as "Zombies" or the soulless, living dead of Hollywood horror films) overseas until the casualty toll in Italy and the Scheldt in late 1944 made it appear otherwise impossible to keep infantry battalions up to strength. Even then, under 13,000 conscripts were shipped to Europe while only 2,463 made it to units of First Canadian Army before the Nazi surrender.[12]

If manpower policy was constrained, politically Canada was more aggressive as a member of the alliance. Its diplomats developed the functional theory – nations with strength in one or two areas must be consulted by the Great Powers in those areas – and parlayed it into representation on some of the (less important) Anglo-US Combined Boards and on the United Nations Relief and Rehabilitation Administration. At various points, to get its way, Canada threatened to withhold monetary and food aid from Britain, and it tried to play off the US against the UK, a task made more difficult because, after Pearl Harbor, the Americans preferred to deal with Britain as the sole representative of the Dominions.[13] However, Canada made no claims for a voice in Allied strategic decisions though, as we shall see, it vigorously contested American claims for strategic and tactical control in Canadian territory.

After 1945, Canada continued to look to Britain to set the lead in foreign policy. Its attitude to the birth of Israel, for example, might have been shaped in London,[14] and it listened closely to, and largely accepted, British views on the developing Cold War. Not until the Suez Crisis of 1956 did London's voice finally and completely lose its power in Ottawa; not until 1956 did the Anglo-Canadian alliance finally wither and die.[15] Anthony Eden's government lied to Ottawa about its intentions to collude with Israel and France and to attack President Nasser, and the hurt – plus the necessity of scurrying to find a way to save Britain's bacon – led Prime Minister Louis St. Laurent to blurt out in Parliament that the days of "the supermen of Europe" were over. Equally damning, the Canadian High Commissioner in London called Britain's actions "the politics of the menopause."[16] The hot flash of British imperialism was over, but Canada had long before paid any debts it owed the old Empire in full – more than one hundred thousand Canadian dead in the two world wars were the proof of that. The new supermen, the Americans, would now determine Canada's course.

This had been clear for decades. Successive Canadian governments in the late nineteenth and early twentieth centuries had sought free trade agreements with the United States, seen as a recipe for prosperity, but had failed because of domestic opposition in both countries. The vocal nineteenth century anti-Americanism in Canada, focussing on the crass materialism, racial violence, and supposed low culture of America, was not toned down after 1900, but huge emigration to the United States suggested Canadians were voting with their feet for a land with greater opportunity – and better weather. The American reluctance to join in the Great War merely fueled the fire.

In fact, the war drove a stake into the heart of Anglo Canada. Britain historically had financed Canadian enterprise, but the City could not do so in wartime. Canada had to turn to Wall Street for financing. Then, as Britain's inability to pay for munitions and foodstuffs began to disappear by 1917, Canada had to turn to the newly belligerent United States to sell its products. Moreover, virtually everything made in Canada required American components, thus creating a huge US dollar shortage. Paradoxically, the more Canada tried to help Britain, the more difficult her balance of payments situation with the United States.[17] And when the Royal Navy refused to assist Canada's efforts to counter U-Boats in her waters in late 1917 and 1918, the United States Navy stepped in.[18]

The old hostile attitudes did not disappear, however. In the 1920s, Canada's tiny group of military staff planners drew up plans for spoiling attacks into the northern US while Canada waited for Britain to send troops to save it in the event of an Anglo-American War. This was a pipedream on all counts, not least that Britain would or could still intervene militarily to save Canada in a war with the United States, although it must he noted that US military planners were drafting their strategy for an attack on Canada well into the 1930s. As Canada's Chief of the General Staff noted, the Americans would not hesitate to invade Canada if they thought it necessary to defend their own nation.[19]

Canadian governments implicitly understood this. Mackenzie King, the prime minister for all but six of the interwar years, worked hard to strengthen relations with Washington, so much so that he knew some critics derisively referred to him as "the American." After 1935 particularly, he and President Franklin Roosevelt met often, and King responded to the American's concerns for Canada's parlous defences by putting more funds into the military and to the strengthening of the navy and air force in particular. Admittedly, the funds were derisory in present-day terms but rather less so in depression-wracked small-government Canada. Then in August 1938, Roosevelt issued an unambiguous pledge to "not stand idly by if domination of Canadian soil is threatened by any other Empire."[20] King responded a few days later by saying that Canada would arm to such an extent that no adversary bent on attacking the US could do so by way of Canada. This was important; so too symbolically was the first ever secret meeting of the two countries' military chiefs in November 1938. When war came in September 1939, the Roosevelt administration all but violated American neutrality laws by letting Canada acquire aircraft in the week between Britain's and Canada's declarations of war.

In May 1940, as the Allied position in France and the Low Countries collapsed, President Roosevelt let Mackenzie King know his grave concerns about the future of the Royal Navy if Britain fell to Hitler.[21] Poor King had to tell Winston Churchill, the new British leader, that the Americans wanted the fleet dispersed to North America in such an event, not handed to the Nazis. Churchill's roar was real, but even he could not guarantee what a Quisling government in occupied London might do. The messenger, the Canadian prime minister, was horrified at what he had had to convey and fretted that the US wanted to save itself at Britain's expense.[22] King felt somewhat better when the "destroyers for bases" deal, an idea that apparently originated in the Canadian Legation in Washington, came on the table. Even so, he was alarmed that the Americans would now have a foothold in Newfoundland, administered since 1933 directly from London, where Canada already had troops and long-standing aspirations to incorporate the Dominion into Canada.

The defence relationship was not formalized until after Dunkirk and the Fall of France. The single Canadian division in England, not yet well-trained, was the best equipped formation in the country, and Ottawa announced plans to dispatch a second division forthwith. Every available ship and aircraft was also sent overseas, leaving Canada essentially undefended. In meetings in April 1940, President Roosevelt had left Mackenzie King in no doubt of his concern "about the inadequacy of the protection to our Canadian coasts" and how this "represented a real danger to the United States."[23] After the defeats of 1940, Canada now had no choice other than to look south for protection. Thus when Roosevelt telephoned King in August 1940 and asked him to meet at Ogdensburg, NY, King leapt at the chance. Without advisers and armed with only a list of badly needed military equipment, he and Roosevelt agreed to create a Permanent Joint Board on Defence and to begin hurried staff talks.

There was some furious grumbling from Opposition figures who feared King was selling out to the Americans,[24] but most Canadians understood that necessity had forced their hand. Britain's military weakness had pressed Canada into a defensive alliance with the United States. Overseas, Churchill was furious that Canada, in his view, was scuttling its British alliance to save itself: if Hitler "cannot invade us ... all these transactions will be judged in a mood different to that prevailing while the issue still hangs in the balance."[25] Churchill's was a total misreading of Canada's situation. King's first duty was to ensure the security of his own nation. He also genuinely believed that he was dragging the neutral United States into a closer relationship with the belligerent Commonwealth and that, having safeguarded Canada, he could continue to strip the Dominion of every available man and gun for Britain's defence. Churchill, understandably enough, thought of British and Imperial interests first (as he would later in dealings with Australia), but it cannot be denied that he completely missed the rationale for the Ogdensburg Agreement. On the other hand, the agreement did mark the point at which Canada passed out of the British defence sphere of influence – it had already left the economic sphere. The point is surely clear: it is very difficult for a small country to be allied to a fading overseas power when it lives next door to a rising one.

The same dynamics compelled Mackenzie King to seek Roosevelt's economic assistance. Just as in the Great War, the more Canada tried to produce arms for Britain, the more it had to import from the United States. This put severe strain on the country's holdings of US dollars, particularly so as the British had stopped the free exchange of sterling, of which Canada had huge amounts. By April 1941, Canada was on the verge of fiscal ruination, but at Roosevelt's home at Hyde Park, NY, the Prime Minister and President struck a deal. The components Canada needed for its arms production could now be charged to Britain's lend-lease account, and the US would buy more raw materials from Canada, thus providing more scarce US dollars. In effect, Canada was mortgaging a part of its economy and future to help win the war. Britain's economic weakness had driven Canada to the south yet again,[26] just as Ogdensburg had demonstrated that militarily Canada had to come under the eagle's wing.[27]

The war set Canada on a seemingly irreversible course. The Ogdensburg Agreement created a civil-military Board with equal national representation. The Americans were ordinarily respectful of their smaller partner, but when they wanted something, they wanted it. The first plan produced by the PJBD was the Joint Canada–United States Basic Defence Plan of 1940. Based on the assumption that Britain was lost and the Royal Navy had ceded control of the North Atlantic, the plan gave strategic control of the Canadian Forces, subject to consultation with the Canadian Chiefs of Staff, to the US. In such dire circumstances, with much of Canada's military presumably in prison camps overseas, this made sense. A second plan, ABC-22, drafted in the spring of 1941 with Britain still in the war, detailed the military necessities when and if the US joined in the war. The Americans wanted strategic control over the Canadian Forces once more, to incorporate Canadian coastal defences on both coasts directly into their military commands and, the Canadians came to believe, they sought tactical control as well. The Canadians resisted, fought strongly, and won; in the end, nothing was conceded except coordination through mutual cooperation.[28]

Nonetheless, the Americans drove the military agenda. The US needed a land route to Alaska, separated from the "lower 48" by British Columbia and, once they argued military necessity, Canada quickly acquiesced. They wanted to set up oil pipelines in the Northwest Territories. Done. Weather stations in the far north. Of course. A chain of airfields in the northwest. By all means. So quickly did the American military presence grow in Canada that Canadians half-seriously joked that the US Army answered its telephones in Edmonton, Alberta, with "Army of Occupation." At one point, the under-secretary in the Department of External Affairs actually feared that the senior official dealing with the Yanks was the secretary of the Alberta Chamber of Commerce and Mines. Ottawa's answer was to appoint an army general as Special Commissioner, give him an aircraft and a large flag, and order him to show it. This worked. More to the point, Ottawa determined to pay full price for every US military installation in Canada at war's end so there would be no doubt which country controlled what.[29]

In fact, however, military relations grew much closer still. The United States Navy took command of the convoy war in the northwest Atlantic off Newfoundland while the Americans were still neutral, and Canadian and American soldiers jointly organized – sometimes uneasily – the defence of Newfoundland. Canada provided an infantry brigade in the summer of 1943 to serve with the American forces attacking (the fortunately just evacuated) Kiska, one of the Aleutian Islands occupied by Japan.[30] Its air force helped defend Alaska, its vessels assisting in the protection of the Pacific coast. Canadians served in substantial numbers in the 1st Special Service Force, a joint Canadian-American force that fought with great distinction in Europe (and for its pains was the subject of a later and dreadful Hollywood film, "The Devil's Brigade"). And for the final assault on Japan, Canada agreed to supply substantial air, sea, and ground forces, including an infantry division tasked with an invasion role. The division, which was organizing itself on a US model and being equipped with American weaponry, fortunately did not prove to be required after the bombing of Hiroshima and Nagasaki.

For Canada, the post-1945 world has been shaped by three things: the Cold War, the disorder that followed the demise of the Soviet Union, and, always, the looming presence of the United States. The Soviet Union was hostile, something most Canadians understood at once when a massive spy ring based in Ottawa was uncovered in 1945–6. The fear of Russian expansionism had much to do with the decision to accept a continuation of military links with the United States. A Military Cooperation Committee took shape in 1946 and the next year, the defence relationship between the two countries was formally extended into the future.

In truth, however, Canada was doing almost nothing in defence. The military chiefs' proposals for peacetime conscription were brushed aside by the government; so too were their recommended force strengths. Although the approved figures did not revert to 1939 levels, the Canadian military was left with almost no capabilities. Where were any credible threats?

What Ottawa was doing was searching for its course. How could the huge weight of the United States be balanced? How could the bilateral imbalance in North America be rectified by multilateral relationships? Initially planners had looked to the new United Nations, but Prime Minister King – and others – returned from the San Francisco conference in summer 1945 convinced that the new world organization would do no better than the League of Nations. Canadians then turned to the British Commonwealth, hoping against hope that the old ties might again help tilt the balance with the United States. But the old Commonwealth was no more, particularly with Britain weak and the former non-white colonies achieving independence. The Commonwealth, if it survived, was destined only to be an organization for the distribution of foreign aid.

Then in 1948, the idea of a North Atlantic Treaty began to take form, Canadians among those pushing very hard for it. The threat of the Soviets was real; so too were the possibilities of Communist electoral victories in Italy and France. Perhaps a new trans-Atlantic alliance could revivify the Western European democracies, still bruised from the war. Canada pressed for this in Europe and pressed the United States, its Republican isolationists very powerful and some, such as Senator Robert Taft, bitterly opposed.

Of course, Canada had its own interests to serve. The shortages of American dollars that afflicted every country after the war were severe in Canada and for a time in 1948, a free trade/customs union arrangement seemed possible. Prime Minister King, still hanging on to power, turned the idea down for fear that he would be portrayed as selling Canada out to the Yanks. With that off the table, perhaps a North Atlantic alliance could encompass more than defence and come to include trade liberalization. Although Canada eventually secured an article in the Treaty calling for economic cooperation, NATO was a military alliance because that was all the United States would accept, and that grudgingly.[31] And in an alliance where only the US had money and soldiers to spare, NATO's value as a counterweight to the Canada-US bilateral relationship was limited. There might have been nine NATO members in the bed, but Uncle Sam ruled the harem in Europe – and North America.

Even after joining NATO in April 1949, Canada did little to improve its defences, but the outbreak of the Korean War changed everything. Under great American pressure, Canada dispatched three destroyers to the area[32] and then, the pressure increasing, agreed to recruit a brigade group for Korean service. Interestingly, the brigade served with the Commonwealth Division, not US forces. A few months later, Ottawa now seized with the reality of the Communist threat, the government agreed to dispatch a brigade group to NATO Europe to serve with the British Army of the Rhine, to provide an air division of fighter aircraft, and to devote the navy to an anti-submarine role in the North Atlantic. Defence spending rose dramatically, exceeding 7 per cent of Gross Domestic Product by the mid-1950s. The regular forces reached 120,000, and Canada's armed forces were at their historic peaks in strength and efficiency. The country's diplomats, even more than in the Second World War years, spoke with weight and force behind them.

That this rearmament had been accomplished under Prime Minister Louis St. Laurent was especially noteworthy. The francophone lawyer was unique – a Quebecker who saw the necessity for strong defences and strong alliances; moreover, he was willing and able to carry that message into his home province. He never swung the opinion polls in French Canada to support of military commitments, but he won the polls that mattered, sweeping Quebec in the federal elections of 1949, 1953, and 1957.

But as the USSR's threat increased, so too did American pressures. The danger of attack from Russian bombers was real, and early warning was critical. Three chains of radar stations developed, each one further north and with Canada providing the geography and some of the funding. It made sense, North America being a single geographical unit and Canadian cities as likely to be targeted as American, to coordinate air defences. In 1957–8, the North American Air Defense Command took to the air, its commander always from the USAF, its deputy from the RCAF. Soon surface-to-air missiles were part of the air defence mix, and the Progressive Conservative government of John Diefenbaker agreed to acquire Bomarc missiles and to arm them with the nuclear warheads needed to make them effective.[33]

John Diefenbaker personified Canadian contradictions.[34] Saddled with a Germanic name, his political career had been hampered, and he had won his party leadership in 1956 because, in part, not many others wanted it. But the long-reigning Liberals had worn out their welcome, and "Dief the Chief" proved a spell-binding orator. He was an Empire man, a monarchist, and someone instinctively suspicious of the United States.[35] He had opposed the Liberals turning of Canada's back on

Britain and France in the Suez Crisis of 1956, for example, and saw this as Ottawa doing Washington's bidding. He had proposed diverting 15 per cent of Canada's trade from the US to Britain in 1957, an impossibility given trade patterns and the shoddy quality of British goods (except Scotch and Harris tweeds).[36] But Prime Minister Diefenbaker nonetheless agreed to join NORAD and to take the Bomarcs, in part at least because President Dwight Eisenhower jollied him along and flattered his enormous vanity. John F. Kennedy would not do that, and from January 1961 on, Canadian-American relations reached their historic nadir.

The main issue hinged around Cuba and Bomarc missiles. When the United States discovered Soviet missiles on the Caribbean island in the autumn of 1962, envoys were dispatched to US allies, including Ottawa, to brief leaders on Kennedy's intentions. All the allies offered immediate support except Diefenbaker. He and his Cabinet were suspicious of American intentions and furious that they had learned of the planning only hours before Kennedy went public. Was this how a close ally was treated? they asked. Thus, Canada's air defence squadrons in NORAD were not ordered to go on alert; neither did the navy get directed to put to sea. The Bomarcs, their installations still incomplete and no decision yet made on when or how their nuclear warheads would be acquired, sat unready. In fact, on their own commander's responsibility, the navy's ships sailed from Halifax into the North Atlantic and patrolled their assigned sectors for Soviet submarines. At the same time, the Defence minister, without approval from Diefenbaker, quietly issued a high-level alert to the Canadian Forces and the Royal Canadian Air Force's Voodoos went to readiness. The Canadian military, if not the prime minister, opted to support the American alliance, instinctively and wholeheartedly. The Americans nonetheless were furious at Diefenbaker, outraged that in the most dangerous crisis of the Cold War their Canadian ally had let them down politically. Once the Canadian public learned of what had occurred – or not occurred – Diefenbaker's government, by then in a minority position, was doomed.

The Bomarcs provided the final push. Anti-Americanism in Canada had been flourishing since the mid-1950s, stoked by increasing American economic control and by anti-nuclear protests. These tendencies combined in the Conservative cabinet with the result that no agreement could be reached among ministers on how or whether to take the nuclear warheads Canada had agreed to use on the Bomarcs. Frustrated, angry, eager to punish Diefenbaker, the US State Department issued a press release that blasted the Canadian government for its failure to do anything credible for North American defence. The Cabinet promptly fell apart, the government lost a confidence vote in the House of Commons, and Canada went into an election. It should have been a walkover for the Liberals, led by Lester Pearson, the Nobel Peace Prize winner, diplomat, and External Affairs minister. But Pearson had reversed his party's long-time position against accepting nuclear warheads just before the Diefenbaker government fell, and the Conservatives painted him as an American lackey. In the most anti-American election in a half-century, Diefenbaker almost saved his skin by touring the country by train and repeatedly harping on the theme that "It's me against the Americans, fighting for the little guy."[37] Almost, but not quite: Pearson formed a minority government and quickly accepted the nuclear warheads.

But Canada was caught up in a frenzy of rampant anti-Americanism, and the Liberal government had its own ministers who were uncomfortable with the American alliance. Finance Minister Walter Gordon, for one, was an economic nationalist, concerned that US investment in Canada had reached the point that the economy was effectively under Wall Street's control. His first budget in 1963 slapped a series of punitive measures on foreign investors, created a furore in business circles and in Washington, and resulted in a quick and humiliating climbdown. Nationalist resentment festered over the battering Gordon received, and the Viet Nam War, then heating up, provided yet another spur to anti-Americanism. In 1965, Prime Minister Pearson, speaking in Philadelphia, called for a halt to the bombing and infuriated President Lyndon Johnson who accused him of "pissing on my rug." Say anything you want in Canada, the message was, but don't bring such calls into the US where they fed American anti-war opinion. No one in Washington truly ought to have been surprised at Pearson's tone. At the UN during the Korean War, he had pressed for the American-led forces to halt at the 38th Parallel, and he had called for a negotiated end to the fighting so persistently that Dean Acheson, the Secretary of State, eventually came to call Pearson and all Canadians "the Stern Voice of the Daughter of God."[38] Preachiness, without carrying a commensurate share of the burdens, was no virtue in the eyes of the US.

Then in 1968 came the emergence of Pierre Trudeau as Liberal leader and prime minister. A stylish and charismatic francophone intellectual, Trudeau was 49 years old. He had opposed Canada taking nuclear warheads, and he believed that military spending was wasteful. Canadian foreign policy, he said, "was largely its policy in NATO, through NATO," not a policy that served Canadian interests.[39] The US and the USSR, to him, were virtually equivalents, and Canada should be equidistant from both. Trudeau was a Québécois, a product of the political debate in his province before, during, and after the Second World War. He wanted Quebec to stay in Canada and be a full partner in it, but he did not admire the direction in which Canada had been going – too close to the US, too hostile to the Soviet Union, and with too much of its effort and money wasted on North Atlantic alliance matters. By 1969, after a defence and foreign policy review, his government cut Canada's military commitment to NATO in half, and defence budgets and military strength began to fall in real terms. Obsolete equipment was allowed to grow older, and the golden age of the Canadian Armed Forces was over. So too was Canada's diplomatic clout.

Arguably, Trudeau's taking the prime ministership – and his almost sixteen years in power – put paid to Canada's American alliance. The close links forged by King and his successor Louis St. Laurent had kept the ties between Ottawa and Washington tight. Yes, Canada had tried repeatedly (but unsuccessfully) to find counterweights to Washington's power, but both ministers and officials could see the vital necessity of working with the US. Diefenbaker's suspicions and the fiascoes over Cuba and the Bomarc had demonstrated that powerful elements in Canada were unhappy with the link to the south. Then Pearson's willingness to tolerate punitive measures against American investors shook Washington as did the vehemence of the anti–Viet Nam War sentiment in Canada. Trudeau's emergence and his quasi-neutralist attitudes were almost the final straw in American eyes. In January 1973, Trudeau's minority government, supported by the socialist New Democratic Party, passed a resolution condemning the prolongation of the Viet Nam War. The American government was furious. There was a similar outraged response from Washington when Trudeau's government in October 1980 imposed a quasi-nationalization on the country's oil industry. The National Energy Program treated US oil companies and investors just as roughly as it dealt with everyone else, including Canadians. After the succession of Trudeau shocks, the formal alliance ties remained intact and the efforts by the Canadian Forces to increase interoperability with their American counterparts did not cease. But the sense that there had been a community of interests, that both nations shared a similar sense of the world and its dangers, was gone for good.[40] To the US, to Britain, and to NATO, Trudeau's Canada seemed to be heading towards neutralism. Trudeau left public life in 1984, deciding to retire, he said, after "a walk in the snow."

The Progressive Conservative Brian Mulroney governed from 1984 to 1993, but even though he negotiated a Free Trade Agreement with the Reagan Administration and generally supported its foreign goals, including the first Iraq War,[41] the sense persists that his governmental policies were an aberration, not least because Mulroney's successor led the Conservatives to the most crushing defeat in Canadian electoral history – two seats in the election of 1993.[42]

The Liberals under Jean Chrétien and his successor, Paul Martin, charted a different, more familiar course. They kept the FTA and its broader cousin, the North American Free Trade Agreement, because they could do no else. But they reinforced the sense that Canada had different values than the US. Canada looked internally, obsessing over Quebec's independentist threats and trying to avoid anything abroad that might increase separatist sentiment or cost money. After supporting the FTA in 1988, Quebec had gradually become increasingly anti-American, the sentiment strong during the first Iraq War and reaching its peak when George W. Bush became President and, after 9/11, waged the war on terror. Quebec always had been and today remains the most anti-military province in Canada by large margins[43] so, with its voters critical for both the Conservatives and the Liberals, funding for the Canadian Forces was scarce.

Although Canada remained in NATO, it effectively had no forces in the Alliance after 1994, the decision to withdraw air and land forces from Europe made by the Mulroney government. Instead the country professed its devotion to peacekeeping, preferably under the UN but under NATO, if necessary. Even after peacekeeping morphed from the benign variety practiced during the Cold War into much more vigorous peace enforcement operations in the new world disorder, Canadians persuaded themselves that they were still the world's natural middlemen, that an 18-year-old Canadian soldier with a blue beret was the answer to the rest of the globe's problems. They continue to believe this,[44] remaining almost completely unaware that the old peacekeeping frequently served American and NATO alliance interests (as at Suez, in the Congo, and in Cyprus) and often depended on American logistics or heavy air lift (as in the UN Iran-Iraq Military Observer Group of 1988). Nor did Canadians even realize that the United States frequently had more soldiers on UN peacekeeping missions than their own nation or that at last count they ranked 34th in providers of troops on UN missions.[45] The lamentable condition of the Canadian Forces (52,000 effectives, no heavy airlift or tanks, obsolete trucks and supply ships, etc., etc.) at the onset of the twenty-first century also largely escaped public – and governmental – notice.[46]

What seemed most important for Canadians was not to appear to follow the United States. Chrétien's Canada refused to support the Iraq War in 2003, its diplomats in New York and elsewhere always pressing for UN resolutions and instinctively preferring a multilateral solution to every question.[47] The government's decision was shaped by overwhelming opposition to the war in French Canada[48] and the coincidence of a Quebec election that seemed likely to throw the separatist Parti Québécois out of power (and did). That all three party leaders appeared in an TV debate wearing anti-war ribbons signaled the Quebec public's mood.[49] If Ottawa opted not to fight in Iraq, it nonetheless deployed troops to Kabul, Afghanistan, freeing up US forces for the campaign against Saddam. One senior army officer resigned in protest at this decision to stay out of the war, but as the war ran into difficulty after the initial successes, the public came to believe that Canada had been saved from Bush's folly.

Then Paul Martin, another Quebecker, became Prime Minister at the end of 2003. Although he had pledged to restore relations with the United States, and although his government had given repeated strong signals that it would support Ballistic Missile Defence, in February 2005 Martin said no to signing on with the US in BMD. The anti-military, anti-American, and anti-Bush opposition in Quebec, the strong anti-Americanism on the left in English Canada, and the manufactured confusion that BMD was really Ronald Reagan's Star Wars in disguise combined with the Liberals' precarious minority government situation to produce an easy, if wrong, decision. For the first time since 1940, an American defence policy decision that directly impinged on Canada's territorial security would be implemented with no Canadian participation whatsoever. The US Ambassador at the time, Paul Cellucci, declared in his memoirs (published in autumn 2005) that the decision left him "astounded," "perplexed," and astonished at the "inept" and "clumsy" way the government handled the decision: "there was," he said, "the fact that the prime minister did not tell the president himself, even though the two men were both at the NATO meeting [in Brussels] and at several points were standing side by side. But not a word was said."[50]

In light of this decision and with the North American Aerospace Defense Agreement due for renewal in 2006, the question of Canadian continuation in the joint defence of North America might well be in question. The Foreign Affairs and National Defence bureaucracies want to renew NORAD and, indeed, expand it to cover naval cooperation in some fashion. But if the Liberals continue in a minority government position in the election expected in Spring 2006, and if the Cabinet continues to remain sensitive to the raging anti-American currents in Canada, the fate of NORAD might turn out to be the same as that of BMD. Complicating matters is that some senior US military figures – for the first time since 1940 – would prefer to go it alone and cut the defence link to an unreliable Canada. Some people in the US military, wrote one journalist, "question whether Canada brings enough to the table in terms of air and naval assets to make a joint command worthwhile."[51]

Martin's government, however, did pledge to deploy some 1,800 troops to Kandahar, Afghanistan to form a Provincial Reconstruction Team in 2005–6 under NATO's aegis. It is easier politically for Canada to work with NATO rather than the US military. The prime minister put a tough-talking and bright Chief of the Defence Staff, one who has worked extensively with US forces, into place in early 2005 and also produced an International Policy Statement and a Defence Policy Statement that called for a vigorous Canadian role in the world.[52] Moreover, his finance minister pledged $13 billion in funding as a start at rebuilding the Canadian Forces. Ninety per cent of the funds, however, were slated for delivery in 2009–10, far beyond the period in which any minority government can make credible promises.

So where is Canada as an ally today?[53] The alliance with Britain is gone, its only remnants the monarchy and regular Commonwealth Heads of Government meetings that do little. Canada's NATO alliance is, the Afghanistan commitment notwithstanding, largely irrelevant: Canada carries little weight in NATO, and NATO matters little to Canada. The alliance with the United States, if not irretrievably finished, is in tatters, exacerbated by antipathy between the countries' leaders and corrosive, long-running trade disputes.[54] Of course, Canada remains inextricably linked economically to the United States with 85 per cent of its exports going to or through the US and 52 per cent or more of its Gross Domestic Product dependent on imports from and exports to the United States. Not surprisingly given those statistics, at least 45 per cent of Canadian jobs depend on trade with the US.[55] To be close to the heart of the global economy should be seen as a strength for any trading nation; in Canada, however, it is popularly perceived as a weakness.

The defence arrangements with the US continue in force. The militaries of the two countries cooperate as closely as they can in a cold political climate, their interoperability hampered by Canada's aging equipment. But turning away from BMD and reducing the Canadian Forces to their present derisory strength means that the historic bargain of 1938–40 has been dishonoured.[56] The United States will defend Canada against any other empire so long as it is in the American national interest to do so. Canada, however, can no longer credibly claim that no power – or no terrorist group – can strike the US through Canada, so weak are its armed forces and security structures. In other words, the United States pretends it doesn't defend Canada, and Canada pretends that it does. But pretence is no rational basis for polity. At some point, in their own national security interests, the Americans may need to make overt efforts to protect themselves through the use of military force on Canadian territory or in its air/sea space. What then of Canadian sovereignty? What then of a historic political and military relationship?[57]

Anti-Americanism and anti-militarism have driven Canadian alliance policies for more than four decades, no matter the country's national interests. French Canada's attitudes have shaped Canadian policy, reinforcing the values of other Canadians of left and left Liberal quasi-neutralist tendencies.[58] No nation can parade its "values" at the expense of its "national interests" for long, however, and the piper soon will demand to be paid.

NOTES

1 "In the of Olympics self-admiration," historian Desmond Morton told a Quebec City meeting on 30 September 2005, "Canadians would compete eagerly – for their traditional bronze medal." ("The Canadian Connection," 22nd International Churchill Conference.)
2 The most recent expositions of Canadian national interests are my *The Importance of Being Less Earnest: Promoting Canada's National Interest through Tighter Ties with the US* (Toronto, ON: C.D. Howe institute, 2003). esp. 7–8, and Denis Stairs et al., *In the National Interest: Canadian Foreign Policy in an Insecure World* (Calgary, AB: Canadian Defence and Foreign Affairs Institute, 2003). Such discussion of Canadian interests is rare; that two appeared all but simultaneously is noteworthy.
3 Quoted in C.P. Stacey, *Canada and the Age of Conflict*, Vol. I (Toronto, ON: Macmillan, 1977), 72.
4 On the Canadian Corps, see J.L. Granatstein, *Canada's Army: Waging War and Keeping the Peace* (Toronto, ON: University of Toronto Press, 2002), chs. III–IV.
5 G.W.L. Nicholson, *Canadian Expeditionary Force, 1914–1919* (Ottawa: Queen's Printer, 1962), 381, and Stephen Harris, "From Subordinate to Ally: The Canadian Corps and National Autonomy," *Revue d'Histoire Militaire* 51 (1982), 109ff.
6 The great American surgeon Harvey Cushing, serving in France with a US Army hospital attached to the British, noted on 1 July 1917 that he was warned by Canadian and Australian doctors in France to expect indolence

and indifference from the Imperials: "The only way to get official action was to kick continually." Michael Bliss, *Harvey Cushing: A Life in Surgery* (Toronto, ON: University of Toronto Press, 2005), 318.

7 Sec Robert Craig Brown, *Robert Laird Borden: A Biography*, Vol. II (Toronto, ON: Macmillan, 1980), chs. VII, XI, XII.

8 See Roger Graham, *Arthur Meighen*, Vol. II (Toronto, ON: Clarke Irwin, 1963), chs. III–IV.

9 On King, see H. Blair Neatby, *William Lyon Mackenzie King*, Vol. III (Toronto, ON: University of Toronto Press, 1976), and Norman Hillmer, "Defence and Ideology: The Anglo-Canadian Military 'Alliance' in the 1930s," *International Journal* 33 (September 1978), 588ff.

10 On the employment of the army, see J.L. Granatstein, *The Generals, The Canadian Army's Senior Commanders in the Second World War* (Calgary, AB: University of Calgary Press, 2005), ch. III.

11 *Uganda* was serving with Royal Navy ships in the Pacific when, in June 1945, the government announced that only volunteers would participate in the war against Japan. Two-thirds of the ship's crew opted to go home, and HMCS *Uganda* returned to Canada, to the chagrin of its captain and Naval Headquarters: John Allemang, "Veteran Recalls a Vote for Home," *Globe and Mail* (Toronto), 12 August 2005. That Canada had a ship named *Uganda* as late as 1945 suggests a woeful lack of imagination and nationalism.

12 On conscription, see J.L. Granatstein and J.M. Hitsman, *Broken Promises: A History of Conscription in Canada* (Toronto, ON: Copp Clark Pitman, 1985), chs., V–VI.

13 J.L. Granatstein, *A Man of Influence: Norman A. Robertson and Canadian Statecraft, 1929–68* (Ottawa, ON: Deneau, 1981) ch. V; J.L. Granatstein, *The Ottawa Men: The Civil Service Mandarins, 1935–1957* (Toronto, ON: University of Toronto Press, 1998), ch. V.

14 David J. Bercuson, *Canada and the Birth of Israel* (Toronto, ON: University of Toronto Press, 1989).

15 This is also the date selected by John English and Norman Hillmer, "Canada's Alliances," *Revue International d'Histoire Militaire* 51 (1982), 31ff.

16 Robert Bothwell et al., *Canada since 1945* (Toronto, ON: University of Toronto Press, 1989), 129; Granatstein, *Man of Influence*, 296ff.

17 See J.L. Granatstein, *How Britain's Weakness Forced Canada into the Arms of the United States* (Toronto, ON: University of Toronto Press, 1989), ch. I.

18 See Michael Hadley and Roger Sarty, *Tin-Pots and Pirate Ships: Canadian Naval Forces and German Sea Raiders, 1880–1918* (Montreal, QC: McGill-Queen's University Press, 1991).

19 Norman Hillmer and J.L. Granatstein, *For Better or For Worse: Canada and the United States into the 21st Century* (Toronto, ON: Thomson Nelson, forthcoming 2006), 132.

20 Quoted in J.L. Granatstein. *Canada's War: The Politics of the Mackenzie King Government, 1939–1945* (Toronto, ON: University of Toronto Press, 1990), 115.
21 Australian Prime Minister Robert Menzies pressed King to appeal for more assistance from the US, including volunteers and every available aircraft. Churchill agreed, but King, who knew the Americans better than either Menzies or Churchill, demurred – correctly. President Roosevelt interpreted the demands as implying that "If you don't help us at once we will let the Germans have the Fleet and you can go to Hell." This was, FDR said, not very helpful. Granatstein, *Canada's War*, 120.
22 Ibid., 120ff.
23 Library and Archives Canada, Mackenzie King Diary, 23–4 April 1940. The whole Diary, a superb source, is available on the Library and Archives Canada website at http://king.collectionscanada.ca/EN/default.asp.
24 Former Conservative prime minister and future party leader Arthur Meighen: "Really I lost my breakfast when I read the account this morning, and gazed on the disgusting picture of these potentates posing like monkeys in the very middle of the blackest crisis of this Empire. We don't want Canadians to get the idea that we don't need to exert ourselves …" Quoted in Granatstein, *Canada's War*, 129–30.
25 J.L. Granatstein, "Mackenzie King and Canada at Ogdensburg, August 1940," in J. Sokolsky and J. Jockel, eds., *Fifty Years of Canada–United States Defence Cooperation* (Lewiston, NY: Edwin Mellen Press, 1992), 22ff.
26 Granatstein, *Britain's Weakness*, ch. II.
27 Extraordinarily, exactly the same situation would arise in 1947–8: Canada again ran short of US dollars because its efforts to assist Britain with loans collided with the end of sterling convertibility and the inability of other trading partners to pay in dollars for Canadian exports. The US bailed out the Dominion once more, but the market to the south was now clearly the only one on which Canada could rely. Granatstein, *Britain's Weakness*, ch. III.
28 Granatstein, *Canada's War*, 131–2.
29 Granatstein, *Man of Influence*, 120ff.
30 Galen Perras, *Stepping Stones to Nowhere: The Aleutian Islands, Alaska, and American Military Strategy, 1867–1945* (Vancouver, BC: University of British Columbia Press, 2003).
31 On Canada, the early Cold War, and the NATO negotiation, see R.D. Cuff and J.L. Granatstein, *Ties that Bind: Canadian-American Relations in Wartime from the Great War to the Cold War* (Toronto: Samuel Stevens Hakkert, 1977), ch. VI, and R.D. Cuff and J.L. Granatstein, *American Dollars/Canadian Prosperity* (Toronto, ON: Samuel Stevens, 1978).
32 This was just a token, American officials said. But it was three destroyers, the Canadians objected. OK, came the response, three tokens.

33 The fullest account of NORAD's origins is Joseph T. Jockel, *No Boundaries Upstairs: Canada, the United States, and the Origins of North American Air Defence, 1945–1958* (Vancouver, BC: University of British Columbia Press, 1987). On the crisis over the Bomarcs, see J.L. Granatstein, *Canada 1957–1967: The Years of Uncertainty and Innovation* (Toronto, ON: McClelland and Stewart, 1986), ch. V.

34 The best study of Diefenbaker is Denis Smith, *Rogue Tory: The life and Legend of John G. Diefenbaker* (Toronto, ON: Macfarlane, Walter and Ross, 1995). Diefenbaker's own (and largely unreliable) memoir is *One Canada*, Vols. I–III (Toronto, ON: Macmillan, 1975–7).

35 For a history of Canadian anti-Americanism, see J.L. Granatstein, *Yankee Go Home? Canadians and Anti-Americanism* (Toronto, ON: HarperCollins, 1996).

36 To his perpetual embarrassment, in the early 1960s the author owned two Hillman automobiles equipped with the Smith's automatic transmission. Neither vehicle worked in winter or summer. A friend owned a British-made refrigerator that had to be chained to stop it moving about his kitchen, so great were its vibrations.

37 Quoted in Hillmer and Granatstein, *For Better or For Worse*, 208.

38 On Canada and Korea, see Denis Stairs, *The Diplomacy of Constraint* (Toronto, ON: University of Toronto Press, 1974). Pearson's memoir is *Mike: The Memoirs of the Rt. Hon. Lester B. Pearson*, Vols. I–III (Toronto, ON: University of Toronto Press, 1972–5). See also John English, *The Life of Lester Pearson*, Vols. I–II (Toronto, ON: Lester and Orpen Dennys, 1989; Knopf, 1992). Acheson's complaints are in his *Present at the Creation* (New York: Norton, 1969) and *Power and Diplomacy* (Cambridge, MA: Harvard University Press, 1958).

39 Quoted in Hillmer and Granatstein, *For Better or For Worse*, 238. The only full account is J.L. Granatstein and Robert Bothwell, *Pirouette: Pierre Trudeau and Canadian Foreign Policy* (Toronto, ON: University of Toronto Press, 1990). One biographical study is Stephen Clarkson and Christina McCall, *Trudeau and Our Times*, Vols. I–II (Toronto, ON: McClelland and Stewart, 1990–4).

40 English and Hillmer, "Canada's Alliances," 32, date the end of Canada's US alliance with the Viet Nam War.

41 See Nelson Michaud and K.R. Nossal, eds., *Diplomatic Departures* (Vancouver, BC: University of British Columbia Press, 2001), and Michael Hart, *Decision at Midnight* (Vancouver, BC: University of British Columbia Press, 1994).

42 A new book on Mulroney based on tapes made by journalist Peter C. Newman, has the former prime minister blaming his successor, Kim Campbell, for blowing the election because she was too busy "screwing around" with her boyfriend, resulting in "the most incompetent campaign I've seen in my life. Peter C. Newman, *The Secret Mulroney Tapes:*

Unguarded Confessions of a Prime Minister (Toronto, ON: Random House, 2005), 369–71. Mulroney also says that when he took power in 1984, after sixteen years of Pierre Trudeau, "the country was fed up to the goddamned teeth with people going around saying the United States is our enemy. They know the United States is our friend ..." Ibid., 305. That was quite likely true, but by 1988 – and the discussions over Free Trade with the US – anti-Americanism was at historic levels.

43 Canadians, a very polite people, do not often talk about things that matter. See my "Canada, Quebec, Anti-Americanism, and Our Leadership Vacuum," Conference of Defence Associations Annual General Meeting, Ottawa, ON, 4 March 2005 [on-line at www.cda-cdai.ca].

44 A public opinion poll taken in late winter 2005 for the Department of National Defence, but not made public until August 2005, showed that Canadians preferred traditional peacekeeping (57 per cent) to peacemaking operations (41 per cent). Québécois (62 per cent) and the university-educated (61 per cent) were most supportive of blue beret peacekeeping. Mike Blanchfield, "Canadians Oppose Tough, New Role for the Military, Poll Shows," *Ottawa Citizen*, 17 August 2005. See also Lane Anker, "Peacekeeping and Public Opinion," *Canadian Military Journal* VI (Summer 2005), 23ff.

45 J.L. Granatstein, *Who Killed the Canadian Military?* (Toronto, ON: HarperCollins, 2004). See John Blaxland, "Strategic Cousins' Reconverging Trajectories: Canada's and Australia's Expeditionary Forces Since the End of the Cold War," in Peter Dennis and Jeffrey Grey, eds., *Battles Near and Far: A Century of Overseas Deployment* (Canberra: Army History Unit, 2005), 221ff.

46 See Douglas Bland, ed., *Canada Without Armed Forces?* (Montreal, QC: McGill-Queen's University Press, 2004), for a detailed examination of the military's condition.

47 There is a very useful collection of essays on the events of this period in David Carment et al., eds., *Canada Among Nations 2004* (Montreal, QC: McGill-Queen's University Press, 2005).

48 In March 2003, an opinion poll done for Global TV found that 77.6 per cent of Québécois held unfavourable views of the US compared to 54.8 per cent favourable views in the rest of Canada. The overall attitude to the coming war in Quebec was "Don't participate." In April, just 20 per cent of Québécois supported the war compared to 62 per cent in the western province of Alberta and a majority in English Canada. Cited in Granatstein, *Who Killed the Canadian Military?*, 194. University of Calgary political scientist Ted Morton observed bitterly that the Iraq War "reminded us [that] Canadian foreign policy is set by Quebec ..." See "Triple E – or Else," *National Post*, 22 May 2005.

49 On Quebec attitudes, see J.-S. Rioux, *Two Solitudes: Quebecers' Attitudes Regarding Canadian Security and Defence Policy* (Calgary, AB: Canadian Defence and Foreign Affairs Institute, 2005); Susan Delacourt, "Cellucci Critical of PM's Stand on Defence," *Toronto Star*, 2 September 2005. Cellucci also apparently believed that the separatist Bloc Québécois leader in Ottawa, Gilles Duceppe, was not anti-American, or so reported Chantal Hébert: "Cellucci's 'Unquiet Diplomacy,'" *Toronto Star*, 2 September 2005. (Only his supporters were!) See Paul Cellucci, *Unquiet Diplomacy* (Toronto, ON: Key Porter, 2005).
50 This decision unusually drew some Canadian media attention to Australia, which did sign on to BMD. Canada, noted one journalist, had sent 15,000 personnel and twenty ships (all told) to Afghanistan and the Persian Gulf since 2002, the largest contributor to the war in Afghanistan other than the US. "Australia has sent a fraction of the soldiers, and yet Australians are seen as model allies, in part because they politically supported the Iraq War." Canadians, on the other hand, are viewed with "some suspicion" because of their criticisms of the US: Luiza Savage, "That Loud BMD Slap," *Maclean's*, 12 September 2005.
51 Luiza Savage, "All for One?," *Maclean's*, 12 September 1950, and a conversation with a senior Washington-based Department of Foreign Affairs official.
52 Department of Foreign Affairs and International Trade, *A Role of Pride and Influence in the World: Overview*, and ibid., *Defence* (Ottawa, ON: DFAIT, 2005).
53 See Allan Gotlieb, *Romanticism and Realism in Canada's Foreign Policy* (Toronto, ON: C.D. Howe Institute, 2004). Many of the essays in "The Troubled Relationship: Papers from the American Assembly," *International Journal* 60 (Spring 2005), bear on the present state of the Canada-US alliance.
54 Americans have noticed, most especially because of Fox News, which might be characterized as the "anti-Canadian" cable network. See, e.g., the book by host John Gibson, *Hating America: The New World Sport* (New York: HarperCollins, 2004), esp. 258.
55 These data are commonly accepted. The only new one is the 52 per cent figure for Canadian GDP dependent on imports from and exports to the US, which is taken from a presentation by Michael Hart at the Wilson Center, Washington, DC, in July 2005 (email, Colin Robertson, Canadian Embassy, Washington, to distribution, 8 July 2005). The weight of the data makes all the more incomprehensible Canada's unwillingness to recognize its interests.
56 This is also the conclusion of the leading Canadian academic expert on BMD: James Fergusson, "Shall We Dance? The Missile Defence Decision, NORAD Renewal, and the Future of Canada-US Defence Relations," *Canadian Military Journal* VI (Summer 2005), 22.

57 The contrast with Australia is clear. The Australian government believes it needs to work at the US relationship in order to be "guaranteed" protection. The Canadian government and people believe the US will protect them, no matter what. This may be true, but with no effort expended by Canadians on their own (and continental) defence, the US may – in its own national interests – simply act rather than consult. There are also indications of a new and close US-Australian intelligence relationship of a kind that only the UK has (Greg Sheridan, "New Ranking Lets Us Share in Secrets," *The Australian*, 1 September 2005). Canada was long a partner in the US-UK intelligence alliance, but recent policies and events may have weakened the link.

58 Pollster Michael Adams, *Fire and Ice* (Toronto, ON: Penguin, 2003), argues that Canadian values have been and will continue to diverge quite sharply from those of the US. Blaxland, "Strategic Cousins' Reconverging Trajectories," 253, hints at Canada's Quebec problem, and Prime Minister Paul Martin told a Vancouver audience on 30 September 2005 that Canada's strong values must be reflected in its foreign policy. Canadian Press, copied on www.GlobeandMail.com.

Chapter Twelve

When the Department of External Affairs Mattered – and When It Shouldn't Have

"Relations with the United States are at the centre of Canada's foreign and domestic policy interests at every level," wrote Michael Hart in his new book, *From Pride to Influence: Towards a New Canadian Foreign Policy*. "The principal foreign policy challenge for Canada is to manage the pervasiveness of this US reality."[1] There can be no question that Hart is right, and his judgment stands as correct at least since the end of the Second World War and arguably from 1938 when American President Franklin Roosevelt and Prime Minister Mackenzie King exchanged defence pledges at Kingston and Woodbridge, Ontario. But our foreign policy-makers have not always recognized reality, sometimes putting other concerns, global or domestic, ahead of the reality of Canadian national interests.

And what are those national interests? Here is my list with which, I suspect, few would quarrel seriously:

1 Canada must protect its territory and the security of its people;
2 Canada must strive to maintain its unity;
3 Canada must protect and enhance its independence;
4 Canada must promote the economic growth of the nation to support the prosperity and welfare of its people;
5 Canada should work with like-minded states for the protection and enhancement of democracy and freedom.

There is nothing remotely contentious here. Of course, these interests are simple enough to state but not always easy to achieve because they sometimes conflict. It is the task of national leaders to sort out the conflicts and determine the best strategy to protect and advance Canada's interests. What is surely clear is that the presence of the United States is omnipresent in most, if not all, of them.

Oscar Douglas Skelton was the senior official in the Department of External Affairs who built and shaped the department. He was the man who did the recruiting in the 1920s and 1930s, and he was the thinker who determined the policy direction, subject to political control. What made Skelton unique is that he thought in terms of the national interest from the time he became under-secretary of state for external affairs in 1925 and indeed before. Other Canadians then accepted that Britain's interests were almost automatically indistinguishable from Canada's,[2] and it was such attitudes that took Canada into the war in 1939 just as they had in 1914. Skelton wrote innumerable memoranda excoriating British policy in Europe in the 1930s and denouncing Britain's Prime Minister Neville Chamberlain's government for the way it treated the Dominions, for assuming (correctly) that they would do what they were told. The under-secretary, who, it is fair to say, missed the necessity of stopping Hitler, did not want Canada to behave as a lapdog and go to war simply because Britain did. But his prime minister, who almost always agreed with Skelton – except on the most important matters – certainly understood English-speaking Canadian opinion better than the under-secretary did and knew that Canada had to go to war in 1939. Prime Minister Mackenzie King, in other words, was a strong minister unafraid to rein in his chief foreign policy adviser when necessary.

Nothing that happened in the first nine months of the Second World War changed Skelton's mind that the war did not serve Canadian interests well. But soon even he could not be blind to the military-political realities. The Anglo-French defeat in the Low Countries and in France in May and June 1940 changed everything. Suddenly, and realistically, Britain's key national interest of survival was critical to Canada. Canada's own national interests demanded that it should work with like-minded states for the protection and enhancement of democracy and freedom, and Skelton saw this at once. "It amuses me a little," King noted in his diary on May 24, "how completely some men swing to opposite extremes. No one could have been more strongly for everything being done for Canada, as against Britain, than Skelton was up to a very short time ago. Yesterday ... he naturally did not want me to suggest any help for Canada, but rather the need for Britain. He now sees that the real place to defend our land is from across the seas."[3]

There was, of course, less contradiction than King perceived. As a national interest thinker, Skelton understood that a Nazi victory, unlikely in September 1939 but very probable in late May 1940, posed a grave threat to North America and to freedom and democracy everywhere. Everything Canada could do to defeat Hitler was necessary – and very much in the national interest. Still, the change in Skelton was marked, and he was quick to realize that Canada could not be protected unless an arrangement with the United States was reached.

The trick now was for Canada to do the maximum possible for the war effort overseas and to guarantee Canada's own security *if* – and it seemed more like *when*, that summer of 1940 – Britain fell to Hitler. This meant getting closer to the still neutral United States and as quickly as possible. Skelton wrote at the end of April 1940 that "the United States is already giving in many respects as much help as if it were in the war, but its further diplomatic and financial and naval and perhaps air support are powerful potentialities. Our task is two fold: to make effective our own share and to speed in every practical and discreet way the cooperation of the United States."[4]

On May 19, Hugh Keenleyside from Skelton's staff went to Washington to see Roosevelt and to deliver the prime minister's appeal for aircraft to replace those Britain now could not supply for the British Commonwealth Air Training Plan. The president offered limited help, but more important, however, was Roosevelt's return message to King of two phrases: "certain possible eventualities which could not be mentioned aloud" and "British fleet."[5] If Hitler forced Britain to sue for peace, what would happen to the Royal Navy? Would it escape to Canada to carry on the fight or would it be turned over to the victors? Questions that had seemed unthinkable on 9 May 1940 were ten days later urgently seizing the attention of the American president and the Canadian prime minister.

Skelton was not the only one who had altered his thinking under the press of events. Informed public opinion, watching the evacuation of allied troops from Dunkirk and the surrender of France, understood that Canada had now been forced to re-think its political and defence relationship with the United States. In mid-July, "A Group of Twenty Canadians," largely associated with the Canadian Institute of International Affairs but including some public servants (Keenleyside, J.W. Pickersgill, and Robert Bryce) and Liberal Members of Parliament (Paul Martin and Brooke Claxton) produced "a programme of Immediate Canadian Action" that called for this reappraisal. "Co-operation with Washington," the programme said bluntly and correctly, "is going to be either voluntary on Canada's part, or else compulsory; in any event it is inevitable." Skelton "took a positive attitude towards the talks," and received the statement "with interest and appreciation."[6] Suggestions for a closer relationship were heard in Washington too, and in mid-August, Roosevelt invited King to meet him at Ogdensburg, in upstate New York.[7]

The result was the Permanent Joint Board on Defence (PJBD), the first Canada–United States defence alliance. As someone who had long believed that "the North American mind"[8] was markedly distinct from that of the Old World and its age-old conflicts, Skelton was overjoyed. It was "the best day's work done for many a year. It did not come by chance," he wrote to King, "but as the inevitable sequence of public policies and personal relationships, based upon the realization of the imperative necessity of close understanding between the English-speaking peoples."[9]

Exactly so. Canada had guaranteed its safety no matter the result of the war in Europe, thanks to the new American alliance. Moreover, with this guarantee, Canada could now offer maximum military support to Britain, sure that its own defence was secure. Even better, public opinion, aside from a few Tory stalwarts who feared Canada being swallowed by the United States,[10] was overwhelmingly supportive.

British Prime Minister Winston Churchill, however, was less pleased, telegraphing King that if Hitler could not invade Britain, all such transactions "will be judged in a mood different to that prevailing while the issue still hangs in the balance."[11] The British leader obviously believed that Canada was scuttling to safety. Skelton prepared a draft response to Churchill's imperial rant – "we can perhaps safely leave the verdict of history for the future to determine" – which was not sent, but it took a propitiatory telegram from Churchill on September 12 before King – and Skelton – were mollified.[12]

The creation of the PJBD was arguably the high point of Skelton's career. Skelton had always insisted that North America was where Canada's "lasting community of interest" and its "current of destiny" resided.[13] But he had never before managed to have the national interest determine the government's actions on questions of war and peace. But now in the midst of a terrible military debacle, he had seen his prime minister take a historic step. In August 1940, the national interest demanded a defence alliance with the United States, for the first time, Canada had put its interests ahead of all others, and Churchill's intemperate, foolish response made this very clear. The British leader saw only the new alliance and a weakening of the old, and failed to note that the PJBD brought the United States closer to Britain's ranking ally and, simultaneously, let that ally do more for Britain. His imperial blinkers on, Churchill missed the point, and Skelton, never having worn those particular blinkers, got it.

Then ten months later and just a few weeks after Skelton's death at the wheel of his car, the Hyde Park Declaration, again reached by Roosevelt and King, secured Canada's wartime economic interests.[14] This again was brilliant prime ministerial negotiation, driven by immediate necessity but also by a clear understanding of future reality. The national interest demanded that Canada promote the economic growth of the nation to support the prosperity and welfare of its people, something that could only be achieved by the closest economic cooperation with the United States. Canada was fighting Canada's war and Britain's, and the Hyde Park Declaration let it keep its factories going, employment and production high, and to do the maximum possible for a financially strapped Britain. Canada was also recognizing at last that it was a North American nation and that its national interests, first and foremost, had to be Canadian.

The turn to the south, the move toward a national interest policy, was Skelton's great achievement, accomplished because he had helped his prime minister prepare the ground. The two men did not always see eye to eye, but in the summer of 1940 they did, and they achieved a historic realignment that protected Canadian interests and advanced the Allied cause.

A very different sequence of events would occur some two decades later, one that changed Canadian politics and came close to jeopardizing the defence relationship with the United States that Skelton and King had created.

One of Skelton's ablest recruits to External Affairs was Norman Robertson, a British Columbia Rhodes Scholar, who joined in 1929 at the age of twenty-five. Robertson had worked mainly on trade questions through the 1930s, but he had greatly impressed King who appointed him, rather than the more senior Lester B. "Mike" Pearson, to succeed Skelton as under-secretary in 1941. He ran the Department of External Affairs throughout the war and held a variety of critical appointments in Ottawa, London, and Washington until his death in 1968. He was a Canadian nationalist but also very much an internationalist, someone who understood that Canada had to work with its friends to advance its interests.

In late 1958, Robertson left his post as ambassador to Washington to become under-secretary for a second time, first for Sidney Smith, a university president turned hapless politician and foreign minister, and then from early June 1959 for his fellow British Columbian Howard Green in the Progressive Conservative government led by Prime Minister John Diefenbaker.

A key national interest for any country is that it must strive to protect and enhance its independence. This was something that concerned the Diefenbaker government, fearful as it was that Washington's sometimes bullying ways might stampede Canada into decisions, whatever the consequences might be. Diefenbaker believed that this had occurred, aided and abetted by the Canadian military, when the North American Air Defense Command (NORAD) was created just after the Tories took power. He may have been right; certainly he suffered attacks from the Liberals who had negotiated the agreement before their defeat in the 1957 election and knew its details better perhaps than the incoming government. Nonetheless, it was Diefenbaker in February 1959 who agreed to install nuclear-armed Bomarc surface-to-air missiles at two bases in Canada and soon after to arm Canada's troops in Europe with nuclear weaponry. The difficulty was that a myriad of details remained to be settled before the weapons were in place, and it was here that Robertson and Green exercised their influence.

Or perhaps it was the under-secretary who exercised his influence on the minister. Howard Green was a fine gentleman without much experience of foreign affairs. He was from birth an Empire-first Tory, and he remained innately suspicious of the United States and fearful of its influence, but he could learn and he quickly came to admire the officers in his department. Still, he was a naif, and disarmament, a subject of interest to Robertson as well, captivated him despite its hopelessness in the darkest period of the Cold War.[15] That led inevitably to the primacy of the nuclear question.

In his various postings, Robertson had dealt with nuclear issues and generally accepted the necessity of the weapons. He understood the need to protect the American deterrent, and he recognized that intimate cooperation in air defence between the two North American nations was necessary. But by 1959, he had begun to worry about the effects of radioactive fallout on humankind's ability to survive, and the mutuality of assured destruction that underlay deterrence theory had begun to trouble him. The nationalist internationalist that he had always been was about to be replaced by the traditional Canadian moralist.

The catalyst that turned Robertson from tacit supporter to opponent of nuclear weapons was an article in the British magazine *The Spectator* that argued that hydrogen bombs had changed the nature of war.

There could be no victor and no chance that civilized life could survive. The answer, author Christopher Hollis said, was unilateral nuclear disarmament and a build-up of conventional forces. The Soviets had no interest in destroying the West for did not Marxist theory postulate that victory over capitalism was certain? Why then destroy what you would eventually take? Robertson sent the article to the prime minister with a note declaring that his "personal views" coincided with Hollis'.[16] Two days later Green became secretary of state for external affairs and the anti-nuclear forces had their champions.

For the next three-and-a-half years, Robertson's fertile mind produced delaying tactic after dilatory response. American policy required United States control of warheads? Then Canada should be for dual control or, even better, no warheads at all on Canadian soil. Should the cabinet discuss the nuclear question, as defence minister Douglas Harkness wanted? No, if word leaked out, this might jeopardize Canadian disarmament efforts at the United Nations. Time and again, the wily diplomat in External Affairs fought off the Department of National Defence's cack-handed efforts to move the nuclear issue along so that Canada could negotiate the arming of the weapons the Diefenbaker government had secured from the United States. Canada's ambassador in Washington, Arnold Heeney, noted that Green's "own attitudes and prejudices, in a curious way, combine with [Robertson]'s cosmic anxieties, particularly in our defence relationships, external and domestic, to produce a negative force of great importance."[17] The issue that was to destroy the Diefenbaker government had been delineated, and the tumbrils of Tory collapse had begun to roll.

The difficulty with the Robertson-Green position was that it flew directly in the face of Canada's national interests. These required Canada to get along with the United States in the interests of its security and its economic well-being, not to mention Canada's reliance on alliances to advance democracy and freedom. The Americans had large burdens to bear in Europe and Asia, but the defence of their homeland was properly their highest priority, and Canada needed to recognize that. Robertson's delaying tactics put his judgment, his values, and his high sense of morality ahead of Washington's – all fine except when the superpower neighbour's security was involved. A refusal or a delay in arming the Canadian component of NORAD with nuclear weapons may not have jeopardized United States security outright – Canadian Bomarcs and interceptors, nuclear-armed or not, did not rule the skies over Canada – but it was a harbinger of even more troubling Canadian attitudes to come during the Cuban missile crisis of October 1962. And these were troubling enough that President John F. Kennedy's frustrated, angry administration moved successfully to topple the dry husk of Diefenbaker's government in January 1963.

Nonetheless the responsibility for the government's collapse should not be placed on the delaying tactics of Robertson and Green. It was John Diefenbaker's alone. His inability to make up his mind on the nuclear question had pitted External Affairs against National Defence, divided his cabinet, caucus, party, and country, and reduced Canadian-American relations to their lowest point in the twentieth century.[18] Still, Robertson, fighting for the moralistic and unrealistic position he believed in and unchecked, indeed encouraged, by his weak minister, seemed to have forgotten the national interest.[19] That was not a mistake Skelton would have made, and there was some irony in the fact that Mike Pearson, the friendly rival Robertson had beaten out (without trying) for the under-secretary's job in 1941, would accept nuclear weapons as soon as he came to power as prime minister in early 1963. Getting on with the Yanks was essential and necessary, and Pearson was nothing if not a practical man.[20]

Skelton had been heard in 1940, and should have been. Robertson was listened to from 1959 to 1963, and ought not to have been. The Canada of 1940 was still psychologically a colony; the nation of the early 1960s was in an age of confidence and wealth, and after the Suez Crisis of 1956 in particular, it had begun to believe that it was a player in foreign policy. It wasn't, not really, and in fact its influence was in the midst of a slow decline after the flush of power and influence created by the Second World War faded.

What Diefenbaker had done was to make the pulling of tail feathers from the American eagle the national sport, and his successors, Brian Mulroney aside, successfully emulated him. The highpoints of this approach came under Prime Ministers Pierre Trudeau, Jean Chrétien, and Paul Martin, with Lloyd Axworthy, Chrétien's foreign minister, as the prime exponent of this tactic. With its security, trade, and economy dependent on the United States, this was never wise policy. Canada was not a great power, not a self-sufficient island, and tail-feather pulling, while one of few sports other than hockey at which Canadians had long excelled, was foolish and appealed to the lowest common denominator of shrill anti-Americanism.

All Canadians want Canada to be independent; certainly Skelton and Robertson did. But wise counsellors understand the limitations within which they must operate, and the most realistic Canadians have understood that their nation's aim should be to be as independent as possible in the circumstances, as one correspondent once told the late Peter Gzowski on the Canadian Broadcast Corporation's radio program, "This Country in the Morning." That is precisely it. Seize an opportunity if it comes, as Skelton did in 1940. But don't, as Robertson did, pretend to be a major player by inventing obstacles to throw in the way of the great power on whom we depend, and especially not on issues, like disarmament, that we can only influence at the margins. Don't shout out that Canada is a moral superpower, in other words, forever telling the Yanks that we know best. Robertson – and Trudeau, Chrétien, Martin, and Axworthy – did that, and they were wrong.

NOTES

1 Michael Hart, *From Pride to Influence* (Vancouver: UBC Press, 2008), 334.
2 This point is made in Norman Hillmer's 2008 Skelton Lecture, "Foreign Policy and the National Interest: Why Skelton Matters," Department of Foreign Affairs and International Trade, Ottawa, 17 December 2008.
3 W.L.M. King Diary, King Papers, 24 May 1940, Library and Archives Canada (LAC).
4 O.D. Skelton, "The Present Outlook," 30 April 1940, Department of External Affairs Records (DEAR), vol. 774, file 353, microfilm reel T-1791, LAC.
5 J.L. Granatstein, *Canada's War: The Politics of the Mackenzie King Government 1939–1945* (Toronto: University of Toronto Press, 1975), 119ff.
6 Copy in Alan Flaunt Papers, box 9, file 1, University of British Columbia Archives [UBCA] and in King Papers, attached to Brooke Claxton to W.L.M. King, 23 August 1940, 241683ff., LAC.
7 For a full account, see J.L. Granatstein, "Mackenzie King and Canada at Ogdensburg, August 1940," in *Fifty Years of Canada-US Defence Cooperation: The Road from Ogdensburg*, ed. J. Jockel and J. Sokolsky (Lewiston, NY: Edwin Mellon Press, 1992), 9–29.
8 Norman Hillmer, "O.D. Skelton and the North American Mind," *International Journal* 60 (Winter 2004–5): 93–110.
9 Skelton to King, 19 August 1940, King Papers, LAC. King used almost the same phrase: "finest day's work in his career," or so Skelton recorded in his memorandum, 18 August 1940, file 5-14, LAC.
10 J.L. Granatstein, "The Conservative Party and the Ogdensburg Agreement," *International Journal* 22 (Winter 1966–7): 73ff.
11 Churchill to King, 22 August 1940, Cabinet War Committee Records, LAC.

12 Skelton to King, 28 August 1940, King Papers, C282306ff., LAC; Granatstein, *Canada's War*, 131; Skelton, Memorandum for Prime Minister, 9 September 1940, King Papers, C282360ff., LAC.
13 Hillmer, Skelton Lecture.
14 See J.L. Granatstein and R.D. Cuff, "The Hyde Park Declaration 1941: Origins and Significance," *Canadian Historical Review* 55 (March 1974): 59–80.
15 J.L. Granatstein, *A Man of Influence: Norman A. Robertson and Canadian Statecraft, 1929–1968* (Ottawa: Deneau, 1981), 333.
16 Ibid., 336ff.; Christopher Hollis in *the Spectator*, 1 May 1959.
17 Heeney Diary, 4 February 1962, Arnold Heeney Papers, vol. 2, LAC.
18 The fullest account is Denis Smith, *Rogue Tory: The Life and Legend of John G. Diefenbaker* (Toronto: Macfarlane Walter & Ross, 1995), chap. XII.
19 I have written on the conflict between interests and values, most especially in *The Importance of Being Less Earnest: Promoting Canada's National Interests through Tighter Ties with the US* (Toronto: C.D. Howe Institute, 2003).
20 See Robert Bothwell, *Alliance and Illusion* (Vancouver: UBC Press, 2007), 172ff., for the most recent analysis of Pearson and nuclear weapons.

Chapter Thirteen

Peacekeeping Is Our Profession?

Peacekeeping as a concept has had its ups and downs. There were some splendid successes in the past as at Suez in 1956 and on the Indo-Pakistani border in 1965. On both occasions the United Nations demonstrated an impressive ability to react with speed and to adapt itself to new situations. But there have been failures too, and lately there have been rather more of these than successes. The disastrous demise of UNEF in 1967 is only the most glaring example of the world organization's catastrophic inability to move from peacekeeping to peacemaking in time to prevent the combatants from taking up arms again. Still, on balance, the peacekeeping ideal has served the United Nations and the world well, damping down a crisis here, separating antagonists there.

For at least a decade, peacekeeping was an important component of Canada's foreign policy. After Mr. Pearson's feats of diplomatic legerdemain at the United Nations in 1956, and particularly after his Nobel peace prize, every Canadian prime minister and secretary of state for external affairs has probably had his dream of a similar coup on the international stage. Suez and the Canadian role in the creation of UNEF had marked the coming of age of Canadian diplomacy, and if it also marked the final shift from Canada's being a tail on the British kite to our being just another American appendage, who would have been so critical as to carp? UNEF, after all, had demonstrated the expertise of Canadian diplomacy at the same time as it resurrected the hoary old cliché about Canada being the linch-pin between the new world and the old. And Suez had also demonstrated the adaptability and skill of the armed forces, then relatively well-equipped with transport aircraft and all the accoutrements of a mini great power. Of course, the Egyptians had complained rather bitterly about Canada's *bona fides* but this was interpreted only as the desperate caterwauling of a militarily defeated state.

In fact, UNEF should have shown us that Canada was not necessarily the most desirable nation for peacekeeping services. Our liabilities were many and obvious. The old ties to empire still manifested themselves in British pattern military equipment and regimental titles that reeked of the Raj. From Canadian representatives at the United Nations and in the editorial pages of the newspapers, expressions of undying regard for Great Britain abounded, albeit tinged with occasional regrets at the failures or follies of Eden's Suez policy. Canadian ties to the United States, too, could be seen as a liability. Was Canada not economically tied to Washington? Did the United States in fact not control Canada? Those were good questions. And Canada, as well, was part of NATO, the imperialist alliance *par excellence.* NATO made Canada an ally of Britain and France, the aggressors of 1956, and it also linked us with Portugal and Belgium, two even more backward colonial powers. Is it any wonder that Canada was considered suspect by the Egyptians?

What was surely extraordinary about the Suez Affair was that Canada was permitted to take part at all. That this was so was primarily attributable to three factors. General E.L.M. Burns was one. Because the General was on the scene as the commander of the United Nations Truce Supervisory Organization, he was the immediate and logical choice for UNEF commander. As a sternly fair man, he was respected if not liked by the Egyptians, and when the General threatened to resign if his compatriots were not included in the force, he could wield enough clout to make his point. The second factor of decisive importance in getting Canadian participation was simply that in its public pronouncements that it was going to send troops to Suez the Canadian government had gone too far to withdraw with any grace. In the various accounts of the formation of UNEF, this becomes increasingly clear. First, Hammarskjöld tried to ease out the Canadians but was persuaded to include them again by Mr. Pearson. Then General Burns was chivvied into finding a new role for the troops – after a long meeting with the indefatigable External Affairs minister. One might be forgiven for believing that Pearson's greatest success at New York in 1956 lay in getting Canadians to Suez in the face of great opposition. Finally, however, what must have been the decisive factor was the military capability of the Canadian forces. No other country that was even remotely acceptable could supply an efficient transport and supply organization. No other could produce effective communications or short-range air transport. These capabilities were needed and so could outweigh every drawback.

What no one troubled to ask then or for a long time was why on God's green earth Canada maintained this overblown capability. Why should a nation of less than twenty millions keep a military apparatus of a microcosmic great power? Why should a small country spend almost $2 billions each year to keep up appearances? Of course, UNEF was one justification and a very substantial one, but characteristically, perhaps, many senior officers looked on this role as a sideshow that diverted attention and resources from other and more important tasks of the Canadian forces. What is truly incredible is that it was not until 1968 that a Canadian government at last began to examine the preconceptions behind its defence policy.

In any case, after Suez Canadian participation became the *sine qua non* of United Nations peacekeeping. In the Lebanon, the Congo, New Guinea, the Yemen, along the Indo-Pakistani border, and in Cyprus, Canadian troops showed the flag – and very well indeed. And if you talk to Canadians who served with these forces, you become convinced that it was only the expertise of our soldiers that held those ill-financed and sometimes ill-conceived operations together. Petty chauvinism aside this is almost believable. The Canadians were professionals and they knew their jobs. Certainly the Canadian public responded enthusiastically to the new role. In the Congo crisis of 1960, for example, it seems clear that the government had no desire to participate in a major way in any United Nations force. Austerity was in force, national survival training was tying the armed forces into knots, and Mr. Diefenbaker was reluctant to press the Treasury Board too hard. What forced the Prime Minister to action in this case was public pressure. The newspapers wanted Canadians in the Congo; public opinion, whatever that is and however one can measure it, seemed to want Canadians at the scene of action; and the United Nations wanted signallers. So in the fullness of time signallers were sent. Peacekeeping had become our profession.

Canadian spokesmen began speaking out at the United Nations for the creation of standard operating procedures. Efforts were made, as at the Ottawa peacekeeping conference of 1964, to pass Canadian expertise along to other nations, and this country became the major advocate of the concept. What very few seem to have noticed at the time was that the new majority at the United Nations, the Afro-Asian states, were less than enthusiastic about the intervention of any force – great power, small power, or United Nations – onto their territory or into their affairs. And when the United Nations bogged down irretrievably in squabbling about who should pay for peacekeeping, the whole idea became tarnished. Along with it, Canada's reputation lost some of its glitter. The Suez success began to appear more and more a one-shot achievement. The .200 hitter had come up with the crucial home run, but he was a .200 hitter nonetheless.

Not even the creation of the 33-nation Special Committee on Peacekeeping Operations at New York in 1965 did much to re-establish the credibility of peacekeeping. For three years almost nothing was accomplished. The great powers pressed their own hard-nosed views, and no accommodation was in sight. In 1969, however, a working group of eight states, including Canada, began to make progress. By keeping its aims limited in scope, by focussing first on the less controversial observer functions, and by taking advantage of the apparently increased willingness of the Russians and Americans to rely on the United Nations to keep the peace in a post-Vietnam world, some small headway was made. Peacekeeping was starting to come back into favour at New York, and the Security Council seemed likely again to play its proper role.

Unfortunately by the time that the climate had begun to change in New York, Canadian opinion had turned against peacekeeping. No longer was it the fair-haired darling of the academics, the politicians, and the press. The professors had begun throwing darts as early as 1964, claiming that peacekeeping was a bar to armed forces training, too often restricted in its locale, and sometimes against Canadian and/or allied interests. Some left-wingers disliked the idea of freezing revolutionary situations, seeing in the interposition of third parties another reactionary device designed to prop up decadent and corrupt régimes. The press began to worry about the terms on which Canadians might be committed to peacekeeping (and after 1967 who could blame them?) and some columnists and writers began to urge against the employment of Canadians on any future operations in the Sinai or in Vietnam. The Trudeau government's review of foreign policy, too, seemed to down-grade peacekeeping at much the same time as it cut into the armed forces' manpower pool. It seemed to be Canada's fate always to be marching to a different drummer.

The question that these volumes raise[1] is whether anyone cares or even notices the Canadian predicament. For one who has studied the Canadian role in peacekeeping, it is somewhat chastening to discover that our role does not seem very significant from the perspective of the outsider. Was it not Paul Martin who, as King Gordon told us in this journal (summer 1964), saved the situation in Cyprus in 1964? Apparently not if one accepts Professor Stegenga's account, for the honourable member for Essex East is relegated to a single footnote. And have Canadians not always pressed without cessation for peacekeeping action in the face of imminent crisis? Not according to India's ambassador, Arthur Lall, who indirectly chides Canadian Ambassador Ignatieff for failing to convene a Security Council meeting when the Middle East was threatening to explode in April 1967 and when Ignatieff was Council president. The absence of such meetings, Lall says, was "regrettable and in some degree inexplicable." That "so dedicated and concerned a representative as the Ambassador of Canada should not have thought it feasible to press for a Security Council meeting ... is an indication of how strong have become the inhibitory factors which arrest timely and peaceful remedial action by the organ of the United Nations specially designed to fulfill just this function." Nor does Professor James allocate much space to Canada. His most favourable reference occurs in connection with a Cyprus incident in 1967, when Canada "fulfilled her accustomed role by putting forward a set of peace proposals, which, characteristically, relied to a large extent on the involvement of the UN." Mrs. Higgins' documents devote most space to Canada when examining the peremptory expulsion of the Canadian contingent from UNEF, hardly a glorious role (if not a discreditable one). All in all, the Canadian part seems rather less important than one might have hoped or expected.

On second thought this should not be surprising. As Professor James correctly points out in *The Politics of Peace-keeping*, the determinant in most peacekeeping actions has been the attitude of the great powers. He sets up six forms of great-power response, James' six laws of peacekeeping: (1) where all the powers are opposed to action, there is little likelihood the United Nations will be able to move; (2) where some of the powers are opposed and others merely acquiesce, there is similarly little likelihood of action; (3) if all the powers acquiesce, then the prospect of action is brighter; (4) where some are in favour and some opposed, then the prospect for action depends on whether those who are best placed procedurally think it worth while offending the minority; (5) where some are enthusiastic and others acquiesce, then United Nations action is likely; and (6) most favourably for action, all the powers are enthusiastic. This formulation, it seems to me, sums up very neatly all the past and probable future cases, and the author richly embroiders his laws by devising his own categories of United Nations action. "Patching-up" is one such category, a function James sees the United Nations carrying out through investigation, mediation, supervision, and administration. Another is "prophylaxis," where through accusation, sedation, obstruction, and refrigeration, the United Nations attempts to prevent dangerous situations from deterioration. Finally the author creates the category of "proselytism," a situation in which the United Nations, either through invalidation or coercion, attempts to alter the course of affairs by eradicating unhealthy situations. This is baldly stated here, and it does no justice to James' argument.

This volume is unquestionably the best we have yet had on the broad subject of peacekeeping, rich in example, well-written, and immensely thoughtful.

Superlatives must also be applied to the documents prepared by Mrs. Higgins for the Royal Institute of International Affairs. Volume I covers the Middle East, and the forthcoming Volumes II and III will focus on Asia and Europe-Africa respectively. All the documents are from United Nations sources, and merely to have the most important culled out from the mass of material makes these volumes of great importance. In addition, Mrs. Higgins has arranged the material for each operation in a consistent fashion under thirteen headings so that, for example, relations with host countries could be compared for UNTSO, UNOGIL, and UNEF with ease. All in all this is a model of the way documents should be presented, and Mrs. Higgins is generally fair – if occasionally tart – in her comments on the material she presents. For example when she prints the correspondence relating to the withdrawal of Canadians from UNEF in 1967, Mrs. Higgins says that "although the Secretary-General clearly states that the sole basis for his decision to accelerate the evacuation of the Canadian contingent was his unwillingness to put the Canadians at risk in a hostile local population, it is perhaps unfortunate that the opportunity was not used clearly to state to Egypt that the Canadian contingent were serving the UN, and were subject to the orders of only the UN and not of the Canadian government." Neatly put.

The volume by Ambassador Lall focusses on minutiae. The role of the United Nations in the fiasco of 1967 is here examined for the period from April to November. The detail is wearisome and the prose legalistic and heavy, but on occasion the author cuts through the thickets with a sure hand. U Thant, we are told, had no alternative other than to withdraw UNEF on Egyptian request. This is direct, straightforward, and clear, although I wonder if it is correct. And the Ambassador concludes that the Soviet Union did everything it could to preserve peace: "Soviet support for the Arab cause ... was subordinate to adherence by the Arabs to a containment of their postures of belligerence within limits that would remain short of actual hostilities."

The study of the Cyprus force is probably more useful. The situation on the island is carefully examined (and Professor Stegenga puts the blame on Archbishop Makarios for deliberately fomenting trouble), and the mechanics, machinery, and politics of UNFICYP are carefully studied. The bulk of the book deals with the functioning of the force, with the frustrations inherent in attempting to resolve a civil conflict with a military force, and with the difficulties of moving from peacekeeping to peacemaking. The author also ventures the conclusion that future peacekeeping forces will likely follow the Cyprus model. They will be "law and order forces that will operate throughout the interiors of single countries to promote internal order ..." The most probable type of armed hostilities, he says, "will pit shaky central governments striving (forcibly if necessary) to maintain national unity against the onslaughts of variously motivated coups, insurgencies, and secession movements." It is difficult to quarrel with this assessment although the difficulties of getting United Nations action will be enormous. However, I suspect that some United Nations bureaucrat in the Office of Acronymic Horrors has already picked out the name for a force in Quebec. Would you believe UNIQUE?

NOTES

1 Arthur Lail, *The UN and the Middle East Crisis, 1967.* New York and London: Columbia University Press [Montreal: McGill University Press]. 1968. x, 322pp. $10.00.

Alan James, *The Politics of Peace-keeping.* London: Chatto and Windus for the Institute for Strategic Studies [Toronto: Clark, Irwin]. 1969. 452pp. $12.60.

James A. Stegenga, *The United Nations Force in Cyprus.* Columbus: Ohio State University Press. 1968. xiv, 227pp. $6.25.

Rosalyn Higgins, *United Nations Peacekeeping, 1946–67: Documents and Commentary.* I. *The Middle East.* London: Toronto: Oxford University Press. 1969. xiv, 674pp. $18.00.

Chapter Fourteen

Peacekeeping: Did Canada Make a Difference? And What Difference Did Peacekeeping Make to Canada?

If there is any one area of foreign and defence policy in which Canada did unquestionably make a difference, it is surely in the area of peacekeeping. Lester Pearson's role during the Suez Crisis of 1956 and his subsequent Nobel Peace Prize fixed Canadian – and global – attention on the idea of interposing troops from many nations between warring armies. Before 1956, UN and other peacekeeping operations were modest efforts, of limited success, and carried out by relatively modest groups of observers; after 1956, peacekeeping was often a large-scale operation, regrettably also of limited success, and carried out by infantry, armoured reconnaissance, and service troops, as well as air force personnel, sometimes in combat roles. The difference was marked, and much of the change had occurred because of Pearson's initiative, diplomatic skill, and assessment of the need at Suez. Later crises in the Congo, Cyprus, the Middle East, Vietnam, the Iran–Iraq borderlands, Latin America, and the Sahara built on the experience of 1956, and in every case Canadian service personnel and peacekeeping expertise played an important part. More to the point, Canada tried hard to ready its armed forces for peacekeeping and to spread its hard-won knowledge to other nations. The designation of a stand-by infantry battalion and of army and air force peacekeeping specialists was one sign of Canada's initiative. A military peacekeeping conference for likeminded nations held in Ottawa in the mid-1960s was another. Repeated efforts to improve the UN's creaky organizational machinery and stabilize its financing of peacekeeping operations were still others. We have done our part and paid our dues in this area, and the world is likely a better place for our efforts.

Has Canada made a difference? There can be no doubt that, in peacekeeping, we have. But to ask only that question is to overlook other, more important ones. Why were Canadians so attracted to the idea of peacekeeping? What was the attitude of the bureaucracy and the armed forces to the concept? Has that attitude changed? and, if so, why and how? And, finally, has the idea of peacekeeping now come to play too large a role, taking precedence in the Canadian mind? Has the support for peacekeeping begun to affect policies in other areas? This brief essay examines these questions.

"Ours is not a divine mission to mediate," diplomatic historian John Holmes wrote in 1984. "Our hand is strengthened by acknowledged success," he went on shrewdly, "but it is weakened if planting the maple leaf becomes the priority."[1] Too often Canada's participation in peacekeeping operations (PKOs) has had some of this "planting the flag" idea about it, a sense that we must maintain our record as the country that has served on more PKOs than any other – whether or not those operations made sense, had much chance of success, or exposed our servicemen and servicewomen to unnecessary risks in an unstable area of the world.

Where did the idea of Canada as peacekeeper *par excellence* originate? Certainly it is not inherent in Canada's origins, which were as violent as those of any nation. The litany of our aboriginal wars, rebellions, bloody strikes, and participation in wars, large and small, is too well known to need reiteration here, and we should accept that violence has been, and might be in the future, as Canadian as apple pie. Probably the idea emerged out of the missionary strain in Canadian Protestantism and Roman Catholicism that saw Canadian men and women go abroad in substantial numbers in the nineteenth and twentieth centuries to bring the word of God to India, Africa, and China. Virtually every church in English and French Canada had a missionary family or religious order in its prayers and as the recipient of its contributions, and letters from the mission fields were staples of Sunday services and church bulletins. Missionaries nowadays do not command good press, the Christian preachers of those simple days before the Second World War more often being painted as despoilers of cultures than as saviours of souls and healers of the sick. But the "do-good" impulse that they represented was a powerful one, and it had its strong resonances in the Department of External Affairs.

So many of External's diplomats were sons of missionaries or of the manse. Some were born in China or in other mission fields; others followed clergyman fathers from parish to parish, imbibing the idealism of the social gospel along with their Bible studies. J.S. Woodsworth exhibited this kind of idealism in political life, and it was not insignificant that one of his sons joined External. Lester Pearson, of course, was another whose Methodist upbringing undoubtedly shaped him profoundly.

But so, too, did Pearson's experiences – and those of his entire generation – in the Great War. The shattering cataclysm of the slaughter on the Western Front cannot be underestimated, especially as it was followed within twenty years by another and even more horrific war. The Great War had sprung from obscure troubles in the Balkans; the 1939 war arose from Hitler's expansionist aims, focused in the summer of 1939 on the Polish Corridor. Small patches of land of relative insignificance, in other words, could lead to global catastrophe. Surely there had to be a better way, and the United Nations was summoned forth in 1945 as an attempt to create a collective security organization with enough teeth to keep aggressor states in check.

Canada had played its part in resisting the aggressors during the world wars, and it had learned something from those two experiences. The most important lesson was that isolation was no guarantee of safety in the modern world and that isolationism as a doctrine was equivalent to fool's gold. Another lesson was that it was sometimes very difficult to get along with your friends. Canadian prime ministers from Macdonald on had realized that about the British, who were certain always that they knew best and that the colonial's duty was to contribute to England's defences and coffers.[2] In the Second World War, however, Canada for the first time cast its lot with that of the United States, and while Ottawa's men got on better with the Americans on a personal basis than they ever had with the British, there were perils, nonetheless. The new superpower was as arrogant in its conviction of rectitude as Britain had ever been, as convinced that God was on Washington's side, and that Ottawa's role was to follow dutifully in its wake. Canadian policy in the postwar world would try to maintain a careful balance between cooperation with the United States and independent action. This was especially true at the United Nations.[3] And peacekeeping, while it often served US interests, to be sure, nonetheless had about it a powerful aura of independence and the implicit sense that it served higher interests than simply those of the United States, or even the West.

The coming of the Cold War paralysed most of the functions of the UN, but peacekeeping, initially by observer forces in areas of the world that were either of little importance to the Great Powers or else too dangerous to be allowed to fester, somehow survived.[4] We have now forgotten that Canada initially was not enthusiastic about the idea of participation in UN peacekeeping operations. At the 1945 San Francisco United Nations Conference on International Organization, at a time when the focus was on large UN military forces to crush aggression, Mackenzie King's Canada inevitably worried about being forced to join in wars without a say in the decisions that led up to them. The United Nations could not become a larger and more powerful replacement for Downing Street and Whitehall, against which Sir Wilfrid Laurier and Mackenzie King had fought for a half-century. The plans of the UN's Military Staff Committee went a-glimmering with the Cold War, but our continuing caution was evident when the UN set up observer missions around the borders of the new states of Israel and in the flashpoint state of Kashmir, strategically located between India and Pakistan. Requests for officer-observers in 1948 were treated very coldly by the Department of National Defence in Ottawa. The army was understrength and not very well trained; no one could be spared; and there might be difficulties with Jewish Canadians or with Commonwealth partners. "Ask someone else, please," was the message.

But, in fact, likely because Pearson had just become secretary of state for External Affairs and because Canada was on the Security Council at the time of the creation of the UN Military Observer Group in India-Pakistan, Canada did reluctantly agree to send four observers from the reserve army early in 1949. That number was increased to eight later that year, and, in 1950, the regular force took over the commitment. Canadian participation in the UN Truce Supervisory Organization (UNTSO) in the Middle East did not begin until 1954, when four officers were seconded for duty there. Before the end of the year, Major-General E.L.M. Burns, a corps commander during the Italian campaign and a senior bureaucrat as the deputy minister of Veterans' Affairs, became UNTSO's commander.[5] Burns's appointment was to have important consequences in shaping Canada's first major peacekeeping contribution.

The same year, Canada found itself unexpectedly asked to participate in a peacekeeping venture outside the ambit of the United Nations. The Geneva Conference, called to wind up the Korean War and provide a cover for France's extrication from the swamp it had made for itself in Indo-China, asked Canada, Poland, and India to create an International Control Commission (ICC) in each of the three successor states of French Indo-China. Canada was a Western democracy and the least objectionable of them to China; Poland was a Soviet satellite, but was deemed acceptable to the West; and India was anti-colonialist, neutral, and a Commonwealth member. Surprised by the request, Ottawa again was genuinely reluctant to participate, not least because the legal basis of the Geneva agreements was hazy and because the Americans were dissociating themselves from them before the ink had dried. Would participating involve us in continuing trouble with Washington? Another reason for Ottawa's reluctance was that the commitment was relatively large; officers, almost all of whom had to be bilingual, were needed, and the armed forces, as usual, were short of such individuals. But Canada found that it could not say no – "If ... by participating ... Canada can assist in establishing ... security and stability in Southeast Asia," the government's press release put it, "we will be serving our own country as well as the cause of peace" – and accepted the commitment. Approximately 150 military personnel and External Affairs diplomats proceeded to Laos, Cambodia, and Vietnam, a group that included three major-generals, eighty army officers, a sprinkling of naval and RCAF officers, and a handful of enlisted men. That was a serious drain on limited resources, one that was resented by National Defence Headquarters at a time when the country's commitments to NATO were large and taken very seriously indeed.

The Indo-China commitment was wearing and wearying. The Indians maintained an air of biased impartiality; the Poles were openly partisan; and the Canadians, after trying to be judicious, soon found that fairness was unfair to the anti-communist elements in all three of the new countries. For the next nineteen years, the ICCs limped along in the midst of war; their presence in Indo-China "radicalized" a generation of military officers and diplomats, in the sense that their experience strengthened their conviction that the communists, Vietnamese and Polish, were totally unscrupulous.[6] On the other hand, Canada's ICC commitment turned out to be a blessing in disguise when the United States became militarily involved in a major way in Vietnam. US allies around the world were pressured to contribute troops to the war, but Canada, sheltering behind its ICC role, was able to deflect Washington's demands. Still, Canadian servicemen and diplomats gathered information for the Americans in North Vietnam and delivered messages from Washington to the leadership in Hanoi. It was obviously sometimes hard to separate the peacekeeper's duty from that of the anti-communist ally.

Canada's military commitment to peacekeeping would soon increase substantially, in 1956, when the Suez Crisis erupted with the Anglo-French-Israeli collusion and attack on Egypt. Prime Ministers Louis St. Laurent and Anthony Eden exchanged heated telegrams as the Canadian fumed over the lies despatched from Downing Street.[7] The "supermen of Europe," St. Laurent said in Parliament, had had their day. So it seemed, and especially so when the militarily weak

British and French had to cut their attacks short, brought to heel by US pressure on the pound sterling and the franc, and by outrage at the UN.

Meanwhile, because General Burns was already on the scene at UNTSO, he was tapped to be the commander of the new United Nations Emergency Force (UNEF), created at New York by Pearson and Secretary General Dag Hammarskjöld. And because Burns was there, he was able to step into the problem caused by President Nasser's objection to having Canadian infantry as part of the UNEF. They marched under the same flag as the British invaders, they wore the same uniforms, and the name of the regiment selected for UNEF duty, the Queen's Own Rifles of Canada, was almost literally a red flag to the Egyptian leader, who feared that incidents between his people and the Canadians might cause serious difficulties. The simple truth is that Nasser was right. Burns found the way out of an increasingly embarrassing situation for the Liberals in Ottawa by suggesting that almost any country could provide infantry, and that what UNEF really needed were logistics personnel, which scarcely any of the potential eligible contributors, other than Canada, could provide.[8] In fact, that was precisely correct. Other than the Great Powers and a few of the Dominions (some of whom, like Australia, had taken too much of a pro-British position in the crisis to be even remotely acceptable to the Egyptians), very few nations had skilled military specialists or an air-transport capability. Canada did, because its military had always been prepared for overseas service and, in the 1950s, was relatively well equipped for its NATO role on the Central European front. The irony is clear: Canada's role as a Cold Warrior had given us the types of military forces that were most useful for peacekeeping. In the end, some one thousand Canadians in the various essential services (and including an armoured reconnaissance squadron to assuage Canada's military ardour) duly went to UNEF duty, where they remained until Nasser ordered them out of Egypt in the run-up to the 1967 Arab-Israeli War. That expulsion caused a traumatic shock to Canadian public opinion, dealing peacekeeping one of its very few blows here in the third of a century after 1956.

The impression persists that Nasser's objections to Canada in 1956 and 1967 came as a great surprise to Pearson and the country. Canadians (or English-speaking ones, at least), while still British in their outlook when the UNEF was established, were not used to having their bona fides questioned, and Pearson's initial idea in the heart of the crisis was that the British and French invaders might lay down the Union Jack and the *tricolore* for the blue flag of the United Nations. The invaders, in other words, could become the peacekeepers. It took almost no time for the Canadian to realize that this was simply not on in the atmosphere of the General Assembly at the end of October 1956, but it was nonetheless revealing that the anglocentric Pearson thought, however briefly, that it might be.[9] The Suez Crisis had made it clear, as it had not been before, that our British connections might not always be an asset in the world.[10]

What made all this even more difficult for the government was that the Progressive Conservative Opposition had had a field-day charging that Canada had sold out Britain and France, its mother countries and historic allies, and had slavishly followed a course laid down by Washington. Peacekeeping, in other words, was not going to be a bed of roses, and if Pearson soon won his well-deserved Nobel Peace Prize and the Liberal leadership, John Diefenbaker and the Conservatives won the general election of 1957. Most accounts agree that Canada's UNEF role cut little ice with the electors, more of them seeming to turn against the Liberals for their "betrayal" of Britain than voting for them for Pearson's UN role.[11] In 1967, Canada's expulsion from Egypt apparently had little political weight, probably because Pearson, then prime minister, seemed to know what he was about and because the war that engulfed the region (and that caused death and injury to other nations' peacekeeping troops still in the Sinai) followed so quickly on the departure of Canadian troops. The prevailing mood here was simply relief.

In 1958, however, once the Liberals had been driven from office, virtually everyone in Canada had basked in the glow of Pearson's Nobel Prize. This was widely interpreted as a sign of Canada's new maturity in the world, and in a curious way that is extraordinarily difficult to trace, peacekeeping became Canada's *métier*. So much so, in fact, that when John Diefenbaker and his Department of National Defence showed little desire to participate in the UN operation in the Congo in 1960 (ONUC), public opinion literally forced the government's hand. It was not that Diefenbaker was against peacekeeping or the UN. While he had been unhappy with Pearson's role at the UN during the Suez affair, he was not backward in claiming that he was the first to advance the very idea of peacekeeping forces;[12] moreover, his government was the first to put an infantry battalion on stand-by for UN service in 1958, and he sent peacekeepers to Lebanon in the same year. But in 1960, the army, as always hampered by the demands of its NATO commitments, by tight budgets, and by a genuine shortage of signals personnel, now had to provide a squadron of the Royal Canadian Corps of Signals and other units, including RCAF transport aircraft and crews, for the new UN force. Once again, there were few other acceptable contributors to ONUC who could possibly provide such technicians. Soon after their arrival in the chaos of a suddenly liberated colonial state, Canadians were attacked and beaten by mobs of soldiery, apparently in the mistaken belief that they were Belgian paratroopers. Later still, Canadian units came under fire on a number of occasions as the UN force became involved in open war with separatist Congolese elements. While they did their tasks well in these difficult situations, it might well be questioned whether Diefenbaker's initial response was not the correct one.

At least the Congo operation ended within a measurable time frame. The next major peacekeeping operation, that in Cyprus, did not. The Mediterranean island, divided between Greek- and Turkish-speaking Cypriots, was in turmoil in 1964. The Greek majority wanted *enosis*, political union with Greece; the Turks (and Turkey) adamantly resisted any such thing, and there was fighting in the streets and in the hills.

What made this crisis unusual was that Cyprus was a Commonwealth state (the British continued to maintain bases on the island), and that Greece and Turkey were both NATO allies. The other NATO partners, not least the United States, looked with dismay on the prospect of fighting between the Greeks and Turks, and contemplated the imminent collapse of NATO's southern flank with horror. It was inevitable that efforts to install a peacekeeping force should proceed with urgency, but neither NATO nor the Commonwealth was able to get President Makarios of Cyprus to agree to receive forces raised by them. It had to be a UN force, Makarios maintained.

Canada had been tapped to provide troops for Cyprus by both the Commonwealth and NATO, and it was asked once more by the UN. For a time, indeed, despite their government's concerns about the way the force was being organized, financed, and administered, the Canadian infantry battalion was the only force the UN had on the island, other than the British, who were exceedingly uncomfortable in their role. Then secretary of state for External Affairs, Paul Martin, began to work the telephones, creating a force out of nothing. The Americans were duly impressed at the way Canada had rescued the situation, President Lyndon Johnson asking Prime Minister Pearson what he could do for him in return. "Nothing at the moment, Mr. President," Pearson replied, noting carefully that he had some credit in the bank of American goodwill.[13]

Canada's concerns about the Cyprus force were more than justified. The commitment begun in 1964, supposedly for a term of six months, has continued to the present, and promises to go on for the foreseeable future. The UN force has survived Turkish invasion, rioting, ennui, and the appalling inefficiencies of the UN's administration,[14] and some Canadian servicemen of long service have put in six, seven, or eight six-month tours of duty on the island. Cyprus was and is an object lesson that peacekeeping is not sufficient and that peacemaking has to be part of every UN mandate. The irony of the situation is that the Canadian military, once unhappy about the Cyprus commitment that took a battalion away from training to fight the Soviets in Germany, now look at the role very differently. With the end of the Cold War, the liberation of Eastern Europe, the dissolution of the Soviet Union, and the coming drastic reduction in Canada's NATO commitment, Cyprus is the only continuing locale for small-unit training in a near-combat situation. The once-dreary duty has become the army's main active role, hailed for its training value; with Canada's other commitments to PKOs, it is now the best argument the Department of National Defence can muster for continuing to maintain any credible forces at all in a world of *détente*.

My account thus far has lightly traced several of the early peacekeeping operations. There is little point in continuing to chronicle the operations and the Canadian role in them. But it is important to remember that Canadians were not asked to participate in any of the PKOs for their inherent neutralism or because our soldiers and airmen were the equivalent of a gendarmerie. Far from it. We were wanted in Cyprus primarily because we were a NATO power; we were needed in the Suez because, as a NATO ally with a tradition of overseas service in two world wars, we had sophisticated technical capabilities; and we were a natural choice for the ICCs because we were a *Western* democracy. Neutralism or military weakness, in other words, had nothing at all to do with our acceptability as a peacekeeper.

And yet, somehow, Canadians came to believe that they did. Partly, this belief came about because peacekeeping was a role that made us noticeably different from the Americans. The Yanks fought wars, Canadians said, pointing at Vietnam, Grenada, and Panama, while Johnny Canuck kept the peace. In an era in which the military called the shots around the world and defence spending ate up superpower budgets, Canada's main claim to fame was its peacekeeping, its *antimilitary* military role. In an era of increasing continentalism, at a time when Canada's independence was seemingly under assault from foreign investors and the all-pervasive force of American culture, such simple myth-making was probably understandable, and perhaps even necessary. All the better, then, that peacekeeping was one of the few roles for our armed forces that could unite all Canadians. New Democrats who disliked NATO, NORAD, and Washington could burst with pride over Canada's UN efforts; Quebeckers, historically averse to overseas commitments, beamed at the exploits of the Vandoos in Cyprus or the gallant efforts of French-speaking officers in the Congo.

Liberals and Tories vied with each other in urging more and more peacekeeping on the government. After all, were we not maintaining order among the fractious nations and peoples of the world? What could be more Canadian than that?

And so we sent a force to Vietnam once more in 1973, our decision aided by strong pressure from Washington, though sensibly, this time, the Trudeau government slapped some tough conditions in place and followed what it called an "open mouth" policy of telling the truth about violations of the truce. More to the point, when the new ICC could not carry out its role with any chance of success, Canada pulled out its forces. There was little criticism of that, however, probably because all Canadians recognized the intractability of the Vietnamese problem. "Canada would act for peace," two historians suggested, "but not in a charade."[15] It remains only to say that the United States was most unhappy at Canada's withdrawal; likely Washington's unhappiness helped mute any criticism that might have fallen on Ottawa from peacekeeping's Canadian supporters.

And those supporters were legion. Let me, in my anecdotage, give one personal example of the support peacekeeping had come to muster. In August 1988 the United Nations authorized the establishment of UNIIMOG, the UN Iran-Iraq Military Observer Group, set up to oversee the cease-fire that brought the eight-year-long war between Iran and Iraq to its end. Canada was asked to participate, once again with a signals unit. I was called by the *Globe and Mail* and asked my opinion of the nation's participation in UNIIMOG, and I suggested that it was a mistake to put Canadian troops into a situation in which they would be at the mercy of what I called "two lunatic governments." That quote, which the next day ended up on page one as the lead story – and which literally made me fall out of bed as I read the newspaper with my coffee – produced some fifteen telephone calls from radio and TV stations and newspapers within three hours, almost all of them vehemently critical of me for daring to suggest that Canada ought not to participate. Both the Iranian and Iraqi governments *were* lunatic, of course, though happily we suffered no casualties in filling our role, probably because exhaustion had temporarily made peace seem to be in the combatants' best interests.

The point I made to the *Globe and Mail*, obviously, was that Canada had to pick its spots and ought not to feel obliged to participate automatically in every peacekeeping operation. We should insist on conditions, there should be a clear mandate, and the financing ought to be levied on all UN member states and not, as has all too often been the case, only on those who feel like contributing. Moreover, since the

Canadian government is responsible to the public for the lives of its men and women in uniform, we ought not to put them in a position where their safety is at risk – as it undoubtedly was in UNIIMOG.

None of this mattered, however, to those who had made participation the *sine qua non* of Canadian nationalism. Peacekeeping was so popular, I had to conclude, because it was useful, to be sure, but primarily because it was something we could do and the Americans could not.[16]

In other words, peacekeeping made us different from our friends and neighbours. And while that was a good thing, it also had about it something of the anti-Americanism that is part and parcel of our identity.

This became all the more obvious to me when Iraq invaded Kuwait in as clear an act of undoubted aggression as the world has witnessed since 1945. The United States mobilized a vast military coalition; Canada took part, though rather more hesitantly than I would have wished; and, in what I have no hesitation in characterizing as a just war under every canonical and legal definition, Iraq was driven from Kuwait at terrible cost to its military and people. This was not a peacekeeping operation, though it was authorized by the United Nations and was, indeed, a throwback to the kind of collective security envisaged by the drafters of the UN Charter in 1945 and practised only once before, in Korea.[17]

Canadian public opinion was sorely divided over the war, but in the end healthy majorities supported Canada's role in it. The Liberals and the New Democrats in Parliament went through conniptions trying to oppose the war while simultaneously supporting our servicemen and -women in the Gulf. The government, one eye fixed on public opinion, gave the troops different and progressively more aggressive mandates several times during the struggle. One of the predominant trends in the public discourse, acerbically characterized by Charlotte Gray in the Canadian Institute for International Peace and Security's magazine as a mixture of "idealism, legalism, internationalism and kneejerk anti-Americanism," was that by participating in the Americans' war Canada was destroying its hard-won credibility as a peacekeeper.[18] There was unquestionably an element of anti-Americanism about all this, not least in the Opposition's stances in Parliament, in much of the media coverage, and in the positions taken by peace groups. And peacekeeping, because it was Canada's particular skill, became one of the main vehicles for expressing it.

The critics who charged that the government had sacrificed Canada's peacekeeping role on the altar of Washington's war over Kuwait and oil were proven wrong almost at once. Within weeks of the end of the Gulf War, Canada was asked to participate – with seven hundred soldiers and the force commander – in a peacekeeping operation (MINURSO) being set up in the Sahara to supervise a referendum designed to end the long war between Polisario guerrillas and Morocco.[19] The country was also expected to participate in a UN force in Cambodia. Our role in Kuwait, in other words, proved to have no immediate effect at all on our ability to operate as peacekeepers. Nor should it have been expected to. We were, as I have suggested repeatedly herein, wanted as peacekeepers because of our military capabilities as much as or more than for our national attributes. Participation in a war in no way altered that, except perhaps to demonstrate that our pilots and ships' crews were as genuinely efficient in combat as Canadian infantry in patrolling the Green Line in Nicosia. It must also be said that, if Canada cuts its armed forces down to nothing, as many of the supporters of a virtually disarmed Canada urge, and if it takes away the military's versatility, our future capacity to act in peacekeeping roles will be severely constrained, if not ended.[20]

The point of all this is that for too many Canadians peacekeeping has become a substitute for policy and thought.[21] Some countries (but no longer our budget-strapped nation) try to deal with problems by throwing money at them; our people and, to some substantial extent, our governments try to deal with the world's problems by sending peacekeepers. This is not an ignoble impulse, but it is one that has to be checked with realism. Canada was right to participate with its allies in the war against Saddam Hussein, and those who objected to our role, whether out of misguided anti-Americanism or concern for our future as a peacekeeper, were wrong. We have also been right to participate in most of the peacekeeping operations in which we have served. But let us, at the very least, retain and enhance our right to consider which PKOs we shall participate in, just as we have the right to consider which wars we shall fight. Governments, like individuals, are supposed to be capable of rational decision making. And automatic responses – whether "My country right or wrong" or "Send in the Canadian peacekeepers" – are no substitutes for thought.

NOTES

1 J.W. Holmes, "Most Safely in the Middle," *International Journal* 39 (Spring 1984): 384.
2 See J.L. Granatstein, *How Britain's Weakness Forced Canada into the Arms of the United States* (Toronto, 1989), chap. 2.
3 See, e.g., J.L. Granatstein and Norman Hillmer, *For Better or For Worse: Canada and the United States to the 1990s* (Toronto, 1991), chaps. 5–6.

4 See J.L. Granatstein, "Canada and Peacekeeping: Image and Reality," *Canadian Forum* 54 (August 1974).
5 See J.L. Granatstein, "Canada: Peacekeeper," in Alastair Taylor et al., *Peacekeeping: International Challenge and Canadian Response* (Toronto, 1968), pp. 100ff., 116–17.
6 The best study of Canada's experience is Douglas Ross, *In the Interests of Peace: Canada and Vietnam 1954–73* (Toronto, 1984). See also Ramesh Thakur, *Peacekeeping in Vietnam: Canada, India, Poland and the International Commission* (Edmonton, 1984).
7 See the account in L.B. Pearson's memoirs, *Mike: The Memoirs of the Rt. Hon. Lester B. Pearson*, Vol. II: *1948–1957* (Toronto, 1973), chap. 10.
8 Burns's account is in his *Between Arab and Israeli* (Toronto, 1962), pp. 208ff.
9 Cited in J.L. Granatstein, "The Anglocentrism of Canadian Diplomacy," in Andrew Cooper, ed., *Canadian Culture: International Dimensions* (Waterloo, 1985), p. 37.
10 Pearson later suggested that his decision to give Canada a flag of its own had its genesis in the Suez Crisis and the troubles over the Canadian contingent. Interview, October 21, 1971.
11 John Meisel, *The Canadian General Election of 1957* (Toronto, 1962), pp. 254–5.
12 See John Diefenbaker, *One Canada: Memoirs of the Rt. Hon. John G. Diefenbaker*, Vol. I: *The Crusading Years 1895–1956* (Toronto, 1975), p. 280.
13 L.B. Pearson, *Mike: The Memoirs of the Rt. Hon. L.B. Pearson*, Vol. III: *1957–1968* (Toronto, 1975), pp. 134–5.
14 On UN administration of peacekeeping, see E.H. Bowman and J.E. Lanning, "The Logistics Problems of a UN Military Force," *International Organization* 17 (1963).
15 See J.L. Granatstein and Robert Bothwell, *Pirouette: Pierre Trudeau and Canadian Foreign Policy* (Toronto, 1990), pp. 55ff.
16 Of course, even this was not true, though not one Canadian in a thousand realized it. The United States participated in the UN Truce Supervisory Organization from its organization in 1948 and in the Multilateral Force of Observers (MFO) set up in the Sinai as one condition of the peace brokered by President Carter between Egypt and Israel. Eventually Canada would serve on the MFO as well. One might add that there is an irony in the way Japan is struggling with the problems posed for its constitution by the possibility of participating in peacekeeping. There, engaging in peacekeeping is largely seen by public and politicians as being obliged to accede to the Americans' wishes; here, the exact opposite is true.
17 See Kim Nossal, "Coalition-Building's Darker Side: Australia and Canada in the Gulf Conflict," a paper presented at the Australasian Political Studies Assn., 1991.

18 Charlotte Gray, "Home Grown Skirmishes: Canada and the War," *Peace & Security*, Autumn 1991, p. 8. See also Don Munton, "From Paardeberg to the Gulf: Canadians' Opinions About Canada's Wars," ibid., Spring 1991, p. 16.
19 See Richard Brûlé, "Western Sahara: A Settlement in Sight," *Peace & Security*, Autumn 1991, p. 15.
20 When the armed forces were unified in 1968, critics charged that Defence minister Paul Hellyer aimed to create a military that could only do peacekeeping, not fulfil a range of mandates. Ironically, a quarter-century later, defence cuts and the virtual end of Canada's NATO role may lead precisely to that result. The point, however, is that without many capabilities even peacekeeping will not be able to be performed well. On unification, see J.L. Granatstein, *Canada 1957–1967* (Toronto, 1986), chap. 9.
21 See Desmond Morton's comment: "Peacekeeping is the great [Canadian] morale builder. It is the only thing the public think the military are any good for. It is a distraction from the military role, but it is unfortunately the one that everybody out there will put as priority one, and one has to respect that political reality": "What Is to Be Done? Canada's Military Security in the 1990s," *Peace & Security*, Summer 1990, p. 5.

Chapter Fifteen

What's Wrong with Peacekeeping?

Canadians know and understand better than any nation on earth how useful peacekeeping can be. We have done it for more than 40 years in virtually every part of the world, 36 United Nations missions in all, I think, and Canada has also done non-UN missions in Indochina, the Sinai, Haiti, and Somalia. We do it as good international citizens and because we are good at it, and it overstates the case only a little to say that Canadians tend to believe that the Nobel Peace Prize for Peacekeepers in 1988 was really intended for them.

Lately, however, our numbers on peacekeeping operations and new UN missions in general have been declining, streamlined in size, or given shorter durations and conditional mandates by the Security Council. The reason is all too obvious: the UN's failures, as in Somalia and Rwanda, led to the hard tasks being taken over by more robustly armed coalitions, as in Former Yugoslavia, or transformed into peacebuilding exercises that are, if anything, even more difficult than traditional peacekeeping. In the circumstances, is it not time to ask what is wrong with peacekeeping?

I want to make nine points, not to knock UN peacekeeping off its pedestal, not to downgrade one of the central props in Canadian foreign policy, but to try to pose a more realistic agenda.

So what is wrong with peacekeeping?

1. The definitional confusion in peacekeeping, peace enforcement, and peacebuilding.

If peacekeeping operations were a child of the Cold War, peace enforcement operations are the product of the post–Cold War world that freed new nations and ethnic groups from superpower restraint. As a result, the line between peacekeeping and peace enforcement has blurred. This definitional problem is a major one, because without clarity we get a serious confusion of purpose. Today we also have peacebuilding – policies that are intended to help countries in conflict achieve stability by mobilizing civilian, military, governmental, and non-governmental expertise. There are preventive deployments such as in the Former Yugoslav province of Macedonia which imply a willingness to use greater force on the part of those nations contributing troops, even though that willingness may not be there, if and when the crunch comes. The UN also engages in human rights promotion, election monitoring, support for good governance, humanitarian assistance, refugee repatriation, disarmament and demobilization, and efforts at mediation to prevent conflicts.

Canada is a major booster of such efforts. For example, the Pearson Peacekeeping Centre in Nova Scotia now offers training for a Neighbourhood Facilitators Project in Bosnia. The Canadian government provides funding to the Guatemala Historical Clarification Committee (in effect, a truth commission), the preparatory commission for the establishment of the International Criminal Court, designed to try those accused of crimes against humanity, and for the work of the joint UN/Organization of African Unity Special Representative for the Great Lakes Region of Central Africa. The government has also put together CANADEM, a roster of Canadian experts on human rights and democracy, and it has expressed its willingness to give $500,000 to establish a Non-Governmental Organization (NGO) foundation in Bosnia to develop civil society on the basis of multi-ethnic cooperation. I fear that more than $500,000, and more than Neighbourhood Facilitators, will be necessary for that.

We also have peacekeepers protecting NGOs – and increasingly NGOs seem to be setting the agenda of soft diplomacy – and not just in Canada: France is said to have 40,000 NGOs. The Department of Foreign Affairs and International Trade has had formal consultations with NGOs for several years now, and I think we can see the impact of these meetings on Canadian policies such as those mentioned. Denis Stairs has called the NGO network the transnational public service left and posited that the NGOs are trying to be a countervailing force to the corporations on the right. He is precisely correct.

All this definitional confusion and mission proliferation is occurring at a time when most conflicts seem to be within countries, not between nations, and civil wars, of course, are notoriously difficult to police. Does the UN need consent to intervene with peacekeepers or peacebuilders? Certainly the line between consent and no consent has blurred, and it should not. How does the UN make war and peace simultaneously on the same territory, as it tried to do in Bosnia? (The only answer, for those who have read the superb articles by Mark Danner in the *New York Review of Books* in late 1997 and early 1998, is badly.) How does it choose which side to support in Rwanda or Bosnia? Or does it decide to opt for strict neutrality and support for the status quo while the killing goes on? The world saw precisely this kind of shameful behaviour occur when the Dutch peacekeeping contingent in Srebrinica stood aside while ethnic cleansing was carried out under its nose. Similarly how does the North Atlantic Treaty Organization play the role of peacekeeper in Former Yugoslavia? Active or passive?

What this confusion too often produces is increasing risk to the peacekeepers. Canadian soldiers have suffered more than one hundred killed on peacekeeping operations and more wounded. The rate of casualties seems to be increasing. Will the public here and in donor countries generally be willing to pay the price if the rules are fuzzy, if atrocities are not prevented, and if their soldiers are put at risk in a succession of political quagmires?

2. What is wrong with peacekeeping? The increasing American influence on and participation in UN and other operations is the second point.

This is not an anti-American comment: Canadians know that the Americans are our best friends, as Social Credit leader Robert Thompson said 35 years ago in one of the great malapropisms of Canadian public life, whether we like it or not. It is simply a statement of reality.

The US is increasingly world weary, fearful of casualties, and simultaneously playing a larger role, so much so that Joel Sokolsky has aptly called the whole process "The Americanization of peacekeeping." The recent peacekeeping operation in Haiti was understandable because of the immigration flow that would have flooded into the US if the problems there were not resolved, but even there, the US, once in, wanted nothing but to get out (and leave the peacekeeping to Canada). The operation in Somalia was humanitarian in intent, but the American military insisted on running the show, an essential condition for all US participation in order to appease Congress and satisfy the Pentagon. But the difficulty with US participation is that the media is always on-site and in strength. This means that any petty warlord can get headlines and shape an issue by killing one – or more – US soldier, as so clearly happened in Somalia. The Americans then feel obliged to over-react or to withdraw; in either case, chaos can be the only result. Even so, for all its concerns about peacekeeping, the United States had 644 troops involved in UN operations at the end of December 1997, while Canada had only 254, the first time in at least forty years that there have been more Americans than Canadians involved in peacekeeping.

There is, nonetheless, a widespread sense that the US only uses the UN when it suits its own purposes, as when it sought UN sanction for the war against Iraq in 1991–2. There is growing concern that Washington is willing to distort threats to regional peace (as defined in Article VII of the UN Charter) to include such crises as Haiti, which stretch the definition very far indeed. And all this goes on, moreover, at a time when the United States doesn't pay its bills to the UN for peacekeeping and, in the autumn of 1997, tried to "blackmail" the world organization into reducing the US contribution to the UN from 25 to 20 per cent (or so the Canadian Ambassador to the UN characterized it in October 1997 with uncommon bluntness). The US failed to reduce its assessment this time, and it has not yet anted up the billions it owes.

But if UN support can sometimes serve American interests, the feeling persists in the US, as *Washington Post* columnist Charles Krauthammer wrote, that "peacekeeping is for chumps." In other words, the US much prefers to be able to use force to "protect its own" and its own interests as defined by Congress and right-wing columnists like Krauthammer, not the UN. Why fool around with the polyglot processes of the United Nations when a simple surgical strike can fix a problem quickly?

Thus, the sense has developed in many national capitals that the US uses other nations when Congress blocks the Administration. For example, Prime Minister Jean Chrétien spoke only the truth when his table talk with the Belgian and Luxembourg leaders was picked up by a microphone at the Madrid NATO summit in 1997: "Clinton goes to Haiti with soldiers. The next year Congress doesn't allow him to go back. So he phones me. OK, I send my soldiers, and then afterward I ask for something in return." (What we might have received in return is hard to determine – certainly it was not a concession in the Pacific salmon negotiations!) Chrétien's partners clucked sympathetically, understanding exactly what he meant and how the game is played.

3. What is wrong with peacekeeping? The disorganization of the United Nations.

The UN in 1994 ran 18 peacekeeping operations with 80,000 soldiers from 82 countries on a budget of $US3.3 billion. At the end of 1997, it was running 17 operations with 23,000 soldiers on a $US1.3 billion budget. The staff of the UN's Peacekeeping Operations Department in 1989 was six civilians and three military officers. Today, matters are somewhat better with 400 civilian and military personnel on staff and a UN Under Secretary-General in charge of Peacekeeping Operations. There is, at last, a round-the-clock Situation Centre that should eliminate the answering machine that used to respond to commanders in the field calling New York for instruction after 5 p.m. EST.

There is also the generally sensible Canadian initiative to establish a UN Rapidly Deployable Mission Headquarters unit of 61 personnel for despatch on short notice to run a peacekeeping operation. But after two years of effort and diplomatic arm-twisting, only half the pittance of money needed to establish this unit has been pledged (perhaps because the countries providing officers pay their costs, not the UN). Moreover, with the plan calling for only eight officers to be recruited specially for this task, with 29 to be provided by the UN's Department of Peacekeeping Operations and serving part-time, and with 24 to be designated, but to remain in their home countries until needed for pre-deployment integration into the Headquarters, one might well question if such a unit can work. How any headquarters can function effectively with officers from different nations and military traditions beginning from a standing start is unclear. There are also complaints from Less Developed Countries, as the current euphemism for the Third World is styled, about this Headquarters, even though Canada, Denmark and the Netherlands have offered to finance LDC participation.

So there is some progress at the UN, but not enough. There still is difficulty getting orders at night; there still is insufficient planning and an alarming weakness in intelligence collection (as bedevilled UNPROFOR in Former Yugoslavia and the UN force in Rwanda), where the UN is literally dependent on US sources which are sometimes withheld, contradictory, or unreliable. The UN's Standing Operation Procedures are still confused and confusing. And the UN Secretariat and its Department of Peacekeeping Operations still cannot be counted upon to back up its commanders or troops in the field.

And now that the UN frequently combines civilian and military personnel on operations and sometimes has to share responsibility in the field with other organizations – e.g., in the Former Yugoslavia where UN and NATO both operate – the complexity of situations is multiplied dramatically. In such circumstances, what is clear is that the ad hoc, amateurish UN peacekeeping organization cannot any longer be tolerated. It is long past time for the UN to get its act together.

※

4. What is wrong with peacekeeping? The contracting out of logistical support for UN peacekeeping.

One aspect of UN peacekeeping's amateurish policy is that, incredibly, the UN continues to rely on civilian contractors to supply most peacekeeping operations. This is an inherently unreliable state of affairs, as with UNPROFOR in Yugoslavia in the first half of the 1990s where supplies could not reach deployed troops because civilian drivers and pilots refused to take the risk. This is one area where US military assistance is likely more valuable than anything else the United States can provide – and, to be sure, the Americans have frequently provided such aid in a pinch. Indeed, it might well be that standby logistical units are more important than infantry for a country such as Canada to consider providing.

※

5. What is wrong with peacekeeping? The new phenomenon of countries selling troops for dollars.

It should not be surprising that some nations have more soldiers than dollars. The Bangladeshis, for example, are frequent contributors to UN peacekeeping in substantial part because the $US1,000 a month paid by the UN for each peacekeeper is a very useful supplement to the country's holdings of scarce foreign exchange. But this can be true even for Canada. The Canadian Forces allow soldiers to keep the UN's monthly shilling, and because the military's pay is so low, many soldiers have eagerly sought UN service as a way of supplementing their income. In effect, Canadian soldiers were selling themselves for UN dollars. Poorly equipped armies can also get new equipment in the UN's service. Germany provided Armoured Personnel Carriers to Pakistani troops in Bosnia, for example.

It is also true that the explosion of countries providing troops for peacekeeping has meant that many contingents are not well-trained. As a result, some experienced nations have stepped in to assist. Sweden trained a Bulgarian unit prior to its despatch to Cambodia, and the Swedes incorporated Latvians into their IFOR unit in Bosnia, as did the Danes. Canada runs a Peacekeeping Centre to train officers and senior non-commissioned officers from many countries and is working directly with the combined Polish-Ukrainian peacekeeping battalion.

---

6. What's wrong with peacekeeping? The almost certain failure of efforts to improve the UN's rapid reaction capability.

The UN has pledges of 80,000 troops on stand-by, but these are non-binding pledges that aren't worth the paper they are printed on. What is needed is a rapid reaction force that can be deployed quickly into a trouble spot. Such a force, for example, might have prevented the bloodbath in Rwanda.

The Canadian government has been pressing an initiative in New York for what it calls "Vanguard" forces, and Ottawa is calling for concrete changes at the UN to ensure speedy, efficient response to crises. There has been some progress, as noted above. The Canadian Vanguard proposal envisages up to 5,000 civilian and military personnel from member states ready for rapid deployment under control of the Rapidly Deployable Mission Headquarters, also suggested by Canada, which would be responsible for planning and advance preparations. The force would have no right to initiate the use of its weaponry but could defend itself vigorously.

Canada is not alone with such suggestions. Sweden's International Command is supposed to be able to deploy a rapid reaction force of 800–1,400 within a month, and there is also a joint Nordic rapid reaction battalion of 1,000. Unfortunately, no one in the Swedish military – or none that I talked to in the autumn of 1997 – seems to believe there is a realistic prospect of this being made operationally effective.

But what do these plans matter when there is widespread resistance to the idea of a UN rapid reaction force, and not least from the US and China? Smaller countries are also suspicious that this proposal amounts to a supranational power grab by richer, bigger nations, and many others believe that such a rapid reaction force could entail a loss of national control over participation in UN operations. Others worry that the existence of such a force would encourage the Security Council to excessive interventionism or, just as bad, encourage the UN Secretariat to interventionist approaches. Then there are the costs – an estimated $US300 million per year for 5,000–10,000 troops.

Nonetheless in December 1996, Canada and six other states, led by Denmark, signed a letter of intent to create a Multilateral UN Stand-By

Forces High Readiness Brigade that would do Chapter VI peacekeeping (the least violent kind). SHIRBRIG, as it is called, has a cumbersome name and an even more unlikely future. Its initial operational and logistical capabilities were supposed to be up and running by January 1998, a deadline that was not met. Indeed, as of the end of November 1997, there had been seventeen drafts of a Memorandum of Understanding on the Operation, Funding and Status of SHIRBRIG – with no agreement in sight. SHIRBRIG is intended to be ready for instant deployment for a maximum six month period, subject to a decision on a case-by-case basis by participating countries. In effect, the rapid reaction force might see its contributors decide not to participate, something that effectively neuters the whole idea, even though the intent is for there to be sufficient forces on standby to replace a drop-out nation. Very simply, this will not work. As a result, the Canadian Foreign Minister, Lloyd Axworthy, sounded less than hopeful at the UN in September 1997: "These improvements ... are feasible, and they should be implemented without delay. Let us learn our lesson, not ignore it once again." But the lesson clearly hadn't been learned: the Non-Aligned member nations at the UN were quick off the mark with protests that SHIRBRIG is premised "on predetermined criteria [resulting] in pre-arranged exclusivistic linkages among a selected few." The Non-Aligned clearly see this initiative as contrary to the intent and spirit of the UN standby system because it has the potential to exclude a significant number of states from participation in UN peacekeeping. The message seems to be "better the shambles of peacekeeping in which all can join in than a more limited system that might actually work."

At the end of 1997, the Carnegie Commission on Preventing Deadly Conflict urged a different kind of rapid reaction force made up of Security Council members' troops, with it being a price of Security Council membership to contribute. The Commission proposed that the US have responsibility for logistics, communications, intelligence, and air transport, and only sometimes for troops on the ground. While that recommendation is eminently sensible, the Commission's proposal would be subject to veto by the Permanent Members of the Security Council. Moreover, such a proposal raises – and even more so – all the fears SHIRBRIG and the Vanguard idea do.

But what is abundantly clear is that continued adhockery in peacekeeping will not work. Something must be done, and the Vanguard/SHIRBRIG idea seems the best solution out there.

7. What is wrong with peacekeeping? Racism among troops doing peacekeeping.

Canadian studies prepared for the Somalia Commission of Inquiry found pervasive racism among Canadian, Belgian, Italian, French, and US troops in Somalia. There seems no reason to doubt that this was so – or that black or Asian troops serving among white populations would be any different. The result is that the local image of peacekeepers among citizens being "helped" is sometimes very bad indeed, with racism added to the usual effects of having young men and women serving away from home, namely, drunkenness and prostitution. This cannot be tolerated any longer, not least in the Canadian Forces, which have been hit with a succession of hammer blows involving racism, sexism, rape, and corruption. The question is how much longer donor countries will accept such behaviour and whether the nations being assisted by peacekeepers will agree to the stationing of UN troops on their territory. The answer is education, training, and discipline. What must be done to train/educate troops better?

8. What's wrong with peacekeeping? The cultivation of the "feel good" effect of peacekeeping.

For 50 years, ever since 1948, the UN has had military observers in Kashmir in UNMOGIP, and India and Pakistan are as close to war today as they have been in the last two decades. For 30 years, Canadians served in Cyprus, patrolling the Green Line separating Greek- and Turkish-Cypriots, and not until the Canadian government pulled its troops out of UNFICYP did the parties really begin to talk, though to no avail.

Simply put, endless missions extended well beyond their original intended lifespan and in defiance of pledges by politicians are very damaging to the concept of peacekeeping. Everyone can feel good when the peacekeepers go in; no one feels good if they must stay in place for a generation with no prospect of a resolution of the crisis that brought them into being in the first place. In other words, peacekeeping must not and cannot be an end in itself. Either it is accompanied by diplomatic efforts at a resolution, or it should not be tried; and if diplomacy fails, then the peacekeepers should be withdrawn.

9. Finally, what is wrong with peacekeeping? The understandable donor fatigue that has gripped or begun to afflict those countries such as Canada that have provided troops to the UN for more than forty years.

These points altogether add up to the sense that peacekeeping has not worked the way it ought to have and, moreover, that since the end of the Cold War, peacekeeping has become much more difficult, confusing, and stressful. Nations and their Finance Ministers want their peace dividends, a sentiment made all the more powerful as their publics feel the apathy born of bad results in UN service.

How can we fix these problems or at least ameliorate their worst effects?

First, is it not time to consider returning to the old conditions that used to govern UN peacekeeping? Consent by the parties involved was a requirement, as was the possibility of a resolution of the crisis. The peacekeeping force needed a clear mandate and a clear line of command and control, no superpowers could be involved on the ground, and the UN force had to be impartial and devoted to upholding international law. Those were sensible rules in the Cold War years, and I think we do need to retain some of them still, especially consent and impartiality. On the other hand, it makes sense in a post–Cold War world to involve Permanent Members of the Security Council in peacekeeping, primarily because they have the resources and reach to be of substantial use.

Secondly, the world has to begin to consider the appropriate role for NGOs. Should NGOs have a role in determining where and how peacekeepers will go and function, as some in Canada have suggested? I think not. The impartiality of NGOs is sometimes suspect, not least because some nations try to use them for intelligence-gathering or for other purposes. The risk of reprisals if NGO members speak out is sometimes great, and NGOs may require military protection. Moreover, and most important, who elected NGOs to make policy?

Third, it seems almost certain that peace enforcement – the toughest kind of peacekeeping permitted under Article VII of the UN Charter – works best outside the UN, most likely with a coalition of nations, operating under a Security Council greenlight. UN peacekeeping should be limited to the low end of the violence scale, to freeze a situation and give the parties a breathing space. In other words, it is time to define clearly what the UN will and will not do.

Fourth, it might also be time to consider subcontracting peacekeeping to regional organizations like the Organization for African Unity and the Organization of American States, which might help make peacekeeping less racist, more sensitive, and even cheaper. The difficulties in using the OAU, for example, are obvious – weak militaries, tribal conflicts, and little money. The US, to its credit, is trying to create an African Crisis Response Force of 10,000 troops with American and other funding, training, and logistics. But only a few countries have signed on, and there is massive criticism of the concept from, among others, President Mandela. The Africans and the UN desperately need such a force.

Then, fifth, countries must decide if they accept peacebuilding, not peacekeeping or peace enforcement, as the wave of the future. In Ottawa, officials are hard at work trying to uncouple peacekeeping from peacebuilding. Peacekeeping is a blunt instrument, they say, while peacebuilding is flexible and doesn't need peacekeeping first to succeed. Police officers, not soldiers; election monitors, not armies, in other words. Should we consider a UN Standing Police Force of cops – an idea that is the trendy one of the moment? How can we mobilize civilian expertise for crises? How then do we protect civilian peacebuilders? Does this mean bringing NGOs directly into the peacebuilding policy-making process? Mr. Axworthy's department has said it will do so. Once again, it is time to ask who elected NGOs to make policy? And who anywhere believes that a Canadian Corps of Airborne Sociologists can resolve anyone's problems?

Sixth, the UN must realize that it cannot be too ambitious and cannot expect to resolve every problem. Hard choices about where to intervene and where not to will be necessary. There are signs that Secretary-General Kofi Annan realizes this. But with so many of the critical factors that affect the ability of peacekeepers to function effectively being within the UN administration or directly under UN control, the one task that cannot be shirked is bringing the UN Secretariat under control. Perhaps the appointment of a Deputy Secretary-General, the former Canadian Deputy Minister of National Defence, will help this process. It must.

Seventh, however much better the UN administration becomes, the UN must recognize that there are serious perils in using force, especially in countries such as Somalia, where there was no larger political framework in place. The UN has to pick and choose its spots and determine which weapons in its arsenal to employ. Certainly, it is easier to minimize the use of force if the United States is not involved.

Finally, Canada and its friends must continue their efforts to develop rapid reaction forces. We must persuade the Non-Aligned and some Great Powers that this is essential, indeed much more important than banning landmines or trying to prohibit the sale of small arms. If Lloyd Axworthy can do this, he might prevent the next Rwanda or forestall the next Bosnia. If he can press the UN to do what it must, then he will deserve the Nobel Peace Prize that he failed to receive for his efforts to eliminate anti-personnel landmines. Nothing Canada can do at the United Nations is more important than to make rapid reaction forces a reality.

Chapter Sixteen

War and Peacekeeping in the Canadian Psyche

The subject of war is not one that Canadians enjoy talking about. We are peacekeepers, we say, and we don't fight wars. This is, of course, completely untrue, for in this century alone Canadians as a nation have fought in the South African War, the First and Second World Wars, the Korean War, the Gulf War, and, most recently, the Kosovo War. Individual Canadians have fought in dozens of conflicts, most notably, perhaps, the Spanish Civil War in the late 1930s. Despite this, we tell ourselves and the world of our presumed virtue: we are the inventors of peacekeeping, the world's first peacekeepers, the best peacekeepers. If only ...

We might wish that war, all wars, should belong in a museum, but as we should know all too well, war unfortunately is still with us. It was with us yesterday and, regrettably, war will be with us tomorrow – and tomorrow and tomorrow. Many native-born Canadians have been directly affected by war, and many of the immigrants who have flooded into the country in the last 60 years or so from Europe, Latin America, and the Far East came here to escape war and civil war. We and they know all too well of the horror and terror that war can bring. But not all wars are avoidable.

These days it is highly unfashionable to say so, but sometimes war is necessary, and sometimes wars must be fought. Canadians tend to blush, stammer, and scrape their foot in the dirt when they talk about subjects like democracy and freedom, but those ideals have been and remain very important to us. This nation has never gone to war for aggressive reasons – we are one of the very few countries anywhere that can say that – but only to defend our own soil and to fight for and with our friends and for concepts like democracy, freedom, and justice. It is our historic willingness to take up arms for just causes, far more than our interest in and support for peacekeeping, important as that is, that has helped to make

Canada the country it is: a nation to which millions of immigrants seek to belong, the nation that is the most favoured place on earth. And to a large extent, it has been war that shaped our society.

For example, Canada went into the Second World War to fight against Hitler, Mussolini, and Tojo, men whose nations aimed to conquer the world. While we did not go to war to save the Jews of Europe, the impact of the Second World War did much to end Canadian anti-Semitism, in particular, and to weaken severely Canadian racism generally. We went to war in Korea in June 1950 to honour our commitments to the United Nations and to support the concept of collective security, the idea that many states should come together to resist aggression against any one nation. We stationed troops in Europe with the North Atlantic Treaty Organization for more than forty years and spent billions of dollars on armaments because we believed that the collective defence and the security of the West in the face of an aggressive Soviet Union was a vital interest to us. And we went into the Gulf War in 1991–2 not for oil, as critics charged at the time and since, but essentially for the same reason – because Canadians believed that small nations like Kuwait have the right to live without fear of invasion from their larger neighbours.

In the Spring of 1999, Canada, as a member of NATO, went to war in Kosovo for similar worthy reasons. Racism, religious hatred, ethnic cleansing, and genocide – the world has seen far too much of these scourges – and the North Atlantic Treaty Organization was right to intervene there. President Vaclav Havel of the Czech Republic, his country one of the newest NATO members, is a man whose commitment to human rights is beyond cavil. Havel defined NATO's aims in Kosovo better than anyone else when he visited Ottawa at the end of April 1999: the alliance, he said, was fighting "in the name of human interest, for the fate of other human beings. It is fighting because decent people cannot sit back and watch systematic, state-directed massacres of other people. Decent people simply cannot tolerate this, and cannot fail to come to the rescue if rescue action is within their power ... It has now been clearly stated," Havel went on, "that it is not permissible to slaughter people, to evict them from their homes, to maltreat them and to deprive them of their property." Those idealistic reasons were at the root of the Czech Republic's, Canada's, and NATO's motives in this war, and the gross violation of those humanistic principles was the reason that an international tribunal has properly and firmly indicted Yugoslav President Slobodan Milosevic and his cronies for their appalling war crimes.

Canada's support for its ideals has not come cheaply. In the Great War, there were 60,000 dead from a nation of just eight million people that somehow put 620,000 men in uniform. The Canadian Corps of four divisions that fought in France and Flanders was an army of amateurs that learned its grisly trade in battle and became a *corps d'élite*, the shock troops of the Allied armies. At Vimy, Paaschendaele, and in the Hundred Days that brought the war to a close, the Canadian Expeditionary Force was an astonishingly effective fighting machine. The war at home saw women working in munitions factories in large numbers, a huge flight from rural Canada to well-paying city jobs, and heightened tensions between French- and English-speaking Canadians over subjects such as conscription for overseas service. The war at the front and at home was hardly a cakewalk, but Canadians of the day believed that they had to participate and that their national interests were at stake.

It was much the same in the Second World War when more than 42,000 Canadians were killed in action in Hong Kong, at Dieppe, on the North Atlantic, in Sicily and Italy, and in and over Northwest Europe. The nation's huge war effort saw more than a million men and women serving in the forces and all of civil society mobilized in a gigantic "total war" that produced a doubling of the Gross Domestic Product in just six years and that saw taxation, rationing, and the control of industrial and agricultural production imposed in ways that would have seemed inconceivable in the Great War. From a standing start in 1939 – the regular forces in all numbered less than ten thousand men – Canada created the First Canadian Army of two corps and five divisions, an air force that was the fourth largest in the world, and the Royal Canadian Navy that escorted half of all convoys across the North Atlantic. This was a simply astonishing war effort from eleven million people almost wholly removed from danger of attack.

After 1945, Canadians seemed determined not to see history repeat itself. The lesson of World War II was that to stop aggression the international community needed a United Nations with teeth, and there were vain efforts, stopped by the budding Cold War, to create a United Nations army. These went nowhere. Even so, when North Korea invaded South Korea on June 25, 1950, the UN put together a limited "police action" to oppose undoubted aggression. Canada committed an infantry brigade group to the war, and more than 500 servicemen did not return home. Few Canadians noticed or, shamefully, seemed to care. Korea was a faraway country, and the booming fifties removed the last traces of the Great Depression from a newly rich Canada. Korea was an American war, a South Korean war, and Canada was simply a choreboy carrying out the demands of its American masters. That, at least, was often how the Korean War was portrayed in an era when anti-Americanism was beginning to re-gather force in a newly nationalistic Canada.

Perhaps that was why peacekeeping became so popular in Canada. When Secretary of State for External Affairs Lester Pearson cobbled together the United Nations Emergency Force in November 1956, few in Canada cheered. Britain and France had colluded with Israel and invaded Egypt, and Pearson's efforts at the UN in New York won scant praise from those who denounced him for selling out Canada's two mother countries, who were resisting a new Hitler in Egypt's Gamal Nasser. But when Pearson was awarded the Nobel Peace Prize the next year, the mood changed at once. Peacekeeping was now Canada's very own contribution to the world. And as peacekeeping developed during the Cold War and for obvious reasons the Great Powers were excluded from UN missions, the tasks fell heaviest on middle powers such as Canada.

Canadians accepted this task readily. There were times, as when the newly independent Congo exploded in 1960, that the Canadian government preferred to stay aloof. Public opinion would have none of this, however, and Ottawa caved in. For years, the national boast was that Canada had participated in every UN force as well as others outside the United Nations.

Why the eagerness? Because Pearson had won the Nobel Peace Prize and soon after the Liberal leadership, other politicians thought that peacekeeping was a route to kudos and their own advancement. But the government also enjoyed the accolades received at the UN in New York, the clout Canada won with the international bureaucracy in return for its soldiers. With the public, peacekeeping was do-goodism writ large, Canada helping keep the world's peace. It was also a military role that differentiated us from the Americans. Canadians never knew that American heavy aircraft frequently had to be called in to move our troops and equipment; nor did they understand that Canadians often performed roles in peacekeeping that directly served Western and US interests. Communal conflict in Cyprus in the 1960s, for example, almost brought Greece and Turkey, both NATO members, to war, and the leading Canadian role in creating a United Nations force there directly served the West's interests.

Of course, even maintaining the peace is costly. Canada has had more than a hundred dead in its manifold peacekeeping and peacemaking missions for the United Nations. Officers and men have died in accidents and under fire, shot down in aircraft or blown up by mines.

Then there is the financial cost of peacekeeping and war. The wars of this century, the preparations to avert it, and the costs of peacekeeping have consumed billions of Canadian taxpayers' dollars. The budget of the Department of National Defence absorbed as much as 7 per cent of the nation's Gross National Product in the immediate post-1950 period. Even in 1999, even after massive cuts stretching over decades, the Canadian Forces still spend in the range of $10 billion a year.

Is it worth it today? Was it ever worth it for Canada to join in the wars and peacekeeping operations of this century? That is a terrible question to pose to a now-aged grandfather who lost his father at Vimy Ridge in 1917, to a widow whose husband was shot down in the air over the Ruhr in 1944, to a bereft mother whose son died on a hilltop in Korea in 1952 or on a peacekeeping mission in Cyprus or Bosnia. The personal grief that is an inevitable by-product of state war-making is unmeasurable other than in terms of tragedy and loss, and Canadians have had to bear their full measure of pain.

Was it worth it nonetheless to play a part in the wars and peacekeeping operations of this century? Yes, if Canada's continuing to live in freedom matters – and it does. Yes, if we accept some responsibility for the state of the world and its people – and we must. Yes, if we belong to alliances in our own interest and then cooperate with our partners in pursuit of shared goals – and we do. Was it worth it? Is it worth it? Yes, without doubt.

That having been said, we know that historically it has been difficult for all Canadians to support all of Canada's wars. In the Great War, for example, German-Canadians suffered abuse and internment and Ukrainian-Canadians were locked up as enemy aliens because parts of Ukraine then lay within the Austro-Hungarian Empire. Many Canadians of German or Ukrainian origin nonetheless enlisted to prove their loyalty to their new homeland, and we can appreciate the emotional turmoil this must have caused them and their families. In the Second World War, the Canadian government again used the sweeping powers of the War Measures Act to round up and intern suspected Nazi sympathizers and Italian *fascisti*, while Japanese Canadians were moved inland from their West Coast homes after Japan entered the war on December 7, 1941. Canadians of German, Italian, and Japanese ethnicity nonetheless fought for Canada. During the Gulf War a half century later, some Iraqi-Canadians complained that the RCMP was watching them for no reason other than their ethnic or national origin. It is almost certain that during the Kosovo War some Serbian-Canadians felt much the same.

In a multicultural nation, this is unfortunately inevitable. Certainly, it would be best if all who immigrated to this nation left their Old World hatreds behind. Canadians do not want to have Irish Catholic immigrants sending money to purchase guns for the IRA any more than they want Jews and Muslims slanging each other in the media.

Who would not have rejoiced during the Kosovo War if Canadians of Serbian origin had left their Balkan politics at the water's edge when they came to Canada? Certainly it would have been best if they had not demonstrated against Canada's role in the NATO action. But it was the Canadian Serbs' democratic right to protest, just as it was the RCMP's duty to ensure that no individual hothead decided to carry peaceful protest to another level. If Canada had been fully at war, however, as opposed to merely having provided a score of aircraft to the war and a small commitment of land forces for the Kosovo Force, then the public, police, and governmental response to protests would certainly have been less tolerant.

Clearly, future wars are always going to be a difficult problem for us in our multicultural Canada. We can understand how the bombings and casualties in Belgrade roused passions in those who came to this country from that unhappy part of the world, and Milosevic's capitulation does not make this any easier to swallow for Serbian-Canadians. We might wish that the plight of the Kosovar refugees and the tales of horror they recounted had generated some public expression of compassion from those who protested against NATO's efforts to stop ethnic cleansing. We might have hoped that Milosevic had been branded the war criminal he is by Canadian Serbs and those others who protested so loudly against the war. But perhaps that is too much to expect in a nation that does not work as hard as it should, as hard as it must in the future, to turn immigrants into Canadians.

What we need to understand is that war and peacekeeping are here to stay. Canada participates in such missions because it serves the country's national interests to do so. In the early years of this century such interests were seen as indistinguishable from those of Britain. Today, our national interests increasingly have merged with those of the United States and of NATO, and we will clearly continue to work and fight with our friends. With a polyglot population, this will continue to cause problems at home, but we must learn to deal with them because, painful as it is to have to say this, war is not about to disappear from the international scene.

Chapter Seventeen

Changing Alliances: Canada and the Soviet Union, 1939–1945

Winston Smith, the protagonist of George Orwell's *1984*, was confused:

> At this moment, for example ... Oceania was at war with Eurasia and in alliance with Eastasia. In no public or private utterance was it ever admitted that the three powers had at any time been grouped along different lines. Actually, as Winston well knew, it was only four years since Oceania had been at war with Eastasia and in alliance with Eurasia ... Officially the change of partners had never happened. Oceania was at war with Eurasia: therefore Oceania had always been at war with Eurasia. The enemy of the moment represented absolute evil, and it followed that any past or future agreement with him was impossible.[1]

The past, in other words, could be erased and made to serve the needs of the present, and the state, with its control over the organs of propaganda (and through such Orwellian devices as the Two Minute Hate), could bring the proles to follow any course it chose.

To claim that the scenario of *1984* represents anything like the twisting course of Canada's relations with and attitudes to the Soviet Union from 1939 to 1945 would be a substantial overstatement. And yet, there are similarities. Under Stalin, the USSR had concluded a pact of convenience with Hitler in August 1939 that freed the Nazis to assault Poland and begin the Second World War. The Russians had gobbled up their share of the Polish spoils, they had invaded Finland, they were soon to swallow the Baltic Republics, and they provided the Nazis with the foods and raw materials they needed. With Britain in a desperate struggle for survival, with Canada as its ranking ally after the collapse of France, the Canadian people inevitably saw the USSR (and domestic Communists)[2] as the literal Antichrist. But the Nazi invasion of Russia in June 1941 turned perceptions around almost at once, and yesterday's devil became today's fighter for freedom. For four years, the Soviets bore the lion's share of the struggle against Hitler, and they received the wild adulation and genuine admiration to which they were entitled from the government and most of the people of Canada. That phase began to end with victory in Europe and especially with the defection of Igor Gouzenko and the revelation that the Soviet Union was operating successful spy rings out of Ottawa. The transition from ally back to Antichrist was underway, and the Cold War had begun. This paper will briefly trace the events of the war years and attempt to show where and how the changes of direction took place.

"[T]he choice by the Soviet of this hour to announce the pact," Vincent Massey, the Canadian high commissioner in London, said to Ottawa on 22 August 1939, "is very disquieting and makes it difficult to accept their good faith."[3] That was Massey's response to the Nazi-Soviet non-aggression pact, and it was an entirely typical one. Less so was that of the under-secretary of state for External Affairs, O.D. Skelton, who, with his dark view of British motives, put the blame on Prime Minister Neville Chamberlain: "It is crushing condemnation of the handling of British foreign policy." London had made commitments to Poland that could not be carried out without the aid of Russia, and Britain's tactics had made it "practically impossible to secure Russian aid on any reasonable terms."[4] The prime minister did not completely share the views of his closest adviser. Mackenzie King wrote in his diary that he felt an "immense" sense of relief that Britain and France had been relieved of the burden of being saddled with a potential ally, the Soviet Union, that would only have betrayed them. "I have never trusted the Russians," he wrote.[5] They were a society in which "reliance has been placed upon force ... All power in hands of one or two men controlling the State and identified with same ... destruction of religion, defiance of agreement and contract."[6]

That attitude was reinforced when Stalin joined in the attack on Poland on 17 September, the Red Army streaming westward toward the advancing Wehrmacht. King noted that "we are fighting the forces of evil,"[7] and Stalin's "ghastly bit of ruthless aggression" two months later when the Red Army crossed the Finnish border again confirmed his stark view of the Soviet Union.[8] Individual Canadians donated money to help the Finns,[9] but however much Soviet policy appalled the prime minister, his government was not prepared to do anything significant to assist Finland, the Cabinet confining itself to a gift of $100,000 made on 18 January 1940 "for the purchase and transport of Canadian foodstuffs for the relief of the people of Finland."[10]

The prime minister, however, did intervene to block the sale of up to 1.25 million bushels of wheat to the Soviet Union in January 1940, the

Cabinet War Committee accomplishing this by the simple expedient of requiring permits for export shipments to European neutrals contiguous to belligerents. Mackenzie King initially had thought of slapping a complete embargo on exports to the Soviet Union, a step that, he believed, might give the United States a reason to proceed with a moral embargo against the aggressor nations. But the prime minister was dissuaded from this course by concerns within the Department of External Affairs that a Canadian embargo on Moscow would make it difficult to refuse to impose one on Tokyo – and that, Norman Robertson told the prime minister, might lead to an alliance between the Soviet Union and Japan.[11]

Ten months later, after the end of the Russo-Finnish war, King still took a principled position against the Soviets' efforts to buy wheat from Canada:

> Russia is ready to pay cash. I took strong exception to anything of the kind on the score that present strategy was blockade and ending the war by ending supplies to gangster nations ... I believe people would be incensed if we sold her wheat which might help to release their wheat for Germany ...[12]

But when London sounded out Ottawa on the possibility of a barter agreement with the Russians, the Department of External Affairs proposed to reply that if trade and political relations between the USSR, Britain, and "other parts of the Empire" were put on a satisfactory footing, "we would be prepared to permit the sale ... for United States dollars or gold, of certain products for which export permits are currently being refused," most notably wheat. The prime minister agreed.[13] If Britain could bring itself to deal with Stalin, then Canada would follow suit. Still, no one expected much, in trade or in any other way. At the end of May 1941, Norman Robertson, the acting under secretary in the Department of External Affairs, sent the prime minister a memorandum bemoaning that "British and Allied diplomacy had never shown much sympathy or imagination in the handling of Russian questions, but," he added, "I do not think there is very much to be salvaged now."[14]

The Nazi attack on the Soviet Union on 22 June 1941 changed almost everything – but not the way Britain regularly acted toward its Dominions overseas. Prime Minister Churchill broadcast his government's decision to "give whatever help we can to Russia and to the Russian people" without the courtesy of seeking Canadian concurrence, a slight that was eased only slightly by a telegram of regret to Ottawa.[15] But in fact Mackenzie King had already issued a statement (to "give a lead to the editorial writers who were floundering," as Norman Robertson put it)[16] that affirmed that "Everyone who engages our enemy advances our cause," a first step in turning public opinion around to the support of the Soviet Union. But as his tortured remarks and explanations suggested, it was obviously difficult for King – and many Canadians – to accept Moscow instantly as an ally:

> Hitler's invasion of Russia is also an attempt to deceive and divide the people of the United States and the peoples of the British Commonwealth by trying to make it again appear that he is the enemy of Bolshevism. Whatever one's opinion may be about the philosophy of the Russian revolution, however strongly some of Russia's international activities may be condemned, the plain fact is today that, as Russia fights Germany, it is not Russia which is a threat to freedom and peace. That threat is Nazi Germany. Indeed one of the effects of Germany's attack on Russia should be to put an end to Communistic activities on the part of Russian sympathizers in other lands.[17]

To Norman Robertson, the new alliance posed some problems for the government. As he told the American minister, Pierrepont Moffat, on 23 June, he was greatly interested in the reactions of Catholics, "who are desperately opposed to the Communists," of Ukrainians, "some of whom might see in the new situation an opportunity for furthering their ambitions for an autonomous Ukraine," and of Finns, "among whom there were more actual Communists than in any other racial group in Canada."[18] But Robertson apparently had no fear of the Canadian elite who soon swung wholeheartedly behind the government's position and, indeed, into criticism of it for not doing enough to help Russia.[19] Moffat wryly observed that, "The Bourbon stronghold of the Rideau Club has gone Bolshevik with a vengeance." The habitués of Ottawa's grandest gathering place denounced any who might suggest that there was little to choose between Nazism and communism. "They said that at least Communism started from a basis of generosity which Nazism didn't, and in any event they claimed that world revolution was on a higher plane than that of world conquest."[20]

But there was little expectation in government circles (perhaps because the purges of the officer corps during the late 1930s and the clumsy handling of the Red Army in the Finnish War had misled observers about its efficiency) that Russia would be able to resist the Wehrmacht's panzers for very long. Robertson and Moffat agreed that "Russia could not be expected to put up much of a military fight." The Canadian, however, suggested that Germany might find that "it would require a greater diversion of strength to organize Russian economy on a paying basis than they calculated." He also "wondered" if Russia might not abandon the war in a few days and accept German terms,[21] thoughts that were widespread in Ottawa and elsewhere.

But the Russians, although suffering huge losses of men and equipment, continued the struggle as they retreated from the frontiers and toward Moscow. As a result, pressure on the King government to do more to help the Soviet Union and to establish closer relations with it increased markedly. Robertson in September told Moffat that "he felt the pressure acutely and that it came in British Canada from a curious alliance between extreme right and extreme left." The prime minister had not yet made up his mind what to do, but he, Robertson, "was still inclined to pussyfoot." He felt Canada should do more for Russia but could do it most effectively in a concealed manner, such as by letting the Joint Metals Board allocate a thousand tons at a time of aluminum for shipment to the USSR. This would "get the aluminum to Russia," Moffat noted, "without running the risk of so stirring the anti-Communist aluminum workers at Arvida that total production might be reduced. It was a delicate problem at best ... damned if you do and damned if you don't."[22]

Supplies were one thing; diplomatic representation another. As early as July, the Soviet ambassador to the United States told a Canadian journalist that there should be direct Soviet representation in Canada. In October, the Soviet ambassador in London asked Vincent Massey if Canada would be willing to receive one or two consular officials, a proposal that Mackenzie King accepted at once,[23] although the agreement between the two countries was not signed until 5 February 1942.[24] By that time, however, the government in Ottawa had already decided that consular representation was insufficient and that legations should be exchanged, and the next month Moscow was approached. Acceptance followed before the end of March 1942, and the agreement on the establishment of direct diplomatic relations was signed on June 12.[25] And lest the Canadian government fear that an exchange of diplomats would lead to "agents of the Comintern ... conducting Communist propaganda in countries to which they were accredited," Novikov, the Counsellor at the Soviet Embassy in London, assured George Ignatieff, a junior diplomat on the staff of the High Commission in London, that "nothing was further from the truth ..."[26]

It is fair to say that the Canadian people as a whole were not convinced of this or of the *bona fides* of the Soviet Union or domestic Communists. Opinion polling at the time found serious divisions. In August 1942, although 57 per cent of a national sample expected the Russians, British, and Americans to make it possible for Europeans to choose their own forms of government, a rather large block of 27 per cent expected the Soviets to try to spread communism throughout Europe. At the same time, an overwhelming number of Canadians – 62 per cent – wanted the Communist party to remain banned in Canada while only 23 per cent thought the party should be permitted to run candidates.[27] Why the divisions? The Wartime Information Board had no doubts as to the reasons. In a major survey of public attitudes in April 1943, the WIB admitted that the "general impressions of the Soviet system built up over the years" constituted a serious obstacle to closer relations and to Canadian acceptance of the USSR as an ally:

> From 1917 onwards, the Soviet regime was widely pictured as synonymous with political slavery, savage cruelty, cynical atheism, destruction of the family and a universal lowering of the standard of living. These stereotypes have sunk deep, and are difficult to alter in the absence of real first-hand contact. They have also been reinforced by the activities and ideology of those who call themselves communists among us, and whose undiscriminating praise of all things Russian has provoked a strongly negative reaction.

The survey then identified the groups in Canadian society "whose acceptance of friendly cooperation with Russia is likely to be slow and reluctant": the Catholic church; business and financial circles who fear a socialist government in Canada; Eastern Europeans keeping alive the fears of Bolshevik oppression current in their homelands; and fundamentalist Protestant sects such as the British Israelites whose prophecies include the destruction of Russia by an Anglo-American alliance. To deal with the "ambivalent and conflicting" attitudes, the authors of the survey suggested that four main points be stressed to the public: first, that the Soviet Union had moved far from its Bolshevik origins in 1917 in such a way as the abandonment of atheism and the restoration of the family; second, that Russia had kept its wartime commitments; third, that the Russians were "people like ourselves"; and finally, that Russia's internal tolerance, its lack of racial or sectional discrimination, suggested external peacefulness.[28]

There was more than a little wishful thinking in those suggested lines of approach, and just as tens of thousands of Canadians supported the Communist and Soviet call for a Second Front, similarly there was no doubt that Canadians increasingly looked forward to better relations with the USSR. A Gallup Poll in April 1943 found 47 per cent who wanted to see Canada and Russia work closely together after the war and only 25 per cent who did not. Every region, except Quebec, was strongly in favour of cooperation; in French Canada, however, 50 per cent wanted no cooperation, the motivation being fear of communism in Canada and the paganism of the Soviet Union. In June, only 30 per cent in Quebec believed that Russia could be trusted to cooperate with Canada after the war, compared to 51 per cent in the national sample and 62 per cent in Ontario. Hostility to cooperation, the Wartime Information Board said, "springs from ignorance and prejudice."[29] But three years later, after intensive propaganda and after the Red Army's victory over the German army, only 27 per cent of French Canadians were confident about Canada's ability to get along with the USSR, compared to 51 per cent outside Quebec.[30] Québécois were also substantially more fearful of the prospect of another war.[31]

Certainly some in Canada were trying to help the Soviet Union directly. The Canadian government allocated substantial amounts of war production to the USSR under the Mutual Aid Act of 1943 or for payment – $102 million worth to the end of 1942 (including a $10 million credit for wheat), $23 million worth in 1943–1944, and in all 6.8 per cent of the total of Canadian Mutual Aid (or $167 million) for the whole war.[32] Substantial quantities of war material (including 1,223 tanks and 1,348 Bren carriers up to 31 March 1944) also went to the USSR from supplies sent by Canada to Britain, and additional quantities of food and clothing went to Russia as a Canadian contribution through the United Nations Relief and Rehabilitation Administration.[33] There was also some scientific information of a military nature that was freely given.[34] Unfortunately, there were problems at the end of the war when the Soviets cancelled orders for industrial equipment amounting to more than $6 million.[35] The National Film Board did its bit with a 1942 film that, one senior Liberal adviser complained to Brooke Claxton, MP, "glorifies ... the communistic faith and is a very insidious piece of propaganda ..." The member of Parliament was not amused by the carping: "If the film about Russia shows Russia sympathetically, thank God for that! It is high time this country began to recognize that it is not decent to kick in the face the ally on whose courage and ability to make sacrifices our security depends."[36]

Most important for its demonstration of public support was the Canadian Aid to Russia Fund, a body formed in mid-1942 as the successor to other, more transitory efforts.[37] CARF was a blue-ribbon operation, its patrons including all the lieutenant-governors, the Archbishop of Quebec and other leading churchmen, and the Chief Justice of Canada. Officers included J.S. McLean, Clifford Sifton, J.E. Atkinson, Sen. Rupert Davies, Samuel Bronfman, Sir Robert Falconer, and Col. R.S. McLaughlin. With support like that, the Fund was extraordinarily successful in raising money; one campaign begun in November 1942 producing $3.08 million by early February 1943, more than double expectations.[38] Moreover, the Fund's rallies drew such notables as Prime Minister King and Eleanor Roosevelt as speakers.[39] By mid-1943, another group was on the ground, the National Council for Canadian-Soviet Friendship, led by Sir Ellsworth Flavelle, John David Eaton, and Malcolm Ross.[40] This group, to which the prime minister was "entirely sympathetic,"[41] started its life with a mass rally in Toronto that was orchestrated down to the last detail.[42] But for a variety of reasons, the Council did not succeed. There was a shortage of funds, primarily because Flavelle, described as "emotionally unbalanced and extremely difficult to work with," refused to approach wealthy friends for contributions. Moreover, the Council's aims – to popularize the Soviet Union, to give material assistance to it by having Canadian cities adopt Russian ones, and to exchange cultural materials – were so grandiose (and some so foolish as to invite ridicule, notably a project to have Canadian trade unionists write to Soviet workers) as to be beyond its scope.[43]

Perhaps the Friendship Council's difficulties were a reflection of that ambivalence to the Soviet Union that still persisted, the brilliant military successes of the Red Army notwithstanding. Indeed, to some Ukrainian Canadians, the success of Soviet arms was a direct blow to their aspirations. One indication of this attitude came in an address in Parliament by Anthony Hlynka, an obscure Social Credit MP from Vegreville, Alberta on 2 February 1942. Hlynka spoke for Ukrainian self-determination and the formation of a government-in-exile, and he argued that the lands of the Ukraine could not be treated as booty because the Ukrainian people had the right to determine their own future.[44] Hlynka's remarks, undoubtedly heartfelt, were completely irrelevant to the political necessities of the day, however. In the spring of 1942, for example, Britain was apparently preparing to recognize Russia's post-war frontiers. Norman Robertson, discussing that pending step with the American minister, expressed the Canadian position: "Of course, the Polish frontiers would be reserved, that nobody worried about Finland, and that Estonia, Latvia and Lithuania was a small price to pay to convince Russia of Britain's trust and earnestness."[45] In that atmosphere of *realpolitik*, one that the war situation fully justified, the claims of Ukrainian nationalists were certain to receive short shrift. The creation of an independent Ukraine, Hume Wrong, the associate under secretary in External Affairs, said flatly the next year, "is entirely out of the question ..."[46]

Still, the Ukrainian irredentists did pose a problem for Canada's relations with Moscow, repeatedly drawing protests from the Soviet mission in Ottawa over their more extreme charges and claims. In May 1943, the Soviet minister to Canada had complained about Ukrainian Canadian newspapers' advocacy of an independent Ukraine, an attitude that he described as "pro-Fascist." In those days before multiculturalism, Norman Robertson had assured the minister that despite their numbers, the Ukrainians "were not a factor in influencing Canadian Government policy ..."[47] Similarly the rabid attacks of Dr. Watson Kirkconnell of McMaster University on the Soviet Union and communist elements among various ethnic groups also drew Soviet censure.[48] In May 1945, for example, the Soviet ambassador complained to the Department of External Affairs about press and radio attacks and, although Zaroubin claimed that one Kirkconnell article contravened the Defence of Canada Regulations, he was assured that "the principle of the freedom of the press did not permit us to interfere with the right of any individual to criticize a foreign government. Such criticisms," J.E. Read of External Affairs said, "were not any more violent than criticism of the United States, United Kingdom or Canadian Governments in our press." As Kirkconnell had claimed to have in his possession a directive issued by the Soviet Government ordering the shooting of intellectuals in the Baltic States, that was a slight exaggeration.[49]

As this Soviet complaint suggested, the formalities of diplomacy were being met between Canada and the USSR. Ministers had been named late in 1942, the first Soviet representative to Canada being Feodor Gusev and Canada's first minister to the Soviet Union (who arrived in Kuibyshev, the administrative capital while Moscow was threatened, several months after the Soviets had come to Ottawa) being Dana Wilgress, the former deputy minister of Trade and Commerce, an expert on Russian trade who was married to a Russian.[50] In November 1943, after a Canadian initiative, the two countries' legations were raised to the status of embassies.[51]

But if there were now embassies in Ottawa and Kuibyshev, there was still relatively little work for the bored diplomatic staffs to do, the technicalities of Mutual Aid notwithstanding. Like all foreign diplomats of this period, Wilgress was kept away from the Russian people, his contacts severely limited. Only on rare occasions (as when his mission was upgraded from legation to embassy) did he see senior officials of the Soviet government,[52] and most of his conversations were confined to his ambassadorial colleagues.[53] The Russians in Ottawa, watched by their own people and the envoys of a paranoiac state, apparently felt similarly isolated, the only staff member who was able to talk freely being Pavlov who "is N.K.V.D.," as Charles Ritchie noted, "and so can say what he likes."[54] And as Ritchie's diary entry of a chat with

Mrs. Zaroubin on 3 March 1945 suggested, there were certain cultural deprivations connected with service in Canada:

> Sat next to the Soviet Ambassadress and asked her how she liked Ottawa after Moscow. She replied with animation, "Moscow wonderful, concerts wonderful, ballet wonderful, opera wonderful, Moscow big city – Ottawa nothing *nichevo*) – cinema, cinema, cinema."[55]

Knowing the Russian people well and able to assess the great war weariness of a society that had been devastated by the slaughter since June 1941, Wilgress' reports tended toward a position of firmness and fairness toward the USSR. General Maurice Pope, sharing similar views, observed simply that Wilgress was "not one who takes a pessimistic view of Russia's postwar policy."[56] In a despatch at the end of June 1944, for example, the ambassador wrote about

> the desire of the Soviet Union for a long period of peace in order to recover from the ravages of the war and to strengthen further the economy of the country. The Soviet Union, however, will continue to represent a distinct social and economic system to that of the United States. This may lead in the more distant future to a conflict of interests if the system of collective security does not function effectively. Canada lies geographically between these two countries of immense potential power. The United States, therefore, may feel compelled to enter into close defence arrangements with Canada.[57]

Ottawa, wrapped up in a Post-Hostilities Problems planning exercise, had been thinking on similar but more apocalyptic lines,[58] and the under secretary replied to Wilgress in slightly incredible terms:

> We have not wanted to over-emphasize the danger of a clash between the US and the Soviet Union. Our fears have been based not so much on the prospect of an actual war over our territory between the USSR and the US. We did fear, however, that the US military policy might be based to such an extent on preparation for a possible war with the Soviet Union, that pressure would be placed upon us to cooperate in defensive measures which the Russians would not consider to be friendly or neutral. Recently, however, there has been evidence of a decline in belief among American military men that a war with the Soviet Union was inevitable.[59]

Ottawa, therefore, planned for the future on the expectation that there was at least "several years" and more likely a decade before the possibility of war between the Soviet Union and the United Slates would become serious.[60]

Wilgress' view of the Soviets was unchallenged in Ottawa until early 1945 when he returned to Canada prior to joining the Canadian delegation to the United Nations Conference on International Organization at San Francisco. In his absence from Moscow, one of his staff, Arnold Smith, began drafting despatches for Ottawa, their line so different from the Ambassador's that Leon Mayrand, the Chargé, refused to sign some of them.[61] Essentially Smith, who as late as July 1944 had taken a position very similar to Wilgress', now argued that since the beginning of 1945 Soviet foreign policy had as its goal the creation of a *cordon sanitaire* in reverse in which Soviet influence would be exclusive. As a paper prepared for Mackenzie King, summarizing one despatch and four memoranda from Smith, put it, "this leaves no alternative to the United States and United Kingdom but to create a strong western bloc, in which western influence would be paramount, and to pursue a firm policy of 'yielding advantage only against advantage' as an 'educational technique' to teach the Soviet Union that non-cooperation does not pay." Even so, Smith continued to adhere reasonably close to the Wilgress approach in his memoranda with his admission that the USSR "has no sinister intentions whatever" nor any intention of being aggressive for the foreseeable future.[62] In a private letter to his friend George Ignatieff, however, he was more blunt: "How sure are you in your own mind, George," he wrote from Moscow, "that a world organization which includes the USSR is really a gain rather than a liability for the long-run security of our civilization?"[63]

Nothing that happened at San Francisco countered the message implicit in Smith's hard-nosed approach. As Lester Pearson wrote in his diary, the Russians "seem determined to pursue a strong Russian nationalist policy in Europe, to extend their influence wherever they desire to extend it, and to use for this purpose those forces of international Communism and Left Wing democracy which habitually sympathize with them."[64]

By the end of the war in Europe, therefore, Canada's relations with the USSR, while good, were already beginning to be caught up in the incipient Cold War. The public, still basking in the euphoria of victory and genuinely moved by the suffering the Russian people had undergone, remained largely unaware of the increasing tensions.

"Mr. Pavlov of the Soviet Embassy telephoned about six o'clock this afternoon to enquire if we had received his note about the disappearance of Mr. Gusenko," Norman Robertson wrote in a memorandum of 9 September 1945. "I told him that it had been translated and referred to the Police, whom we had asked to make enquiries."[65] A few days later, he added: "I think of the Russian Embassy being only a few doors away and of there being there a centre of intrigue. During this period of war, while Canada has been helping Russia and doing all we can to foment[?] Canada-Russian Friendship, there has been ... spying ..."[66] Canadian public opinion was no less dramatically affected. In December 1945, even before the public had been informed of Gouzenko's revelations, the Canadian Institute of Public Opinion had reported that 58 per cent of a national sample wanted the secrets of the atomic bomb to remain secret from Russia.[67] Four months later, as the Royal Commission investigation into the Gouzenko case did its work, 52 per cent of a CIPO survey sample expressed dark views of Soviet policy while only 17 per cent offered sympathy for the Russians. And in May, 93 per cent of a sample said they had heard of the spy cases and, despite the criticisms of civil libertarians about the government's and the Royal Commission's tactics, 61 per cent said the King government had acted wisely and only 16 per cent disapproved. Finally, in June 1946, the CIPO asked its sample if "Russia's attitude in the past few months has been due mainly to our withholding the secret of the atomic bomb." Fifty-six per cent said no and only 25 per cent agreed.[68] Without question, the data was clear in its direction if not entirely conclusive. The bloom was off the Red Rose.

NOTES

1 George Orwell, *1984* (New York, 1959), 31–2.
2 See on this subject, not treated here, Reg Whitaker, "Official Repression of Communism During World War II," *Labour/Le Travail* XVII (Spring 1986), 135ff.
3 John Munro, ed., *Documents on Canadian External Relations*, VI, *1936–1939* (Ottawa, 1972), 1232–3. [Cited hereafter as *DCER*.]
4 Ibid., 1233.
5 NAC, W.L.M. King Papers, Diary, 22 August 1939.
6 Ibid., "Memorandum re Broadcast: War Aims," 17 October 1939, ff. C285909.
7 Ibid., Diary, 17 September 1939.
8 Ibid., 30 November 1939. For the reaction of Canadian communists to the Nazi-Soviet Pact, see Merrily Weisbord, *The Strangest Dream* (Toronto, 1983), chap. 8, and Ivan Avukomovic, *The Communist Party in Canada* (Toronto, 1975), chap. 5.
9 *DCER*, VIII, 1049.
10 Ibid., 1055.

11 Ibid., 1090ff.; King Diary, 20 January 1940.
12 Ibid., 1 October 1940.
13 *DCER*, VIII, 1097–8.
14 Ibid., 1098–9.
15 Ibid., 1099–1100.
16 Harvard University, J. Pierrepont Moffat Papers, XLVII, Memorandum, 23 June 1941.
17 *DCER*, VIII, 1100–2. For Communist Party response, see Weisbord, chap. 10.
18 Moffat Papers, Memorandum, 23 June 1941.
19 *DCER*, VIII, 1106–9.
20 Moffat Papers, Memorandum, 6 September 1941.
21 Ibid., Memorandum, 23 June 1941. Harry Ferns maintains that he believed the USSR would win. *Reading From Left to Right* (Toronto, 1983), 157.
22 Moffat Papers, Memorandum, 16 September 1941. See also King Papers, Memorandum for the Prime Minister, 16 September 1941, f.C250926.
23 *DCER*, VII, 94–5, 356.
24 Ibid., IX, 44.
25 Ibid., 44ff. The account in A. Balawyder, ed., *Canada-Soviet Relations 1939–1980* (Oakville, 1981), 4–5, is slightly garbled. See also Department of External Affairs, John Starnes Papers, Robertson's memoranda for the Prime Minister of 11, 23 December 1941, and 4 March 1942.
26 Department of External Affairs, External Affairs Records, file 2462-40, Massey to Ottawa, 10 April 1942. The Comintern was declared dissolved in October 1943.
27 *Public Opinion Quarterly* (Winter 1942), 655, 665.
28 Wartime Information Board, "Public Attitudes: Canada and Soviet Russia," *Survey No. 8*, 10 April 1943, Copy in the National Library, Ottawa. The WIB sounded very similar to CCF leader M.J. Coldwell. See House of Commons *Debates*, 23 February 1943, 633.
29 Wartime Information Board, "Public Attitudes: Canadian-Russian Cooperation," *Survey No. 21*, 9 October 1943. Copy in National Library, Ottawa.
30 PAC, Wartime Information Board Records, IV, WIB Survey file. *Survey No. 63*, 19 May 1945.
31 *Public Opinion Quarterly* (Summer 1945), 257.
32 King Papers, "Materials and Equipments ... to 31 December 1942," 12 January 1943, ff. C259001–2; *DCER*, IX, 437ff.; *Public Accounts* (1944), p. xxxi.
33 *Report of the Canadian Mutual Aid Board*, 20 May 1943 to 31 March 1944 (Ottawa, 1944), 23; *Final Report*, 1946, Canadian Mutual Aid Board (Ottawa, n.d.), 38–9, 44–5.
34 See Donald Avery, "Secrets Between Different Kinds of Friends: Canada's Wartime Exchange of Scientific Military Information with the United States and the USSR, 1940–1945," *Historical Papers 1986*, 251.

35 Balawyder, 9.
36 NAC, Brooke Claxton Papers, XLIV, H.E. Kidd to Claxton, 12 June 1942, and reply, 18 June 1942.
37 The Canadian Aid to Russia Fund records are in the PAC. Earlier groups were apparently subject to investigation to determine if they were Communist-backed. See NAC, Department of National War Services Records, VII, Russian Relief file, E.W. Stapleford to J.T. Thorson, 20 October 1941, and ibid., Russian Groups file, Thorson to M. Gould, 5 September 1942.
38 King Papers, J2, vol. 369, file W-307-4, Interim Report of Canadian Aid to Russia Fund, 17 February 1943. Balawyder, 7, gives totals to 30 September 1945, as $3.86 million in cash and $3.3 million in clothing.
39 King Papers, "Remarks by the Prime Minister ...," 19 January 1943, ff. C238067ff.
40 Ibid., National Council Labour Committee Bulletin, 3 January 1944, ff. C238133ff., lists the executive.
41 Ibid., Memorandum for Council, 14 January 1943, f. C23078.
42 Ibid., "Canadian Soviet Friendship Council Rally – 22 June 1943," ff. C238089ff. King's remarks are in Wartime Information Board Papers, XIX, file 10.A.12.
43 King Papers, Note for Mr. Wrong, 26 February 1944, ff. C238142–3.
44 House of Commons *Debates*, 2 February 1942, 231–5. See Whitaker, 156–9; John Kolasky, *The Shattered Illusion* (Toronto, 1979); B. Kordan and L.Y. Luciuk, "Security, Loyalty and Nationbuilding: Ukrainian Canadians and the Politics of State, 1939–1945," a paper presented at the Canadian Committee on the History of the Second World War Conference, September 1986; and Samuel Nesdoly, "Changing Perspectives: The Ukrainian-Canadians Role in Canadian-Soviet Relations," in Balawyder, 111–12. See also Watson Kirkconnell, "The Ukrainian Canadians and the War," Oxford Pamphlets on World Affairs (1940); his *Seven Pillars of Freedom* (Toronto, 1944), and his memoir, *A Slice of Canada* (Toronto, 1967), chap. 24.
45 Moffat Papers, Memorandum, 13 April 1942.
46 King Papers, "Restoration of Property of Ukrainian Farmer Labour Temples," 7 June 1943, ff. C231869–70.
47 Kordan and Luciuk, op. cit.; *DCER*, IX, 1863–5.
48 E.g., *Globe and Mail*, 2 February 1943.
49 King Papers, J4, vol. 414, file 3990, Memorandum for Prime Minister, 12 May 1945. See also William Christian, ed., *Innis on Russia* (Toronto, 1981), diary entry, 30 June 1945: "Attack of *Moscow News* on Kirkconnell illustrates lack of sense of proportion ... magnify Kirkconnell in Canada ..."
50 See Wilgress' anodyne *Memoirs* (Toronto, 1967) and his article, "From Siberia to Kuibyshev: Reflections on Russia," *International Journal*,

XXII (Summer 1967), 372ff. See also R.M. Macdonnell, "The Mission to Kuibyshev," *International Perspectives* (July/August 1973), 53ff.
51 *DCER*, IX, 76ff.; King Papers, Canadian Minister to USSR to Ottawa, 17 November 1943, ff. C238126-7 and ibid., 4 March 1944, ff. C237691-2.
52 When Wilgress did see senior officials, his despatches to Ottawa were regularly sent to the British Foreign Office, where they drew favourable comment. See docs. on PRO, Foreign Office Records, FO 371/43413, and PRO, Dominions Office Records, DO 35/1601, minutes. See also Don Page, "The Wilgress Despatches from Moscow, 1943–1946," a paper presented to the Canadian Committee for the History of the Second World War Conference, 1977.
53 Donald Page, "Getting to Know the Russians – 1943–1948," in Balawyder, 16.
54 Charles Ritchie, *The Siren Years* (Toronto, 1974), 186. See also Ferns, *Reading From Left to Right*, 184ff.
55 Ritchie, *The Siren Years*, 186.
56 NAC, Maurice Pope Papers, I, Diary 1945, entry, 16 April 1945.
57 Department of External Affairs, External Affairs Records, file 7-AB(s), "Wilgress to Ottawa," 30 June 1944.
58 See James Eayrs, *In Defence of Canada: Peacemaking and Deterrence* (Toronto, 1972), 320ff., and generally D. Munton and D. Page, "Planning in the East Block: The Post-Hostilities Problems Committees in Canada 1943–1945," *International Journal*, XXXII (Autumn 1977), 687ff.
59 Department of External Affairs, External Affairs Records, file 7AB(s), Robertson to Wilgress, 5 August 1944. See also FO 371/43413, Garner to Costar, 17 July 1944 and attached minutes.
60 Donald Munton and Donald Page, "The Operations of the Post-War Hostilities Planning Group in Canada, 1943–1945," CHA paper, 1976, 31. This material did not appear in the published version of this paper, cited above.
61 Arnold Smith interview, 18 February 1978.
62 King Papers, Memorandum for the Prime Minister, 20 June 1945, ff. C237899ff. Smith's despatch and memos are in Department of External Affairs, External Affairs Records, file 2-AE(s).
63 George Ignatieff, *The Making of a Peacemonger* (Toronto, 1985), 86.
64 NAC, L.B. Pearson Papers, N8, vol. 2, San Francisco diary, 72. W.L. Morton took a surprisingly benign view: Russia, he said, "is going ahead and making its own arrangements in special areas on its borders ... This may be regrettable, but after all here is a chance that may not return and no Russian statesman can pass it up." "Behind Dumbarton Oaks," *Behind the Headlines* V (1945), 14.
65 Department of External Affairs, External Affairs Records, file 8159-40C, Memorandum for the File, 9 September 1945.

66 Ibid., 24 September 1945.
67 *Public Opinion Quarterly* (Winter 1945–6), 537. For a useful assessment of the information on the atomic bomb and other secret projects the Russian spy ring did secure, see Don Avery, *Historical Papers 1986*, 245ff.
68 *Public Opinion Quarterly* (Summer 1946), 264–5.

Chapter Eighteen

From Gouzenko to Gorbachev: Canada's Cold War

For Canadians, the Cold War was a matter of great importance – some of the time. For them, it began in September 1945 with the defection of Soviet embassy cipher officer Igor Gouzenko and revelations of major Soviet spy rings in Canada. Moscow's brutalist policies under Stalin did nothing to ease growing concerns. Because they shared a continent with the superpower leading the democracies, their largest trading partner and "best friend," they soon found themselves living under the flight path for bombers and missiles from the Soviet Union and that sharpened the collective mind and pushed them toward continued military cooperation with the United States. At the same time, Canada's two mother countries, Britain and France, and nations such as Belgium, Netherlands, and Italy that Canadians had fought to liberate, were under threat from what was generally perceived as an expansionist Soviet communism. These and economic concerns led to a newly internationalist Canada being an enthusiastic supporter of a North Atlantic Treaty and the first peacetime stationing of troops abroad. In Asia, the Hong Kong debacle of 1941 aside, Canada had never been active until the Korean War opened another front in the "Cold" War. Again Canadians participated with troops.

Defence spending rose sharply in a booming economy, but very soon pressures began to arise. There were widespread concerns about US policy, Canadian nationalists and anti-Americans began to kick against the pricks, and demands for expensive and expansive domestic social welfare policies led to pressures for defence cuts. By 1968 and the advent of Pierre Trudeau as Prime Minister, the calls for foreign policy change had become unstoppable, and until the arrival of Mikhail Gorbachev and the subsequent demise of the Cold War, Canadian policy was one of limited cooperation with Alliance partners, defence spending cutbacks, and planned military obsolescence. The Cold War if necessary, therefore, but not necessarily the Cold War, or at least not all Cold War all the time.

⁂

The Canadian view of the origins of the Cold War was stark and focussed. "The chief menace now," Lester Pearson said in 1948, the year he left the foreign service to enter the Cabinet as Secretary of State for External Affairs, "is subversive aggressive Communism, the servant of power politics ... Our frontier now is not even on the Rhine or rivers further east. It is wherever free men are struggling against totalitarian tyranny," wherever the "struggle of free, expanding progressive democracy against tyrannical and reactionary communism was being fought ..."[1] Pearson had a subtle mind, but to him the conflict was one painted in black and white. "Western democratic governments have no aggressive or imperialistic designs," he said a decade later. "This is as true of the most powerful, the United States of America, as it is of ... Iceland ... Americans are not by nature or desire wandering empire builders ... They are homebodies, and their 'westerns' give them an adequate if vicarious sense of adventure."[2] For remarks offered in 1958, these might charitably be described as naïve or at best hopeful, and Pearson knew better. On the other hand when he was asked if it were better to be dead than red, Pearson sensibly refused to agree, something that was used by political opponents to paint him as soft on Communism for decades.

Pearson had been shaped by his personal experiences. He had served overseas in the Great War and as a young diplomat during the disillusioning 1930s. He had watched the democracies crumble in the face of the dictators and, as a senior official, he had cheered as the United States had stepped forward – with substantial help from the British Commonwealth and especially the Soviet Union – to save freedom and democracy. To him, to his generation of Canadians, the only way democracy could be saved from the new totalitarian threat was if the Americans, sometimes much too reluctant in Canadian eyes, could be encouraged to accept their responsibilities for world power. If they could, Canadians and others would participate in helping to create a *Pax Americana*. The involvement of the United States was the *sine qua non* in preserving the free world – that was an article of faith.

Canadians knew this, but as neighbours of the US they had their concerns. Britain's economic and military weakness in 1940 and 1941 had forced Ottawa into its first military alliance with the United States, the Permanent Joint Board on Defence created at Ogdensburg, NY, in August 1940. That meant that the growing Canadian forces could put all their efforts into the defence of Britain, sure that the United States would protect their home base. A few months later, Mackenzie King struck an economic arrangement with Franklin Roosevelt that let Canada avoid taking Lend-Lease, something no one wanted for fear of the future economic power this would give Washington over Canada. Instead, FDR agreed to cover Canada's shortage of American dollars, the only hard currency in the world, in other ways, notably by buying more raw materials. The result was much the same: by the coming of the peace, Canada's only postwar commercial market was the US, with virtually all of the nation's trade with other nations financed by Canadian loans and grants.[3]

Ottawa's Post-Hostilities planners had watched carefully as the strains on the wartime Grand Alliance festered and developed over issues such as Poland. They understood that if they developed into open antagonism, Canada's geographical position and economic situation meant that neutrality was not an option. Nor could Canada any longer rely on Britain for protection. Canada had to be aligned with the US. The Gouzenko case made this clear.

Igor Gouzenko fled the Soviet Embassy in Ottawa with a sheaf of carefully selected documents just weeks after the atomic bombs brought the Second World War to its ghastly end. His telegrams and memos made evident that the GRU, Soviet military intelligence, had spies in Parliament, the Canadian civil service and the military, in the British High Commission, and in scientific establishments including those working on atomic research. Gouzenko knew of additional spy rings run by the NKVD, and he told his interrogators what he knew of rings in the US, and his accounts eventually led to Alger Hiss, Harry Dexter White, and Julius and Ethel Rosenberg.[4]

Gouzenko mattered. First, his defection and his documents, made public beginning in February 1946 and the subject of an extraordinary Royal Commission investigation, demonstrated that the wartime friendship between the Soviets and the West was over; indeed, it demonstrated that Moscow's war against the capitalist democracies had not even been put on hold during the struggle against Hitler. Second, for Canadians accustomed to being a backwater of little importance, Gouzenko demonstrated that Canada was a player, a nation worth spying on for nuclear and scientific secrets as well as for details on British and American policy. Third, his documents showed that the assumptions of loyalty and trust that had been assumed to bind those working for government had been misplaced. Now ideas and ideology had to be probed; now positive vetting had to be put in place; now character weaknesses began to be rooted out. It took time to implement this modest variant of McCarthyism but before the end of the 1940s, some public servants' careers had been ruined and some had been hounded out of the bureaucracy.[5] One diplomat, Herbert Norman, the Ambassador to Egypt, had been driven to suicide by witch-hunting US congressmen convinced – correctly – that he had been a Communist and fearful he might have been a mole.[6] By the mid- to late 1950s, homosexuals too had been singled out and forced from senior positions, not least in the Department of External Affairs.[7] There was some irony in this. The Department of External Affairs, believing that Stalinist Moscow was a posting too dreadful for married diplomats with families, had sent three successive single men – all closet homosexuals – to Canada's embassy in the late 1940s and early 1950s. All had been targeted by the KGB, apparently with only limited success.[8]

The Gouzenko case had altered attitudes, helping to shift Canadians away from their heartfelt admiration for the Red Army's extraordinary fight against the Wehrmacht. The revelations of spying had been manipulated to point to a Communist and Soviet threat, to be sure, the Royal Commission report on the Gouzenko case written in a reader-friendly way (by an officer from External Affairs), the press making much of it and anti-Communists and anti-socialists using it as a weapon. But Gouzenko was not a Canadian creation; Moscow had committed the espionage – and it publicly admitted this, however unlikely that might seem. Moreover, Stalin's acts in Eastern Europe and his representatives' actions in various postwar forums hardly stressed eternal friendship. There is blame enough to go around on the origins of the Cold War, but Canada has none, and Moscow, of the Great Powers, carries the lion's share.[9]

Those in Canada who had anticipated that the new United Nations could enforce collective security on an unruly world had seen most of their hopes shattered within a few years by Soviet obstruction and the wielding of the veto in the Security Council. That was depressing enough, but Moscow's pressure on Iran and Greece, its swallowing of Eastern Europe, especially the crushing of Czechoslovakian independence, and soon the triumph of Mao Tse-tung's Communism in China made all deeply concerned for the future. Josef Stalin's speech in Moscow in February 1946, one week before the Gouzenko case became public, declaring capitalism and Communism incompatible and pointing to the inevitability of another war added to the growing unease.[10] What frightened Canadians and others silly, however, was the fear that Communist parties might come to power in free elections in Italy and France. The West, the democracies, had to be spiritually rearmed and made ready to resist the Red tide. Perhaps, just perhaps, the democracies could create a new alliance for collective security to replace the veto-prone talk shop that the UN had quickly become.

The first stage in this process was the Marshall Plan. The European economies lay in ruins, their cities shattered, food scarce and rationed, and the will to re-establish pre-war patterns of life not much in evidence. Only the Communist parties flourished, and the view in the US State Department – and in Ottawa – was that only American aid could turn the tide. The United States had already stepped in to assist Greece, proclaiming the Truman Doctrine as the way to help a faltering government and to replace Britain, economically too impoverished by war and reconstruction, to continue its efforts there. On June 5, 1947, Secretary of State George C. Marshall told a Harvard University convocation that the European countries should create a collective plan for reconstruction and put a proposal for assistance before the United States. The road to Europe's economic salvation had been discerned.

Canada's too. Like the US and a few other countries that had not been devastated by war, Canada had emerged in 1945 economically and politically far stronger than it had been when it went to war. The nation's military had fought well and that conveyed prestige and power. Its Gross Domestic Product had doubled, its industries boomed, and its well-fed people had money in the bank. But Ottawa knew this privileged position could not last without markets for the nation's goods. The government had tried hard to re-build its British and European markets. A 1946 loan of $1.25 billion at 2 per cent to Britain (especially when compared to the US loan of $3.75 billion) and of $600 million to other trading partners was simply huge in Canadian terms,[11] the country's GDP being only $11 billion.

But American dollars, the world's hard currency, again were growing scarce all over the globe; in Canada, the developing crisis was precipitated by soaring imports of everything from jukeboxes to oranges to consumer goods as Canadians tried to spend the money wartime wages and unlimited overtime had let them save. In 1947, Canada had no choice except to impose import restrictions on American products to try to conserve its dollar supplies. The Marshall Plan, if the US could be persuaded to allow "off-shore procurement" in its provisions, could resolve much of the Canadian difficulty. If France, say, which had too few dollars to buy Canadian goods could pay with Marshall funds, then Canada would both sell trade goods and increase its holdings of American dollars. There was much struggle along the way, but off-shore procurement eventually saved Canada's bacon – and its wheat exports too – by authorizing purchases of $1.1 billion US in Canada.[12]

But for a superpower supposedly poised to step in to save the world and scoop up the rewards, the US – at least according to the way Canadian diplomats in Washington saw it – seemed remarkably reluctant to approve the Marshall Plan. Senators and congressmen objected to bailing out the Europeans and, if they had to do that, then, they said, every penny must benefit American farmers and workers, not Canadians. Still, events drove the agenda. The Communists seized control in Prague in February 1948. The next month, General Lucius Clay, commanding the US Zone in Germany, sent a message to Washington that seemed to suggest war with the Soviet Union was imminent. In March, President Truman asked Congress to implement conscription, and overseas the Brussels Pact was signed, linking Britain, France, and the Low Countries. The Berlin Airlift soon began (with Canada declining to provide either aircraft or crews). The first preliminary discussions for a North Atlantic Treaty began. The drumbeats for war with the Russians were increasing in tempo. But Republican Senator Robert Taft and his isolationist friends still balked at American engagement in Europe, and Canadians feared the United States might yet fall back into its "prewar aloofness."[13]

Canadian Ambassador Hume Wrong, a man with a steel trap mind and, as a lifelong friend of Dean Acheson, the very best of contacts in Washington, shrewdly observed in September 1947 that "There is truth in the paradox that, to secure the adoption of a plan for world economic recovery, it is necessary to emphasize the division of the world between the Soviet bloc and the rest."[14] Frighten the American people, in other words. A few months later, the Ambassador added that "The contest between the US and the USSR is providing the necessary popular foundation for a vigorous foreign policy and it has put those leaders who still possess strong isolationist leanings, such as Senator Taft and Speaker Martin, in the position of opening themselves to charges of lack of patriotism if they attack the general trend; they are therefore reduced to the role of critics of its details." Wrong understood that the whipping up of anti-Communist hysteria was unfortunate, but perhaps inevitable in the American context. Certainly such excesses were useful. For example, he reported to Ottawa, "they are part of the price to be paid for the Marshall Plan."[15] Ambassador Hume Wrong and his colleagues (one of whom incredibly was named Hume Wright) had had serious concerns that isolationism might prevail. Most in Ottawa did not believe that war was imminent, but if the American Congress and people could be frightened into believing that it was ...

Once again this served Canadian interests. Canada's leaders understood that their nation could not defend itself, and they accepted grudgingly that this realization meant the subordination of their policies and military plans to those of the US. The Second World War had pushed Canada into a bilateral defence alliance with the US, a position that left Canada trying to deal all by itself with a partner fifteen times its weight. The war had also demonstrated that Canadian interests and concerns could frequently be brushed aside by the great powers. Now, if Britain and Western Europe could be brought into the equation, if the US could be persuaded to join a permanent North Atlantic alliance, this would be good for the security of the West and, by creating a new and strong multilateral alliance, certainly better for Canada than a purely bilateral relationship with Washington in which it could only ever be a very subordinate partner. The Soviet threat facilitated the desire of Canadian leaders to have the United States, not all that enthusiastic as Ottawa and its diplomats perceived it, join a permanent military alliance and to take a multilateral, rather than unilateral, approach to the exercise of its powers and responsibilities. Ottawa's goal, at once idealistic and self-interested, was to see American power exercised in association with Canada and other powers.

Indeed, a trans-Atlantic alliance held out the possibility of resolving one of the great Canadian dilemmas. Norman Robertson, the Canadian High Commissioner in London and the most far-sighted of Canadian officials, wrote in April 1948 that "A situation in which our special relationship with the United Kingdom can be identified with our special relationships with other countries in western Europe and in which the United States will be providing a firm basis, both economically and probably militarily, seems to me such a providential solution for so many of our problems that we should go to great lengths ... to ensure our proper place in this new partnership."[16] The North Atlantic Triangle was very much in Robertson's mind.

The negotiation of the North Atlantic Treaty is a large subject. What needs to be said is that Canada, perhaps instinctively as suggested by Robertson, sought to broaden the discussions to include economic clauses. Robertson was the initiator of the idea of Article 2 of the Treaty. How could nations unite for defence, he asked, if they fought trade wars against each other? How much better if the new alliance included a clause binding the parties "to make every effort ... to eliminate conflict in their economic policies and to develop to the full the great possibilities of trade between them"?[17] A version of Robertson's formulation eventually was included in the Treaty, a tribute to the negotiating skills of Ambassador Wrong in Washington. Lester Pearson noted that there were domestic political reasons behind Article 2: "We did not think that the Canadian people, especially in Quebec, would whole-heartedly take on far-reaching external commitments if they were exclusively military in character ..."[18] But no party to the Treaty other than the Canadians wanted Article 2, and the Americans in particular, worried sick about what they saw as the almost insuperable difficulty of securing public and Congressional support for a peacetime military alliance, wanted nothing to do with a trade clause that might threaten the treaty for no important benefit. As Dean Acheson, becoming Secretary of State at the beginning of 1949, put it, "The plain fact ... is that NATO is a military alliance." Article 2, to him, was "typical Canadian moralizing that meant 'next to nothing.'"[19] He was right, and Hume Wrong, the Canadian negotiator, knew it. For all the successful Canadian efforts, for all that Acheson began to characterize the Canadian demands as coming (*pace* William Woodsworth) from "The Stern Daughter of the Voice of God," Article 2 in the end, in fact, amounted to nothing.

Neither did the Canadian signature on the North Atlantic Treaty, at least not immediately. Signing on in April 1949, Canada did nothing very much to improve its armed forces, to rearm, or substantially to increase defence spending. The Defence budget in 1947 was $227 million, in 1948, $236 million, in 1949, $361 million, and in 1950, $493 million, satisfactory increases but nothing to suggest urgency to create a great host. The Korean War, beginning in June 1950, changed everything, especially the Chinese intervention in December 1950 that drove the UN forces reeling to the south. The Communist attack and the winter 1950–1 defeat in Korea led to fears in Western capitals that the Soviet Union, now with nuclear weapons in its arsenal, was turning to military aggression to achieve its goals and that Europe might be next. For Canada that led to the despatch of an army brigade group to Korea and a second brigade group and an air division of fighter aircraft, more than ten thousand troops in all, to Europe in 1951.[20]

At the same time as it was fighting on the Korean peninsula, for the first time in its history Canada began to create an effective, well-equipped professional military. Defence spending in 1951 was $1.16 billion; the next year it was $1.8 billion or 7.5 per cent of GDP, and in 1953–4, the Canadian Forces, now with a regular force strength of 118,000, received $1.9 billion or 7.6 per cent of Canada's GDP of just above $25 billion.[21] Such figures were huge for Canada but small beside the enormous sums Washington was devoting to defence.

Clearly, Stalin had made a huge error in giving Pyongyang the go-ahead to strike south. As Escott Reid, a senior External Affairs official in Ottawa and one of the originators of the idea of the North Atlantic Treaty, told a journalist friend, there were two key events that had saved the world: "the intervention in Korea and the defeat of the UN army.

Had it not been for these events, the West would never have faced up to rearmament," he maintained rightly.[22]

At the same time, Canadian policymakers had real concerns about US leadership. Writing in May 1948, Pearson noted that in the event of war the United States would be the dominant partner, but, he said, if the Western European countries are not occupied, they will be able to make some effective contribution to the political direction of the war. "I have more confidence in the wisdom of their political views," he said, "than in the wisdom of the political views of the United States ..."[23] NATO and the "police action" in Korea had been designed to contain the Soviet Union. In Canadian eyes, however, containing the United States was also necessary, and disputes between Ottawa and Washington over the conduct of the Korean War and the possibility of a negotiated armistice to end it sometimes became very sharp. The Americans, bearing the heaviest burdens of the war, resented being told how the war should be fought by the Canadians with a single brigade and a handful of ships committed to the struggle. Pearson expressed the frustrations best in a speech in April 1951. The United Nations was not the instrument of any one country, and Canada had the right to criticize American actions "if we feel it necessary. The days of relatively easy and automatic political relations with our neighbour are, I think, over." Now the Canadian concern was not *"whether* the United States will discharge her international responsibilities, but how she will do it and whether the rest of us will be involved."[24]

The Liberal government led by Louis St. Laurent, a francophone lawyer from Quebec City, that had taken Canada into NATO and Korea was genuinely committed to the alliance and to the Cold War. For a francophone prime minister to act this way so soon after the manpower crises of wartime was highly unusual and demonstrated, to use one Australian's acerbic description, that he was not a "neurotically-introverted, isolationist Québécois," a "millstone perpetually limiting Canadian freedom of action in strategic affairs."[25] Far from it: St. Laurent's internationalist foreign and defence policies were not cheered in a Quebec that historically was suspicious of the military and of overseas commitments, but his French Canadian compatriots trusted his judgment and gave him big majorities in three successive elections. To the Prime Minister, the Soviets and Mao's Communists were a threat to Canadian and Western interests, and indeed all three mainstream political parties in Canada agreed with this with varying degrees of enthusiasm in the 1950s. Moreover, despite its general lack of interest in Asia, the Canadian government saw it as a duty to respond positively when asked – without any prior notice from the powers involved – to send military officers and diplomats to Indo-China in 1954 to serve on the International Control Commissions. This burdensome quasi-peacekeeping role later proved a blessing when the Vietnam War exploded into a major confrontation, and Canada could say that the ICC, continuing to work ineffectually while the fighting went on, prevented it from joining the United States in the war. As it was, Canadians on the ICC provided intelligence to the US and the nation's diplomats carried carrot-and-stick messages between Washington and Hanoi.[26]

St. Laurent's Canada believed that there were virtues in accepting reality. It had been on the verge of recognizing Beijing when China intervened in Korea, for one thing, despite opposition in Washington. It wanted to talk to the Soviets, and Foreign Minister Pearson was the first NATO leader to visit Moscow in October 1955, where he was abused roundly by Nikita Khrushchev for the sins of the West while he and all his party got thoroughly sozzled on the endless toasts offered by their hosts.[27] And St. Laurent and Pearson worked hard at the United Nations to rescue Britain and France, mother countries and NATO partners, from the consequences of their folly in ineptly invading Egypt in collusion with the Israelis in the fall of 1956. As a Western power, as a member of NATO, Canada had a vital national interest in trying to repair the split between Britain and France, the aggressors, and the United States. Canada's actions were directed as much to repairing the breach among allies as to restoring peace in the area. Indeed, the two goals were positively inseparable. That the Suez Crisis occurred at the same time as the Hungarian revolt and the Soviets' brutal intervention, that it took place during a US presidential election, only compounded the difficulties. Pearson won the Nobel Peace Prize for his efforts at saving the world and, not least, the NATO alliance, but the Canadian public, unhappy that Canada had turned its back on London and Paris, voted the Liberals out of power at the first opportunity.[28]

The new Progressive Conservative Prime Minister, the lawyer and Prairie populist John Diefenbaker, was militantly anti-Communist. Unfortunately he also proved to be virulently anti-American, falling into difficulties with President John Kennedy that turned primarily around nuclear weapons. In 1957–8, Canada and the US had created the North American Air Defense Command to combine and coordinate their air defences against Soviet bombers with their nuclear payloads. NORAD was readily agreed to by the Chief, as he liked to be called, but soon became the cause of political difficulty. Was it part of NATO, as Diefenbaker claimed, or was it not, as the Pentagon argued? Then in 1959 Diefenbaker had cancelled work on the CF-105 Avro Arrow, much to his political cost, and instead decided to acquire US-made Bomarc surface-to-air missiles to defend Canada and the northeastern United States against Soviet bombers. The Bomarcs, as well as newly acquired surface-to-surface Honest John missiles and fighter bombers for the Canadian contingent in NATO, were effective only when armed with nuclear warheads. In 1959, no one appeared to notice the warheads question.[29] By 1962, however, Diefenbaker's government, now a minority, began to be torn apart by the nuclear yes/nuclear no question, and public opinion, pushed hard by peace groups, was divided (but still supportive of acquiring the warheads).[30] The US administrations of Eisenhower and Kennedy had watched angrily as Canada tried to scoop up the Cuban trade that US companies lost after Fidel Castro came to power in Havana, and the Kennedy Pentagon was furious that there was a hole in their northern defences while Diefenbaker delayed a decision on accepting the nuclear warheads he had earlier wanted. Matters worsened dramatically during the sharpest crisis of the Cold War when complete prime ministerial indecision during the Cuban missile crisis of October 1962 resulted in serious delays in putting Canadian interceptors in NORAD on alert. (In fact, the Defence minister acted on his own in ordering a full alert, while naval commanders put their ships to sea to shadow Soviet submarines on their own responsibility.) The result, with White House approval, was the issuing of a press release by the State Department that delineated Diefenbaker's wavering and parsed his speeches for inconsistencies and outright lies. Within days, the Cabinet splintered, the government fell early in 1963, and after a brilliantly mendacious anti-American campaign that almost carried the day, Diefenbaker was gone.[31]

The new prime minister, Liberal L.B. Pearson, accepted the nuclear weapons, and everyone expected continental harmony to reign anew. But soon Kennedy was dead, Lyndon Johnson was in office, and the Vietnam War became messier. Some of Pearson's ministers were every bit as anti-nuclear weapons and anti-American as Diefenbaker, Finance Minister Walter Gordon in particular. Gordon, who wanted to cut the flow of American investment into Canada, failed in his efforts when Canadian businessmen and the US government protested vigorously, and then he turned to the war. Pearson in fact had called on the US to halt the bombing of North Vietnam in a speech in Philadelphia in March 1965, a futile gesture that earned him Johnson's contempt. "Here are the loyal Germans, always with us when it matters," LBJ told a gathering of diplomats in Washington. "And then there are the Canadians."[32] Canada was not a totally compliant ally – it had never been so – and Canadian nationalism, always drawing its strength from magnifying differences with the Americans, flourished. The nuclear stalemate with its potential doomsday effects if war ever began reinforced anti-Americanism in Canada, certainly more than it fed anti-Communism.

But Canada was still a helpful fixer, ready to send in the peacekeepers when the West's interests were at stake. In Cyprus in 1964, where Britain had bases and interests in a former colony, two NATO members, Greece and Turkey, were on the verge of war over the island they both wanted to control. Prime Minister Pearson initially was dubious about sending Canadian troops – "Let them cut each other up," he told Paul Hellyer, his Defence minister. "We certainly won't go in just to help the British."[33] A war would have had disastrous effects on NATO's southern flank, however, quite possibly destroying the alliance, and the Pearson government's External Affairs minister Paul Martin went to work on the telephones, calling foreign ministers around the world. The result was the establishment of a UN force. On March 13, 1964, Canada sent an infantry battalion, and UNFICYP, the United Nations Force in Cyprus, hit the ground running. This served Canada's desire to be a peacekeeper, already demonstrated in innumerable missions, but it also saved a critical part of the Western alliance, exactly as in 1956. Canadian foreign ministers from Pearson's successor onward began to hope that, if they called in their markers in the world capitals and at UN headquarters in New York, they too might create a peacekeeping force and help freeze a crisis. Then, perhaps, a Nobel Peace Prize just might come their way. After all, it had worked for Lester Pearson, hadn't it? Didn't the Peace Prize help him become Liberal leader and then prime minister? Nobelitis, Canadians called it, and not in an unkindly way.

In the decade after Pearson's Nobel Prize, as the Cold War continued and as the United States became ever more embroiled in the morass of Vietnam, the Canadian public began to believe as an article of faith that peacekeeping was their métier. We were the world's master peacekeepers, the indispensable UN players absolutely necessary for each and every mission. The Americans, always bumptious and too aggressive, fought wars, but Canadians, nature's neutral middlemen, kept the peace. This became a mantra, a powerful idea that successive governments scarcely ever challenged. War was foreign to Canadian thinking, and peacekeeping was the natural role to play. For the public, peacekeeping was do-goodism writ large, proof that Canada really was a moral superpower, loved by all. It was also a military role that differentiated Canada from the Americans' focus on nuclear deterrence and Mutual Assured Destruction. And if some worried that Canadians weren't pulling their military weight in the Cold War, the easy answer was that the nation's peacekeeping was useful, and it did not require huge armies, large fleets, and vast air forces. Governments liked that low cost factor. Being the globe's pre-eminent peacekeepers was good for Canadian nationalism, peaking in a frenzy in 1967, the centennial of Canada's creation (and ironically the year that President Nasser tossed UN peacekeepers out of his country, much to Canadian chagrin, just prior to the Six Day War).

This nationalism would reach another peak when the charismatic, stylish 48-year-old bachelor Pierre Trudeau succeeded Pearson in the spring of 1968. Trudeau opposed Quebec separatism, and he was skeptical of nationalism in all its forms. He was a new man, the fluently bilingual quintessential Canadian, or so many thought in 1968. What Trudeau was, in fact, was typically French Canadian in his attitude to the military, to NATO, and to the Cold War. He was no isolationist, but he was not one to believe in the military or one to want to take on the difficult global tasks that kept the peace. Puzzlingly, given his views on nationalism, he would become a nationalist icon in English-speaking Canada; predictably, he would be the key figure in weakening the country's support for the verities of the Cold War.

Trudeau was a trickster, always looking to shock. As a young civil servant in the Privy Council Office in Ottawa, he opposed Canada's joining in the Korean War or sending troops to Europe for NATO. Then after leaving the public service, he had visited Moscow to attend an economics conference in 1952, telling everyone he was a Communist, something noted by US Embassy officials. He also, at age 41, had tried to paddle a canoe from Florida to Cuba in 1960. Just good fun, his biographer said, as if the fellow-travelling Trudeau had been unaware of US hostility to the new Castro regime.[34] Both of those actions suggested he knew little of the US (though he had spent a wartime year at Harvard), and perhaps that he was far from convinced that the Soviet Union was a major threat to peace (though Moscow's repression of the Czech "spring" occurred soon after he took office). He was scornful of Canada's "helpful fixer" approach to the world, and he claimed to want to shape Canadian policy from national interests.[35]

In fact, what Trudeau wanted was an end to Canada's nuclear role, to get Canadian troops out of Europe, and to focus the Canadian public and policymakers on domestic concerns such as Quebec separatism. His efforts at reducing the NATO role came close to tearing his Cabinet apart in 1969. He and his ministers had examined all the options – among them, astonishingly and flying square in the face of geography, joining the non-aligned group of nations. Finally the government announced a re-ordering of defence priorities, with NATO ranked third behind the protection of national sovereignty, North American defence, and just ahead of peacekeeping.[36] Canada subsequently cut in half its

NATO forces in Europe and announced a phase-out of nuclear weapons. That was enough to gut the air force and to turn the brigade group, well capable of punching above its weight and a key part of the NATO line in northern Germany, into a weak reserve formation in the rear. A man who had little regard for the military in general, Trudeau also cut the Canadian Forces by 20 per cent to 80,000 and froze the defence budget at $1.8 billion; ironically, when terrorism erupted in Quebec in October 1970, the military performed well in securing a volatile situation.

Trudeau epitomized the growing feeling in Canada that the Cold War had lasted too long and had distorted national priorities. For two decades, Trudeau said, "Canada's foreign policy was largely its policy in NATO, through NATO."[37] That was no longer good enough. His government recognized China at last in 1970 and signed a Protocol on Consultations with Moscow, an agreement that Washington feared was a sign that Canada was sliding toward neutrality, a view shared by some in the Cabinet in Ottawa, which extraordinarily had not been consulted about the Protocol. As Trudeau put it in Moscow, "Canada has increasingly found it important to diversify its channels of communication because of the overpowering presence of the United States and that is reflected in a growing consciousness amongst Canadians of the danger to our national identity from a cultural, economic and perhaps even from a military point of view."[38] In Moscow, such rhetoric sounded different than it might have in Moosonee, but most Canadian nationalists loved it. So did the Russians. He visited Castro in Havana in 1973 and shouted "Viva Castro" to end one speech. He visited Beijing in 1973 and expounded on the wonderful system Mao had given his people. It was little wonder that some in Washington believed Trudeau a Communist sympathizer. Then in 1982 in a speech at Notre Dame University, Trudeau suggested that Canada was edging toward equidistance between the two superpowers, an astonishing comment from the leader of a nation almost wholly dependent for its defence and prosperity on the United States.[39] That was a mistake, Allan Gotlieb, the Ambassador to Washington who accompanied Trudeau to South Bend, wrote in his diary: "The Americans ... don't like the notion that they and the Soviets are equally responsible for world tensions" and, Gotlieb added, it offends the policymakers and the elites, "people we can't allow ourselves to alienate."[40]

The period of détente and the cooling of hostility between the West and the Communist world that Trudeau perhaps had some small part in fostering came to its end with the 1979 invasion of Afghanistan, the West's subsequent boycott of the Moscow Olympics in 1980, and the Soviets shooting down of a Korean airliner in 1983. Trudeau's response, his time in power coming to a close, was to launch a quixotic peace mission that saw him travel the globe urging the nuclear weapons powers to reduce their arsenals. The Reagan administration distrusted Trudeau and his efforts, and one official at the Canadian embassy in Washington said the Americans "hated" Trudeau's rhetoric that Canada was good, a peacemaker, and morally equidistant from the "naughty boys" with nuclear weapons. "A leftist high on pot," one senior Administration official said undiplomatically after Trudeau's visit to Washington on his quest.[41] Ambassador Gotlieb noted in his diary that Trudeau "is playing with other people's marbles."[42]

Nonetheless, Trudeau's pitch to Reagan was not ineffective. "You are a man of peace," he told the President in the Oval Office, "but your peace signals are not getting through." Yes, Reagan said, "The press has distorted my image ..."[43] There were some signs that presidential rhetoric cooled after Trudeau's visit, though no American officials believed Trudeau had anything to do with this. Overall, however, the peace mission had little effect. When asked about his impact some years later, however, Trudeau said with a characteristic shrug, "Well, there was no war."[44] That at least was so.

Arguably the most important formative role Trudeau played in easing tensions with Moscow was the friendship he developed with Alexander Yakovlev, Moscow's Ambassador to Canada. Urbane and intelligent, Yakovlev spent a decade in exile in Canada, punishment for his sins in calling for more effort to integrate Central Asian minorities into the USSR.[45] In May 1983, Yakovlev arranged a ten-day visit to study Canadian agriculture for Mikhail Gorbachev, a rising Central Committee member. It was his first trip to Canada and one of his few trips to the West, and Gorbachev reportedly was impressed by Canadian agricultural efficiency and, said one Cabinet minister who escorted him around, by the quantities of food in and the opulence of Canadian supermarkets.[46] Demonstrating that he was something different than the usual Politburo hack, Gorbachev even appeared before a joint meeting of a House of Commons and Senate Committee, a first anywhere. The Russian amiably sparred with the Canadian parliamentarians, parrying their criticisms with admissions that the Soviet Union was not perfect. None of the MPs and senators laid a glove on him.

Trudeau also had lunch and dinner with the visitor, observing later that Gorbachev was the first Soviet leader with whom one could have a freewheeling conversation.[47] The Canadian defended his own (very reluctant) decision to allow the US to test Cruise missiles over Canada and NATO's policy on the deployment of missiles in Europe to counter Moscow's SS-20 deployment. Trudeau told Gorbachev that, while he found President Reagan's rhetoric distasteful, it would be a mistake to believe that Reagan didn't reflect American public opinion. "Trudeau the hardliner," wrote Ambassador Gotlieb in Washington. "Go figure."[48] Gorbachev must have been puzzled that Trudeau had not behaved as his briefing notes portrayed him. Coming to power in 1985, the new Soviet leader brought his Ambassador to Canada back to Moscow and made Yakovlev, a proponent of *glasnost* (openness) and *perestroika* (restructuring), one of his key advisors as the Soviet Union began to change course.

The Cold War was not yet finished, however, but Trudeau was. He departed in 1984, the Canadian public cheering him to the echo for his still-born peace mission. There was not much reason to cheer, either for the short-term results or the long-term effects Trudeau had had. Arguably, his prime ministership – with almost sixteen years in power – almost put paid to Canada's American alliance. His quasi-neutralist attitudes had led the US to all but write off Canada as an ally. The formal alliance ties remained intact and the efforts by the Canadian Forces to increase interoperability with their American counterparts did not cease. But the sense that there had been a community of interests, that both nations shared a similar sense of the world and its dangers, was gone. To the US, to Margaret Thatcher's Britain, and to NATO, Trudeau's Canada had seemed to be heading towards neutralism.

Matters could still change, however. John Turner, Trudeau's lacklustre Liberal successor, lasted only months before losing an election. In charge now was the Progressive Conservative Brian Mulroney, an Irish Quebecker, smooth, charming, unabashedly pro-American, and desirous of "good relations, super relations" with Washington. Mulroney negotiated a Free Trade Agreement with the US and won an election on the issue in 1988. He had also promised to restore the Canadian Forces, its equipment increasingly obsolete, its budgets constrained, and there were pledges aplenty made to the public and to the Reagan Administration with which Canada shared responsibility for North American air defence. But huge budget deficits constrained government actions, there were initially cuts instead of increases for the military, and by the time a bright young Defence minister, Perrin Beatty, took over, the Cold War was drawing to an end. Beatty produced a Defence White Paper filled with sharp anti-Soviet language in 1987. *Challenge and Commitment* called for Canada to have a fleet of ten to twelve nuclear submarines ostensibly to protect Canadian sovereignty in the Arctic, where American, French, British and Soviet submarines roamed at will under the polar ice.[49] But would Canadian subs fire on the intruders? Would they try to sink the USN boats? The idea of Canadian nuclear subs, hugely expensive and sharply opposed by the Americans, who did not want to share their nuclear technology yet feared Canada might acquire French power plants, disappeared from the table as the Berlin Wall came down and the long Cold War drew to its end. So too did Canada's commitment to the defence of Western Europe. Without consulting their NATO allies, the Conservatives in 1992 announced a total withdrawal of Canadian forces from Europe, a process completed in July 1993 at a projected budgetary saving of $2.2 billion. Canada was now committed, but not present, insofar as NATO was concerned.

In fact, Canada had been committed but not psychologically present to the defence of Western Europe and indeed of North America for years. The peace dividend had been cashed in and spent since Trudeau's NATO cuts of 1969.

Three streams of opinion shaped Canada's Cold War: internationalism, continentalism, and nationalism. The diplomats and some of the politicians who took Canada into the Western alliance were internationalists who believed this was the way to foster a sane nationalism. They were aware, however, that Canada's economic prosperity and its defence ultimately depended on the United States, and the scarcity of US dollars and British economic weakness drove Canada southward. So too did Canadian businesses' desire for rich, easy-to-serve markets, and a shared North American view of the world. Canadian nationalism, exemplified by John Diefenbaker and especially Pierre Trudeau, however, looked on the costs of defence with a wary eye and resented the United States for the way it sometimes bullied the Dominion. Diefenbaker fought with President Kennedy and was toppled. Trudeau wanted a Canadian foreign policy that served the national interests and peace, but he never appeared to understand that Canada was attached physically, economically, and militarily to the US, and could not act as if it were an island. All Canadian leaders from Louis St. Laurent on focussed on peacekeeping, which sometimes served the interests of the Western alliance. But peacekeeping, because it alone was popular with the public and came to form a key component of Canadian nationalism, ultimately put paid to the nation's psychological participation in the Cold War, long before its end in Soviet collapse.

Curiously, however, it was continentalism that achieved dominance among the competing Canadian ideologies. By the end of the Cold War, a free trade agreement with the United States was in place, a huge proportion of Canadian trade went south, and US corporations operated everywhere in Canada. That anti-Americanism was the key component of Canadian nationalism could not hide the reality of almost complete integration; nor could Canadian internationalism, strong among youth and NGOs, dispel the fact that Canada from the 1960s to the turn of the century received scant regard from its friends abroad and none from its enemies. Canadians had forgotten that reliability in foreign policy and the ability to deploy force when necessary both mattered. They had even forgotten that the ability to defend their own people and territory is the essential national interest for every nation-state. National interests have always mattered, and they still do.

NOTES

1 L.B. Pearson, *Words and Occasions* (Toronto, 1970), pp. 72, 75. The fullest new account of postwar Canadian foreign policy is Robert Bothwell, *Alliance and Illusion: Canada and the World, 1945–1984* (Vancouver, 2007).
2 L.B. Pearson, *Diplomacy in a Nuclear Age* (Cambridge, MA, 1959), p. 53.
3 See J.L. Granatstein, *How Britain's Weakness Forced Canada into the Arms of the United States* (Toronto, 1989), Chapter 2.
4 The best study is Amy Knight, *How the Cold War Began* (Toronto, 2005).
5 R. Whitaker and G. Marcuse, *Canada: The Making of a National Insecurity State 1945–1957* (Toronto, 1994), passim.
6 See J. Barros, *No Sense of Evil: Espionage, the Case of Herbert Norman* (Ottawa, 1986), and R. Bowen, *Innocence Is Not Enough* (Vancouver, 1986).
7 Gary Kinsman and Patrizia Gentle, *The Canadian War on Queers: National Security as Sexual Regulation* (Vancouver, 2010), esp. Chapter 3.
8 See Adam Chapnick, *Canada's Voice: The Public Life of John Wendell Holmes* (Vancouver, 2010).
9 A largely contrarian view can be found in Reg Whitaker and S. Hewitt, *Canada and the Cold War* (Halifax, 2003).
10 Gregor Dallas, *Poisoned Peace: 1945 – The War That Never Ended* (London, 2006), p. 576.
11 R.D. Cuff and J.L. Granatstein, *American Dollars – Canadian Prosperity* (Toronto, 1978), p. 28.
12 Ibid., p. 203
13 Ibid., p. 135. Canada declined to participate in the Berlin Airlift, arguing that this would be incompatible with its Security Council membership. See *Documents on Canadian External Relations* [DCER], Vol. XIV: *1948*, Chapter 5, www.dfait-maeci.gc.ca/department/history/dcer.

14 Department of External Affairs, Records, file 264(s), Wrong to Secretary of State for External Affairs, 26 September 1947. These documents were examined at the Pearson Building but are now in Library and Archives Canada.
15 *DCER*, Vol. XIII, document 243, Wrong addendum to Hume Wright, "Influences Shaping the Policy of the United States to the Soviet Union," 4 December 1947, att. to Wrong to Pearson, 5 December 1947, www.dfait-maeci.gc.ca/department/history/dcer.
16 Quoted in Escott Reid, *Time of Fear and Hope* (Toronto, 1977), p. 132.
17 J.L. Granatstein, *A Man of Influence: Norman Robertson and Canadian Statecraft 1929–1968* (Ottawa, 1981), pp. 236–7.
18 L.B. Pearson, *Mike*, Vol. II: *1948–1957* (Toronto, 1973), pp. 55–6.
19 Ibid., p. 56; Dean Acheson, *Present at the Creation* (New York, 1969), p. 277. The best work on Canadian diplomacy during the Korean War remains Denis Stairs, *The Diplomacy of Constraint* (Toronto, 1972).
20 A good history of the NATO brigade is Sean Maloney, *War Without Battles: Canada's NATO Brigade in Germany 1951–1993* (Toronto, 1997).
21 Cuff and Granatstein, p. 224
22 Queen's University Archives, Grant Dexter Papers, memo, 22 February 1951.
23 Department of External Affairs Records, file 2-AE(s), Pearson to Wrong, 21 May 1948. This file is now at LAC.
24 John English, *The Worldly Years: The Life of Lester Pearson 1949–1972* (Toronto, 1992), p. 59.
25 Neil James in *Defender* [Australia Defence Association] (Summer 2006–7), p. 40.
26 The best study is Douglas Ross, *In the Interests of Peace: Canada and Vietnam 1954–73* (Toronto, 1984). See also Shane B. Schreiber, "The Road to Hell: Canada in Viet Nam 1954–1973," *Canadian Army Journal* (Spring 2007).
27 English, pp. 98ff.
28 Ibid., Chapter 4; Granatstein, *Man of Influence,* Chapter 10. For peacekeeping as part of the Cold War, see Sean Maloney, *Canada and UN Peacekeeping: Cold War by Other Means, 1945–1970* (St. Catharines, 2002).
29 The Cabinet minutes in *DCER*, Vol. XXVI (1959), Chapter 4, www.dfait-maeci.gc.ca/department/history/dcer, leave no doubt of the decision to go nuclear.
30 See J.L. Granatstein, *Canada 1957–1967* (Toronto, 1986), Chapter 5.
31 Ibid. See also Denis Smith, *Rogue Tory* (Toronto, 1995), Chapter 12. Cf. Diefenbaker's memoirs, *One Canada*, 3 vols. (Toronto, 1975–7), esp. vol. III.
32 English, pp. 362ff.
33 Paul Hellyer, *Damn the Torpedoes: My Fight to Unify Canada's Armed Forces* (Toronto, 1990), p. 65.
34 English, pp. 263ff., 336.

35 *Foreign Policy for Canadians*, a six-pack of policy pamphlets, appeared in June 1970. They rejected the helpful fixer role, made economic growth the focus of foreign policy, along with social justice and quality of life. See J.L. Granatstein and Robert Bothwell, *Pirouette: Pierre Trudeau and Canadian Foreign Policy* (Toronto, 1990), pp. 32–3.
36 Ibid., p. 25.
37 Ibid., p. 8.
38 Ibid., p. 195.
39 Prime Minister's Office, Ottawa, Transcript of Remarks at Notre Dame University, 16 May 1982.
40 Allan Gotlieb, *The Washington Diaries* (Toronto, 2006), p. 61.
41 Patrick Gossage, *Close to the Charisma* (Toronto, 1986), p. 260.
42 Gotlieb, p. 180.
43 Ibid., pp. 190–1. The Canadian press in Washington were unhappy that Trudeau hadn't attacked Reagan. "I have no sympathy with this posse," said Gotlieb. "Their problem is that they are anti-American ... All they want to hear is that Trudeau dumped on Reagan." Ibid., p. 192.
44 Author interview with Pierre Trudeau, Montreal, 30 June 1988.
45 On Yakovlev, see Christopher Shulgan, *The Soviet Ambassador* (Toronto, 2008), and John English, *Just Watch Me: The Life of Pierre Elliott Trudeau 1968–2000* (Toronto, 2009), pp. 205, 469–70, 589–90.
46 Eugene Whelan and R. Archbold, *Whelan: The Man in the Green Stetson* (Toronto, 1986).
47 Trudeau interview.
48 Gotlieb, p. 159.
49 Ambassador Gotlieb supported the idea of nuclear subs: they would end Canada's nuclear virginity and the situation where the US protected Canada's Arctic. Ibid., p. 479.

Chapter Nineteen

Multiculturalism and Canadian Foreign Policy

Let me begin this chapter with two quotations that suggest the problematic relationship of multiculturalism and Canadian foreign policy. The first is by the Toronto journalist Zuhair Kashmeri, who published *The Gulf Within: Canadian Arabs, Racism and the Gulf War* in 1991. Kashmeri argued that Canada had failed to consider "the views of its large Arab and Muslim communities before it decided to join the US-sponsored coalition in the Gulf." Such action was simply unacceptable to him, and he then quoted the views of a Reverend Tad Mitsui of the United Church of Canada, who saw "race involved in judging who is an enemy and who is a friend. For example, Canadians will never think of America as an enemy, and neither can they think of British or the French as enemies ... But it is so easy to think of Arabs as the enemy. I think this is not fair." Mitsui goes on: "Why can't Pakistan be our friend no matter what? Why can't Iraq ...? And if you expand that logic, if Canada should exist as a multicultural, multiracial country, you cannot take sides with anybody." Kashmeri picks this up to argue that "Since multiculturalism advocates celebrating the differences, allowing the traditions and cultures to co-exist, the extension of that policy in foreign policy is a stance of neutrality."[1]

The second quotation comes almost fifteen years later from the political columnist John Ibbitson of the *Globe and Mail*, who wrote in August 2005 about Canada's new governor general, Mme. Michaëlle Jean. At her press conference the day she was named, the governor general designate spoke about the situation in Haiti, where she was born. Ibbitson wrote that her words were important: "reflecting a subtle but profound shift in recent Canadian foreign policy priorities, the tsunami of last year, the chaos in Haiti, the exploding troubles in Sudan are not foreign-*aid* issues for Canada, they are foreign-*policy* priorities. They reflect our demographic transformation, from predominantly European to truly multinational. Problems in India and China and Haiti are *our* problems because India and China and Haiti are *our* motherlands"[2] (emphasis in original).

Both these quotes, fifteen years apart, in my view reflect a fundamental misunderstanding of the roots and sources of a nation's foreign policy. Both are advocating policies of the heart, not policies of the head. They are values-oriented, not founded on national interests. Foreign policy is not about loving everyone or even helping everyone. It is not about saying a nation cannot do anything or cannot go to war, for example, for fear of offending some group within the country. It cannot be about doing something only to satisfy one or another group's ties to its mother country. Foreign policy instead must spring from the fundamental bases of a state – its geographical location, its history, its form of government, its economic imperatives, its alliances, and yes, of course, its people. In other words, national interests are and must be key.

No nation like Canada can do what its citizens of Sri Lankan or Pakistani or Somalian or Jewish or Muslim or Ukrainian origin want – all the time. No nation like Canada can do what its provinces, or founding peoples, or some of them may want – all the time. A nation must do what its national interests determine it must. And that requires that a nation like Canada know what its national interests are.

Canadian national interests, while difficult to prioritize and harder still to put into effect, are not very difficult to state:

1 Canada must protect its territory and the security of its people;
2 Canada must strive to maintain its unity;
3 Canada must protect and enhance its independence;
4 Canada must promote the economic growth of the nation to support the prosperity and welfare of its people;
5 Canada should work with like-minded states for the protection and enhancement of democracy and freedom.

These are very easy to list, but they can and do fluctuate in importance from time to time. In wartime, national interest 1 might be supreme, but at the time of the Quebec referendums in 1980 and 1995, 2 might have been at the top of the list. The key point, however, is that the five national interests are all important all the time, though with varying weight.

The first four interests are unquestionably our domestic goals and are what any nation must do. The foremost goal, the basic task as acknowledged by the government, is to secure and protect the Canadian people and their territory. Unity is a key interest but is difficult to achieve, as

Canadian history amply confirms. Nothing we do should tear us apart, but at the same time we must be careful lest *not* doing something strain the polity. Maintaining unity is the test for any and every government, and we judge our prime ministers by their success in this area. Sir Robert Borden, for example, has frequently been judged a failure for his inability to hold the country together during the Great War, while Mackenzie King has earned kudos from historians for his successes in the Second World War.[3]

The third national interest, protecting Canada's independence, demands that the nation strive to resist the pull of the United States, the only nation that threatens our independence – in a benign way, thus far in the twentieth and twenty-first centuries – through the attractiveness of its culture and institutions and the power of its corporations. This is very hard to do, primarily because the next interest, the fourth, is most easily met if we work with the United States. The US takes more than 85 per cent of our trade today and sustains 52 per cent of our gross domestic product. The United States, moreover, is where we draw our foreign investment from and where most Canadian foreign investment goes. There is simply no other market on which we can depend and none – neither China nor India nor Europe nor Latin America – to which we can look with any confidence as a replacement for the foreseeable future. Thus we must balance the need to be independent with the need to be able to live and prosper.

Finally, the last national interest is based on our history and institutions. We have always fought for freedom and democracy, for our friends and allies, when we chose to do so. *When we chose to do so.* We did our part in the war against the Nazi Germany and during the Cold War because Canadians believed it – correctly – in our national interest to do so. Stopping oligarchies and advancing freedom and democracy remain goals for Canada, and the government recognizes that Canada is not a great power, that it cannot save the world by itself. We need alliances of the like-minded, and Canadians have sought for this. The last of our national interests reflects this necessity.

Canadian Values

Sometimes, the Canadian people's desire to press their values overrides their good sense to the point that we seem to believe Canada to be the moral superpower of the world. We want equality at home and abroad. We want freedom of religion for all. We believe in human rights, the rule of law, good governance, and a long list of additional virtuous values. These are important, but we have not gone to war for such things. Canada is unlikely to wage a war for gender equality, however important it is. Moreover, our values can and do change, and some of the values Canadians trumpet today are fairly new – gender equality, multiculturalism, and respect for diversity. But our national interests are long-lived. Canada might go to war, Canada has fought wars, to protect its national interests.

But we have gone to war for ethnicity, too. Let us be honest enough to admit that in 1914, the Canadian war effort was shaped by the British connection, not by national interests, at least not initially. Yes, Canada was a colony and thus bound by the British declaration of war. But the size of the Canadian war effort was shaped by the government's and the English-speaking Canadian public's desire to be British, to be part of the Empire, and to accept the burdens and glory of a British war. In the Second World War, Canada was no longer a colony; after the Statute of Westminster (1931), Canada was independent in its foreign policy, but we used this power only to wait one week after Britain went to war on 3 September 1939, before we too plunged in. Were Canada's national interests threatened in 1939? The United States next door certainly did not think its interests were, nor did any other independent state in the Western Hemisphere. Was Canadian unity not endangered by the war? Of course, it was. Canadians went to war in 1939 because Britain did, because English-speaking Canadians wanted to support the Mother Country. Few cared what Quebec thought or wanted.

Certainly Prime Minister King handled the strains far better than Borden had a quarter-century before, and King's government constructed a vast war effort that did its full share in defeating the monstrous Nazi regime. No one should doubt that Canadian national interests were ultimately threatened in the 1939–45 war. On the other hand, every Canadian historian knows that French Canada's version of the events of 1939–45 is far different and that the Second World War goes into the long list of issues on which English Canada forced its will on Quebec against the desires of its people. Opinion polls during the war made clear that Quebec took a different view of the war than did English-speaking Canadians, and not just on the subject of military conscription. But conscription is an important measure – the 1942 plebiscite, for example, showed huge support in English Canada for freeing the government's hands to deploy conscripts abroad, while Quebec showed equally high numbers against. Indeed francophones all across the country voted "no" in very large numbers. Almost always forgotten is that other ethnic groups such as the German- and Ukrainian-Canadians also voted heavily "no."[4] The Second World War, like the Great War, was in Canadian terms a British ethnic war in which everyone else was dragged along.

But Canada grew up as a nation and began to recognize its own national interests. In August 1940, alter Dunkirk and the fall of France, Canada struck its first defence arrangement with the United States because Canadians recognized that Britain could no longer be counted on to defend them. They continued their defence relations with the United States after 1945 because of the threat posed by the Soviet Union. Canada went into the North Atlantic Treaty in 1949, into Korea in 1950, and into the North American Air Defense Command in 1957–8 for the same reason. Canada's national interests were to the fore. Ethnicity seemed to be very secondary. But it wasn't, or at least not for very long. And certainly not among Canada's ethnic groups.

There are many examples in the recent past. Sikhs based in British Columbia blew up an airliner in the late 1980s to express their support for an independent Khalistan in the Indian subcontinent. This mass murder was plotted by Canadians on Canadian soil. It stands as a cautionary tale about the importation of a homeland conflict to Canada and of the utter inability of the Canadian Government to respond before terror struck or to resolve the matter in the courts after the fact. Similarly, Canadian Sri Lankans continue to raise money for the Tamil Tigers, a terrorist group – and succeeded a few years ago in getting the then-finance minister of Canada to attend a fundraising dinner in Toronto.

Then during the collapse of former Yugoslavia into warring ethnicities, Serb- and Croat-Canadians got into scuffles on the streets of Toronto, raised funds for the Old Country, and many returned to Serbia or Croatia to lend their political and military muscle to the struggle. One Serb-Canadian was sentenced to three years in jail in September 2005 for taking United Nations personnel – including Canadians – hostage in Serbia in May 1995. Clearly Canada had failed to integrate these people into its nationality.

Carol Off, in her book *The Ghosts of Medak Pocket*,[5] wrote of the quarter-million Croats who arrived in Canada from the 1960s on. "Their continuing identity as Croats was powerful – and much encouraged by the Canadian government," she said. "In 1971 Canada declared itself officially multicultural; and Ottawa began to offer millions of dollars to ethnic communities in Canada to preserve their immigrant identities, a well-meaning policy that unfortunately exacerbated the problem of the angry émigrés who weren't even trying to fit into the society of their adopted country." That was, of course, true for more than Croats. The government, Off goes on, funded language schools and folklore centres and also, as it turned out, publications disseminating radical right-wing messages. What Ottawa did not do was try to make Canadians out of them.

Off continues by noting the pro-Nazi Ustase connections among Canadian Croats, and the fact that the very idea of a Croatian state, including part of Bosnia, was born at the Norval Community Centre, set up by Croatian-Canadians not far from Toronto. This Centre became the heart of Gojko Susak territory.

An Ottawa restaurant owner and house painter when Franjo Tudjman took over the Government of Croatia in 1990, Susak heeded his leader's call for the Croatian diaspora to come home. He quickly became an extremist and provocateur, literally firing what Off calls "the first shot" in the Croatian war for independence. Soon, he was Croatia's defence minister. He used his connections in Canada to raise money for Croatia, up to $200 million, Off suggests, for weapons and aid.[6] Susak eventually presided over the "ethnic cleansing" of Serbs in the Medak Pocket – where Canadian soldiers, trying to prevent the slaughter of Serbs, killed Croats in a large pitched battle. It is fair to say that Susak was a war criminal, and if he had not died before the International Criminal Court was set up he would almost certainly have been tried.

The point of the Croatian events in this context is that Canada failed to turn Susak into a Canadian. He had arrived here in 1969 and lived in Canada for more than two decades, but his allegiance was to Croatia first, last, and always. Was he any different than the Sikh terrorists? The Tamils? Or the other ethnic Canadians who send money for political purposes, or for guns, to their homelands? Why has Canada failed? Why does the link of "blood and soil" remain so strong? Why don't the people who live here give their first allegiance to Canada's national interests?

In early 1939, a young civil servant, Norman A. Robertson of the Department of External Affairs, was given the task of working out what was to be done about German pro-Nazi Bundists and Italian Fascisti groups in Canada in the event of war. Robertson proposed that the government make full use of the law to block the import of seditious, disloyal, or scurrilous propaganda. He urged the government to refrain from any administrative encouragement by stopping advertising, for example, in suspect newspapers. He called for tax audits of suspected Nazis and Fascists and Royal Canadian Mounted Police investigations of applicants for naturalization. In other words, Robertson wanted to use the resources of the state to control propaganda.[7]

Robertson could be tough, but he knew that toughness was not enough. He wanted to integrate immigrants and to make them into

Canadians. He recommended English classes for newcomers, the assistance of social workers, legal aid, access to medical care, the use of the CBC and NFB, taking immigrants into political parties, and the enlistment of churches and other groups into making all who came here Canadians. His goal, he said, was "a positive affirmation of the concept of Canadian Citizenship based on loyalty & domicile and a repudiation of 'blood & soil.'"[8] Robertson was right, but unfortunately he was largely ignored.

Multiculturalism

Sixty-five years later we have still not done as Robertson suggested, or not done it very well. The result, for example, is that a Canadian becomes defence minister in Croatia. The result is that Canadian Jews pressed Prime Minister Joe Clark to promise to move the Canadian Embassy in Israel from Tel Aviv to Jerusalem, no matter whether it made sense there or not. The result is that Canadian Jews in 2004 urged Prime Minister Paul Martin's government to "tilt" toward Israel. Canadian Muslims, naturally enough, argue the reverse.[9] Canadian Ukrainians encouraged Brian Mulroney's government to take the lead in supporting an independent Ukraine, just as those from the Baltic states did for their former homelands.

These things may be right or wrong in and of themselves; some of them unquestionably are right. They ought only to be Canadian policy, however, if they meet the test of Canada's national interests. They are not good foreign policy if they are done only to win support from the "padrones" of the ethnic groups who are supposed to be able to deliver votes during Canadian elections.

Even those who do not usually agree with Naomi Klein will recognize that she was surely right when she wrote in summer 2005 after the terrorist attacks in London "that the brand of multiculturalism practiced in Britain (and France, Germany, Canada ...) has little to do with genuine equality. It is instead a Faustian bargain, struck between vote-seeking politicians and self-appointed community leaders, one that keeps ethnic minorities tucked away in state-funded peripheral ghettoes while the centres of public life remain largely unaffected by seismic shifts in the national ethnic makeup."[10] Mme. Jean, if we can trust quotes from her life before Rideau Hall, shares this view of multicultural ghettoization.

Canada needs and wants immigrants, and most of us believe that the influx of people from all over the world is good for the country. But we must make Canadians of those who come here. Experiences in Holland and Britain and elsewhere suggest that it is not enough to leave immigrants alone and let them become adapted or not as they choose. We need to make clear to those we choose to admit to Canada that we are a nation with national interests, that we are a formed society with values, and if they wish to join us, they must understand this. That is what Canadians want: a Strategic Counsel poll in August 2005 showed 69 per cent wanting immigrants to integrate into Canada and only 20 per cent saying that immigrants should maintain their own identity and culture.[11] Canadians want immigrants to understand that Canada is part of Western Civilization with all its values; that we are not a community of ethnic, linguistic, regional, and religious groups, but a nation. Women must have equal rights, and religion does not and cannot rule. Canada is a secular, pluralist, democratic nation.

Yes, Canadians want to be multicultural and to let all flourish here, but at the same time the government and people absolutely must stress that it is a requirement that immigrants come to accept the values of our society, the values of Western Civilization, the values of Canada, which surely are broad enough to accommodate a wide range of behaviours. Canadians somehow do not even realize that to not do this causes a problem, and we tell ourselves that Canadian multiculturalism is far more successful than British or Dutch multiculturalism. We couldn't have filmmakers assassinated on the street for making the films they choose; we couldn't have subway bombings, or so we say. But there is no evidence whatsoever to suggest that Canada's multiculturalism is any better at integrating immigrant groups than the British or Dutch models.[12]

To paraphrase David Rieff (the word "Europe" and its derivatives have been replaced here by "Canada" and its derivatives): the multicultural fantasy in Canada was that, in due course, assuming that the proper resources were committed and benevolence deployed, Islamic and other immigrants would eventually become liberals. As it's said, they would come to "accept" the values of their new countries. It was never clear how this vision was supposed to coexist with multiculturalism's other main assumption, which was that group identity should be maintained. But by now that question is largely academic: the Canadian vision of multiculturalism, in all its simultaneous good will and self-congratulation, is no longer sustainable. And most Canadians know it. What they don't know is what to do next.[13]

Most Canadians recognize that, if we can make multiculturalism work, if our citizens from every origin can accept Canada's values and add their own traditions to them – over time – and become integrated into the polity, then Canada can gain a huge advantage in trade, foreign policy, and even defence. But to make this work Canada needs its leaders to lead, to speak the truth, and to help integrate those who come to join our society. Among other things, that means not pandering for votes by twisting Canadian foreign policy.

Quebec and Foreign Policy

Now let me turn to another aspect of Canadian ethnicity. If British-Canadians shaped foreign policy questions in World Wars I and II, French-speaking Canadians have largely shaped our defence and foreign policies since Pierre Trudeau became prime minister in 1968. There is no doubt – according to opinion polls – that Quebec attitudes to the military and defence spending and to war are very different than those of English-speaking Canadians; moreover, francophone attitudes to imperialism (historically British, and now American) are much cooler. A recent paper by Jean-Sebastian Rioux for the Canadian Defence and Foreign Affairs Institute makes this clear.[14] Canada has had a string of long-lived prime ministers of Quebec origin – Trudeau, Mulroney, and Chrétien – all of whom were exquisitely cognizant of these attitudes and, of course, all too aware of the *indépendantiste* attitudes in Quebec, ebbing and rising with events and the years. If it is bad policy to let Canadian Jews or Muslims have undue influence on policy to Israel, it is similarly bad policy to let Quebec, or any one province, determine Canadian defence and foreign policy.

Is it too strong to say that Quebec has determined policy? Quebec opinion, if we believe the present leaders of the Bloc Québécois and the Parti Québécois, is pacifist. If we accept the argument made by Stéphane Roussel and Charles-Alexandre Theoret, it is motivated by Pearsonian internationalism in that it supports the United Nations, peace, development, and international law.[15] My instinct is to believe the politicians, not least because Pearsonian-style internationalism, while it believed in all the good things noted above, also took Canada into NATO and the Korean War, not only into UN peacekeeping operations. Pearson had been a soldier in the Great War, a diplomat in the Second World War, and a Cold War protagonist. He was no pacifist, his Nobel Peace Prize notwithstanding.

To me, the decision to stay out of the Iraq War in 2003 was almost certainly shaped by Quebec's anti-military and anti-imperialist (or anti-American) views. These were reflected in the overwhelmingly negative attitudes toward the war in opinion polls in Quebec and by the coincidence of the provincial election (where all three leaders wore anti-war ribbons during the leaders' debate on television). Prime

Minister Chrétien saw this – and he heard anti-war attitudes expressed in his own Quebec caucus, from the Bloc Québécois, and also the very anglo-Canadian NDP. The decision by Paul Martin's government to refuse to join the United States in Ballistic Missile Defence early in 2005 again was shaped by overwhelmingly hostile Quebec opinion poll numbers, the same forces in the House of Commons, and by the Liberals' minority government situation. The prospect of winning seats in Quebec, ultimately frustrated for Martin in the January 2006 election, largely drove the issue.

There were good arguments for supporting the United States in Iraq and joining in BMD. The best reasons were based on Canadian national interests. Canada's economy depends on trade with the US, and that is unlikely to change. If Washington being unhappy with us impedes trade, for example, if border crossings are slowed for even a few minutes more for each truck, or if passports are required to cross the border, that will have huge impact on us. In my opinion, the economy, one of Canada's key national interests, ought to have determined those issues for us.

But what of national unity, another of Canada's interests? This is difficult, and there is no doubt that initially on both Iraq and BMD Quebec was of a very different mind than the rest of Canada. Professor David Haglund in fact called Quebec opinion on BMD "unanimity, with near total agreement that missile defence must be bad."[16] The key point, however, is that in neither the Iraq nor the BMD case was there any leadership from Ottawa to try to persuade Quebecers that the economy, their jobs, and their pocketbooks might actually matter more than whether or not Canada supported the US in Iraq or joined it in missile defence. The latter case is strikingly clear – Prime Minister Martin had indicated early on that he supported BMD, but once he saw the opinion poll numbers, once the NDP (a strong anti-war voice in English Canada) and some in the Liberal caucus began a vigorous opposition, he backed away. The BMD issue was decided by a lack of leadership.

It is bad for Canadian unity to have Quebec driving the agenda on Iraq or BMD.[17] On both issues, the poll numbers were initially supportive in English-speaking Canada; on Iraq, there was at one point more than a thirty point difference between Alberta and Quebec on support for the war. Trying to give Quebec, or any other single province, what it wants can hurt the country; trying to follow clear national interests might help keep it together – if we have prime ministers who are willing to educate, explain, and lead – in Alberta and in Quebec.

Leadership actually can be exercised by politicians on sensitive foreign policy issues. Take the example of Louis St. Laurent, prime minister from 1948 to 1957. St. Laurent took Canada into NATO, into the Korean War, and he raised defence expenditures to more than 7 per cent of gross domestic product in the mid-1950s. He spoke of these things in Quebec, and he did so while memories of the wartime conscription crises were still very fresh. He toured the service clubs and business groups, and he made the case that Canada was threatened by the Soviet Union and needed to re-arm and to work with its allies. Opinion polls showed that Quebec remained opposed to sending troops to Korea or to NATO, that Quebec opposed any idea of peacetime conscription, and that the province was not especially happy with high defence spending. There were even great difficulties in recruiting enough francophones to man the battalions of the Royal 22ᵉ Régiment fighting in Korea. Nevertheless, Quebecers still voted for St. Laurent: in the three elections he fought (1949, 1953, and 1957) he swept Quebec every time.[18] Why? Because he led. Because he didn't try to shape policy by opinion polls. Because he explained why he was acting, told people what was necessary, and won their acquiescence, if not their wholehearted support. This was leadership. It was also a recognition of the country's national interests and a willingness to make sure people understood them and why they were important. A prime minister needs to talk national interests to Quebec – and to all Canada – and tell the same story from Montreal to Vancouver.

Understanding what our national interests are is the way to make foreign policy, a better way than pandering to opinion polls and ethnic pols, a better way than – *pace* Ibbitson – looking for new motherlands. We have only one motherland now: Canada. Our foreign policy must be based on what is important to Canadians as a whole, not to Canadians wearing only their Old Country/ethnicity/religious hat. Anything else is a recipe for fragmentation, division, and discord.

It may be entirely appropriate that Canada, as Zuhair Kashmeri would prefer, be neutral in all or almost all wars. But not on the grounds he suggested: that a multicultural nation cannot go to war. Neutrality is an option – but only if it serves our national interests. Advancing democracy and freedom and cooperation with our friends – that should be the test, along with the impact of neutrality on the remainder of our interests.

Conclusions

Canadians should care for and about the world and be idealistic. They want to help in tsunami and hurricane relief and to help clean up Port-au-Prince. But such things are not national interests, however; they are issues that test our values. They are important, but they are not, for

Canada as a nation-state, life-or-death issues. These are the national interests: security, unity, economics, democracy, and freedom. It will help greatly if Canadians and their leaders can make the distinction.

This chapter began with two foolish quotes from journalists. It is therefore appropriate to end with the ordinarily sensible James Travers of the *Toronto Star*, writing in mid-July 2005: "Paul Martin's government ... must send a zero-tolerance message to those who bring to a new country the troubles that make it so attractive to leave an old one. This isn't racism or cultural insensitivity. It is a categorical rejection of bombs, guns and hatreds as legitimate expressions of political will."[19]

It will also help greatly if our leaders can focus on the aspects of foreign policy that are important to the nation as a whole and stop playing to the ethnicities that make up our population. Prime ministers must lead nationally. Look after the nation's interests first and its values second. Think for more than the present moment. Lead.

NOTES

1 Zuhair Kashmeri, *The Gulf Within: Canadian Arabs, Racism and the Gulf War* (Toronto, 1991), 126ff.
2 "She Is the New Canada," *Globe and Mail*, 5 August 2005.
3 See the accounts in J.L. Granatstein and Norman Hillmer, *Prime Ministers: Ranking Canada's Leaders* (Toronto, 1999).
4 See J.L. Granatstein and J.M. Hitsman, *Broken Promises: A History of Conscription in Canada* (Toronto, 1977).
5 J.L. Granatstein, *Who Killed the Canadian Military?* (Toronto, 2004), chapter 1.
6 Ibid., 48ff.
7 I suspect that in the 1980s and 1990s governments and political parties advertised in the Canadian Croatian (and Serbian, Bosnian, Slovenian, and Montenegrin) newspapers that called for slaughtering their overseas neighbours.
8 J.L. Granatstein, *A Man of Influence: Norman A. Robertson and Canadian Statecraft, 1929–68* (Ottawa, 1981), 82ff.
9 E.g., John Ivison, "'Pro-Israel' Federal Advisor Must Go, Elmasry Says," *National Post*, 17 August 2005.
10 "Terror's Greatest Recruiting Tool," *The Nation*, 29 August 2005.
11 "Canadian Attitudes Harden on Immigration," *Globe and Mail*, 12 August 2005. Similar results can be found in a Dominion Institute/CDFAI/Innovative Research Group poll. See *Ottawa Citizen*, 31 October 2005.

12 I will say, however, that the young – those who have gone through our public school systems – seem remarkably colour-blind and tolerant of diversity. Whether that applies to those educated in madrassas, Hebrew schools, and Christian fundamentalist schools, I do not know.
13 *New York Times Magazine*, 14 August 2005, "An Islamic Alienation."
14 "Two Solitudes: Quebecers' Attitudes Regarding Canadian Security and Defence Policy," Calgary: CDFAI, 2005.
15 See *The World in Canada: Diaspora, Demography, and Domestic Politics*, ed. David Carment and David Bercuson (Montreal: McGill-Queen's University Press, 2008); but perhaps Roussel and Théoret need a different descriptor for Quebec.
16 David Haglund, "Does Quebec Have an 'Obsession Anti-Américaine'?," unpublished paper, 2005.
17 It is also bad for sovereignists to have Quebec so anti-American that it is bound to make the US even more concerned than it might otherwise be should Quebec ever succeed in separating from Canada. Somehow this fact does not appear to enter the debate in Quebec.
18 See Granatstein, *Who Killed the Canadian Military?*, 109–11.
19 "Underscoring a Message of Zero Tolerance," *Toronto Star*, 14 July 2005.

Chapter Twenty

Can Canada Have a Grand Strategy?

Great Powers can have Grand Strategies. Alliances can have Grand Strategies. This we know. In June 1940, Britain and its Commonwealth-Empire was left to fight against a triumphant Germany singlehanded and thus devoted all its military, industrial, diplomatic, and financial resources to the survival of its home base and some key strategic outposts while trying to persuade the United States into the war, an aim achieved in December 1941. This was Grand Strategy, and it succeeded. And after Pearl Harbor, Britain and the United States decided to defeat Hitler first before concentrating their power against Japan. Germany directly threatened Britain and the Soviet Union, and its military and industrial power far exceeded that of Imperial Japan, which could be fended off with subsidiary forces. This Grand Strategy was successful.

Then, after the war, as the Soviet Union became a threat, the US and its allies followed a Grand Strategy of containment, mobilizing alliances and resources to prevent Moscow from extending its control into Western Europe and the parts of Asia and Africa into which its reach did not extend. This Grand Strategy also succeeded four decades later in bringing down the USSR, a signal victory without a general war (though there were still limited wars with terrible costs) and a demonstration that skillfully wielded economic and military power can destroy an empire. Thus, there can be no doubt that Grand Strategies can be derived, followed, and be successful – by Great Powers or great alliances.

Similarly as we watch the United States lurch and stagger about in the Middle East and North Africa today, the absence of a credible Grand Strategy can lead to the loss of allies and, perhaps, the triumph of enemies. To be successful, therefore, a Grand Strategy must be clear and potent enough to sustain itself in the face of setbacks and be seen as such by those small nations that seek shelter in a Great Power alliance. In other words, Grand Strategies can fail or turn out to be not so grand.

But can a small or middle power have a Grand Strategy? Former diplomat Daryl Copeland defined Grand Strategy as "a unifying, long-term vision of a country's global values and interests; an expression of where the country is, and where it wants to go in the world; and an analysis of its potential and capacity to achieve its objective. I consider it a core element of statecraft." That sounds difficult to derive for most nation-states, but to me it does not sound like Grand Strategy, at least not for smaller powers.

Smaller countries can fight wars against other smaller powers or manoeuvre to avoid them. They can join Great Power alliances or not. They can follow particular economic policies or decide not to. But – and here I disagree with the able former Defence minister David Pratt in his Ellis Lectures at the University of Calgary – they do not have Grand Strategies because they lack the human, industrial, and military resources to sustain them. In other words, the God of Grand Strategy is only found on the side of the big battalions.

But small countries do have, like every other state, national interests, and their policies are (or should be) focussed on advancing or protecting these interests and on their national survival. For example, Canada has in the past skilfully balanced the aims of Britain and the United States against each other in an effort to keep Britain interested enough in the Dominion to prevent it being swallowed by the United States. This worked so long as Britain had military, economic, and diplomatic power, but by the summer of 1940, as Britain lay naked before the Nazis, Canada in the interest of its own survival had no option but to scramble to tie its defences to those of the US and the next year to integrate its war economy with that of its neighbour. If balance in the North Atlantic Triangle had been a Grand Strategy, by 1940 it was a strategy in shreds. The psychological impact of this failed Grand Strategy, if that is what it was, might be seen in the bitter writings of Canadian Tory nationalists like historians Donald Creighton and W.L. Morton.

Canada then tried in the postwar years to keep Britain and Europe alive as a counterweight to overweening American power. The creation of NATO and the successful Canadian effort to get Article 2 into the Treaty mark the high-water line of this effort. Canada certainly was present at the creation, and Ottawa mattered more in the years from 1947 to 1949 than it ever has before or since in peacetime. But Britain and Europe remained weak into the 1950s, the US grew ever stronger, and Canada, not for want of effort, essentially found itself left as the junior partner in a bipolar relationship. NATO had its moments in the next fifty years, but its members' performance in Former Yugoslavia, in Afghanistan, and now in Libya do not suggest that it can be relied on as a prop of Canadian foreign policy, let alone as a repository of a credible Grand Strategy. Few in Ottawa any longer believe in NATO as a military or political alliance of crucial relevance to us.

Sometimes, of course, small country national leaders may formulate an overarching policy – the functional principle, for example, that Canada derived during the Second World War in an effort to get itself a voice in Great Power decisions where it had the resources to matter, Secretary of State for External Affairs Louis St. Laurent's 1947 Gray lecture that defined the principles of Canadian foreign policy, the Paul Martin government's International Policy Strategy, or the present government's Canada First strategy – to describe their intent, but these are at best small market policies aimed at protecting or advancing limited-scope national interests. Copeland's definition seems to fit here.

But the leaders of every smaller nation know from hard experience that at base their interests may be sacrificed or overridden by superpowers following their own Grand Strategy or, sometimes, selfishly or in a fit of absence of mind advancing their own national interests. Britain historically had no qualms in sacrificing Canadian interests to advance its own. The United States, more shrewdly, has generally been reasonably accommodating of Canadian interests in the post-war years and it has let Canadian political and business leaders initially make the case for ever-closer ties.

A nation such as Canada has never gone to war in its own national interests, some might argue, including me, but only to advance or protect the interests of its colonial masters (Britain) or its allies (the United States). In other words, Canada – and many other nations, too – has always served the Grand Strategy of others.

This is the way of the world, and while we may grumble, there is little that can be done about this. Great powers think in grandiose terms and fight to protect their global interests; small powers are small and think small – or, at best, in medium-size terms. Their aim, and here I come close to Pratt's minimalist definition of Grand Strategy, is to survive and prosper and to be left alone to do so, and a judicious use of their limited power, management of their alliances, and maximization of their resources to these ends is assuredly their best strategy.

In this vein, Senator Hugh Segal put it well a few years ago: "it is really vital that we develop a 'grand strategy for a small country' that integrates military, diplomatic, and foreign aid instruments in a thrust that preserves security and opportunity at home, advances leverage with our allies, and responds in an integrated way to the threats that are real from abroad. We need to shape a strategy that, as we learn from the experiences of East Timor, Bosnia, Kosovo, Haiti and Iraq, combines military, civil, private sector, democratizing, and post-conflict transition skills. These need to be built into real plans and models that maximize the ability of each to engage constructively on Canada's behalf, and that enhance the leverage of a combined application where appropriate and helpful." This sounds very much as what we have now come to call a Whole of Government approach, and it is not yet something Canada has made work. We should.

But whatever else this is, it's not Grand Strategy as it has been traditionally understood. So for a country like Canada, the once-again popular refrain from "South Pacific" remains true: "What ain't we got? We ain't got ..." not dames, which we do have, but a Grand Strategy, which we cannot have.

www.ingramcontent.com/pod-product-compliance
Lightning Source LLC
Chambersburg PA
CBHW020350080526
44584CB00014B/968